D0958519

DEATH AND LIFE IN THE TENTH CENTURY

Death and Life in the Tenth Century

by Eleanor Duckett

Ann Arbor Paperbacks
The University of Michigan Press

First edition as an Ann Arbor Paperback 1971
Copyright © by The University of Michigan 1967
All rights reserved
ISBN 0-472-06172-0
Published in the United States of America by
The University of Michigan Press and
in Don Mills, Canada, by Longmans Canada Limited
Manufactured in the United States of America

Bibliothecarum praefectis ministrisque citra ultraque Oceanum studia foventibus, qui summa cum sollertia, patientia, immo vero suavitate animum meum sitientem liberaliter aluerunt, hoc opusculum qualecumque dedicavi.

FOREWORD

The tenth century in its course knew well the evils of the world, the flesh, and the devil: battle, murder, and devastation; plague, pestilence, and famine; rebellion and riot; fornication and lust in places high and low, secular and sacred; ignorance, brutality, silence, and despair.

Yet surely, seen as a whole, it does not deserve the name of an "age of lead," sunk inert amid the night of barbarism. This may indeed be held true of its first eighteen years, dead in the winter of its history. But with the 920's there arose a spring of renewed life which was to turn, from the 960's onward, into a summer of vision and hope for the nations of regained empire, civilized and uncivilized alike. Constantly, malicious force interrupted and barred the path of progress; but ever the warring of good against evil went on. As there were pagan invaders, rebel citizens, a multitude of uncultured men, unworthy rulers in Church and state, so were there emperors striving to bring their peoples into peace and harmony, bishops caring as true fathers for those in their charge, missionaries boldly facing martyrdom, scholars eager to teach and to learn. That the summer of vision was broken by storms and ended at last in death does not destroy its truth. If the tenth century did nothing else in its struggle to bring light into darkness, order into chaos, emptiness into harvest, it was at least preparing the way for happier and more blessed days to come.

My book has been written for those who are interested in medieval times, who know little concerning these hundred years. The twentieth century has seen a marked revival of probing into the hidden events and character of the tenth. Nor has the Church failed to recognize this millenium: a fact perhaps most widely impressed upon us by the baptism in 966 of Miesko, duke of the Poles, and the conversion of Poland to the Catholic faith. It has therefore seemed worth while to try in more modest and less original manner once more to recall some memory of this age: an effort complicated by the need to include, as all writers have included, history of Church and state in medieval Germany, Italy, France, Burgundy, Provence, Poland, and Bohemia.

The reader, therefore, on his side, will need patience. I have dealt with my complex subject as simply as I could, but I could not deny it its necessary detail. Doubtless among the wheat, if wheat there be, tares will be found, faults in date or detail. These errors are my own.

For aid in my effort I gladly render thanks to my friends: to the members of the University of Michigan Press for their unfailing courtesy, skill, and care; in Smith College, to Margaret Johnson, librarian, to Patricia Delks, Grace Holt, Emma Kaplan, and Ruth Noble, of the Library staff; to Virginia Corwin, Paul Graham, Charles Henderson, Sidney Packard, and Edna Williams, professors of religion, German, classics, history, and English; in the University of Cambridge, to Arthur Tillotson, secretary to the Syndics of the University Library, to Harold Pink, under-librarian, to Dr. Nora Chadwick, and to Professor Bruce Dickins. To these I owe deep gratitude for the gift of their learning, as I do likewise to others, many and well remembered, who in darker moments have held a candle to light me to work.

E. S. D.

CONTENTS

TABLES

MAPS

Part One

The Tenth Century in Its Seasons
Winter, Spring, and Summer

CHAPTER ONE

Approach of Winter, 885-99
Charles the Fat; Arnulf of Carinthia

1

FIFTEEN YEARS before the ninth century ended, the shadow which had darkened its course on the continent of Europe seemed for a moment likely to lift. In 885 one prince alone, of legal birth and mature age, remained to carry on the Carolingian imperial line. History knows him as Charles III, great grandson of that Charles the Great who had been crowned by Pope Leo III in 800 as emperor of the West.

In 814 Charles the Great had died, and for seventy years the empire which he had won and controlled had been breaking up through division and discord among his heirs. Now at last, in 885, hope of reuniting its severed parts under one ruler rose again. Success, great and easily won, had fallen to this Charles III.

He was the youngest son of Louis "the German," king of the East Franks who dwelt in the modern Germany; his father had given him as a young man the rule of Swabia, a country of the Upper Rhine and the Danube. In 879 through the chronic illness of his eldest brother, Carloman, he had won the homage of Italian nobles and their crown. When he had returned across the Alps from Italy to aid his Carolingian kinsmen, fighting for their land, he had brought with him a strong hope that his holding of this royal crown would in time open his way to solemn consecration in St. Peter's at Rome as emperor of the West. The pope of these years, John VIII, was longing for his support, as he well knew. War was threatening Rome itself. In July 880, John had written to him: "We have sought to elect you above all men as defender and protector of the Holy See, as one deeply aware of its distress. It is for us a sheer necessity that our friends give us their help, not only against wicked Christians but against the Saracens, those brigands swarming over our country, robbing and plundering without cease."

The hope of Charles had been fulfilled. He had deserted his kinsmen in the midst of battle and he had slipped off again across the Alps to receive, in February 881, that coveted coronation from the hands of Pope John. The pope had gained nothing. A few weeks later he had written to Charles to complain: "It is your duty to hold in mind the sufferings of your Mother, the Church of Rome, and to help us with all speed. You know very well how many, how great miseries and evils are coming upon us daily, and more and more as time goes on. It were better that we should die than endure what we now endure. My son, emperor as you are, we beseech you, for your love of Almighty God and of His saints, Peter and Paul, hasten to bring hither that army which you promised you would bring. Come quickly, that the peoples all around us cry no longer. 'Where is the emperor?' "

Charles had done nothing but cross the mountains once more for vague discussion with the pope at Ravenna. Of far greater interest to him than the needs of Rome was the news of the death in January 882 of his second brother, Louis the Younger, king in Germany. How could he think of papal worries when he was being called to the German throne? He had left Pope John to his fate—brutal murder, in December of this same year by, so it was said, one of his own family. Charles himself had eagerly hastened to assume kingship over his own German land.

The enemies of the Holy See, both heathen Saracens and "wicked Christians," natives of Italy itself, had now turned to distract John's successor, Pope Marinus I. Chief among the Italians was Guy (Wido), duke of Spoleto, south of Perugia, whose family had long been hostile to papal authority. Marinus, also, had appealed to the Emperor Charles. Again, in April 883, Charles had crossed the Alps. At Verona he had called an assembly of loyal nobles and with their support had ordered the duke of Spoleto and his fellow disturbers of the peace to be deprived of all the benefices which they and their fathers had held from time immemorial. The enraged defendants had promptly led out their vassals to plunder and ravage Italian lands, and thus had gained far more than they had lost. A charge of high treason had been brought against Guy; in revenge he had fled to join the enemy Saracens. Then Berengar, marquis of

Friuli, at the head of the Adriatic Sea, as faithful an adherent of his kinsman Charles and the Carolingian-German line as he was rival in bitter hatred of this duke of Spoleto, had marched out to punish Guy. An epidemic of fever raging in northern Italy had driven him home and had sent the Emperor Charles, caught by its infection, hurrying back to Germany. In the autumn of 884 he had returned—it was his fifth journey westward through Alpine passes—and in 885 peace had been made. Guy had sworn an oath of fidelity to Charles before an assembly of nobles held in Pavia, capital of Italy's Lombard-Frankish kingdom.

The emperor was still in Italy when envoys reached him to tell of the death, in December 884, of another Carloman, a distant cousin of his. This Carloman had been king of France. He had been killed, men declared, by accident, wounded fatally by one of his friends in the excitement of hunting the wild boar of the forest. Now these messengers had come to make formal supplication: Would Charles accept the crown of France? No other choice, indeed, seemed possible. Carloman, it was true, had left a half-brother; but he was a little child, only five years old.

The prospect of this reunion of France, Italy, and Germany, including Lotharingia, under the rule of one man, Charles III, emperor of the West, brought to their leaders both hope and fear. Many problems were staring them in the face. Provence had been torn away from the Carolingian House in 879, when Boso, its duke, had persuaded its nobles to make it a kingdom and to give him the crown. That country of Lotharingia, lying between France and Germany and perpetually a cause of conflict between their kings, by bribery and corruption had at last by 881 passed to German rule. But not for permanent peace. One Hugh, an illegitimate son of King Lothar II, from whom Lotharingia had gained its name, was even now plotting to seize its land as his own to command, by right or by wrong.

Far worse were the questions concerning the fate of France. Pirates from Scandinavia were still laying waste and ravaging the regions of the Seine, the Somme, the Oise, and the Loire. Only the year before, in 884, the chronicler of the abbey of Saint-Vaast, near Arras in the Pas-de-Calais, had written of the misery of his world: "Never do the Northmen cease to take captive and to kill Christian people, to destroy churches and ramparts, to burn our houses in flames. Through all the open streets the dead are lying: priests, layfolk noble and humble, women and men, youth and little children.

Everywhere tribulation and sorrow meet our eyes, seeing Christian folk brought to utter ruin and desolation."

At Compiègne in 884, shortly before the death of Carloman of France, his counselors had met to debate what they should do. Their king was young and lacked experience. At last in despair they had decided to send an envoy to ask for terms of peace from the Danes, then encamped for the winter at Amiens on the Somme. Their messenger was himself a Dane, but a convert to Christianity and a sworn friend of France. Argument had been long and difficult. Finally, at the price of twelve thousand pounds of silver, to be reckoned and paid according to Danish measure, the invaders had consented to depart. Depart they did, but only to Louvain in Lotharingia.

Inside these lands of the empire the nobles of each country were taking up arms, not only for their defense against raiders from without but for robbing, pillage, and murder of their own neighbors. In March 884 Carloman had sent out from his palace at Ver, near Senlis, a protest, drawn up by his advisers, against the "poison of this malice, spread so far and wide throughout France that all men seem freely to hold within them the accursed and deadly disease." "How," the king had asked, "how shall we conquer our pirate enemies, when the blood of our own brethren stains our hands, when these hands can scarcely contain the load of booty snatched from our poor and wretched fellow citizens?"

Then, what about the emperor, Charles himself? For years the Carolingian House had held kings frail in health, kings who died young, kings unreliable in character who came to their end through their own folly, their own grasping ambition. In body Charles was heavy; the twelfth century was to name him Charles the Fat. In mind he was erratic, impetuous, highly strung, given, if story be true, to dream or delusion. Hincmar, archbishop of Reims, had told in the *Annals of Saint Bertin* that in the year 873 young Prince Charles at his father's court of Frankfurt had seen a vision of Satan, transformed into an angel of light. "God," the devil had said, "is angry with your father, the king of Germany, and is going to take away his crown and give it to you." In terror Charles had fled into the royal chapel and Satan had followed him. "Why this fear?" he had complained. "Do you think that I would enter a church with lies in my mouth? Receive from me, God's angel, the Host from the altar, and believe that I bear this message from the Lord of Heaven himself." Whereupon, so Hincmar had declared, Charles had received holy sacrament as from a priest of the Church, and with this deceit Satan had entered into him. So firmly the evil power had possessed him that no one, not even the archbishop of Mainz, could cast it out. It only departed when his father, Louis "the German," was preparing to send him to the pope at Rome for his release. We cannot say that Hincmar's story has any basis in fact, but many people must have heard it.

Nor had Charles proved himself a hero on the march to battle. As emperor and king of Germany in 882 he had gathered a great army to attack Danish invaders in their camp on the bank of the Meuse. Face to face with them he had yielded to foolish counsel and had made peace. Two Danish chieftains had received his bribes; to the one, Godfrid, he had given feudal tenure of Frisia, northeastern district of the Netherlands; to the other, Sigfrid, he had made rich payment of money. His only demands had been a treaty of alliance and, from Godfrid, Christian baptism.

There was, it is true, some comfort amid the doubt. As emperor and king, Charles III had loyal friends. There was Hugh, called "the Abbot," because, layman though he was, he held the rule and dispensed the revenue of the famous abbey of Saint-Martin, Tours. Hugh was also count both of Tours and of Anjou and had won high importance as the protector of Neustria, that part of France lying between the Seine and the Loire, against the assault of pirates; through endless strife and danger he had fought for the Carolingian line. If Charles III were to neglect France, by staying in his native Germany, by journeying to Italy as emperor and king to give aid against the Saracens or to deal with those ambitious rivals for power, Guy of Spoleto and Berengar of Friuli, Hugh "the Abbot" could be counted on to lead out an army for the defense of France and her people. If only nothing happened to him himself; rumor told that he was failing in health.

There was Count Henry of Swabia, another military adviser to Charles, and chief in command of the fighting force in Germany. In vain he had tried to keep his king from making peace with Godfrid in 882; even now he was watching Godfrid and the Danish camp at Louvain as substitute for the emperor.

There was Liutward, bishop of Vercelli in Italy by appointment of Charles, and archchancellor also in Germany. To him the emperor confided all his secret plans, desires, and fears; he trusted him well. Nevertheless, men shook their heads when they spoke of him; they had scant respect for his character.

Above all, Charles III was of the direct Carolingian line, and France was firmly attached to the descendants of Charlemagne.

In 885 the emperor was in France, ordering its fighting men to march against Louvain in Lotharingia. As they drew near, worried because sickness had prevented Hugh "the Abbot" from leading them forward, they heard the Northmen shout in mockery: "Why come to us? No need! We know you and what you want. You want us to come back against you! And we will!" The men of France lost courage and turned to retreat.

At this moment the Danish chieftain Godfrid, now duke of Frisia, was meditating plans for his own profit. Frisia, he had decided, was not enough for him; he must squeeze more out of this Emperor Charles. Moreover, the land of Frisia was not fertile. Why not demand from Charles the wine-producing country around Coblenz and Andernach on the Rhine in Germany? He was making up his mind to do this when he received welcome encouragement. Hugh, that son of Lothar II, still eager to regain Lotharingia for his own, sent envoys to him, suggesting a union of their forces. Hugh was his brother-in-law; Godfrid had married Hugh's sister, Gisela.

Godfrid promptly sent off messengers to Charles, boldly asking for the land on the Rhine: a reward, he said, for his faithfulness in keeping his feudal oath regarding Frisia. The emperor had no idea how to answer this request. But Henry, count of Swabia, was ready enough. He went off to settle matters and took with him Willibert, archbishop of Cologne, and Count Eberhard of Franconia in Germany, both declared supporters of Charles. They met in secret conference with Godfrid upon an island, surrounded by the waters of the Rhine and the Waal. Angry words broke out as they talked, swords were raised, and Godfrid was killed. It was no accident, no sudden act of rage. Shortly afterward Hugh of Lotharingia, partner of Godfrid, was invited by Count Henry to meet him at Gondreville, near Toul in that land. He came readily, and there, by order of Charles himself, he was seized, blinded, and sent into monastic prison, first at Saint-Gall in Switzerland and then at Prüm, near Trier in Germany.

The following month, June 885, saw Charles received as king of France at Ponthion, near Châlons-sur-Marne, and the nobles of France offering him their homage. As soon as he decently could, he left France for his home in Germany. The matter of the succession to the German crown, he had decided, must be arranged at once; he had no lawful heir except that child, his remote kinsman of France, who was to be known later on as Charles the Simple. At Frankfurt he commanded his German nobles to elect as his heir Bernard, a son of his born out of wedlock. As Charles of France at the age of five could not possibly succeed him, Bernard, illegitimate though he was, must inherit the kingdom.

To his surprise and wrath he could wring no consent from these subjects of his. He turned to the Church. Would the pope, Hadrian III, travel to Germany, he asked in a letter addressed to him in Rome, that this matter might be settled once and for all by apostolic authority? Hadrian, no doubt hoping for aid against Saracens and disloyal Christians, started on his way. Death overtook him before he had left Italy, and his successor was at once elected as Pope Stephen V.

The news of this happening drove even the thought of the German succession from the emperor's mind. In a violent rage he asked what right had Rome to appoint a ruler of the Holy See without his imperial assent and confirmation? He ordered Liutward, bishop of Vercelli and his own trusted counselor, to start for Italy at once. Moreover, certain other bishops who held office under the papacy were to join him in Rome; by this combined force of authority Stephen was forthwith to be deposed on the ground of irregular election. Finally, that all might be carried out as he required, Charles announced that he, the emperor, would travel with Liutward.

His courage, however, did not carry him to argue his cause at Rome. He remained in northern Italy, and Liutward won no success against the Roman nobles. They were completely satisfied, and so was Stephen V. Had his election not been authorized by the signatures of more than thirty bishops, of cardinal priests and deacons of Rome, and of its leading laymen?

Soon Charles had more serious trouble to face. Revolt broke out among his subjects at Pavia; many were killed and he himself had a narrow escape. To make matters worse, a crisis in France called him home.

Two important sources tell us of the great and lasting siege of Paris carried on by the Danes during 885 and 886: the annals written in prose by a monk of the abbey of Saint-Vaast near Arras, and the verse of Abbo, monk of the monastery of Saint-Germain-des-Prés in Paris. Both are contemporary writers; Abbo, indeed, saw with his own eyes the scenes which he described.

In July 885 the Northmen were at Rouen; from there they made their way to Paris, burning and working destruction by the axe and the spear. They arrived before the city on November 24 and quickly opened attack. The island on which Paris stands was at this early time connected with the mainland by a bridge on either side: the Grand Pont—the Great Bridge—on the right bank, the Petit Pont—the Little Bridge—on the left. Both bridges were fortified by towers, one at each end, as guard against the enemy's approach. Protection of all—city, island, connecting bridges—was directed by two leaders: Odo, often known as Eudes, count of Paris, and Gozlin, recently appointed its bishop. Odo had inherited his title from his father, Robert the Strong, who had held command against the Northmen between the Seine and the Loire before Hugh "the Abbot," his successor in this post of duty. In 866 Robert had fallen, boldly fighting the enemy at Brissarthe, near Châteauneuf-sur-Sarthe. He left two little sons, Odo and Robert. Now, in 885, nearly twenty years later, since Hugh was seriously ill, Odo had taken his place. By November he had already fortified Paris, and in calm confidence, side by side with Gozlin, he awaited the coming of the Viking warships, three hundred of them, bearing more than thirty thousand men.

For two days, November 26 and 27, assault was made from sunrise to sundown upon the outer tower of the Great Bridge; all night long the defenders, tired out by the day's fighting, worked to repair the damage done. Then the invaders settled down in grim determination outside Paris. With utter disregard of injury and death, the Danes built a strongly reinforced station opposite the city and from it bombarded Paris with missiles and rockets of flame. Charles the Fat, king of France, remained in Germany; but not because he knew nothing of what was going on in his realm. Already Fulk, successor of Hincmar as archbishop of Reims, had written to warn him: "Paris," he had said, "that chief city, that city which gives entrance to the kingdoms of Neustria and Burgundy, is surrounded by barbarian blockade. Soon, unless by God's mercy rescue be at hand, it must fall to the enemy. And if this come about, the whole of France will be ruined."

During the night of February 6, 886, the Petit Pont, which connected Paris with the river's left bank, suddenly fell apart, destroyed by floods pouring along the Seine. Gozlin, in despair, sent a messenger to Germany. Would Count Henry hurry to their aid? The count eluded the Danish sentries and came. It was the season of Lent, March or April; his coming, we are told, did no good and soon he went back to tell what he had seen. He left Gozlin on the point of yielding to terms of peace exacted by the Danes. But Gozlin did not yield; in mid-April he died.

Odo was left alone to carry on. In May he slipped secretly out-

side the walls to reach men of power and influence in France. Would
they themselves, he begged them, go on a mission to their emperor
and king, Charles the Fat? Unless he came, they were to say, with
all the force which he could gather, Paris was doomed.

On his return journey Count Odo nearly lost his life. He had
escaped capture by immense skill and care, and he was already within a mile from the city's gate when suddenly scouts of the Danish
blockade rushed out from their hidden watch beside the road. Only
the speed of his horse and the power of his sword, striking on either
hand, carried him to safety.

It was August 886 when Charles the Fat finally marched into
France. Toward the end of the month he was at the royal manor of
Quierzy-sur-Oise, near Laon, with an "immense army." There he
stayed, and sent ahead Count Henry to see what could be done. The
count, thanks to a formidable force of fighting men and to his own
strategy, arrived in Paris. He decided that before launching an attack it would be prudent to spy out the enemy's position and numbers. With a small escort he rode out in the darkness of night; his
horse fell into one of many holes carefully dug and lightly covered
by the Danes; he was thrown to the ground and killed on the spot by
Danish guards.

At last, late in September or early in October, the citizens of
Paris, exhausted by famine, sickness, wounds, and the constant presence of death, caught sight of their emperor and his army, moving
into camp below the heights of Montmartre. Their hope, their joy
flared up again, only to be quenched within a few weeks; in November Charles, their king, was negotiating terms of peace at a price.
The winter was coming on; he had no wish to face what his subjects
had long known. France, he said to himself, was not his native land.
Moreover, there was word that another army of these Viking pirates
was on the march toward Paris. Caution was better than foolish
hardihood. Promptly seven hundred pounds of silver were promised
to the invaders if all would leave for Scandinavia by March 887.
Meanwhile, to make persuasion even stronger, Charles declared that
the Danes might spend the winter in plundering Burgundy; this was
exactly what they longed to do. "O Burgundy, little didst thou reck
of war in days past!" wrote Abbo. "But now thou knowest well the
names of those whose iron assault thou hast endured."

From this point the story of Charles the Fat comes quickly to
its end. There was no delay; he left Paris and reached Germany. It
is only just to tell that sickness had long been creeping upon him. As

he lay upon his bed he heard that Boso, the usurper king of Provence, had died and that his widow, Ermengard, desired greatly to see him. He received her and with her their little son Louis in gracious hospitality; it was even said that he welcomed the boy as his own child.

But his power, whatever power he had had, was gone. His chieftains in Germany turned from loyalty to their own devices and desires. They cast accusation of grievous scandal against his beloved Liutward, bishop of Vercelli, and finally Charles was forced to dismiss this favorite adviser from his court. His empress, Richarde, would have no more of life with him; she left the court for peace and security within a convent. In November 887 the reign of Charles ended. At Tribur, near Mainz, his leading men carried a vote by overwhelming voices: that he be straightway deposed and that the kingship over Germany and all land subject to him be given to his nephew, Arnulf; at Frankfurt this nephew was declared sovereign.

Arnulf was duke of Carinthia, son of Carloman, eldest brother of Charles. His birth, it is true, was illegitimate, for he had been born to a mistress of Carloman, and his uncle had consistently neglected him. But he was young and courageous; he had done good service for the German kingdom in its battles against invaders. Men hoped that this German duke of Carolingian blood might win for them renown, now so badly wanting.

Charles made no resistance, even when all his possessions save a few bare necessities were taken from him. Contemporary record tells that he sent to Arnulf a parting gift, a relic of the true cross, so he said, on which Arnulf had once sworn allegiance to him as his lord. With it came a cry of reproach: "Why, Arnulf, why show thyself so barbarous and cruel?" In answer Arnulf, moved by pity, allowed to this uncle of his some few acres in Swabia, once kingdom of Charles. Here he spent in solitude and increasing misery the little that remained of his life; he died, mourned by none, on January 13, 888.

2

The deposing and the death of the Carolingian emperor, Charles the Fat, tore his empire into fragments. For years no man held the imperial crown, and when a pale succession of ghost emperors one after another gained it for a while, it was by power of arms. In the well-known words of Regino of Prüm, a tenth-century chronicler: "Now the kingdoms which had been subject to Charles, holding themselves bereft of lawful heirs, cut loose into separate realms. Now they looked for no prince of hereditary descent; each divided part elected a king for itself from itself." Each now chose for its king the man whom its nobles judged best prepared to administer and to defend it in these days of danger from without and within. This impulse of division also worked for individual nationality. The Frankish peoples of the West and of the East were already divided in language; now, born anew as France and Germany, each land was eager to prove its independence.

From Germany young Arnulf, elected and crowned king, watched events in France and in Italy. Like Charles the Fat, he too was ambitious to hold the imperial crown of the West, to reunite the divided countries under his overlordship as emperor.

From France came word of a fierce conflict of will and judgment. Its chief archbishop, Fulk of Reims, was driven by that same zeal for politics which had so often brought his predecessor, Hincmar, into conflict. He, also, had been carefully trained in diplomatic experience at the Carolingian court. Men everywhere were now saying that Odo, the brave defender of Paris, was the one and only choice for the empty throne; Fulk was determined to prevent this stranger to the Carolingian line from becoming king of France. He therefore wrote to the pope, Stephen V, in support of his own candidate for the throne: Guy, duke of Spoleto in central Italy. Had not Guy made his peace with the Emperor Charles and with the Holy See? Was not Pope Stephen calling him his "one and only adopted son?" He was also a relative of Fulk himself. Above all, he had friends in France, men of his own family.

In high hope Duke Guy crossed the Alps and found a following, aided by Fulk's influence. At Langres near the Marne its bishop, in the spring of 888, even dared to proclaim and crown him king of France. The act was soon rejected. Guy heard that Odo had been chosen by overwhelming force; his own hope was gone and he returned to Italy. There was still a throne there in his native land which he might gain.

Odo had indeed been crowned king at Compiègne on February 29, 888. It was now for him to prove his right to rule, and at first he shouldered bravely the burden of drawing together the people of France; partly by grace of favor, partly by threat and menace. For ten years he was to struggle against many who, like Fulk, held him an alien usurper; against the constant raids of pirates from Denmark; against Aquitaine, that duchy of his realm which as of old held itself independent under its present duke, Ramnulf.

In Italy Guy failed to win the crown for which he had hoped in his retreat from France. While he had been lingering there, his rival, Berengar, marquis of Friuli, had seized his chance. In January 888 he was elected Italy's king. He, too, claimed Carolingian heritage; his mother, Gisela, was a granddaughter of Charlemagne. Only, however, in his own northern land could Berengar hope to prove himself sovereign; Guy, jealous as ever, settled down in central Italy to build up strength for war.

Another, a new kingdom of "Burgundy," now arose under one of Swabia's nobles: Rudolf, nephew of Hugh "the Abbot." At Saint-Maurice in the Valais, Switzerland, the capital center of his power, Rudolf in 888 was crowned king of Transjurane Burgundy, which stretched across southwestern Switzerland, from the Saône River in France to the Pennine Alps. He tried also, through an assembly of bishops and lay chieftains gathered at Toul in Lotharingia, to make himself lord of that land, in defiance of Lotharingia's sovereign, Arnulf of Germany. For a moment he was successful, actually declared king. But soon, pursued by Arnulf's army and deserted by his friends, he fled back to his realm, protected by the mountains of Switzerland.

The kingdom of Provence, founded by the usurper Boso, continued as an independent realm under Louis, son of Boso, the child so graciously welcomed three years before by Charles the Fat. As soon as his years allowed, Louis received in 890 solemn coronation as king at the special bidding of Pope Stephen V himself. Stephen had been earnestly urged to intervene; the archbishop of Vienne had vividly held up before him the sufferings of Provence through the turmoil caused by rebellious nobles, hungry for power, and by Saracen invasion which never ceased. A king upon its throne, if only ten years old, would at least mark some turning toward order in the midst of chaos.

Over these "kinglets," as in contempt they were called, of France, Italy, Burgundy, and Provence, Arnulf soon won the supremacy which was his aim. Odo of France, probably worn down by the long struggle of 885-86, as crowned king was now disappointing all. He seemed to lack all confidence, all ambition for victory; the resolution which had marked the beginning of his reign had crumbled away. France was devastated by Danish plunderers; her people were living in bewilderment, anger, and shame. At last Archbishop Fulk felt driven to take action. The heir, Charles the Simple, now eight years old, was far too young to hold the throne in these perilous times. Some other must be made king of France. And what man now, thought Fulk, could bring to an end the struggle between Carolingian and non-Carolingian, who, as a bold and shrewd leader, could give France both peace and victory, except the ambitious Arnulf of Germany?

Fulk went, then, to Arnulf in Germany, carrying with him knowledge of support from Rudolf, abbot of Saint-Bertin in northern France, and Baldwin, count of Flanders, men high in political power. It seemed as though Arnulf must yield to his long argument. But as Arnulf still hesitated, the decision was made for him. Messengers arrived at the German royal court, and Fulk's words fell dead. Odo, king of France, was once more a ruler to be reckoned with. On June 24, 888, with only a small army, he had brilliantly defeated the Danes at Montfaucon in the Argonne, between the rivers Aisne and Meuse. At once Arnulf refused to supplant this victor. He called Odo to an assembly at Worms, swore in a great oath to protect him, received his promise of adherence, and thus gave content both to himself and to this king of France, now, if not his vassal, at least in some measure dependent on Arnulf's aid.

The other rulers also came into line. In Italy Guy of Spoleto prepared this same year, through the assistance of troops brought by him from France, to march out against King Berengar. A battle was fought near Brescia, between Verona and Milan; although Berengar claimed the field was his, he yet had good reason to fear. He needed support, and he hurried to meet Arnulf amid the mountains of the Trentino, a region on either side of the Adige in northern Italy, easily reached by Arnulf from Bavaria. There Berengar gave his own pledge of loyalty and gained in return Arnulf's assurance of protection. So promised Rudolf of Burgundy at Regensburg in 888, after judicious pressure from the German king. Finally, the official decree which announced in August 890 the election of young Louis as king of Provence made it clear that this had been brought about with Arnulf's assistance and consent.

Under Arnulf as overlord these "kinglets" might be expected to live in peace. Yet, the year 889, even before Louis gained his crown, saw Berengar and Guy meeting once more for battle, this time on the river Trebbia. Berengar was utterly defeated; he returned to his marquisate of Friuli and lost control over Italy. In February of this

year a council of bishops, gathered at the royal city of Pavia, declared that "after horrible warning and unspeakable disasters" they
had met to declare Guy their rightful king. They then issued an edict
to inform the Italian people that Guy, attacked by "furtive and fraud-
ulent menace and twice put to flight," was now their ruler and sovereign lord.

Fear promptly sprang up in the heart of Stephen V, pope of
Rome. The dukes of Spoleto had been openly hostile to the papacy
in former days. Why not again? The pope could not forget that this
same Guy had once made common cause with the Saracens, those
perpetual enemies of Italy and the Holy See. By indirect channel he
sent a message to Arnulf. It was given to the king of Germany in 890
while he was on an expedition to Pannonia (covering parts of Aus-
tria, Hungary, and Yugoslavia) by Svatopluk I, king of Moravia, land
of the river Morava, a tributary of the Danube. Svatopluk and his
people were Christian, converted by the famous Saints Cyril and
Methodius earlier in the ninth century. Relations between Moravia
and the See of Rome were harmonious. Moravia and Germany frequently fought when Moravians invaded the German borderland,
but at this moment there was truce of friendship between Arnulf and
Svatopluk.

Arnulf did not enter Italy to help Stephen in 890. He was busy
defending his kingdom from the raids of neighboring Slavonic tribes
and keeping a firm hand over his own chieftains, especially those of
Swabia. The inevitable result followed. On February 21, 891, Pope
Stephen, sorely against his will, was compelled to crown Guy, king
of Italy, as emperor of the West in St. Peter's at Rome. A pale ghost
of the imperial state had risen from the grave of empire. The news
caused Arnulf deep anguish. Had he gone to Italy, might not the
pope have given him this crown? Who knew?

During September 891 this pope died, and election as his successor
came to Formosus, bishop of Porto, one of the several sees around
Rome.

The history of Formosus is of interest. In 866 Pope Nicholas I
had sent him on a mission to the Bulgarians, at the request of Boris,
their king. Boris had become so greatly attached to Formosus that he
had begged the Holy See to appoint him archbishop of Bulgaria: a
petition repeatedly refused. The bishop had finally returned to his
see of Porto and had thrown himself eagerly into Roman ecclesiastical affairs. His ambition had betrayed him. He had fallen under bit-

ter censure from John VIII, pope from 872 until 882. In a synod held at Rome on April 19, 876, John had deprived him of his bishopric and had even threatened him with excommunication unless he hastened to Rome at once to plead his case. Formosus did not appear, and the sentence of excommunication was pronounced at two councils held in France: at Ponthion in 876, and in 878 at Troyes, where the pope himself was present.

The reasons for this action were put forward by John VIII in 876, through a letter addressed "to all in the lands of Gaul and Germany." "So greatly," declared the pope, "had Formosus by his shrewd cunning corrupted the heart of Boris of Bulgaria that he had bound the king in terrible oath never to receive any other but himself as bishop from the Holy See as long as he, Formosus, should live. So high," the accusation continued, "had his ambition soared that he had hoped to be elected holder of the papal seat itself; so deep had been his treachery that he had deserted his own diocese and had plotted evil against the highest power in the State."

But before the Council of 878 broke up at Troyes, Formosus had found a chance to plead before John VIII in person. On his taking solemn oath that he would never again function as bishop or as priest, never even set foot again in Rome, he had at last been permitted communion at the altars of the Church; but only as a layman, among the crowd. Then in 882 Pope John had died, and all had been changed. Boldly Formosus had returned to Rome, to be set free from his oath and to be restored to his see of Porto by John's successor, Marinus I, pope from 882 to 884.

In 891 Formosus, then, was elected pope. His life, men now maintained, was beyond reproach; he was known everywhere for his strict austerity and Christian zeal. It was true that his promotion to the Holy See was against the letter of canon law; this held it illegal to transfer a bishop from one see to another. Yet, was this not true of Marinus also? He had been bishop of Caere, some twenty miles from Rome, before his attainment of the Apostolic See.

In Germany the year 891 was bringing further trouble to King Arnulf. Danish pirates had moved from Brittany to Belgium, part of German Lotharingia. They had pitched camp and had gone out to plunder with all their will. Arnulf quickly sent an army to put an end to this assault, ordering its leaders to make their station on the river Meuse. Under no condition were they to allow the Danes to cross the river. But the enemy escaped and crossed the Meuse near

Liège before the German force reached camp at Maastricht, and, so messengers told, were at the moment making havoc in the forests and marshes around Aachen. Arnulf's army hurried after them, here and there, unable to find the Northmen at their work. Had they reached Cologne or Prüm or Trier? Or were they hurrying to their ships in fear of their enemy? On June 25, after the Germans had made their way through a rushing stream called La Gueule near Maastricht and the borderline of Holland and Belgium, this uncertainty turned into terror. The Danes suddenly and savagely attacked as the Germans were advancing in slow and irregular march. Driven to flight, Arnulf's men ran in all directions; more were killed than could be counted. On the following day the pirate invaders deliberately put to death their prisoners and carried everything of value which they could snatch from the dead to their ships standing in harbor on the coast.

News of this shame to his pride came to Arnulf in Bavaria. He was fighting the daring inroads of Slavs on his border. But the Danish invasion was an even greater peril; he gathered another army from eastern Germany and hastened at once to cross the Rhine and to encamp on the bank of the Meuse. The Danes, elated by victory, were busy in wrecking the countryside when they heard of his approach. Hastily fortifying a rampart built of timber and mud by the river Dyle, close to Louvain in Belgium, they settled there, full of confidence in their power. When the long German lines were seen marching toward the rampart they were met by shouts of laughter and taunts of mockery. "Remember La Gueule!" rang again and again in their ears. It was the first of November. Arnulf, as he drew near had been hesitating, trying to think out the best method of attack. But now, when he heard this laughter, his quick temper flared up. "Off your horses," he roared to his troops; "Rush them with all that is in you!" The Danish rampart yielded to the storm, the Danes turned to run; blocked by the river, many lost their lives. Regino of Prüm proudly wrote in his record for 891: "God gave our men strength to extinguish their adversaries with the sword, to lay them low upon the ground, so to destroy them that scarcely one man of them was left to carry word back to their fleet." The annalist of Fulda in Germany added: "The river stayed its course, dammed by the bodies of the dead. Two Danish kings were killed, and sixteen Danish standards were borne back in triumph to Bavaria."

The next year saw an incident long to be remembered. Arnulf was trying with all his power to thrust back an invasion by the Mora-

vian king, Svatopluk, who was bent upon entrance into Bavaria; in
support of his defense he called in a band of wild Magyar warriors.

The Magyars were originally a people of Asiatic home and Fin-
nish-Ugrian tongue who dwelt among the Ural Mountains. Pressed
forward by migrants behind them on the east, they had streamed
through Russia, and onward from the lower course of the Don to the
Danube. Late in the ninth century many of them were finding settlement in Hungary, and, therefore, were becoming known as Hungarians; the tenth century was to dread the name as intensely as the
ninth had feared that of the Northmen from Scandinavia. Their manner of assault, however, was very different. Instead of encamping in
stations on rivers from which they roamed far and wide to rob and
destroy cities, churches, monasteries, fields, and harvests in the manner of the Northmen, the Hungarians rode fast and fiercely to the
attack, felling with sure aim a multitude of victims by their arrows,
then as swiftly wheeling round to disappear in search of further destruction.

Men down the years have blamed King Arnulf as one who by his
appeal to these barbarians brought about their unceasing raids during the tenth century. This is not so; they had made their way into
Central Europe before Arnulf called upon them. Ludwig M. Hartmann, historian of medieval Italy, a land which suffered intensely at
their hands, has more widely seen a deeper reason in the force which
pushed these invaders ever further forward, seeking food and pasture
as they wandered west. They fought for their living; in time they
came to delight in the skill through which their arrows found each
its victim, in the lively satisfaction of a nomad life which gave them
far more than their fathers had known. Like the Danish pirates, these
new enemies were hungry, not only for adventure but for a living
rich and fat.

Meanwhile, in Italy, like Pope Stephen V before him, Pope Formosus
was growing more and more worried as the power of Guy of Spoleto,
now emperor, continued to threaten Rome. Reluctantly, he decided
that he must bring himself to do as Stephen had done; the Saracen
menace was at his door. On April 30, 892, at Ravenna, having wrung
from Guy a promise of help, he anointed and crowned Guy's son
Lambert as co-emperor with his father. A dynasty was being created
for the House of Spoleto, thought the pope in his misery, and as Stephen had done three years before, in 893 he, too, sent an appeal to
King Arnulf of Germany. The realm of Italy and its See of Peter, he

declared, were in grave danger of attack. This time Arnulf answered the call; in January 894 he invaded Italy at the head of an army. Opposition faced him at Bergamo, near Lake Como, and he ordered his men to batter down the walls of the city, their shields raised high to their heads and locked in Roman form. The walls fell; the citizens of Bergamo fled; Count Ambrose, leader of the resistance for the Emperor Guy, was dragged from his refuge in one of the city's towers and hanged from a tree at its gate; the bishop of Bergamo was seized and handed over as prisoner to Hatto, archbishop of Mainz, who had marched to Italy with his king.

Promptly, Milan and Pavia surrendered; various nobles of Italy, showing stubborn pride and refusing to submit, were also held captive until they swore allegiance to Germany. Arnulf was hailed as Italy's king.

Here the triumph ended. This king, courageous and ambitious as he was at home, here seemed to lack patience and perseverance and the power of inspiring his followers with the same. Soon the Italian nobles were breaking their word of loyalty and escaping by secret paths to the support of Guy; Arnulf's men quickly lost enthusiasm, grew weary of the march, and longed to return to Germany. At Piacenza, south of Milan, Arnulf was compelled to give the order for retreat. The journey back gave one of his vassals opportunity to harass this overlord; the road through the mountains was barred by order of Rudolf, king of Transjurane Burgundy, always eager to assert his independence against the German power. The Germans, then, were forced to find a way wherever they could. With enormous difficulty, seizing upon such guidance as they chanced to meet, they scrambled up and down and over rocks and precipices in the Alps. But in May 894 they were at home, and Arnulf sent his son Zwentibold to ravage Burgundy in retaliation. Much of its land was laid waste, and its people fled in great numbers to find safety in Alpine crevices and caves.

In France, like Arnulf in Lotharingia, King Odo had been in conflict with Danish pirates. He had also met opposition from his lay nobles, especially from Baldwin, count of Flanders, his own vassal in feudal tenure; and from his bishops, many of whom were agreeing with Fulk, archbishop of Reims, that now the best course for France was to place the Carolingian Charles the Simple on its throne. At last, in the autumn of 892, the Northmen, realizing that France had been drained empty of wealth through their plundering, resolved to leave its shores and to cross the Channel to find new hunting in England.

In the same year Fulk and his friends had a new idea. France must now profit by rest from fighting. The pirates had gone. There was peace from outside, at least for a while; there must be peace within. But the king, Odo, by his very presence was encouraging men's ambition for war. What could be better than that he should retire for the winter of 892-93 to Aquitaine, that he should leave the harried land north of the Seine for that south of the Loire? Aquitaine had not suffered the ravage wrought elsewhere in France. Moreover, the old Duke Ramnulf was dead, and Odo's presence would influence for good his successors in that independently minded duchy.

Thus, by crafty argument Odo was persuaded to retreat; once he had departed, his enemies prepared for action. At Reims on January 28, 893, Charles the Carolingian was declared and crowned true king of France in a ceremony which saw many of its nobles kneeling to yield him homage. He was thirteen years old.

We still possess, imbedded in Flodoard's *History of the Church of Reims,* the very careful letter written by Fulk, its archbishop, in an endeavor to explain this act to Arnulf, king of Germany. He had heard that Arnulf, who in 888 had promised his support to Odo, had burst into angry words at the news of this coronation of the boy Charles. With all adroitness Fulk chose his words:

"After the Emperor Charles [the Fat] had died, in 888 I turned to you, his nephew, in my desire to receive you as lord and ruler of France. At that time, O King, you dismissed me without counsel or comfort. Since no hope was left for me in you, I was forced to submit to the reigning of one Odo, a stranger to our royal house: a man who since he has been king over us in France has made tyrannical use of his power. Unwillingly I have endured his rule. At last sheer necessity has driven me to my only recourse, to elect as king one truly born of our line, one whose predecessors, whose brothers, themselves bore a crown. In 888 Charles was a child, unable to reign. Now he is older, old enough to follow the guidance of wise counselors, of those who see in his reign good both for Germany and for France. It is true, King Arnulf, I admit, that I did not ask your advice before we elected Charles. But will you remember that it has ever been the custom of France to elect her kings from her royal house without seeking counsel, without calling for aid from any sovereign, however more powerful he may be? Now that he is crowned king among us, it is our desire in all confidence to entrust

him and all his realm to your protection, counsel, and ordinance."

Pope Formosus wrote to congratulate Charles and to send him token of blessing. To Fulk he sent frank advice: he must work for peace between Charles and Odo and rebuke Odo for his transgressions. To Odo himself he sent command that he do nothing against King Charles, that he keep truce steadily until Fulk, archbishop of Reims, should be able to come to Rome for consultation with the Holy See.

Uneasy peace followed for two years, in 893 and 894, marked by negotiations between the rival kings; marked, too, by secret plans for battle. Shortly after Easter 894 Odo decided on action. He marched against Reims, where Charles was stationed under the protection of Fulk. Soon Odo was besieging the city and the friends of Charles were carrying him off under cover of night to Germany, to ask help from Arnulf as his overlord. Perhaps Arnulf had been influenced by that letter from Fulk; perhaps, now that Charles was growing in years and intelligence, Arnulf himself preferred to see a Carolingian kinsman of his on the throne of France. At any rate, he dismissed his oath of protection given to Odo in 888. He received young Charles with kindness at Worms and declared his right to rule the land which his ancestors had ruled. The bishops and nobles of the region of the Meuse, he ordered, were to give Charles their support as king over France. Encouraged by this welcome, the guardians of Charles made further truce with Odo.

In the same year, 894, men heard of the death of the Emperor Guy in Italy and of the installing of his son and colleague, Lambert, as sole holder of the imperial crown. Pope Formosus wrote to Fulk in praise of his "loyal and zealous affection for Lambert, kinsman of Fulk himself." The words were false; Formosus had no love for any duke of Spoleto, emperor or not. With the same diplomacy Fulk replied that he looked upon Lambert as his dear son, rejoicing in his devotion to the pope. At the same time he prayed the pope to foster friendship between the Emperor Lambert and Charles, king of France by right of inheritance. Certainly, it was not possible at the moment that Charles should hold under his rule all its lands; but surely some part, in keeping with his royal dignity, should be his in permanence.

Evidently, not even the ambition of Fulk for his youthful protegé could claim kingship over France as a whole in the face of Odo's possession. The division of monarchy in France was also worrying Arnulf. It was for him, he determined, to act; had he not been acknowledged as overlord of both these rivals for power? In 895 he summoned both of them to his presence at Worms, "that the evil of this great tragedy be ended." Word had reached him that in 894 Charles had been obliged to retreat before Odo, once again breaking the peace, to find shelter in the French duchy of Burgundy, ruled by his friend, Richard "the Justiciary," a brother of Boso, once king of Provence. There, however, Charles could not restrain his soldiers from plundering the land; they received scant reward for service and their hunger was great.

The situation was critical. But the advisers of Charles told him on no account to go to Worms. He might well be detained there; they would send to Arnulf men of less importance than their king. As a precaution, however, Archbishop Fulk wrote to the German court, assuring Arnulf that Charles had no intention of breaking his loyalty to his overlord. He was working hard, doing his best to defend his throne against Odo, who was ever preparing assault upon him; an enemy insidious, treacherous, and of immense force.

Charles obeyed his advisers, but it cost him dear. Odo went to Worms, escorted by his most able followers; he carried many gifts and his own pledge of loyalty. In return Arnulf again changed his mind. Angered at the absence of Charles and pleased by the deference of Odo, he welcomed Odo during a great assembly which met at Worms in May 895; there he promised to support him, as one crowned king of France in 888.

At this same Assembly of Worms and in Odo's presence Arnulf boldly bestowed upon his favorite but illegitimate son, Zwentibold, a crown as king of Lotharingia. The move was never to find success. For many years Lotharingia had held no king; it was the home of warrior nobles, quick to assert their independence. Two of them, Count Reginar, known as "Long-Neck," and Count Matfrid, fought continually against Zwentibold; in vain Arnulf tried repeatedly to settle the land in peace. Zwentibold was young and courageous, but uncertain in temper, quick to act upon impulse; he lacked political sense and tact.

Perhaps it is worth while to recall for the honor of Arnulf another famous council held in his presence this same month. To Tribur near Mainz came three archbishops, at least nineteen bishops, abbots, and other dignitaries, from the kingdom of Lotharingia and the various states of Germany: Saxony, Bavaria, Franconia, Swabia. After a general fast, ordered for three days, and the chanting of

litanies in preparation, King Arnulf marched with splendid pageant
to receive homage in the great hall of his palace; then his clergy,
wearing the robes of their calling, met in the palace chapel, where
they received the royal consent to the opening of a crusade against
sinners and assailants of the Church in Germany. The chapel reechoed their voices, crying "Hear us, O Christ! Long live our great
king, Arnulf!" Then they all settled to their work and in time produced fifty-eight decrees, still ours to read.

The power of King Arnulf was rising and he was glad. Nobles of high
rank, indeed, not only ecclesiastic but also secular, supported his
rule during his days of power; only in Swabia did he have to rely on
the Church for aid against a rebel count. Once more he felt ready for
a call which should bring him yet wider influence, the supreme moment of his life. It came: another appeal from Pope Formosus that he
invade Italy for Rome's protection. Could he not redeem the failure
of 894?
     He spent some months in preparation, and in October 895 he
set out with an army gathered chiefly from Franconia and Swabia.
Pavia in the north of Italy was reached by December. From there
by way of Piacenza he went on to Parma, where he divided his
force: the Swabians were ordered to proceed through Bologna to
Florence, while he with the Franconians made their way through the
passes of the upper Apennines.
     The march through the mountains was beset for the king with
every kind of trouble. Rain poured down in torrents, flooding the
trails along which Arnulf and his long line of soldiers picked their
foothold here and there, lost and floundering, regaining the path at
infinite cost of time and energy. Plague struck the horses so heavily
that at last nearly all the packs had to be carried by oxen. As the
men struggled onward, bad news arrived. Arnulf had felt sure that
Berengar of Friuli, still in retreat after the battle of 889 for Italy's
crown, would eagerly come to his support against the House of Spoleto. Now he heard that Berengar would have nothing to do with
this invasion; he was sternly remaining aloof in his northern land.
     But neither Nature nor man held back Arnulf from his will, and
in February 896, outwardly bold but tense at heart, he was outside
Rome. Against him its gates stood fast closed by order of the Empress Agiltrude, widow of Guy, with whom she had been crowned
in 891. Their son Lambert, king and emperor, was busy elsewhere.
But she was a woman of great valor and ambition; in her son's ab-

sence she was ready at all cost to defend his right, as she held it. The people of Rome were standing firmly with her, and Pope Formosus was powerless against them. St. Peter's basilica, therefore, also refused all approach.

The morning after his arrival Arnulf called the whole of his force, officers and those under their command, to a general debate. They gathered near the church of Saint Pancras, where they heard Mass and then listened to their king. What, he asked them all, did they wish to do? With the help of God, they shouted, they would carry on; they would take Rome by assault.

The Lord God was on their side, wrote the annalist of Fulda. Arnulf, with some of his leaders, stole out from their camp to spy upon the defense; Roman soldiers caught sight of them and the spark of battle flared up. It was entirely unexpected; but the king's men rushed to the walls of Rome in a furious passion of attack. They hurled stones; they threw themselves upon the gates; they hacked and tore at the iron barriers with axes and swords; they brought ladders and climbed, striking down all whom they met. Toward evening the city fell into Arnulf's hands.

Soon all was open for his entry; the empress fled and senators of Rome came forward to escort him on his way. With banners and crosses held high, the procession marched to the Ponte Molle and from there to St. Peter's itself. On the steps Pope Formosus stood waiting to receive the victor and to lead him within; before its altar he placed the imperial crown on Arnulf's head and declared him emperor in the place of Lambert, deposed and dethroned. It was February 22, 896.

Some days later, in the basilica of St. Paul-Outside-the-Walls, Arnulf held audience of state to receive homage from the nobles of Rome. They gave oath in these words, in common assent:

"I swear by all these mysteries of God here present that, reserving only my own honor and law, and my loyalty due to the pope, Formosus, I am now, and all my life I shall be, faithful to the Emperor Arnulf. Never will I conspire against him in company of any other man; never will I aid Lambert, or Agiltrude his mother, to attain honor of this world; nor will I through any device or argument deliver to either of them this city of Rome."

Arnulf stayed in the city only two weeks. His chief act as its lord and master was to arrest on a charge of high treason two leaders of its senate, Constantine and Stephen, who had committed Rome

ITALY

into the hands of Agiltrude; they were to be carried as prisoners to Germany. Early in March he left the city in the care of one of his vassals, Farold, and turned away to face the formidable empress herself. He heard that she had retreated to Spoleto, and toward that duchy he gave order to march.

He was never to see her. His fate was nonetheless tragic in that it may well have been, unknown to him, inherited from his father Carloman, who had been forced by sickness to hand over to his brother, Charles the Fat, his dream of empire. Now, as Arnulf hurried to storm the fortress in which Agiltrude stubbornly awaited his coming, he, too, was suddenly seized by fearful pain and numbness in the head—paralysis, Regino called it. He could go no further. He sent his little son Ratold, like Zwentibold, of illegitimate birth, to refuge in Milan and was himself carried home to Germany. By May 896 he was in Bavaria.

Another ghost of empire had disappeared. Ratold fled back to his father, and in 897 Lambert was again in possession of Italy. He was also reconciled to his rival, Berengar. In 896 Berengar had marched southward from Friuli, taking advantage of the disturbed state of central Italy to make inroad upon its lands. Lambert had thought it wise to make terms of peace, and Berengar had accepted what he offered. As before, the north was to lie under Berengar, the central and southern regions under Lambert; Lambert, as before, held the crown of empire. The rivers Adda and Po marked the division of their authority.

In France Odo, relying on the promise made to him by Arnulf at Worms in 895, was steadily winning support from chieftains who had once upheld Charles the Simple. In that same year of 895 the few friends still left to Charles had decided in their distress to plead with Arnulf. Could not Arnulf induce Odo to grant Charles at least some share in the kingdom of his ancestors? Arnulf had received the legates graciously and had promised to consider their petition. Nevertheless, soon Charles knew only one sure source of hope, the clergy and citizens of Reims. Even his constant friend and protector, Fulk, was losing faith; after all, Charles was only sixteen and France needed a skilled head. The year 896 had not ended when he received the most bitter blow of his young, harassed life; Fulk had been caught by nobles of Odo and, against his will, it was said, had been forced to seek out Odo and to promise obedience to his command.

To Charles it seemed the end of all things, and he left France in 896 to seek retreat in Lotharingia, where Zwentibold for his own ends offered him a home.

There is some interest to be found in a letter which Fulk wrote to him in this exile, a letter of anger, whether diplomatic or sincere. In the summer of 896 Danish pirates had again appeared in France; under a leader named Huncdeus they had entered the Seine and had done great harm by their raids. After spending the winter in camp on the bank of the Oise, they moved in 897 to begin new work of evil on the Meuse. For some reason, at Eastertide Charles the Simple invited Huncdeus to visit him in Lotharingia. The two talked together in friendly fashion, and finally Charles received Huncdeus, the pagan pirate, from the font as his godfather in Christian baptism.

Of course men said that Charles in his despair was asking pagan aid from the enemies of France to reestablish himself on its throne. Fulk heard the rumors and in his anxiety, whether for himself or for Charles, promptly sent him this letter.

"What truly faithful follower of yours," the archbishop wrote, "would not be filled with fear, hearing that you desire friendship with those who fight against God, that you are making accursed alliance for the destruction of the Christian faith? To make common cause with heathen men is no whit different from denying God and worshiping idols! What you consort with, that you will imitate, that will bind you in practice and lead you to crime. Did not your ancestors forsake pagan error and seek that divine support which brought them to prosperity? Never, believe me, will you establish your rule in France by this means; nay, rather God in His wrath will swiftly bring you to destruction. I had hoped for better things from you. I beseech you, for God's sake, cease to follow such counsel, lest you bring lasting sorrow to me and to others who are loyal to your cause. Better had you never been born than be king by the Devil's aid!"

It was Fulk, however, and his supporters who sent Charles to Odo, in the hope that he might concede part of the kingdom of France to him. Odo proved gracious and kindly; he declared that he would in truth grant him as much of France for his governing as should seem right at the moment, with a promise of a larger portion in days to come. This declaration was made good by act. The portion allowed Charles was probably indwelt by nobles who had no love for Odo; we do not know where it was.

In any case the unexpected yielding by Odo was no doubt due to failure of strength and health. He was weary of struggle against

Charles and his nobles, against Danish invasion of the land. Let Charles have what was asked, provided that his own honor was secure. As for the pirates, "willing to redeem his country at a price" Odo offered them money, and they retired into winter quarters for 897-98 upon the Loire.

He did more. Not long before he died, on the first of January 898, he made known his wish that the Carolingian Charles the Simple should rule the realm. He was buried with royal honor in the abbey of Saint-Denis and his will was respected; Charles was declared sole king of France.

In Italy the Emperor Lambert early in the summer of 898 called his advisers, including seventy-three bishops, together at Ravenna for the making of a covenant, which he hoped would be a lasting one, between his imperial throne and the Holy See. Formal agreement was exchanged; Berengar was left, as before, to his discontent in his northern marquisate of Friuli.

During the autumn this discontent ripened into action. Berengar marched to attack Lambert's capital city of Pavia, and the emperor was forced to leave his sport of hunting around Marengo, a village south of the river Po, to gather all the men on whom he could lay command and to lead them out against his enemy, encamped at Borgo San Donnino (now Fidenza), near Parma. Victory fell to him, and, well content, he hastened back to Marengo's forest and his chase of the wild boar. On the fifteenth of October he was killed there, either by a murderer's hand or by a fall from his horse. No heir inherited his titles. His son, Guy the fourth, met his own death shortly afterward at the hands of one Alberic, who then seized the duchy of Spoleto. We shall hear of Alberic again.

Now, his chief rival removed from his path, Berengar of Friuli could hope. Once more he gained the royal crown of Italy. But his power was weak, and he spent the months to come in gathering every man he could for its extension southward. Then, before he could hold himself in truth Italy's ruler, the Hungarians, swarming into northern Italy, destroyed his hope. The huge force which he had mustered went out indeed to battle, attacked them time after time, and wrung from them an offer of peace. This in his joy of success Berengar foolishly refused; whereupon the invaders with bold determination rallied all their strength and in September 899 suddenly rushed upon his men on the bank of the Brenta, a river of the northeast. The Hungarian victory which followed gave untold disaster to the king; many Italian nobles were killed and the survivors fled in panic. The enemy stayed in northern Italy, laying waste its land, until in 900 through surrender of hostages and immense bribery Berengar at last induced them to leave.

From 896 onward the king of Germany had been helpless, lying sick with disappointment, worry, and fear. The raiders from Moravia and Hungary were continually descending on his realm; Lotharingia was in revolt year after year against his son, King Zwentibold. It was Arnulf's intense desire that in spite of his irregular birth this son of his should inherit the German crown. A story was told that in his eagerness he rejected the boy, Louis, born to him in 893 from his lawful marriage with his queen, Ota, maintaining that Ota had been unfaithful to him and that Louis was no child of his. Thus, three years passed, while Italy was lost to him, while France no longer felt his influence, while his control of his own German kingdom slipped away, while German chieftains ruled independently their several provinces and drove invaders away by their own power. On December 8, 899, Arnulf died.

The winter of Europe's tenth century was approaching. The lawful heir to the German throne was only six years old; in France a youth of twenty held the royal crown; in Italy there was no royal power, no emperor of the West. Guy and Lambert of Spoleto were dead; Berengar by his failure to resist the Hungarian invaders had lost the support of Italian people, great and little.

Yet, perhaps the coming of the winter of history can be seen no less clearly in the annals of the papacy during this ninth century's last years.

In April 896 Pope Formosus died, and after a tenure of two weeks by a pope named Boniface VI, the Holy See came by election to Stephen VI. He ruled only until 897, but his name is remembered. Possessed by an intense hatred of Formosus and his doings, as one condemned by John VIII and illegally placed in the seat of St. Peter, Stephen assembled a synod at Rome in January 897 for the satisfaction of his resentful mind. Formosus, he decided, should meet after death the judgment which he had escaped in his life on earth. By papal command his dead remains, which had now lain nine months in the tomb, were dragged out, put together into some shape, arrayed in the vestments of apostolic holiness and propped up in the papal chair within St. Peter's basilica for all to look upon in scorn—bishops, priests, deacons, and laymen of high rank present at the council. Against this silent figure accusations were cast, one after another: Formosus had disobeyed canon law in passing from a first episcopal see to a second; he had broken his oath after swearing never to return to Rome, never to exercise priestly function again; he had been ordered to receive communion only as a layman and after this he had dared to accept election as pope. Nothing, however, was said regarding Stephen's chief resentment against Formosus; it was he who had crowned Arnulf of Germany as emperor of the West while Lambert was living, banished from Rome. Pope Stephen VI was a close friend of the House of Spoleto.

To give more realistic character to this "trial," a deacon was ordered to act as defender of the accused. In terror this "friend" stammered out that if Formosus had been bishop of Porto before becoming pope, so had Stephen himself been bishop of Anagni in central Italy.

The pope listened undisturbed, and promptly moved that Formosus be found guilty of the crimes charged against him. All who were present cried aloud, "So be it." At once the papal vestments were torn away and the three fingers of the right hand which Formosus so often had raised in blessing were hacked off. Then the mutilated remains, wrapped in sackcloth, were again dragged along the nave of St. Peter's, to be flung into a "Potter's Field," the burial ground of strangers and aliens. Even there they found no rest. Attracted, it would seem, by the sight of a grave recently dug, robbers in search of plunder opened it, found nothing of value, and threw the relics into the Tiber.

Nor did Pope Stephen spare the living. By his edict letters were sent to all the clergy who had been ordained by Formosus, requiring their "resignation" from sacred office. At this, angry voices rose from many men in Rome. Heaven itself had made clear its wrath at the blasphemous doings of this Pope Stephen, they said; the walls of the Lateran Church had collapsed soon after the "Synod of the Corpse" had been held. Before the end of 897 hired ruffians—by whose order or where we do not know—seized Stephen VI, cast him into a dark and narrow prison, and shortly afterward made an end of him by strangling.

He was followed in the Holy See by Romanus, who died before he had ruled four months and was succeeded by Theodore II. Theodore himself lived as pope but three weeks, but he used them well. In November or December 897 he held a council for the reestablishing in all honor of the clergy who had been deprived and put to shame. About the same time the relics of Formosus were driven by a strong current to the bank of the Tiber at Porto. Theodore heard of this and at once had them brought back to St. Peter's, to lie for some days in state before its altar. Solemn Mass of Requiem was sung, and then at last they were once more laid side by side with those of former popes.

For a short while after the death of Theodore the Holy See was in dispute between Sergius, bishop of Caere, and a Roman priest named John. Sergius actually established himself in the Lateran, but early in 898 John won the victory and was consecrated pope as John IX. Under him, as one ordained priest by Formosus, the acts of the "Synod of the Corpse" were formally condemned; the papers containing its decrees were burned to ashes, and those who had thrown the relics into the river were threatened with excommunication, did they not do penance for their crime.

The story of this "trial" and its annulling has been told by Robert Browning in *The Ring and the Book, X, The Pope:*

> Read—*How there was a ghastly trial once*
> *Of a dead man by a live man, and both, Popes:*
> *Thus—in the antique penman's very phrase.*

He is speaking of Liutprand, bishop of Cremona, whose vivid and unsparing story we shall reach later on. In 900 Pope John IX died, and his successor, Benedict IV, ruled until 903. Then once again struggle for papal supremacy set in. Two priests in turn held briefly the seat of Saint Peter: Leo V and Christopher. Christopher seized Pope Leo and cast him into prison; soon afterward he himself suffered the same fate. Both vanished from sight, and in January 904 that Sergius who had lost to John IX triumphantly sat as pope. The seed of this bitter fruit of dissension and rivalry lay in the "Synod of the Corpse." Was the seat of Saint Peter to be held by one who supported or by one who condemned Pope Formosus? With this question began the record of papal rule in the tenth century.

CHAPTER TWO

Winter, 900-918
Louis the Child; Conrad of Franconia

1

On February 4, 900, the little six-year-old son of Arnulf was declared king of Germany in an assembly of dignitaries of Church and state—archbishops, bishops, and secular nobles—at Forchheim, on the river Regnitz. History knows him as Louis the Child, and his brief reign of less than eleven years was to leave a record of failure and misery, tragic and complete.

As ever, the Church gave its support to a son of the Carolingian line. The counselors of the German kingdom at this time were its great prelates, the archbishops of Mainz, Cologne, and Trier, and they did all that was possible to direct and control affairs for their infant king. But they had a twofold problem on their hands, on either side too great to overcome.

Within the kingdom trouble faced them in their own fellow countrymen, the nobles of Germany. Since 896, during the years when Arnulf was held from action by sickness, strife had been rising among these chieftains, a struggle for power in their own parts of the kingdom. The kingship of Louis the Child extended over five regions of German land: Saxony, Bavaria, Franconia, Swabia, and Lotharingia.

In the later tenth century we shall be able to think of these regions as "duchies" and of their rulers as "dukes" in the sense of the words as commonly understood; the peoples who dwelt in them will have become distinct in character, and their lands will have developed into acknowledged and individual states. At this date, however, the word "duke" still had its original Latin meaning of "leader" in battle. In Saxony, Bavaria, Franconia, and Swabia there was need of such a leader who was strong in power, who could gather under his command the people living around him and march out at their head to beat back invaders of their borders. Already this "leadership" was becoming hereditary here and there; father was handing down his power in legacy to son. If, then, for the sake of convenience we now already call these regions "states" or "duchies" and their chieftains "dukes," it must be remembered that during much of the tenth century these "duchies" were only gradually gaining their right to be thus known as definite territories, ruled by nobles of definite status. Not from gift or grace of the crown of Germany did the German ducal office come into being; it rose from within the people of each region, independent of benefit from outside. Later days will show an opposite course.

The leading House of Saxony in the north had been founded in the ninth century by a Count Liudolf; his younger son, Otto, now held power among its dwellers in this reign of Louis. The people of Bavaria, in southern Germany, looked for protection to Liutpold, their first chieftain. Fear of Hungarian invaders induced them in 901 to make peace with Moravia, that land on their border through which the Hungarians again and again rode to attack them. Nevertheless, Hungarian invasion continued; in 907 Liutpold was killed as he fought its savage descent. His son, Arnulf, inherited his command as Bavaria's "duke by divine providence."

In Saxony and in Bavaria the claims of Otto and of Arnulf as leaders of their people met no opposition. But Franconia, northwest of Bavaria and in the region of the river Main, during the reign of Louis the Child was rocked by bitter struggle between two rival families, fighting for supremacy within it. One was the House of Babenberg, whose head was Adalbert; the other was the House of the Conradins, led by Conrad the Old. In 906 these two chieftains met in battle at Fritzlar on the bank of the river Eder in Hessen; Adalbert won the victory and Conrad the Old was killed. His success, however, won nothing for Adalbert. In the same year, on September 9, he was accused of treason against his country and was promptly put to death; the warrant of execution was signed by King Louis himself, now a boy of thirteen. The leadership of Franconia at once came to the Conradins, in the person of Conrad the Younger, son of Conrad the Old.

The fourth "state," Swabia, in southwest Germany, lay between the rivers Rhine and Lech and included part of Switzerland. It also was harassed by a quarrel ending in death. But here no chieftain had as yet gained recognition as "leader" of his people against their enemies from without. There were indeed claimants for this honor. But no one among them could make good his claim against the determination of Salamo III, bishop of Constance and abbot of Saint-Gall, that his own power should prevail. Strongest among the seculars who struggled was Burchard, a chieftain of Rhaetia (Burchard I).

Lotharingia was still a kingdom when Louis the Child came to the German throne, that kingdom given by Arnulf of Germany to his favorite son, Zwentibold, in 895; but for only a few months, however, did he continue to hold its crown. Lotharingian nobles complained constantly of "the insolence of his ways"; they declared that he ordered the business of the realm in company with women and vulgar folk, that he stripped those high in dignity of their due and valid rights. On August 13, 900, Zwentibold was killed in battle against his rebel subjects on the bank of the Meuse. Lotharingia now recognized Louis the Child as king; its people were always ready to acknowledge the rule of a Carolingian prince. Yet the power of its chieftains remained strong in menace.

King Louis, therefore, acting through his advisers, decided to allow Lotharingia independent administration under his crown; he appointed one Gebhard to govern and protect it as "duke." His act worked little good. Lotharingian nobles cherished a peculiar and special devotion to their own land and as keen a jealousy in regard to their own rights. Gebhard was an outsider, a Conradin from Franconia. Soon Count Matfrid, who had opposed the kingship of Zwentibold, rose again in rebellion and war broke out. In 906 Matfrid was driven into exile; in 910 Duke Gebhard died in battle with the Hungarians and the control over Lotharingia was seized by Reginar "the Long-Neck."

Into this German kingdom, torn by its own dissension and quarrel, there came year after year the onrush of Hungarian enemies, bent upon slaughter and destruction or capture of possessions. In 906 they were victors over Moravia, the gate to Germany; in the same year they fell upon Saxony at the call of Slavs for aid against Henry, son of Duke Otto. Henry fiercely drove out these invaders, but in 908 they were ravaging both Saxon land and that of Thuringia, southeast of Saxony. The people of Bavaria fled before them in 907; the Bavarian army was annihilated, bishops and counts fell in the effort to defend, and, as we have seen, their leader, Liutpold, was killed. Once again Germany's fortune turned for a moment. In August 909 Duke Arnulf won a hard-fought battle against the Hungarians on the river Rott, tributary of the Inn. The same year saw the invaders in Swabia, taking home a prize of prisoners and of cattle in droves; in 910 they were victors once again on the borders of Bavaria and Franconia. When, on September 24, 911, Louis the Child found relief in death from his hopeless reign, two facts were clear to the counselors of Church and state in Germany: its land was exhausted, drained of life by unrest and struggle within, by continual raid from without; and for its people, the Eastern Franks, the royal Carolingian line had come to an end.

It is good to remember that this year, 911, brought hope of peace and comfort to the Franks of the Western realm. About October, and probably some weeks after the death of Louis in Germany, the king of France, still Charles the Simple, signed a treaty at Saint-Clair-sur-Epte which for a while and to some extent banished from Europe the terror of the Northmen and their presence for evil on the banks of the Seine and the Loire. Its provisions yielded to Rollo, now leader of these Vikings from Scandinavia, the territory stretching from the river Epte northward to the sea: the region of Rouen, Lisieux, and Eureux. The act of treaty gave birth to the duchy of Normandy; from this time the Northmen held in France their own lawful home and estate.

2

Louis the Child, eighteen years old at his death, left no heir. Election to kingship was made by nobles of Franconia and Saxony, once more assembled at Forchheim; on November 10, 911, they chose as their sovereign Conrad the Younger, duke of Franconia. Bavaria and Swabia accepted the choice. Conrad was the first non-Carolingian king of German-Frankish birth elected by Germans to hold German duchies under his supremacy. Brave and courageous he was known to be; but his ability to rule his varied peoples in the despair now facing them was open to question.

Franconia, it would seem, now passed to the control of the crown itself; it was Conrad's own duchy. The bishops of Germany gave their support to the king. But other leaders in the realm were by no means minded to yield their independence; they were prepared individually to defend their rights as chieftains within their own borders.

Saxony was quick to show this decision. In 912 Henry, son of
Otto, became its duke upon his father's death. He was not inclined
to bow in reverence before either Church or crown. With Hatto,
archbishop of Mainz, who had been chief counselor of Louis the
Child, Henry had at this moment a quarrel in regard to Thuringian
land on Saxony's southern border. In 915 he dared to rebel against
King Conrad, also involved in this quarrel. The king sent his brother
Eberhard into Saxony with an army. We are told by Widukind, historian of this tenth century, that as Eberhard marched on his road he
complained that no Saxons were bold enough to appear before their
walls to fight with him. He had hardly spoken when Saxons appeared in hordes, to inflict on Eberhard so crushing a defeat that
afterward in jest strolling players in Saxony asked: "Where is there
a hell big enough to hold all the multitude of the royal army that
fell on that day?" So, at least, ran the folktale of Germany which
Widukind loved to repeat. More soberly he added: "The king's
brother feared no longer the absence of Saxon fighters. He had seen
them face to face, and in shame he fled home."

Equally independent of both king and bishops was Arnulf, duke
of Bavaria. At last in 914 Conrad felt compelled to march into Bavaria; in 916 the royal army laid siege to Arnulf's capital city of
Regensburg, captured it, worked much damage by plunder, and
compelled Arnulf to seek refuge among Hungarian enemies of his
land.

In Swabia that chieftain of Rhaetia, Burchard I, had lost his
life in 911 through his endeavor to attain leadership under the persistent hostility of Salamo III, bishop of Constance. The struggle of
secular ambition here was continued by this Burchard's successor,
Erchanger, who in 914 captured the bishop and held him prisoner.
This was a grievous offense against the Church, and evil in the eyes
of the crown, which leaned on episcopal support. Promptly Erchanger was sent into exile by King Conrad. Soon, however, he returned to Swabia, where to his high content he won the dignity of
duke and remained firmly opposed to his king.

But the most definite move against King Conrad was taken by
Lotharingia. Its nobles would have nothing to do with a sovereign
who was not of the Carolingian line, and, therefore, in 911 they
yielded their duchy to France and their homage to its king, Charles
the Simple. In 915, or early in 916, after the death of Reginar, his
son Gilbert became leader of Lotharingia. For long Conrad, bitter
at the loss, had fought in campaign after campaign for this duchy's

recapture by Germany; in 912 he had marched with an army to Aachen, in 913 he had again invaded Lotharingian land. The land stayed in the keeping of France.

September 20, 916, saw at last a firm effort on the part of the bishops of Germany to bring the independent, rebel heads of German duchies into due loyalty and reverent submission to their king. They met at Hohenaltheim in Swabia, together with the priests and abbots of their dioceses and—an important happening—with a legate sent by the pope, John X. Severe action was taken, but gained little success. Henry, duke of Saxony, was not brought to trial; he had made a nominal peace with King Conrad, although he neither consulted him nor desired his approval. Arnulf, duke of Bavaria, and Erchanger of Swabia treated the council's acts of judgment with contempt. Then, in anger Conrad issued sentence against Erchanger; he was arrested, and in January 917 he was put to death. The rule of his duchy passed to another man of independent character and force, Duke Burchard II by name; he seemed to be the best candidate available for the assuring of Swabia's defense from invasion. Arnulf, driven for a while from his Bavarian city of Regensburg, in retaliation set violently to work at plundering the Church's monasteries far and wide; their treasure he then divided between himself and his liege men: misdeeds which earned for him the description of Arnulf "the Bad." In 918 the king marched into Bavaria to punish him. The march brought nothing to Conrad but serious injury and sickness; Arnulf, once more in his capital, held his own as duke.

Throughout this reign, then, Saxony, Bavaria, and Swabia had constantly been rising in rebellion against the crown. Lotharingia had been lost from the beginning. Bishops and lesser clergy had done what they could, only to end in failure. Among secular nobles those alone of Conrad's own duchy of Franconia had given him support.

Once more, also, German annals tell of Hungarian assault, awaited by German people in terror year after year. Once again Arnulf of Bavaria drove the invaders back in flight. With the aid of Erchanger of Swabia he defeated them on the bank of the river Inn in 913; the victory saved Arnulf from destruction, but its memory did not extinguish the wrath of Conrad against the rebel Erchanger.

The reign from which much had been hoped lasted only seven years and once more left Germany in anarchy. Conrad died as Louis the Child had died, exhausted by despair, in December 918. He, too, left no son, and his brother Eberhard, we may suppose, had hoped to succeed him. But the king in his last days ordered Eberhard to convey the German royal heritage and crown to Henry, duke of Saxony. Doubtless Eberhard, when he in loyalty fulfilled his mission, did not actually repeat the words attributed to Conrad by Widukind. But they may well represent Conrad's mind: "Fortune, brother Eberhard, yields its kindest gifts to Henry; power in public affairs lies with the Saxons." Conrad, in spite of his failure as king, could look with discerning eyes upon the character of men; behind the Duke Henry, so often a rebel against his king's weakness, Conrad saw, or thought he saw, a ruler of determination and resource. He trusted that he saw aright; but it was a heavy burden of disorganization and disorder which he handed down to his successor.

CHAPTER THREE

Spring, 919-36
Henry I, the Fowler

Now BEGINS the story of the Saxon kings of Germany who were to lead their people from the long hopeless winter of death toward a new springtide of life. In May 919 Eberhard, before an assembly gathered at Fritzlar, declared Duke Henry well and truly elected king of Germany. Its nobles, willingly and unwillingly, listened with approval or in silence. Only Saxony and Franconia assented to the election; not all five dukes even came to Fritzlar for this day. In hazard and in peril Duke Henry gained his crown. Since the twelfth century, through, it was said, his love of sport, he has been known as Henry the Fowler.

But Eberhard's declaration, bold as it was, proved worthy. Unlike his two predecessors, this king conceived a calculated, shrewd, and wise policy for his rule. He would be in truth head of his realm; he would work for its defense against foreign enemies and he would establish peace within its borders. Rebellion and disorder among his magnates must be replaced by submission to himself as their sovereign. This done, he would leave each of his dukes to administer and protect his duchy freely, as he willed. In a word, he would be not only king of Germany but also the first and foremost of its chieftains, in friendly alliance with his fellow leaders.

From this policy sprang at once Henry's action in regard to the ceremony of kingly coronation. No crowning or anointing after sacred tradition would he accept from the archbishop of Mainz, now Heriger, who was to bestow these rites. The refusal did not spring from humility, as Widukind asserted. The words which in his *History of Saxony* he put into the mouth of Henry as declared to his future subjects are mere fiction: "It is enough for me that for the merit of my ancestors I be named and appointed king by the will of divine grace and your loyalty. Let anointing and a crown be given to those better than I; of so great an honor I deem myself unworthy." The Saxon people were delighted, Widukind said; they lifted high their hands and voices in applause. Henry, however, wanted to receive his kingship from the will of his fellow dukes rather than from the hands of the Church.

With quick decision he set out to bring order into the duchies of Germany. Saxony henceforward, his own land, would be under the control of the crown as long as he was king. It was also entirely natural that Franconia, which had been under the crown during the reign of the late King Conrad, should now receive Eberhard, his brother, as duke.

In other duchies Henry found trouble awaiting him. Duke Burchard II of Swabia was ready to resist all yielding of homage. He was a bold leader, and he had deliberately refused to attend the assembly at Fritzlar. In 919 the king marched against him with an army of full force, and Burchard, "realizing that his power was not equal to this menace, prudently surrendered, with all his strongholds and his people." Henry accepted his submission and left him wide liberty of administration in matters both spiritual and secular. This concession, however, was only partly successful. Although Duke Burchard in secular matters from 920 onwards remained acquiescent, the bishops and clergy of Swabia were constantly encouraged by him in their hostility to Henry as king. Not until this Burchard II died in 926 and one Hermann was appointed duke of Swabia by Henry himself, did the king receive loyal support from Swabia as a whole, from its subjects both ecclesiastic and lay.

In Bavaria King Henry also faced serious rebellion. Arnulf "the Bad," its duke ever independent, spurred on by his victory over the Hungarians in 913, upon the death of Conrad had thought of claiming the crown of Germany for himself; only the opposition of Bavarian prelates had stopped him in mid-course. But his secular nobles were firmly behind him, and when in 921 Henry entered Bavaria with an army to conquer this resistance to his rule and attacked Arnulf's capital city, Regensburg, the duke held out to the utmost of his power. In the end he yielded, to the immense relief of his king, who badly needed the aid of this bold and able fighter in the continuing crises of Hungarian invasion. Arnulf was graciously received into friendship by his conqueror and, alone of all the German dukes under this king, received from him the privilege of appointing the bishops in his duchy. Confirmation of all episcopal appointments, nevertheless, in Bavaria as throughout the kingdom, remained in Henry's hands. For his other duchies Henry reserved to himself the right of naming and investing bishops for German sees.

There remained the duchy of Lotharingia, which Henry was determined to win back from France. The king of France was still the Carolingian Charles the Simple. Gilbert, duke of Lotharingia now some five years, in 920 allowed himself to be declared its king; he was no loyal friend of Charles and his realm. He was indeed a man who cared little for king or country, ready to give his support wherever it would serve him best. Lotharingian he was; but if the king of Germany would promise him more than Charles of France, to Germany he would turn. To his trusted companions he admitted his ambition to follow Lothar II and Zwentibold, to see Lotharingia a kingdom in permanence, and himself possessed securely of its throne. Of all this Henry of Germany was well aware.

The years from 920 onward were full of tragedy for the man to whom, in the minds of many Lotharingian people, Gilbert owed his allegiance, Charles the Simple. The nobles of this Charles, however, led by Robert, a brother of Odo, once king of France, were even now rebelling against him in high discontent because of his persistent affection for a lowborn man named Hagano, with whom he was constantly to be seen, whose advice he sought on all occasions. Many had warned him against his folly, as they termed it, but in vain. Already at Soissons in 920 armed revolt broke out and Charles was captured. He escaped through the contrivance of Hervé, since 900 successor of Fulk as archbishop of Reims; its see, like the duchy of Lotharingia, was traditionally faithful to a Carolingian king.

Meanwhile Gilbert, eager to promote his power as duke, and possibly his crowning as king in Lotharingia, made overtures to Henry of Germany, who seized this chance of winning back Lotharingia's land. Preparation for battle was made by both France and Germany; Charles even marched across the German border with an army. Yet, he knew well the weakness of his crown; Henry, also, had no desire to win his way by open war. November 7, 921, therefore, found both kings meeting to make peace one with another on a boat anchored in the Rhine near Bonn. It was agreed that Lotharingia should remain a duchy of France. The words spoken sounded pleasant in the ears of Charles; but Henry was nonetheless determined that sooner or later that duchy should be within his own realm.

In 922 rebellion in France came to decisive result. Its nobles openly rejected Charles the Simple, and on Sunday, June 30, they gathered in solemn assembly at Reims itself to witness the crowning of their leader, Robert, by Walter, archbishop of Sens. No doubt Archbishop Hervé was weary of upholding the cause of his royal protegé; but perhaps he was relieved that illness prevented him from placing the crown of France in his own cathedral upon a rival's head. Three days later he died.

Nevertheless, Charles the Simple still clung to his throne. The next year, 923, Robert sought support from Henry of Germany in a meeting near the river Rur, a tributary of the Meuse. Friendly conversation was exchanged; Henry wished success, he declared, for this rival king of France. In his eager ambition he even pushed aside his "peace" made with Charles the Simple in November 921 and left the two kings to fight for their claims. On Sunday, June 15, 923, Charles fell upon the army of Robert, encamped at Soissons; in the battle which followed Robert was killed, but his men, struggling to avenge their leader, forced the Carolingian to flee for his life. Nor did they delay election of a successor for their rule. On July 13, only some four weeks later, in St. Médard's abbey at Soissons the archbishop of Sens crowned as king of France Raoul, duke of Burgundy and son-in-law of Robert.

In this same year, 923, Charles the Simple was forced by tragedy to leave the crown of France under the rule of Raoul. To no purpose had he appealed in his despair to those among the nobles of his land from whom he hoped for support. One of them, Count Herbert of Vermandois, invited him under pledge of security to visit him in his fortress of Saint-Quentin on the Somme. It was a traitor's act. The king was seized and held a prisoner, first at Château-Thierry on the Maine and afterward at Péronne, near Cambrai.

King Henry of Germany was quick to grasp this opportunity given by confusion in France. In 923 he invaded Lotharingia; in 925 it was his. He settled its governing under the administration of Gilbert as duke; in 928 he confirmed this possession by giving to Gilbert his daughter Gerberga in marriage. His long endeavor had reached its end; five duchies of Germany were now subject to his crown.

Meanwhile Charles the Simple remained in the hands of his guards. Six years, with brief interval, he lay captive, until death released him in 929. His wife, the Lady Eadgifu, a daughter of King Edward the Elder of England, had long since left France for the shelter of the English court. With her she had taken their son Louis, only a little child when his father fell into Count Herbert's power. From 929 until 936 Raoul of Burgundy was to be sole king of France.

In Germany, in spite of internal peace, the Hungarians still continued to cause trouble from without. From 919 to 926 they raided the kingdom, swooping down on their swift horses to carry off plunder here and there; constantly Henry and his people remained helpless under their attack.

At last in 926 this terror ended for a while. A happy chance brought a leading Hungarian chieftain as prize of war to the royal court; Hungarian envoys promptly appeared, offering ransom without limit if the German king would set him free. Henry refused every offer; he would only accept as ransom a Hungarian pledge of truce with Saxony, to last nine years, from 926 until 935. If this demand were allowed, he on his side promised yearly tribute of money to these invaders of his land. The pledge was given, and at this price his kingdom for a while gained release from assault.

It was worth the price. Wisely Henry used the years of truce in fortifying centers of shelter, castles for defense, throughout Saxony; his vassal dukes recognized his shrewd tactics and followed his lead within their own regions. Saxon men were called in levy to form a great armed force; Saxon cavalry was now at last made effective, drilled and trained to meet and ward off Hungarian riders; Saxon civilians were ordered to build, furnish, and provide food and provision, for the soldiers and the city-fortresses protecting them and theirs. All, indeed, who could work were required to give of their strength and skill under strict organization; even convicted robbers, able in body and forceful in attack, were allowed to exchange penance for service to the state. Franconia and Bavaria, Swabia and Lotharingia, did their best to cooperate with Saxony, the guide. Raids here and there still descended; but for Saxony and the regions on its borders there was release from fear.

Not only, however, was Henry fortifying and preparing his Saxons against the Hungarians; he took advantage of these years of peace to march against other peoples.

Of special interest is his action in regard to Wenceslas (Wenzel), duke of Bohemia, a country on the Bavarian border. The duke was the son of Vratislav, a noble chieftain of Bohemia, killed about 920 in fighting the Hungarians. From Moravia Christianity had penetrated his land, and the work had been continued by missionaries from Bavaria. Wenzel was its enthusiastic supporter. As a boy he had received training, both spiritual and secular, from his grandmother, Ludmila, a lady of high rank; he had learned to read writings both Slavic and Latin. So eagerly had Ludmila instilled into him her own faith in the teachings and practice of her religion that she had aroused resentment in the mind of the Princess Drahomira, the boy's mother: a woman outwardly Christian but no follower of Christian precepts and morals. Resentment had ripened into hatred; hatred had driven Drahomira to murder, and she had ordered her rival strangled by men ready to serve her command. For some years Drahomira had held office as duchess-regent of Bohemia while Wenzel was still too young to rule; at last about 925 he was able to take his place as its duke. Then in 929 Henry of Germany, anxious to extend and to secure his power, came marching into Bohemia and pitched his camp before Prague. Duke Wenzel had no wish to subject his land to a siege which could only end in defeat and misery; he surrendered to the king and promised to pay tribute. In return he won peace and an alliance with Germany which was to last during the few months left to him of life.

Many of the nobles of Bohemia not only disliked, as did Drahomira, the firm adherence of Wenzel to the Christian Church; they also resented his yielding to the Saxon king. Independence in matters civil and religious was their keen desire for their duchy. Before long their smouldering hostility broke out into act, brought about by a younger brother of the duke, named Boleslav, who, Christian though he was, had been very angry at the decision of Wenzel to make no resistance to the invader of his land. In the autumn of 929 (the date which seems preferable; the year 935 is also put forward) Boleslav invited the duke to visit him at his castle. Early one morning—it was September 28—Wenzel was struck by this brother of his and finally killed by three other traitors as he was on his way to church in Bunzlau.

The tenth century had not reached its end when Wenzel was revered as national hero and saint in Bohemia; his name still appears in the calendar year, Czech and Polish. In England his memory has been handed down by legend as "Good King Wenceslas," through the Christmas carol written by John Mason Neale in the nineteenth century.

There were also the Slavonic peoples on the Elbe, always ready to rise for invasion of German land. Soon after Henry had settled his peace with Bohemia, the "Redarii," a Slavonic tribe dwelling around the Elbe, destroyed the fortified town of Walsleben near

Arneburg and killed many of its inhabitants. This led to a general rising of Slavonic peoples; promptly two of Henry's leading commanders were ordered by him to besiege the town of Lenzen, a center of disturbance on the river. For five days their fighters blockaded its gates. On the fifth day messengers arrived who told that an army of Slavs was near at hand, marching in massive force for the relief of Lenzen that very night, the third of September, 929.

Widukind vividly describes the varied feelings of Henry's soldiers as they received this report, as they looked, some with fear, some with eager joy, for the setting of the sun and the night of battle. "By grace of God," he tells, "the night was very dark and rain poured down in sheets; those savage barbarians could not carry out their evil design. All night long the Saxons waited, armed and ready; at the first break of dawn they, one and all, leaders and men, gave oath to each other that they would do their duty as true soldiers on the field. The sun rose clear in the sky, and they marched to battle from their camp outside Lenzen. Now they saw the Slavs approaching: few of them mounted, but those on foot, soaked to the skin, so many in number that the riders behind could scarcely push them forward. Steam flowed like smoke from their dripping tunics, encouraging the Germans as, with a ringing shout, they dashed forward to attack. But they could not penetrate the dense mass facing them; soon they turned to break in wherever this was possible, here and there, separating small sections, right and left, for the kill. For long the Slavs held firm, while many fell on either side and the struggle drew ever more fierce and grim. At last one of Henry's generals sent a lieutenant with fifty men to rush upon the enemy's flank. This manoeuvre took the Slavs by surprise; sudden panic sent them running in confusion to gain refuge within the walls of Lenzen. Hurled back by the Saxon general, who had foreseen this move, they met quick death, cut down by the sword or driven forward relentlessly to drown in the waters of a lake close by."

Now the battle was over; the town surrendered, and its men, with their allies, their women and children, were in German hands. Very happily the king welcomed his army on the return home: "So small a German force to win by God's clemency so splendid a success."

In the autumn of 932, three years before Henry's pact with the Hungarians was to end, he felt that he had had enough of payment of tribute, and of life under truce with these invaders. He was ready, he judged, to act, and his Saxon people gladly rallied in support.

Therefore, he now refused Hungarians the sum which, as usual, they came to demand. In the first days of spring 933 their horsemen were again rushing forward, arrows poised for flight. It was too late; Henry's use of the years of peace had done its work. Again and again the enemy in multitude tried to enter Saxony; the Saxons drove them back to die of hunger and cold. Finally on a marshy plain at "Riade," very probably near the river Unstrut, the king of Germany stood to face them, surrounded by his soldiers, disciplined and ready, the standard of Saint Michael the Archangel flying by his side. There on March 15, 933, he bade them admit defeat; the Christian God was with him and his victory was sure. They accepted peace and swiftly disappeared from his presence, leaving their camp and prisoners to his will. From this time a new feeling of confidence in this overlord swept through the duchies of Germany.

From his victories over Slavonic and Hungarian menace the king turned to deal with Scandinavians. In 934 he led an army against these marauders from the North who were invading Frisia, on Saxony's northwestern line of march. From Chnuba, of Swedish blood but a prince of Denmark, he exacted tribute and Christian baptism by conquest in Danish land, and he forced Gorm the Old, king of Denmark, to ask for terms of peace.

As the years of his rule progressed, Henry the Fowler, who had once for political reason refused his crowning by the Church, saw more and more clearly that his working in union with the bishops and priests of his realm brought good to all his subjects. Before he died his royal court held not only its chancellor but also its chaplains; churches, abbeys, and convents were receiving his aid; missionary campaign was planned and set on foot among the Slavonic tribes who had felt his hand in conquest. Thus, Germany, through the endeavor of both state and Church, was rising in power.

Before, however, we can understand the course of this German king's ambition for the influence of his crown we must see something of the history of countries over which he might hope still further to extend it. Italy, in particular, was constantly in his mind.

We last saw Italy's secular history in 900, when its king, Berengar of Friuli, defeated and harassed for many months by Hungarian invaders, was losing the confidence of his Italian subjects in northern and central regions. Now in their discontent they turned to seek another to rule them. Across the Alps in 900, urgently invited by Berengar's

former friends, came young Louis, king of Provence. Wild enthusiasm greeted his arrival; on October 12, 900, a vast assembly saw him
crowned king of Italy at Pavia. The nobles who gave him their homage on this day conveniently forgot that he was the son of Boso, the
usurper, who twenty years before, in 879, had seized Provence and
made it a kingdom for himself. Had not this Louis been blessed by
the pope himself at Rome? The Holy See was to do more; in 901 Benedict IV, successor of John IX, gave yet another blessing to Louis
and in St. Peter's declared him emperor of the West.

Nothing followed. Only in name was Louis of Provence king and
emperor. Italy's joyful welcome died down, and in the mind of Berengar, long since in retreat at his home of Friuli, hope began to
revive. Once again Italian nobles turned to him, and in 902 he mustered his men once more for battle. In the face of growing distrust
and hostility Louis speedily collapsed. He resigned the crown which
he had held less than two years; he swore in terror never to enter
Italy again; and he was then allowed to hurry back to Provence, dismissed but alive. In July 902, Berengar regained his royal throne.

For three years Louis lay in his kingdom of Provence across the
Alps, brooding over his failure, listening to those who told him to go
forth and dare again. What was an oath wrung from him by force
compared with a crown which his own grandfather had worn? Was
not his mother the daughter of Louis II, himself king of Italy and
emperor in his time?

At last he could resist no longer, and in June 905 he entered
Pavia at the head of an army. Berengar fled a second time; even, if
report is true, as far as Bavaria. In confidence Louis dismissed his
men and advanced with only a few followers to Verona; its bishop,
Adalard, had promised him support. The bishop acted alone; the
citizens of Verona sent messengers in haste to Berengar. Was he not
their king? Why in God's name, had he fled? Louis of Provence, the
intruder, they declared, had only small escort with him. Berengar
must return at once.

He did return in this same year and entered the gates of Verona
under cover of night. In the darkness just before dawn his friends
led him, and the men-at-arms whom he had hurriedly picked up
here and there upon his way, to the house where Louis was said to
be hiding. He was not there; warned of his enemy's march upon
Verona, he had fled to seek sanctuary in its church of St. Peter. Berengar heeded no sanctuary. His soldiers found the church, and there
the fugitive was seized and blinded by them for the crime of this

return which he had sworn never to attempt. Back to Provence he went, and as Louis "the Blind" he lived there until 928, king in name alone for twenty-three years.

Kingship in Italy remained with Berengar, but only his own northern duchy of Friuli felt his power. Yet, he still clung to the hope which he had held for many years, that he might win the throne of empire in the West.

The pope who ruled from 904 until 911, Sergius III, had no sympathy with this ambition of Berengar, and the two popes who succeeded him lived but a short while and were of no importance to history. Under the next holder of the papal throne, however, John X, whose tenure lasted from 914 to 928, peril and crisis in Italy did for Berengar what ambition could not do. During the earlier years of this pope's rule Saracens from Spain were tormenting the south of Italy by invasion; also, strongly entrenched in an encampment high above the mouth of the river Garigliano, they were constantly descending in raids upon the lands of Campania. Against this evil, John X as pope and Berengar as king united their efforts, supported by Alberic, duke of Spoleto in central Italy. In 915 they were rewarded; the Saracens at length were driven from their station near the Garigliano and central Italy at last knew the joy of peace. It was time, the pope decided, to show gratitude to his fellow fighter. Late in 915 he crowned and blessed Berengar as emperor.

Six years later, Italian nobles once more were in revolt against him and he was again facing defeat and shame. But, as it happened, the Hungarians were once more invading Italian land, and now, in his panic, to this enemy of his people he secretly sent an appeal for aid. With the appeal went guides who could lead Hungarian archers to attack the determined Italians, already gathered in camp for war. Thus led, a strong band of Hungarians stole secretly to the camp, took it by surprise, killed many whom they found within it and carried off many more in hope of ransom.

His treachery did Berengar no good and much harm; it only increased Italian determination to reject him as king. Now for the second time the leaders in Italy's politics offered their royal throne to a man reigning across the Alps: Rudolf II, since the death about 912 of his father, Rudolf I, king of that realm of Burgundy founded in 888 beyond the Jura mountains.

It took a month of negotiations to induce Rudolf to accept; he remembered the fate of Louis of Provence and he feared to assume control in a land so long divided by civil strife. But in 922 he sat as king in Pavia among bishops and secular lords of the north.

Berengar, rejected and dishonored as he was, still had his adherents in Friuli, and they urged him to avenge this insult, to drive from Italy this alien intruder. In Verona he had sought refuge from the wrath of his fellow countrymen; from there, gathering up his courage, he marched out to battle. Near Piacenza, south of Milan, in 923 he fought Rudolf's army with what strength he could muster, and was hopelessly defeated. Back to Verona he fled in all haste, and there on April 7, 924, he was murdered by one of his own vassals, one whom he had admired and loved. With him the imperial throne of the West disappeared, to lie unrecognized for nearly forty years.

The fear of Rudolf of Burgundy proved well founded; the Italians of this time were notoriously fickle, ever veering from point to point in their allegiance. For a while he held his rule both in Burgundy and in Italy, now living in one kingdom, now in the other. In Provence Louis "the Blind" was still king in name, but its ruler in reality was one Hugh of Arles, that old city in its land. Report of the energetic, forceful character of this Hugh reached Italy and promptly persuaded its faithless nobles to invite him to visit them. The visit did its work. Early in 926, Rudolf II, finding it no longer possible to keep any loyal unity among his Italian subjects, went back, disappointed and defeated, to his little realm of Burgundy in the region around Besançon. At Pavia on July 6 in the same year, 926, Hugh of Arles was declared Italy's king.

It may be worth while to look here upon an incident of considerable interest to historians but surrounded by doubt through lack of sure tradition: the handing over of the Holy Lance, so famous in these early medieval times, by Rudolf II to Henry the Fowler, king of Germany. The date of this handing over has provided difference of opinion; Reginald Poole and Martin Lintzel have preferred this year of 926, Robert Holtzmann and Walther Holtzmann that of 935. The year 926 seems the better choice.

Liutprand of Cremona tells us that men looked upon the Lance as a sacred relic which would bestow "arms, defiant of conquest, and perpetual victory against foes visible and invisible" upon him who owned it. It held, so tradition declared, a nail from the cross itself of Calvary. According to Liutprand, Henry was eager to possess this treasure, held by Rudolf of Burgundy; he tried to persuade Rudolf to surrender it by means both peaceful and hostile, by offer of gifts and by a threat to burn his lands. At last Rudolf yielded, and Henry's joy was shown in his giving to him not only gold and silver but also a wide tract of land in the duchy of Swabia. The land donated, we may believe, was that of Basel and the region surrounding it, near Rudolf's realm.

It may seem strange that Henry the Fowler, ambitious to see Germany established as the chief power in Europe, should give Swabian territory to the king of Burgundy. Rudolf II was a son-in-law of Burchard II, duke of Swabia. Both Swabia and Burgundy were conveniently situated for him who would march upon Italy; the duke of Swabia and the king of Burgundy were therefore especially open to temptation in this respect.

All this Henry knew well. But in 926 Burchard II was killed by enemies across the Alps, and without delay Henry appointed a loyal supporter of his, Hermann by name, as duke of Swabia. The moment of change of rule was convenient for the changing of Swabia's extent. The fact that part of the duchy had been cut away by the gift to Rudolf would not only earn adherence to Henry and his plans from him, but it would also lessen Hermann's power to act, should he, friend of Henry though he was, be tempted to use Swabia as a road into Italy.

Very possibly Henry shared with other men of his time a belief that the Holy Lance had belonged to Constantine the Great, emperor of Rome in the East in the fourth century, and that therefore its possession symbolized imperial dignity for its owner. And, lastly, in 926 Rudolf II was driven from Italy. He might well have been willing after this disaster to further, for his own sake, alliance with King Henry of Germany by handing over a symbol which had not brought hope of imperial power to himself. The imperial throne in Italy was now held by no man. If he, the king of Burgundy, could not be emperor of the West, perhaps he would find aid from one who might be in the future.

The rise and the fall of kings and emperors in Italy of this tenth century make a tale as complicated as it is grim.

But behind this tale stands a record even more grim. Early in the century, while in their turn Berengar of Friuli, Louis of Provence, Rudolf of Burgundy, and Hugh of Arles held the Italian crown, while Berengar from 905 to 915 was struggling to become emperor, there had been in Rome a gradual rising of the power of the lay nobility. Kings and emperors might come and go, but the nobles of Rome remained; control, in matters secular and ecclesiastic, had been falling more and more into their grasp. At their head from 911 onward stood one Theophylact, who called himself consul and senator of Rome; as Duchesne observes, "he was not a consul, but *the* Consul, not a senator, but *the* Senator" in the city. With him in his rise to power stood his wife, Theodora, who claimed the title of "senatrix." Together they governed Roman policy, made Roman appointments, guided Roman business; at last they held under their hands not only the people of Rome, noble and common alike, but the rulers of the Holy See itself. Their two daughters, Theodora the younger and Marozia, grew up to share their mother's ambition.

A writer of the tenth century described Rome as sinking into corruption under the influence of these women. He was that Liutprand whom we have met before, born about 920 in Lombard, Italy; in his eyes the elder Theodora was "a shameless harlot, who held dominion over Rome as if she were a man," and her daughters "were not only her equals in lustful ways of sex but even more ready for sin." Marozia, Liutprand declared, and the *Book of the Popes* supports him here, was mistress of Pope Sergius III and bore him a son who was himself to be pope as John XI: a story most probably true. Her mother, also according to Liutprand, made Pope John X a victim of her adulterous desire. It was she, we are told, who had driven him in his earlier years to desert his bishop's see of Bologna in northern Italy for the archbishopric of Ravenna, against the canon law of the Church. Not even then was she content. As wife of Theophylact the consul she lived in Rome, and Rome was two hundred miles away from Ravenna and its Archbishop John. In 914 the Holy See fell vacant through the death of an insignificant pope named Lando; Theodora forced John to leave Ravenna in haste, bound for Rome and his promotion to the papacy through her will, and her desire.

So the story runs; but whether we are to believe its details on the authority of Liutprand is a matter of dispute. At any rate this Archbishop John became pope in 914, and he was still pope in 926 when Hugh of Arles became king of Italy. John was looking forward to alliance once again between the royal crown and the papacy, for the defense of Italy and of Rome. Italy was still threatened by the Hungarians and Rome was under the power of Marozia, a power even greater, more dangerous, more grasping than that of her mother. Quickly she felt the pope's opposition to this power and she did not hesitate to act. In 928, working through her husband, Guy of Tuscany, she threw him into prison, where, either through murder—suffocated by a pillow, men said—or, it may be, through the misery of his soul, he died.

By 926 Marozia had twice been married. Her first husband was Alberic, duke of Spoleto, and of this union had been born a son, known to history as Alberic II. After the death of Alberic I she had found a second husband in Guy, marquis of Tuscany. From 928, as before, she continued her domination over Rome and over its Holy See. The death of John X was followed by the succession, in each case won by her naming, of two popes who left nothing worthy of record. Then in 931 her working gave the papal crown to one who was to be known as John XI and, in tradition, as her son by Pope Sergius III.

In 932 Hugh of Arles came to visit Rome. He was now in his sixth year as king of Italy and in 931 he had raised his young son, Lothar, to share his royal rule as co-king. Liutprand tells that Hugh, now a widower, had come to the city at the invitation of Marozia, also left alone; Guy of Tuscany had recently died, and she was again a widow. She needed support; her power, she feared, would fade away without a man of assured dignity and rank by her side. Naturally, her choice fell upon Hugh; she carefully hinted how much she could do in Rome as queen and wife. On his part, also, King Hugh had been uneasy; some rival might try to seize his crown.

There was, however, a barrier standing between Hugh of Arles and a marriage with Marozia. Her late husband, Guy of Tuscany, and Hugh of Arles had been born of the same mother, Bertha; Hugh by her first, and Guy by her second marriage. That made Marozia related by law to Hugh, and the Church frowned upon a union of two persons thus connected.

Yet the influence of Marozia, supported by murderous violence and fraud on the part of Hugh, contesting that the relationship had no basis in fact, brought about their wish, and a ceremony was carried out within the castle of Sant'Angelo, that ancient fortress so often appearing in the story of this time. It stood upon a bridge at the entrance to Rome; on its wall rested the church of Saint Michael the Archangel.

Hardly had the two been declared man and wife when the hope which sprang from their union died. Marozia had brought to Hugh as stepson Alberic II, the child of her first marriage. He was a youth of sixteen, of high spirit and shrewd, eager mind. Perhaps he was jealous of Hugh; perhaps he feared Hugh's power over Rome, over himself, Marozia's son. In the pages of Liutprand, again our source, we read a tale of rude and unkind behavior of Hugh during the wedding feast. Marozia had told her son to serve water to his step-father for the washing of his hands. The boy obeyed reluctantly and in careless manner; in anger Hugh slapped his face.

Young Alberic went directly from the castle to lay complaint against his mother and Hugh, king of Italy, in the presence of nobles of Rome. "Where is this city's pride," he stormed, "that it should do the will of one loose woman? Are the Romans to obey a man from Provence that once was subject to their rule? If my stepfather treats me, his son, in this way when he is new to our house, what do you think he will do to you when he has come to know Rome and you, its nobles?"

Hugh and his bride were still at Sant'Angelo when suddenly a regiment of armed soldiers appeared. In a moment the fortress was surrounded. Hugh, the king, just managed to escape on a rope let down over the wall; he left Marozia to her fate under the anger of her son Alberic.

Young as he was, from this time Alberic was in command of Rome. Hugh of Arles was at once banished, though he continued to hold the title of king in Italy and year after year he attempted to invade the city by armed assault. He did not succeed. In Alberic the people of Rome had at last gained a ruler whom they could both admire and fear, strong to control the swaying moods and quickly changing wills of the lords of its palaces and to check tumult of the mob so readily excited in its streets and squares. He governed Rome for twenty-two years, from 932 until 954, and steadily his power increased: "Prince of all the Romans, great was his strength. Exceedingly to be dreaded, his yoke lay heavy upon those who dwelt in Rome, even upon him who sat in the Apostolic See." So wrote a monk in the tenth century as he looked down toward Rome from his monastery of St. Andrew on Mount Soracte. His name was Benedict, and he left us a chronicle of these years. Though his Latin is terrible, his comments are of great interest and value. The experience of his time recalled to him the words of the prophet Isaiah: "The effeminate shall rule Jerusalem"; so, he declared, "the power of Rome has been made subject to a woman." Also he told that Hugh of Arles, in his rage against the victory of his stepson Alberic II, plotted to tear out Alberic's eyes and thus to win again mastery over Rome.

If he did plot this revenge, he did not carry it out. Rome was lost to Hugh and to his wife, Marozia; from 932 her power and her presence were dead to her world. And more: all control in secular matters was now cut off from the pope whom that world held as her son, and, therefore, brother of Alberic himself. For some time Alberic kept John XI in prison. Finally, he was released, but he was allowed to work only in matters of his own spiritual office. In 936 he died.

Trouble also continued to visit Hugh in his kingdom of northern and central Italy. About 933 the faithless Italians, despising a ruler who had been driven from Rome, were proposing to recall once more Rudolf II, king of Burgundy, to hold their crown. Hugh felt it wise to conciliate Rudolf and arrest any thought of invasion on his part by yielding to him lands claimed by himself, Hugh, within that realm of Provence which the death of Louis "the Blind" in 928 had left open to conflict. Louis had no heir of legal birth.

Such, then, was the position of Rome and of Italy in 935 when Henry I of Germany was making himself the chief power on the continent of western Europe. Raoul, still king of France, the easier in his mind since the Carolingian Charles the Simple had died in 929, had sent his envoys to ask aid from Germany; there was bitter quarrel between him and Herbert, count of Vermandois, who had held Charles prisoner. Herbert, also, and Rudolf of Burgundy had sought counsel and support from the German crown. Now in this year Henry invited Raoul of France and Rudolf of Burgundy, with Herbert of Vermandois, to meet him for a frank discussion of their aims and desires. The three kings came together in June at Ivois on the river Chiers, near Sedan. Here at last Henry's influence brought about the end for which he had hoped. Intrigue and quarrel sank before it, at least for the time, and all declared a will for peace.

It was a happy moment for the king of Germany. He himself controlled the loyal people of his own Saxony. His dukes were aware of his power; so were France and Burgundy. His son Otto was married to Edith, sister of Athelstan, king of Wessex in England.

There remained Italy; since the murder of Berengar in 924 no man, even in name, had held the imperial crown of the West at Rome. Arnulf, duke of Bavaria, had indeed showed clearly his ambition to gain the crown of Italy, and he had failed. Would it be possible for him, Henry, king of Germany, to deprive Arnulf of further plotting and planning, to overcome the resistance of Alberic, master of Rome, to drive Hugh of Arles from his nominal kingship?

Did such thoughts stir within Henry? On this problem Eugenio Duprè-Theseider has an interesting discussion. Widukind states that he meant to go to Rome. Was he to go as pilgrim to its holy places, as the historian Thietmar had heard? At the head of an army as rival of Alberic and Hugh? As one who hoped to win royalty at Pavia, empire from the hands of the pope in St. Peter's? Or did he, thinking back upon the struggles with enemies from within and from without his land, judge it better to rest content with what it had been given him to win for Germany?

Fate decided the matter for him. In the early autumn of 935, while he was taking a brief holiday, hunting in the Harz Mountains, a paralyzing stroke ended whatever hope or fear he had held. All the winter he lay helpless in his bed. In the spring of 936 he was able to call together, at Erfurt in Germany, leading men from Saxony and Franconia and to declare before them his son Otto his heir and successor to his throne.

Surprise, discontent, and disappointment followed the words he spoke. Many, including his queen, Matilda, had looked for the name of a younger son, Otto's brother Henry, who was far more popular at court. They at once raised the question: Had not Henry the better right, since his father was already king of Germany when he was born? Otto had been born before 919, son of a mere duke of Saxony. At this time the realm of Germany recognized no natural right of the firstborn to inheritance.

King Henry changed neither his word nor his certainty, won by watching, that Otto would make the better king. He had, indeed, another son, the eldest of all. His name was Thankmar, and his mother, Hatheburg, had broken a vow to follow the religious life when Henry had pleaded for their union while he was young, irresponsible, and impulsive. Because of this sacrilege, as the Church had held it, Thankmar, their son, had been declared illegitimate and Hatheburg no true wife. Henry had not rebelled or resisted this judgment; he had fallen in love with another woman. The Henry of these younger days was not the Henry who became king of Germany. The woman he had now married in due order of law was Matilda, and she bore him five children: three sons, Otto, Henry, and Bruno, and two daughters, Gerberga and Hedwig. Gerberga we have seen as wife of Gilbert, duke of Lotharingia; Hedwig was married to Hugh, duke of the Franks. In point of policy and international alliance Henry of Germany had seen his daughters wisely wedded.

The Council of Erfurt was the last event of importance in his life. His reign was over. Much had been done; much remained to do. It had not been given to him, the Saxon, to unite under his imperial throne the lands held by the Frank, Charles the Great, the king who year after year had relentlessly conquered and driven to death Henry's own Saxon ancestors. That ambition, that hope of empire, he was leaving to the son he had called to follow where he had led. At least he himself had done all in his power to make ready the way. The thought was strong within him when a second stroke brought death on July 2, 936.

CHAPTER FOUR

Spring into Summer, 936-83
Otto I, the Great; Otto II

1

Kingship in Germany for many years was to continue to spring into life, amid difficulties innumerable and crises which threatened to destroy all hope. The son whom Henry the Fowler had chosen as inheritor of his crown was both like and unlike his father, in aim and in character. It was for him, he knew well, to rule his own kingdom in firm authority, to attach his nobles to himself in proper subjection, to protect and to extend German power, to march out to conquer the barbarian and the heathen. As king he was openly loyal to the Church. Day after day he rose from his bed to hear Mass and office; he was to use the energy and the skill of his prelates not only in matters ecclesiastical but also secular. He himself was no scholar and not even passably educated, though we find him speaking Old French and also Slavonic now and then. Hunting was his recreation out-of-doors; at home he sometimes gave an hour of leisure to a game of chess or draughts. He was quiet and reserved in manner; but he enjoyed talk, light or serious, at table with his friends: a relaxation for the moment from the hard realities of his life. At the time of his election in 936 he was twenty-four years old; from his marriage in 929 with Edith of England he had two children: a son, Liudolf, and a daughter, Liutgard.

Saxon as Otto was, and determined as Saxon king of Germany, yet his admiration of his great predecessor, Charlemagne, lent joy to his crowning in Aachen, where that Charles the Great had ruled, where he had welcomed ambassadors from many lands, where he had gathered much treasure, where he had delighted in sport and in debate with all his energy, where at last he had been laid to rest.

The Saxon historian Widukind and, in less generous detail, Thietmar, chronicler of the early eleventh century, give us a picture of the ritual carried out on August 7, 936. Escorted and followed by a great company, the young king-elect arrived at the palace church of Saint Mary the Virgin, built by this same Charlemagne. Already the dukes and chieftains, military and civilian, of the German realm had taken their places in due order of rank at its entrance, around which rose high the pillars of its outer hall. There they set him upon a high seat before them; and then, one after another, putting their hands in his, they promised him with solemn oath their loyal support against all enemies. While these nobles of secular office were thus acknowledging their ruler-to-be, Archbishop Hildebert of Mainz, with his clergy and a congregation of humbler folk, was awaiting sight of the procession which was to conduct Otto from the outer hall into the church itself. When it appeared, Hildebert, splendid in the vestments of his dignity and carrying the crozier, moved forward to take Otto by the hand and to lead him into the center of the church. It was octagonal in form, and there were galleries running around it on two levels, so that every one present could see what was going on. Looking up and around, "Behold," the archbishop said, "I bring to you one chosen by God and named by your lord of former days, King Henry. Now he has been declared king by all the nobles of our realm; if this election finds favor with you, show your consent by lifting toward heaven your right hands." All at once raised their hands and cried aloud, "Hail to our new Leader!" Then Hildebert and the king, who after the Frankish custom was wearing a simple tunic, walked slowly to a place behind the altar, on which were lying the royal insignia: the sword with its shoulder-belt, the mantle, the sceptre, and the crown. One by one, with words which warned him of the symbolic meaning of each for himself and his people, Hildebert invested the young man of twenty-four with these outward marks of his burden of power; last of all, he and Wikfried, archbishop of Cologne, anointed him and placed his crown upon his head. Then amid renewed shouting of the crowd Otto was led to his high throne.

Once more the procession formed, to move up the slope toward the royal palace on its height, where all was ready for the coronation banquet. The king sat with his bishops; service was offered them by the great dukes of Germany, now vassals of Otto. Arnulf of Bavaria had charge of hospitality and lodging for the guests; Eberhard of Franconia superintended the serving of the feast; Hermann of Swabia was steward of the wine; Gilbert of Lotharingia kept a keen eye on all that was done, since Aachen lay in his duchy.

So the great day came to its end in revel and merriment, and then Otto said farewell to his dukes and bishops with giving of thanks and of rich presents as marks of his joy.

This joy of a few hours quickly passed away, and Germany's king faced the future. Action was needed for the protection of German frontiers. The Danes were rising in new invasion from the north; so were the Slavonic peoples on the Elbe. For defense against the Slavs he put one Hermann Billung in charge of the region on the northern border of Germany. This Hermann, who must not be confused with Hermann, duke of Swabia, was loyal, able, and energetic, but the honor given him at first caused trouble. His elder brother, Wichmann, angry because he had not been appointed, promptly left Otto's army under pretense of sickness; the quick success of Hermann against the Slavs even drove Wichmann in his jealousy to rebel against the king. Prudence, however, soon brought him to submission.

In 937 the constant restlessness of Slavonic tribes forced Otto to send north another count of the border, one Gero. Against him the Slavs plotted murder, which Gero forestalled by stealing upon their camp one night when they were holding high revel and by killing some thirty of their men. Nevertheless, they continued to plunder and to burn German fields and buildings. Nothing seemed to deter them. Widukind wrote in discouragement: "They are a race hardy and enduring, accustomed to live on next to nothing. What to us in Germany seems a heavy burden, the Slavs count as some sort of pleasure." Again and again Otto himself led out his army to battle, but still "they preferred war to peace, choosing to live in all hardship if only they might be free." At last the united efforts of Hermann Billung and Gero, supported by the king, brought them to surrender a wide area, in the land reaching from the Elbe as far as the river Oder.

Further trouble came from Bohemia, where Boleslav I, who was now its duke in the place of the brother whom he had murdered, rose also in rebellion. And so he continued for fourteen years until in 950 Otto marched against him with so strong a force that the duke found it prudent to promise loyalty for the future rather than lose his duchy and probably his life. The dreaded Hungarians also rode to plunder, "to put to the test the courage of this new king." At the beginning of 937 they were in Franconia on their way to Saxony, and Otto drove them back; in 938 he defeated them in Saxony, and from that time they left his Saxon duchy alone.

These were the worries which early in his reign fell upon Otto from outside his kingdom. During these earlier years he also faced peril from within, rising both from his family and from the nobles of his realm.

In 937 Arnulf "the Bad," duke of Bavaria, died, and his son Eberhard succeeded him. Upon this change in rule Otto as overlord decided that the time had come to increase his own royal power by diminishing privilege for Bavaria's duke. Arnulf, as we have seen, alone among dukes in the German kingdom had been allowed by Henry the Fowler to choose and to name those who should be consecrated bishops for his duchy. It was most important, Otto knew well, that crown and Church should work hand in hand, and he was determined to possess what he believed to be his right. So now he announced to Duke Eberhard that the right of nominating bishops, for Bavaria as for the rest of Germany, was his as king and his alone.

This at once provoked Eberhard to rebel; soon Bavaria was divided between those who supported him and those who kept loyalty toward the crown.

Another who broke his allegiance to Otto was Eberhard, duke of Franconia. The historian Widukind traces this rebellion first of all to the Franconian's wrath at what he considered Saxon arrogance. "The Saxons," wrote Widukind, himself a Saxon, "were so proud because King Otto was one of their own people that they disdained to serve or to accept as liege lord any man who was not of Saxon birth." In 937 a Saxon named Bruning who held a town, Hellmern, in feudal tenure under Eberhard, refused to treat his Franconian lord with proper respect; in his anger Eberhard burned Hellmern with the farms surrounding it and killed those who lived in them. When Otto heard of this working of revenge by a duke subject to his crown, he ordered him to hand over to that crown horses to the value of one hundred talents of silver. It was a heavy penalty. But far more offensive in Franconian eyes was the punishment ordered by the king for those who had aided Eberhard in Hellmern's destruction. They were to appear in shame and disgrace, carrying dogs in their arms, at Otto's royal palace in Magdeburg, Saxony. Franconia now burst into open revolt; in vain during May 938 the king endeavored to calm its rebels in a council at Steele, on the Ruhr near Essen.

A third to rise against the Ottonian House was Otto's half-brother, the Thankmar who had been held ineligible for kingship in Germany. Thankmar was not only jealous of Otto but also of Otto's own brother, Henry; as son of Hatheburg he believed that he had been defrauded of property left to him at her death. He therefore joined Eberhard of Franconia in battle; they laid siege to the town of Belecke on the river Möhne, captured Henry himself, and took possession of a strongly fortified center, Eresburg, placed where afterward was to stand the town of Ober-Marsberg on the Diemel.

The year was still 938 when Otto decided to take vigorous action. Toward Eresburg he marched, and in their fear its citizens surrendered without resistance. Thankmar fled to sanctuary in its church of St. Peter. Without Otto's knowledge some of Henry's men struck down the door of this refuge with their hatchets and rushed in; Thankmar was seen standing before the altar, on which he had laid his sword and chain of gold. Perhaps, as Percy Ernst Schramm has thought, this was an act of symbol; perhaps in this way Thankmar had shown his will to yield homage to his king and brother. But the soldiers who were hunting him understood nothing of this; they had found the enemy and they ran to kill. A brief time Thankmar resisted, fighting with courage; then a spear thrown through a window near the altar caught him in the back and he died.

Henry, taken prisoner by him and guarded by Eberhard of Franconia, was now set free and there was peace for a while between Franconia and the crown of Germany. Otto turned to reduce Bavaria to submission; in 938 its duke, Eberhard, son of Arnulf, was sent into exile and its duchy was entrusted to the rule of his uncle, Arnulf's brother Berchtold, a man loyal to his king.

Not for long did peace endure; in 939 there were again three nobles of Germany busy in preparing plans for the overthrow of Otto and the success of their own ambition: Duke Eberhard of Franconia, Henry, brother of Otto, and another partner who longed for power, Duke Gilbert of Lotharingia. War followed. In March of this year Otto was standing with the main part of his army on the bank of the Rhine at Birten, near Xanten. Ferryboats had just begun the long business of carrying his men across the river; at the moment only about a hundred had landed on the further shore. Suddenly, as he looked across, to his horror he saw a strong force of the enemy, led by Henry and Gilbert, riding to attack this little band, divided from him and from their fellow soldiers by waters impossibly wide. The king could do nothing but pray Heaven for help, holding the Holy Lance close within his hand.

His men served him well. Fifty in one rush and fifty in another, they fell upon the rebels, on the front and on the rear. Despair gave them strength, and to their effort the enemy at last began to yield.

Then strategy, thought up by some quick mind, came to the rescue. Some of Otto's German soldiers could speak the Old French language familiar to so many of Duke Gilbert's Lotharingians. In its words they shouted to them to save their lives by flight; and the words were taken as a command from Gilbert himself. So Widukind tells. At any rate by a miracle the battle ended in victory for Otto, in a record of rebels killed, captured, or driven from the field, of baggage seized and divided among the conquerors. Henry fled to Merseburg in Saxony, where he shut himself in with its townspeople and his own followers, to resist blockade from Otto during two weary months. Then he surrendered and was given a truce of thirty days.

Later in 939, not Otto himself but a force sent by him was on watch in the region of the Rhine, searching for Eberhard of Franconia and his ally, Gilbert, Lotharingia's duke. Both leaders were busy in plundering the country around when Otto's soldiers, led by Hermann, duke of Swabia, heard that the two were near at hand; quickly they hurried forward to find and to attack. Chance gave them good fortune; they caught both men near Andernach, peacefully sitting to enjoy a meal by the river. It was October the second, and the situation somewhat resembled that of March. But this time most of the rebel army had been carried to the further side of the river; Eberhard and Gilbert were waiting to be ferried across, guarded only by the few who remained. The victory was easy for Hermann. Those of the enemy on the opposite bank of the Rhine, left without command, promptly fled. Duke Eberhard fought stubbornly, only to die, exhausted by his wounds; Duke Gilbert rushed to a boat arriving near by and was drowned when it sank under the weight of many, all trying to climb on board at once.

Otto now endeavored to work for peace. To Hermann and his brother Udo, Hermann's fellow general in the battle, he gave his grateful thanks. Franconia, he ordered, was from this time to be under the rule of the crown of Germany. In his relief and joy of victory and in hope of an end of struggle with the third rebel, his brother Henry, the king conferred upon him administration of Lotharingia; Henry had sought retreat there after his surrender. But the Lotharingians would have nothing of Henry as their duke. Soon he was forced to abandon his rule; in 940 this was given to a noble of Lotharingia's own land, Otto, son of Ricwin of Verdun.

Of these rebels, then, Henry now remained. Humiliation gave rise to even deeper resentment and jealousy in his mind. He had never

been able to forget that his mother Matilda and many German nobles
would gladly have seen him as their king. In 941 we find him plotting a move more evil than rebellion. Easter was approaching and
Otto intended to spend its days at his palace of Quedlinburg, pleas-
antly situated near the Harz Mountains. There, Henry decided, he
would remove for ever this brother who stood between him and the
German throne; men were always at hand who would gladly kill for
money.

But the king had an efficient staff, and word of this plot was
brought to him in time for his defense. He went to Quedlinburg and
celebrated Easter with all ceremony, protected day and night by
armed guards; the conspirators, whose names were known, could
not reach him. Once Easter was over, they were all arrested, except
Henry who escaped. He stayed eight months in hiding, and then
suddenly on Christmas Day 941 he appeared before Otto, clad as a
penitent in sackcloth, to swear oath of loyalty in return for pardon.
Again and again he pleaded, and Otto could not bring himself to
refuse. Year after year Henry kept his word, and at last Otto resolved
to reward and encourage him. Bavaria in 947 had lost by death its
ruler, Berchtold; Henry became its duke.

It was Otto's hope that by giving administration of the duchies
of Germany to members of his own family he might bind them in
faithful service to the crown; by the year 950 each of the duchies
was in the keeping of a ruler connected with the Ottonian House.
Saxony and Franconia were under his own control as king; Bavaria
was governed by his brother Henry; in 944 upon Duke Otto's death
Lotharingia had come by his royal will to Conrad the Red, a nephew
of Conrad I, king of Germany, and in 947 this duke of Lotharingia
had become the son-in-law of Otto the king by marriage with Liutgard, daughter of Otto and Edith of England; in 949, Swabia's duchy,
left without a ruler through the death of Hermann I, had been entrusted to Liudolf, King Otto's son by that same first wife.

It is time to look at France and her history in these years. The relation of Otto of Germany to the realm of France during the eighteen
years from 936 to 954 cost him also intense thought, planning, and
effort. On June 19, 936, some six weeks before he himself was
crowned at Aachen, Louis IV, now fifteen years old, had been elected
king of France upon the death of Raoul. Louis was a son of Charles
the Simple and therefore of true Carolingian lineage. His accession
for a while troubled the German king. Might the descent of this

Louis from the great Charlemagne give him a prior claim to the throne of empire which was already in the vision of Otto's mind? Moreover, Louis had been brought up at the royal court of England to which his mother had fled from France. He was known as Louis d'Outremer; the English would surely be his friends.

Fate, however, was to prove cruel to this Louis d'Outremer. His rule was threatened by the nobles who held chief power at this time in France: Hugh, duke of the Franks, and Herbert, that count of Vermandois who had seized and held his father. He longed for the return of Lotharingia to his crown, and many of its people also longed to see it in Carolingian hands; in 939 Lotharingian nobles were giving him their homage, in rebellion against Germany. But Hugh and Herbert did their utmost to oppose him, and naturally Otto, who held himself king over Lotharingia, made common cause with them. In 940 he invaded France. By the work of these three, determined in an allied effort, Louis was driven from Lotharingia and took refuge in Burgundy.

Two years later, in November 942, we find Otto in a different mood. King Louis was his brother-in-law; he had married Gerberga, sister of Otto, after her first husband, Gilbert of Lotharingia, had been drowned in the Rhine. Gerberga was naturally eager for peace between Germany and France.

Now Otto and Louis met to make agreement one with another, probably at Visé-sur-Meuse, near Liège; from this time Louis left Lotharingia in peace under German rule. Soon Otto induced Hugh to submit to the king of France as his lord, and in 943 Herbert of Vermandois died.

Yet, in spite of that reconciliation Duke Hugh of the Franks did not keep faith with his king. In 945 Louis IV was captured at Rouen by a treacherous move of Danes from the North, who promptly delivered him to Hugh as prisoner. Protest came from two directions, requiring his release; from Edmund, who in 939 had succeeded his brother Athelstan as king of Wessex in England, and from Queen Gerberga, who sent envoys to Otto of Germany, begging for his aid. In July 946 Louis was free, mainly through the intervention of Otto, who had gathered a great army "from all his dominions" and had once more invaded France.

Time after time this Louis of France was to seek support from Otto against his rebellious magnates. In April 947 he was at Aachen, keeping Easter with the king of Germany; in August the two were together near Mouzon and the river Meuse. The month of June 948

saw the assembling of a council in the church of Saint Remi at Ingelheim on the Rhine near Mainz. The pope himself, now Agapetus II,
had sent his legate, Marinus, to Otto for its convoking; so, too, he
had ordered bishops of Germany and France to attend. More than
thirty were present, the greater part from Germany, together with
Otto and Louis. There Louis declared his grievance against Hugh,
duke of the Franks, and ended, according to Flodoard, annalist of
the times, with this appeal: "Many, many troubles I have suffered
since I received the crown of France. Should any one declare that I
have brought them upon myself by my own evil doing, I will rest
my cause either upon the judgment of this synod and the decision
of King Otto, or I will defend myself by my own argument."

The debate lasted two days. It upheld the king of France; it
threatened his enemy, Hugh, with excommunication unless he should
justify his past action before a council called for this purpose.

Hugh offered no such action, and Otto sent his son-in-law, Conrad the Red, duke of Lotharingia, into France for the support of
Louis. In September another synod, meeting at Trier, excommunicated Hugh as one stubborn and defiant. The sentence was moved
by a legate and chaplain of Otto. In the following year Pope Agapetus II, before a synod held in St. Peter's at Rome, confirmed the
decree.

At last in 950 peace was given to the distracted land of France.
King Louis IV and Duke Hugh of the Franks stood on the banks of
the Marne, one on either side, and negotiated agreement of harmony through their several envoys, who crossed and recrossed the
river. Among them Conrad the Red was prominent. The peace lasted,
and Otto showed friendship to both parties. In 951 he was again
listening to Louis, asking help in further trouble, and during Easter
at his palace of Aachen in Lotharingia he was entertaining Hugh as
his guest.

Once again, in 953, this harmony was renewed when Louis and
Hugh declared their good faith before an assembly at Soissons. The
next year King Louis d'Outremer died, and his widow, Gerberga,
sent to ask Duke Hugh for his advice and assistance. He gave both,
and thus, Lothair, son of Louis and Gerberga, at this time only thirteen years old, was declared and crowned king of France in November 954.

So much for the power of Otto the Great amid the troubles of France
during the earlier years of his reign. What was happening in Italy?

Here a chain of events was also leading to his intervention. We left Rome in 936—the year of Otto's coronation and of the death of Pope John XI—under the supreme control of Alberic II. For eighteen years, from 936 until 954, Alberic continued to rule the city, intolerant of any rival, while pope after pope submitted to his will. Hugh of Arles was king of Italy, conscious of Otto's ambition to gain the imperial crown. Since that same crown was also hovering before his own mind, Hugh persevered, year in and year out, in two paths of policy. Constantly he attacked Alberic, while constantly he met defeat in the end; he did all that he could devise to propitiate Otto, while secretly he plotted against him. Otto, in spite of all the rebellions in his own land, was already thinking of an advance upon Rome. He knew well that he who would enter Italy must dominate Burgundy, which would lie in his path. Rudolf II, king of Burgundy, had died in 937, and Hugh had seen a chance of seizing its crown; Rudolf's son and successor was only fifteen years old. Prudently Hugh, now freed by Marozia's death, had married Rudolf's widow, Bertha. With equal prudence Otto had countered this move by carrying off Rudolf's son, known later on as Conrad the Peaceful. He had kept him at the German court and had wrung from him a solemn assurance of loyalty.

But Hugh of Arles had another to contend with in Italy besides Alberic. A rival for his own kingship appeared in Berengar, count of Ivrea in Lombardy, a grandson of that Berengar of Friuli who had been crowned emperor of the West in 915. By 941, however, Berengar was fleeing for protection to Hermann, duke of Swabia, who escorted him on his way to seek help from Otto. Berengar received nothing except courtesy; Otto had his private thoughts concerning Italy and its kingdom.

Four years later Berengar was in Italy once more with fresh hope of success, and soon his hope was fulfilled. Hugh, now king only in name, left Italy for the shelter of Provence, still dreaming of revenge and return. He lived only a few months, and his death in 947 was followed in 950 by that of his son and co-king, Lothar. Lothar in vain had tried to strengthen his position by marrying a girl of sixteen: Adelaide, daughter of Rudolf II of Burgundy. In December 950 Berengar, count of Ivrea, and his eldest son, Adalbert, were crowned joint-kings of Lombard Italy in its capital city of Pavia.

This Berengar II was to reign in Italy from 950 to 961. Widukind calls him "a man fierce and greedy, who would sell all justice for money." The words rise from Berengar's cruelty to Lothar's widow, Adelaide; not yet twenty, beautiful and charming, she had won the hearts of her husband's Italian subjects. Moreover, she was of royal blood. Berengar had good reason to fear that she might soon find a second husband, some powerful Italian noble who would use her influence in the land to hurl him himself from his throne. In April 951 he shut her up in prison at Como and after a while transferred her for still safer keeping to a fortress on the Lago di Garda.

Her friends worked hard to rescue her. At last in August, through the aid of Adelard, bishop of Reggio nell 'Emilia, she escaped to the fortress of Canossa, near Reggio, owned by a liege man of Adelard. Nobles of her land, together with her brother, Conrad the Peaceful of Burgundy, implored Otto to invade Italy for her defense.

No invitation could have been more welcome; Otto lost no time. In September 951 he was already marching with an army toward Italy, accompanied by two of his brothers: Henry, duke of Bavaria, and the youngest, Bruno, whom two years later he was to appoint archbishop of Cologne. At his approach Berengar fled. Otto then entered Pavia and declared himself king of Lombard Italy. With no hesitation he sent messengers to Adelaide. Would she be his wife and queen? His marriage with Edith of England had ended with her death in 946. Before the end of 951 Otto and Adelaide were married in Pavia.

As husband of one who had been queen of Lothar, Otto felt that confirmation of his claim to kingship over Italy was sure. And not only to kingship. Now he sent from Pavia his envoys, Frederick, archbishop of Mainz, and Hartbert, bishop of Chur, to Pope Agapetus II at Rome, praying for approval of himself as Italy's king and suggesting that the pope look graciously upon his entry into Rome for coronation in St. Peter's as emperor.

He did not realize the strength of the force marshalled against him. Alberic, master of Rome, was absolutely determined that no other man should displace or even dispute his authority there. The pope was helpless; he could only refuse consent. Otto in 952 saw that there was nothing for him but a retreat with his bride to Germany. Duke Conrad the Red was left in Italy by him to do all that could be done in dealing with Berengar, who of course returned with all speed as king of Italy.

Conrad worked hard. He managed to persuade Berengar that a visit to Otto at his German court would serve his interests. Berengar

came, and at first received but scant hospitality. Eventually, however, he was welcomed with honor, doubtless through advice of Conrad to his king, and he received invitation to a council to be held
near Augsburg in August 952. There, on the bank of the river Lech,
in the presence of the archbishops of Ravenna and Milan from Italy,
and of a multitude of nobles from the duchies of Germany, Berengar
and his son Adalbert swore homage to Otto as their overlord. They
then returned to Italy, and King Berengar, thus supported, hoped
for peace.

In 954 Alberic died. Benedict, the monastic chronicler of St.
Andrew-on-Mount-Soracte, records that in his last days he called
the leading nobles of Rome to his house and drew from them assurance on their sworn word that when the hour arrived they would
elect his son Octavian as pope in succession to Agapetus II, still at
this time ruler of the Holy See. That was for the future; now in 954
Octavian followed his father as "prince" in Rome.

During 953 and 954 Otto was too much occupied with his German
kingdom and its problems to think of intervening in the affairs of
Italy. After his first wife, Queen Edith, had died in 946 he had formally declared their child, Liudolf, heir to the crown of Germany;
Liudolf was then about sixteen years old. The next year his father
had seen him married to Ida, daughter of Hermann I, duke of
Swabia; and, as we have noted, after, in December 949, Hermann
had died, Otto had entrusted the duchy to this, his eldest son. He
loved Liudolf with all his heart and he was preparing him for his
future destiny.

But, even before the king, his father, had marched into Italy in
951, Liudolf had gone there on his own account, eager to raise his
standing wherever he could. Then came the marriage of Otto with
the widowed Adelaide. This deeply troubled his young heir; it happened so suddenly and it brought with it a menace to his own hope.
Of course in due time a son would be born of this royal union, was
his thought, and Adelaide's child might well be named successor to
the throne instead of himself. He returned to Germany in angry
mood.

As time went on, other factors, unfortunate but real, sharpened
this feeling. Conrad the Red, duke of Lotharingia, was also angry
with Otto. Had not Otto in his scorn kept King Berengar of Italy,

whom Conrad with all zeal had conducted to the German court, waiting for three whole days before he consented to grant him audience? Berengar had held this an insult, and he had thrown the blame upon Conrad, his escort. In addition, both Liudolf and Conrad were on bad terms with Henry, Otto's brother, who as duke of Bavaria was now in high favor at court. Had not the king, Liudolf remembered with growing resentment, handed over to Henry, this uncle of his, rule over the marches of Friuli, Istria and Verona?

So their wrath increased day by day until they, like their elders before them, burst into revolt. On the side of Liudolf stood the men of Swabia, his duchy, with Conrad the Red and Frederick, archbishop of Mainz, a prelate devoted to a strict life of prayer and fasting, but also jealous for his see and in politics determined to maintain his own views. Many from his diocese upheld him in revolt. Against Liudolf and in loyalty to Otto, the king, were ranged the duchies of Saxony, a land subject to the crown; of Bavaria, ruled by Henry; and of Lotharingia, whose men heartily disliked their duke, Conrad the Red.

Otto decided to call an assembly to meet in May 953 at Fritzlar in Hessen. He was weary of rebellion in his family; it was time for strong measures. Frederick, vehemently accused by Henry of Bavaria, was deprived of the office of archchancellor which he had held together with his archbishopric; Conrad lost his duchy and, thoroughly alarmed, hurried to find refuge in Mainz. To Mainz also came Liudolf with armed troops. Soon Otto marched to besiege the city. Widukind gives a full description of the struggle between those within and those outside the walls: "The son, in battle array, awaited his father. There a war began, more bitter than civil strife and all tragedy. Many engines of war were moved up against the ramparts of Mainz, only to be split into fragments or burned by the defenders. Again and again the soldiers of the king assaulted its gates, and only rarely were they driven to retreat by Liudolf's men. Day by day fortune varied; at one time those within were in terror of Otto, Lord of their kingdom, attacking their walls; at another, it was Otto's men who feared. And so, with victory now here, now there, the siege went on two months before there was talk of peace. Then Egbert, cousin of the king, was delivered by him to the citizens of Mainz as hostage for a truce and discussion was made of terms of surrender. Liudolf and Conrad the Red in their loyalty to Mainz and its people demanded audience from the king; they were ready, they said, to endure all punishment if only the friends to whom they had pledged faith came to no harm."

This Otto would not allow, and the negotiations broke down. The men of Bavaria deserted their Duke Henry and joined Liudolf. Through this encouragement Liudolf boldly seized the city of Regensburg, drove out Henry's wife, his sons and his friends, and divided its wealth among the rebels.

Otto was forced to abandon the siege of Mainz. But his will to conquer did not fail; he marched into Bavaria and attacked Regensburg. One great source of support was given him now in his brother Bruno. Bruno stands out in the tangled history of Otto's reign as an ally loyal, able, and shrewd; Otto could always depend upon him, in peace or in war. The king had given him office both spiritual and secular; from 953 onwards he was not only archbishop of Cologne but duke of Lotharingia, replacing the deposed Conrad the Red. It was an unusual combination of honors.

Yet, it was Otto himself who finally won the battle with Liudolf. At Langenzenn, near Nürnberg, during an assembly held in June 954 Conrad the Red and Archbishop Frederick submitted and owned their defeat; Liudolf himself remained obstinate. Widukind seizes the chance to indulge his sense of drama and again puts words on the lips of a hero; "I would bear all," Otto here declares, "if the wrath of my son and of his fellows in intrigue hurt me alone and did not bring confusion upon all people of Christian name. It would cost me less that they invaded my cities as robbers and seized the lands of my dominion, had they not soaked them in the blood of my kinsmen and of my dearest friends. Here I sit, a man bereft, my son my most eager enemy. That man whom I loved so well and raised from an obscure life to the highest rank and dignity, Conrad the Red, that man has turned my son against me. Even this might be endured, if the enemies of God and man had not been given a share in these doings. Now they have laid waste my kingdom, they have seized and killed my people. My towns lie in ruins, the temples burned, the priests slain, the very streets running red with blood. Through bribe of that gold and silver with which I made rich Liudolf, my son, and Conrad, my son-in-law, the enemy are now returning to their homes laden with the plunder of their raids."

The words, indeed, may well picture the anger of Otto, held at Regensburg while the Hungarians were ravaging German land. Thietmar reports that Liudolf asked aid of the Hungarians; Widukind tells that he gave them guides to further their plundering. They cared, of course, nothing for Germans, either loyal or rebel; but money or an invitation to plunder from a German source was more than welcome.

From Langenzenn Liudolf returned to the city of Regensburg and Otto returned to the assault outside its walls. In Widukind's words: "Now all the people decided that it was worse to be tormented by hunger than to die bravely in battle." Command was given that riders on horseback should rush out from its western gate. Otto's men, it was hoped, would at once leave their camp to attack them; while this battle was going on, others from the besieged city would board the boats lying on the river near at hand and move secretly round to storm that camp, now deserted by its defenders. The order was carried out; but when those on the boats flung themselves on shore to raid the camp, they found themselves face to face, not with emptiness, but with a strong body of armed fighters. Word of their plan must have reached Otto. "In the terror of surprise they fled in all directions. Some were cut down; others, stumbling through panic, fell into the river and were drowned. Many managed to gain footing upon the boats that still awaited them; so many that boat after boat sank under their weight. In all, few were saved. Even the horsemen who had gone out to battle from the western gate were soon driven back to refuge within the city's walls, many of them badly wounded."

Suffering through hunger now was increasing daily; yet, the citizens of Regensburg in their anger at this blockade by Otto stubbornly refused to yield. It was too much for Liudolf to bear, watching men, women, and children enduring evil for his sake; once again he offered to surrender his own person if his followers might be relieved. A council was ordered, to meet at Fritzlar for debate on this matter; but before the day of its assembling Otto, who had left Bavaria for Saxony and Thuringia, was suddenly surprised, as he was finding a brief rest in hunting game amid the Thuringian Forest, by the appearance of his rebel son. As his uncle Henry had done in 941, so Liudolf cast himself at the king's feet and prayed for pardon. Once more Otto could not refuse. In December 954, at the Diet of Arnstadt on the river Gera in Thuringia, south of Erfurt, Liudolf, forgiven but not without punishment, was declared deprived of his duchy of Swabia. This was handed over to a son-in-law of Duke Henry of Bavaria, known to us as Burchard III. Frederick, archbishop of Mainz, had died shortly before; William, a natural son of the king, was appointed by him as successor in the see.

Early in 955 Regensburg gave up resistance and a truce was made. Thus, justice was mingled with mercy and the summer of this year found the people of Bavaria subject in peace to the German crown.

Revolt in Otto's family had once more been crushed by him; his son Liudolf and his son-in-law Conrad were under his control. Now he would gladly have found some rest from battle. It was not possible; armed struggle faced him on two sides. Savage hordes of Hungarian invaders were again sweeping across Bavaria in terrific force to rob and destroy; Duke Henry was calling urgently for help. The Slavs were again rising in revolt upon the Elbe. Without delay the king gathered an army from his duchies and went forward to meet the Hungarians; "he would rather die," he said, according to Thietmar, "than tolerate such evil." Adalbert, monk of Saint-Maximin of Trier, who continued the *Chronicle* of Regino of Prüm as far as 967, described the multitude of Hungarian riders as terrific; they boasted that "the earth would open and the heavens fall upon them before they could be conquered by any man." Eight "legions" were drawn up in order by Otto near Augsburg, on the Lechfeld, the plain lying along the bank of the river Lech. The first, second, and third were commanded by three Bavarian nobles acting for their duke, Henry, already crippled by the sickness which was soon to cause his death; the fourth consisted of Franconians, led by Conrad, now bravely loyal in spite of his lost duchy; the fifth, the "royal legion," was under Otto himself, made up of fighters picked out for their keen and energetic daring; Swabians, under Duke Burchard III, formed the sixth and the seventh; in the eighth marched Bohemians, chosen and led by Duke Boleslav I, still keeping his vow of homage to the German crown. To the care of this eighth legion was entrusted the heavy equipment necessary for Otto's army; the Bohemians, he had decided, would hold it with greater hope of safety, since they marched in the rear. Here his decision was to prove wrong.

It was the tenth of August 955, the Feast of Saint Laurence the Martyr. Early on its morning the king at Mass vowed that if the Lord would grant him victory, he would found and endow in Merseburg, near Halle, a bishopric in honor of this saint, "victor over fire." Then, the Holy Lance in his hand, with the banner of Michael the Archangel flying before him, he gave the signal for battle.

He had hardly raised his arm when word of disaster reached him. A large force of Hungarians had already crossed the river and had ridden around to send countless flights of arrows against his rear. Even now, with yells and shouts of mockery, they were killing and capturing Otto's men and seizing the baggage so carefully placed. Already not only the Bohemians of the eighth legion but the Swabians of the sixth and the seventh had broken their ranks and were running for their lives.

Otto acted swiftly, with extraordinary shrewdness and courage. He sent Conrad the Red with the Franconians of the fourth legion to rescue both men and material. His confidence in this son-in-law, so recently a rebel, took many by surprise; but it saved the day. In a fury of passion Conrad freed the prisoners, recaptured the baggage, and sent all he could find, men and machinery, into safety or into ordered battle under his direction. Meanwhile the "royal legion," with the king at its head, rushed against the main host of the Hungarians in a drive so bitterly determined and persistent that at last the barbarian invaders turned their horses and fled. Otto's army pursued them, killing and seizing, as far as Regensburg, where their chieftains were promptly hanged within sight of all. Among these was the famous Bulksu, leader, called in tradition "king," of the Hungarian invaders.

The victory was complete and its power was to last; Hungarians no longer troubled Germany. Widukind in his pride compared it with the stand of Charles Martel against the Saracens at Poitiers in 732: "So great a triumph had not been the glad good fortune of any king for the last two hundred years." He even wrote that "the king was hailed by his army as 'Father of his fatherland and Emperor.' " From this time the savage Hungarian riders began to learn the decency of civilized life; among them the knowledge, even the practice, of Christian men was to find early and increasing reception.

Only one message brought grief to Otto in his joy: Conrad the Red had fallen, pierced in the throat by an arrow at a moment when, hot and panting, he had carelessly thrown back the visor from his face to get a breath of air. He was buried with all reverence at Worms, and the Lotharingians, who had once cared so little for him, mourned his death.

The sickness of Henry, duke of Bavaria, ended in death during November 955. His duchy was administered for the time by his widow, Judith, as regent for their little son, Henry, Otto's nephew;

later on he was to govern Bavaria and to be known as Henry the Quarreler.

From fighting against Hungarians Otto turned to battle with the Slavs. Their present rising had been encouraged by two brothers, Wichmann and Egbert, nephews of Hermann Billung, count of the border. Egbert, who had lost an eye in a brawl, is known to history as Egbert the One-Eyed; both men had caused much trouble in Saxony during the war against Liudolf. For some time Otto had held Wichmann prisoner in the palace at Quedlinburg; then, after his release, he had aroused rebellion anew in Saxon land. This was too much for a loyal uncle; Hermann Billung had driven him with his brother Egbert into exile north of the Elbe.

It was a rash and foolish act; for the Slavs across the Elbe were only too eager to rise against Otto, their conqueror. Wichmann and Egbert found welcome support from two Slavonic chieftains, Stoinef and Naco. In March and April of 955 Hermann had tried to suppress the rebels, with no success; the Slavs—or Wends, as they were called —were still on the march in the north, killing and capturing, when Otto returned from the Lechfeld. The news of his victory spread fear among northern peoples; some of the Slavonic tribes even sent envoys to the king of Germany, promising tribute and peace if the lands which they had invaded might be theirs to keep. Otto not only demanded reparation for the harm which they had done but in October led an army northwards to encamp amid the woods and marshes of the river Recknitz in Mecklenburg. The position was dangerous. His enemy faced him, hidden but likely at any moment of day or night to attack; sickness and lack of food before long threatened the endurance of his fighters.

For several days he waited. Nothing happened, and at last he sent Gero, who shared with Hermann the guarding of the lands on Germany's border, to Stoinef with a call to yield himself; "in the king," Gero was told to say, "Stoinef would find no enemy, but a friend." But the Slavonic chieftain knew well the troubles of Otto's army; Gero met nothing but ridicule, abuse, and scorn, and he returned to his king to arouse wrath equal to his own. That same night Otto ordered his soldiers, armed with arrows, to force their way across the river and its swamps; at the same time Count Gero, with a band of volunteers, secretly crept a mile down the bank of the Recknitz to throw in all haste three bridges over its stream. Directly the work was done he sent word to the king. Then Otto launched battle; the Wends resisted stubbornly but were conquered with great loss. Stoinef was among those killed; both the German rebels, Wichmann and Egbert the One-Eyed, managed to escape, to reach France and the protection of Duke Hugh of the Franks. Egbert finally won a pardon from Otto through the intercession of Archbishop Bruno; Wichmann returned to Slavonic lands and continued to stir up revolt. In 958 he decided to submit and swore "a terrific oath" that he would do no more harm to Germany; hereafter he aided Gero in fighting against Miesko, duke of the Poles.

Now Otto for a moment could stand still in this year of 955 and look around him with content in his Germany. His duchies were at peace; his rebel kinsmen had returned to their allegiance to the crown; the Hungarians had been conquered; the Slavs of the north, if not well and truly subdued, were at least under the watchful eyes of efficient and trustworthy officers. Toward the end of 955 Adelaide bore him a son, who was to be Otto II.

In France the young king, Lothair, was under the guidance of his mother Gerberga and, more especially, of Bruno, archbishop of Cologne and duke of Lotharingia; Gerberga was sister and Bruno was brother of Otto. In June 956 Hugh, duke of the Franks, died; his widow Hedwig was also sister of the German king and of Bruno.

Again with increasing force the thought of Italy rose in Otto's mind. There Berengar II of Ivrea and his son Adalbert, kings over Lombard Italy but subject through their oath of 952 to Otto's overlordship, were doing their utmost to maintain their power by harsh treatment of even its chief citizens. In Rome Octavian, son of Alberic, upon the death of Pope Agapetus II in December 955, had been elected, as Rome's nobles had sworn he should be elected, to ruling of the Holy See. He was head of the Church of Rome as Pope John XII, and he was also, as heir of Alberic, in control of Rome's secular government.

He was not yet twenty years of age. To the ambition which was to mark the hectic course of his life as pope those who have told its story have added a dark stain of immorality, license, and vice. The writer of the *Liber Pontificalis* himself declared that "his years were spent in doings both adulterous and vain." Flodoard wrote in his *Annals* that "Octavian was rebuked for his lack of religion." Benedict of Mount Soracte went further: "a lewd man," he described him, "bold, and brash as a pagan. Often he went out hunting in the field, not as the head of the Apostolic See, but as one who dwelt in the wilds. His thoughts were but vanity, and he loved to be with women." Above all, Liutprand of Cremona told evil tales against him. Political motive prompted some of this story; yet, much of it had good foundation. Octavian was no true father of the Church, and Otto was to know it.

In the autumn of 956 the king sent his son Liudolf in full confidence to Lombard Italy "to suppress the tyranny of Berengar," as the "Continuator of Regino" put it. Liudolf resolutely atoned for the past. He won a remarkable victory; he drove Berengar and his son from power; and by 957 he was on the point, we may think, of receiving from his father the Italian crown as king in their place. Then, suddenly he was caught by the malaria which haunted the land, and in September 957 he died, to the great grief of German king and people. His body was carried home for burial in the church of Saint Alban at Mainz.

Berengar and Adalbert, saved by his death, recovered kingship and continued their rule of tyranny while Otto was waiting for his chance to interfere. By 960 bishops and secular nobles of Italy's land were so full of resentment against both holders of the crown that they were crossing the Alps to seek refuge with the most powerful Lord in Western Europe, Otto of Germany. Others, who did not leave their homes, wrote to Otto, begging him to come to Italy for their rescue.

Among these was Pope John XII himself. He had decided that the presence of this German king, so loyal to the papacy and so famed through his subduing of Christian rebels and heathen barbarians, would keep Berengar and his son from infringing upon the rights and dominion of the Holy See. Now he sent to Germany two envoys, the Cardinal-Deacon John, and Azo, papal secretary, with a letter to Otto: "For the love of God and the Apostles Peter and Paul, come to free the Church of Rome and restore it to its former safety and freedom!"

Of course, once again this exactly matched Otto's will; gratitude from the pope would surely lead to imperial crowning at his hands. The king, therefore, made ready for departure. As a precaution in case of disaster, at a council at Worms in May 961, his son Otto, five years old, was declared king of Germany in union with his father; once again, as in 936, the coronation and sacring were celebrated at Aachen. Rule of the kingdom in Otto's absence was handed over to Bruno, and care of the little boy to William, archbishop of Mainz.

Now all was in hand. During Eastertide of 959 Lothair of France in a meeting at Cologne had given his pledge to his uncle, Bruno, that Lotharingia should remain firmly under the German crown. Lothair, it is true, was to break his word in future time, and in this year of 959 nobles of Lotharingia had risen in revolt against their duke, Bruno. Bruno with shrewd tact had offered to share his title and administration in Lotharingia with one of its own people, Friedrich, count of Metz. Thus, peace had been restored.

With his queen, Adelaide, and a formidable army Otto marched through the Brenner Pass in August 961. In Italy bishops and lay nobles gave him eager welcome; without hindrance he and his son were acclaimed at Pavia as co-kings of its realm. Berengar, with his wife and sons, had already found refuge in the mountains of the north. Before he left Pavia he had destroyed its royal palace, and one of King Otto's first acts was to order its rebuilding. He kept Christmas in the city, and he sent Hatto, abbot of Fulda, who had accompanied him, to prepare the way for his arrival in Rome by reverent greeting of the pope and by securing suitable quarters there for his own royal self and for his followers, high and low.

In the new year he set out on his final journey and found near Rome due residence prepared on the Monte Mario and the plain below, just outside and within sight of the city's walls. One thing remained for him before he could enter within; he must give his oath to maintain papal security. Thus, then, in these words he declared:

"To thee, John, Lord and Pope, I, King Otto, do promise and swear in the name of the Father and of the Son and of the Holy Spirit and on this wood of the life-giving cross and these relics of the saints, that if by God's will I enter Rome I will glorify its holy Church and thee, its ruler, to the utmost of my power. Never shalt thou lose life or limb or the honor which now thou hast and which thou shalt hold, through me, by my own will or consent, by my counsel or encouraging. In Rome no measure, no policy, will I take in hand concerning all matters which touch either thee or thy Roman people, without thy consent. Whatever shall come into my power from the land of holy Peter, that I will restore to thee. The man, whoever he may be, to whom I shall entrust the kingdom of Italy, him I will make swear to support thee in the defense of the land of holy Peter, so far as in him lies."

He had reached the camp of Monte Mario on January 31, 962. Three days later, on February 2, Feast of Candlemas, the ritual of imperial coronation was celebrated for Otto in St. Peter's by the young pope with all due solemnity and magnificence. With him also his consort, Adelaide, was crowned empress. Then the pope and the Roman people gave to him pledge of faithful adherence. Once more, after a lapse of thirty-seven years, an emperor held his throne in the West: a Saxon, a king of Germany, a man of alien race. Otto had gained his ambition. Yet, it may be that fear was mingled with his joy. Thietmar tells us that as he entered Rome Otto said to his sword-bearer: "While today I make my prayer at the sacred shrine of the apostles do thou cease not to hold the sword over my head. Well I know that the faith of the Roman people has very often been matter of doubt for our predecessors."

The story may not be true, but it could well reflect Otto's thought. Pope John XII, with the nobles and the people of Rome, surely resented the rule of a foreign overlord. Did not this Pope John, this Octavian, son of Alberic, by inheritance hold office secular as well as spiritual? Benedict of Mount Soracte recorded of this time: "The realm of Italy and the imperial dominion of Rome were now made subject to a Saxon king."

Eleven days later, on February 13, the new emperor issued at Rome a decree in which he confirmed for John XII his continued possession of territories hitherto held by the Papal See. On the other hand, the pope had perforce to yield to the emperor his right to legal and judicial authority in Rome.

Time hastened to erase this show of courtesy. It found Otto I resolved to hold power in the city, to support a pope whom he respected, not one whom he scorned as he did John XII, to be emperor not by blessing from the pope alone, but by wielding of his own control. On the fourteenth of February he left Rome to appear first in imperial honor at Pavia and then to deal with Berengar and with Willa, Berengar's wife.

Soon the pope was bitterly regretting his act in acknowledging Otto. Berengar was helpless, in refuge within the stronghold of San Leo, near Montefeltro. Adalbert was still at large, although in his fear of Otto he had fled for the time to the Saracen enemy, settled at Fraxinetum (Garde-Freinet) in Provence.

The emperor carried out his business in Pavia and was occupied there and in other places of the neighborhood until the spring of 963. From May of that year until its autumn he was besieging Berengar's fortress, encamped before the walls of San Leo. During his absence from Rome envoys came and returned between Pope John in the city and the emperor in northern Italy. The pope complained that Otto had broken his sworn word. In reply the emperor sent to Rome this message: "We have promised to restore all territory of St. Peter which should come under our power, and that is the reason why we are toiling to drive Berengar and his family from this fortress of San Leo. How can we restore this territory unless we capture it from the hands of violent men and bring it into our own? We have *not* seen nor have we received here the bishop Leo, and John, cardinal-deacon, as the pope accuses us of doing: men disloyal to him, he declares. They were caught at Capua, we heard, on their way to Constantinople by order of the pope, there to do us harm. And with them was Saleccus, a Bulgarian brought up among Hungarians and a special friend of the pope; also Zacheus, a man of very bad character and utterly ignorant of culture both spiritual and secular, whom the pope recently consecrated bishop. He was going to urge the Hungarians to attack us; we learned this when Saleccus and Zacheus were captured. We would not have believed such action by the lord pope on the word of any man; but the letters they carried gave us proof: letters that were sealed with the pope's seal and signed with his name."

The story comes from Liutprand, bishop of Cremona, who certainly was much given to relating scandalous stories exaggerated or wholly without foundation. But he was highly aware of political matters at this time and he knew his country's happenings, good and bad.

In October 963 Otto left to his supporters the blockading of San Leo and marched south to Rome. Pope John XII had summoned Adalbert, son of Berengar and sharer of his throne, to the city; he had given Adalbert welcome and had promised his support against Otto, the emperor. When, on November 3, Otto again entered Rome's gates, the pope had fled with Adalbert. The people of Rome once more swore lasting faith. They were overcome at the sight of Otto's army; never, they vowed, would they elect or appoint any pope without the consent and decision of the august Lord Emperor Otto and his royal son.

Some days later, on November 6, the emperor assembled a synod of bishops, priests, and deacons, together with secular nobles of Rome. It met in St. Peter's; but Pope John XII had not given permission for its holding nor did he appear. Its purpose was to hear in detail charges of evil in his daily life as man and as priest, put forward against him. Our information, telling the names of the council's members and the words of its proceedings, is again due to Liut-

prand, who was present. "Why is the pope not here?" Otto inquired
of those gathered in the great basilica. Bishops, priests, deacons, and
people answered with one voice: "He is about the Devil's business
and he does not try to hide it." At which the emperor commanded
that the accusations should be plainly and fully declared, one by one,
that debate and judgment might decide the action proper for this
case. One by one, by prelate after prelate, they were named: grave
and grievous irregularity in celebrating Holy Mass, in ordaining to
Holy Order; simony and sacrilege; adultery and lust, so constant that
the sacred palace of the popes now was a brothel and a house of
prostitution; hunting for sport in public; violence, murder, and arson;
playing with dice and praying for aid from Jupiter, Venus, and foul
demonic spirits; neglect of matins and the canonical hours.

This hideous tale of sin may be seen in Liutprand's *Historia
Ottonis*. He informs his readers that, as the Romans would not understand the emperor, speaking in his native Saxon, Otto now ordered
him, Liutprand, to state in Latin the authority required in evidence,
as basis for these charges. Otto's Latin was little and halting. From
Liutprand's mouth the words rolled out, definite and determined:
"Unworthy as I am, by the authority of the high office given to me,
I require you all in the name of God, Whom no man can deceive,
though he will it, and of His holy Mother, the pure Virgin Mary, and
by the most precious body of the prince of the apostles, in whose
church these words are read aloud, that no crimes of abuse be cast
upon the lord pope which have not been committed by him and witnessed by men of utter honesty."

Session followed session; letters passed between the synod and
the pope. In the end, on December 4, when the emperor had added
to all the other charges that of disloyalty to himself, the assembly
declared its will that John XII be deposed and that another be
elected in his place. Ready approval was given by Otto, and then
again bishops, clergy, and laymen cried with one accord that one
Leo, who as *protoscrinarius* directed the business of papal correspondence, of records and archives at Rome, should be elected pope.
They knew well that Leo was favored by the emperor. He was a
layman, but this caused no debate. Step by step—*per saltum*—he
was ordained to successive degrees of Holy Order, until at last he
received consecration as pontiff of Rome in St. Peter's on December
6, 963. He took the title of Leo VIII.

This settled, Otto hurried back to San Leo to take over again the
direction of its blockade, which had now lasted from May until De-

cember; Berengar had for two years been, at first refugee, then prisoner, inside the walls. The fear was ending when he at last surrendered; the emperor sent him with his wife, Willa, to live in exile
at Bamberg, Bavaria. There in 966 he died.

Otto returned to Rome and as a measure of mercy decided to
send back home across the Alps many of his fighting men; their
maintenance in food and lodging was a heavy burden for the Roman
people. John XII, deposed and in exile, heard of this dismissal of
Otto's soldiers with joy; he knew the Roman temper, resentful of
the emperor's power among and over all who dwelt within the city.
He knew, also, that the Romans were easily tempted by the hope of
money. From Tivoli, to which he had fled, he sent messengers, offering bribes; the treasury of St. Peter, the wealth of all Rome's
churches, he promised, would amply reward those who worked
against Otto and the pope of his choice, Leo VIII. Word ran around
that the emperor was now guarded only by a slender force. Ambition to drive out this foreign ruler, to recall Pope John, arose in the
minds of many; on January 3, 964, Rome's people rushed along its
streets in multitude to seize, even to murder, both Otto and Leo
alike.

The passion of this sudden rising was for the moment intense.
But how was a mob of badly armed citizens to resist even a small
army of soldiers cool and sober, trained for war? In the words of
Liutprand, these were "as hawks spreading terror among a flock of
sparrows." The Roman crowds soon broke up; they ran to seek shelter and could find none; Otto's men killed and wounded at their will,
until the emperor ordered punishment to cease. On the next day the
survivors acknowledged defeat, offered a hundred hostages as guarantee of their submission, and swore on the tomb of St. Peter that
for the future they would be loyal to the emperor and to Pope Leo
VIII. At Leo's prayer Otto set the hostages free; in a few days, feeling that peace was safely recovered, he left Rome for Spoleto in
pursuit of Adalbert.

Promises made under duress are easily forgotten; the emperor
had hardly disappeared from sight when Rome's citizens again rose
in revolt. John XII was recalled from exile; the city was no longer
safe for Pope Leo VIII and he hastened to protection at Otto's side.

Why the Roman people should so promptly drive out Leo, who
had restored to them their hundred hostages, and recall John, the
pope whom they had condemned for unbridled wantonness and lust,
finds strange explanation in Liutprand's *History of Otto*. He tells that

the women of Rome with whom John XII "had enjoyed his sport of pleasure," women many in number and high in rank, had induced these acts by vigorous persuading and argument. If this is true, they must once more have inflamed men's minds against the "tyranny" of the emperor. At any rate, John XII, now once more acclaimed pope in Rome, fell at once to vengeance. His two former envoys, the Cardinal-Deacon John and the papal secretary, Azo, were tortured in barbarous mutilation for deserting his cause. Then he ordered a synod to convene in St. Peter's on February 26 of this year, 964. Many of those present had been prominent in the assembly which on December 4, 963, had cried aloud for his deposing; now he was presiding, and they thought it well to change their minds. The decree of deposition was formally cancelled and the synod which had approved it was condemned "for all eternity." Leo VIII was stripped of all honor and function in the Church, under pain of excommunication; anathema was also held out for any one who should support his claim to the Holy See. Those who had been ordained to office in the Church by him were commanded to appear before the synod, arrayed in the vestments of their orders, and then and there were forced to declare in their own writing that these orders were null and void, as received from one "who had nothing to give." The bishop of Ostia, see of Rome's port, who had ordained, step by step, "Leo, this neophyte and perjurer," who had raised him from layman to bishop, was also deposed, "without hope of restoration."

Thus, John XII exulted in his joy of recall. But soon fear returned and he decided to ask peace from the emperor. It was too late; his misspent life was ended on May 14, 964, by a stroke of paralysis. The emperor was still absent from Rome, and its people had no intention of restoring his adherent, Leo; in place of John they now showed their independence of foreign imperial rule by electing their own pope. He was known to Rome as Benedict "Grammaticus" and he was, in the words of that other Benedict, of Soracte, "a man very wise in experience, skilled in the knowledge of letters." For long he had lectured in Rome's schools, until his fame for learning had brought him honor in the Church, where he was now cardinal-deacon. With great satisfaction the clergy and laity of Rome saw him consecrated as Benedict V in St. Peter's before the end of May. They took oath never to desert him; they would defend him with all loyalty against the emperor.

Caution, based on fear, nevertheless was mingled with this bold show of independence; before they ventured upon Benedict's consecration as pope the Romans had thought it well to send envoys to inform the emperor of their decision and to ask his confirming of their will. The envoys found Otto at Rieti, between Spoleto and Rome; they presented their message and Otto burst into a passion of anger. "Sooner will I throw away my sword," he swore, "than fail to restore Leo, the pope, to the seat of holy Peter." When afterward he heard that Benedict's consecration had actually been carried out, he started for Rome. Outside its gates he raised high barricades and thus allowed no one to leave the city, declaring by message to the people within that the blockade would continue until they recalled Leo and brought Benedict, "that invader of the Holy See," to his presence for judgment. In reply Benedict, from the height of the city's walls, hurled threat of excommunication against the emperor and those under his command.

The blockade continued until hunger forced Rome to yield; on June 23, 964, Otto and his soldiers entered its open gates. Benedict was surrendered and Leo again sat on the papal throne; the Roman people once more promised obedience to this Otto of Saxony. Some days later Pope Leo VIII and the emperor presided at the Lateran over a synod of many bishops and minor clergy, Roman, Italian, Lotharingian, and Saxon. Before them all came Benedict, clothed in pontifical vestments. A moment of silence, and the cardinal-archdeacon, also named Benedict, rose from his seat: "By what authority," he demanded, "by what law, hast thou usurped this pontifical array while our Lord Pope Leo is still living, him whom thou thyself, accusing and upbraiding John XII, didst elect for the Apostolic See? Canst thou deny that thou didst vow by oath to this, our lord emperor, that never wouldst thou, and all the Roman people, elect or appoint a pope without the consent of himself and of his son, King Otto?"

The accused, Benedict Grammaticus, was a man not only learned but of honest and Christian character. Now he humbly replied: "If I have sinned, have pity upon me." So, at least, Liutprand reports, and doubtless he heard the words. He goes on to tell that Otto, moved to tears, asked that fair treatment be given; that if Benedict would and could, he should be allowed to speak in his defense; that, if he admitted his guilt, for fear of God he should find some mercy from his accusers.

Upon this Benedict threw himself at the feet of Leo and the emperor, crying that he had sinned, an intruder upon the Holy See. Stripping from his shoulders the pallium, symbol of his high dignity, he returned it with his pontifical staff to the pope. At once Leo broke the staff into pieces, then held them out for all to see. Next he ordered Benedict to sit upon the ground; he tore from him his chasuble and stole, and finally declared him deposed from all pontifical and priestly office. Only through Otto's intercession would he allow him to remain a simple deacon of the Church.

The emperor was weary; in the autumn of 964 he went off for a holiday, spent in hunting game among the mountains and forests of Piedmont. At Christmas he was in Pavia; then, early in 965, he set out for Germany. With Adaldag, archbishop of Hamburg-Bremen, Benedict also crossed the Alps, to live in exile under his charge. Adam of Bremen, historian who wrote in the eleventh century, recorded: "The archbishop held Benedict in high honor until his death." This was but a brief while; the exile died on July 4, 965, at Hamburg.

Not long was it given to Otto to live undisturbed among his people of Germany. Soon after his return home he heard that men of Lombard Italy in rebellion against his rule had brought back Adalbert, formerly their king in union with his father, Berengar of Ivrea, to reign over them once more. The emperor did not hesitate. He sent Burchard III, duke of Swabia, to Italy, and Adalbert fled from him to hide in the mountains. The same year, 965, saw the death of Pope Leo VIII, and the Roman people, taught by hard experience, sent delegates to Germany to ask whom it would please the emperor to appoint in his place. In answer Otto instructed Otger, bishop of Speyer, and Liutprand, bishop of Cremona, to proceed at once to Rome for direction and control of this business. Under his imperial and supreme authority they ordered on October 1, 965, the enthroning as pope of the bishop of Narni in Umbria, appointed as John XIII. Thus did the Emperor Otto the First himself disregard canon law by this transferring a prelate from one episcopal see to another.

The election led to further trouble. John XIII, relying on imperial support, tried to subdue the nobles of Rome with a heavy hand. In December, led by Peter, prefect of the city, they rose in their wrath and seized the pope in the Lateran; with every insult they imprisoned him in the fortress of Sant'Angelo, and afterward somewhere in the Campagna, while the Roman people raised the cry reechoed by Benedict of Soracte: "That Saxon kings come not to destroy our realm and lead out our children captive, pray for us, O Peter Apostle!"

In the autumn of 966 Rome heard that Otto was returning to

Italy. This was a matter unexpected. Its citizens, in fear of his anger, decided to send for the banished John XIII; by November he was again in his see. Their fear had reason. On his way the emperor crushed the ambition of Adalbert and his supporters, still holding out in the north; Christmas of this year he kept in Rome and then promptly dealt out punishment for the suffering of the pope whom he had appointed. A lurid story is found in the *Liber Pontificalis, the Book of the Popes*. We read that Otto arrested the consuls of the Romans and drove them across the Alps; he hanged by the neck twelve prominent citizens; he ordered the prefect, Peter, to be handed over for judgment by John XIII. Pope John then, we are told, gave sentence that the prefect's beard be shorn away and that he be suspended by the hair of his head from the "Horse of Constantine" (in reality the equestrian statue of Marcus Aurelius, now in the Piazza del Campidoglio, but at the time standing in front of the Lateran). After this disgrace the usual punishment was given; Peter was placed upon a donkey, sitting backward to face its tail; holding fast to this he was forced to ride through the streets of the city. Three great bunches of feathers adorned his head and his sides, and a bell tied to the donkey's neck rang constantly to summon Roman people to this sight of shame. Prison followed, and, after that, exile in Germany.

Otto remained in Italy six years, from 966 until 972. His power over Rome and the northern kingdom was established; the pope, John XIII, was ruling, and he was to rule until 972. Four aims now filled the emperor's mind. If the Lombard realm of north and central Italy was to remain safely under his crown, he must protect it against attack by Byzantine invasion from Italy's southern lands; his power must be acknowledged by the Byzantine Empire which from Constantinople claimed dominion over southern Italy; alliance of his own empire of the West with that empire of the East must be brought about, with all proper understanding of the sphere of control of each; the future of his own standing as emperor in the West must be assured.

Assurance of his authority in Italy began with its central region. In January 967 Otto won influence there by issuing in favor of Pandulf Ironhead, lord of Capua and Benevento, already a friend of his, a decree in which he declared Pandulf invested with the duchy of Spoleto. It was a shrewd move, if audacious; henceforth, Pandulf was not only Otto's friend, but his vassal in respect to this duchy.

Now Otto turned to prepare an alliance with the empire of the East.

In 959 Constantine VII, known to history as Porphyrogenitus, "born to the purple," and also as the earnest ally of scholars and the author of a mass of writings, some of which happily still survive, by his death had left the imperial throne of the East in Constantinople to his son, Romanus II. Some years before his accession, this Romanus had fallen in love with a young woman, eighteen years old, beautiful and charming, daughter of an innkeeper. He had made her his wife, and now she was crowned empress under the name of Theophano. She was as able in mind, and that an evil mind, as she was attractive. In 963 Romanus II died and she was declared regent in government for her two little sons. Immediately her ambition set to work, planning power for herself in years to come. A second husband, she realized, would best assure this, and her choice fell upon Nicephorus, a general in the army of the East, famous for his victories over the Arab and Saracen enemy, and highly admired in Constantinople. He surrendered at once to her will; the wedding took place a few weeks after (in August 963) he had been proclaimed emperor of the East as Nicephorus Phocas.

Four years later, in 967, ambassadors arrived in Italy from Nicephorus, bearing to Otto, then in Ravenna, presents and a desire for peace and goodwill between them. In the same year Otto sent off his own envoy, Dominic of Venice, to Nicephorus with a proposal for the marriage of his son, Otto II, with an imperial princess of the East. Dominic by accident met Nicephorus in Macedonia and he had a bad reception. The emperor of the East knew well Otto's ambition regarding the southern lands of Italy; he at once told the envoy that, before he would even think of such a marriage, the German king must declare his formal renunciation of any design upon them. Dominic replied that Otto had no intention of invading land which belonged to the Eastern Empire, and then started back for Rome.

Before he arrived there with his report, Otto had sent a messenger to this son, now twelve years old; he was to join him in Italy without delay. On Christmas Day 967 in St. Peter's at Rome Pope John XIII crowned the boy co-emperor with his father.

Since the scheme of alliance by marriage had been rejected by Nicephorus, Otto decided to defend and to maintain his position in Italy by strong measures. During March 968 he marched southward with his army, entered Apulia and attacked the city of Bari. Its walls stood firm, and the temper of Nicephorus rose from irritation to fury.

Now, however, Otto determined to make another attempt at alliance. This time he chose as his legate the bishop of Cremona, and Liutprand has left us a spicy account of his experience. Nicephorus, he told Otto when he returned from his errand, hot with anger, had been utterly insulting. He would have no alliance with the West; he would not discuss negotiation. Was not he, the emperor in Constantinople, lord of Rome both East and West? It was entirely lawless for the king of Germany to come in arms to raid Byzantine land, Byzantine subjects, in southern Italy.

Late in 968 Otto was still invading Apulia. At Christmas he was there, and for six months in 969 he fought the Byzantine menace while his friend, Pandulf Ironhead, gave him support. Then for a while he gave over the struggle to Pandulf; necessity required his presence in northern Italy. Success and defeat fell in turn to each side, German and Byzantine; plundering and blockade went on during the rest of the year. In the spring of 970 the German army welcomed their emperor's return to the south and with energy laid siege to Apulia's city of Bovino; like Bari, it stubbornly resisted attack.

Meanwhile, fate had been descending upon Constantinople; its story was told by Leo the Deacon, a Byzantine historian in the tenth century. The Empress Theophano, growing discontented with her marriage to Nicephorus, had turned her attention to another renowned soldier of the Eastern Empire, John Tzimisces. Like herself, John Tzimisces also was eager for power. Why, she thought, should they not work together to gain and to share it?

This was no easy task. Soon they both realized that the only way to success was by murder of the Emperor Nicephorus. Accordingly they proceeded to plan, and on the night of December 10-11, 969, they went into action. An icy wind was blowing and snow was falling fast when John Tzimisces, with other men bribed for his aid, came by boat to the shore of the Bosphorus, and landed near the palace where Nicephorus lay asleep. Signal of their arriving was then given by a low whistle to other conspirators stationed at an opening high upon the palace wall; here a net woven of rope was lowered to draw up each man in turn, John himself last of all. They had been told where to find the emperor's room; its door would be open. "Please do not close it," his wife had said to him; "I will do this when I join you, later in the night." In peace Nicephorus had gone to rest. The murderers; sword in hand, silently entered, heard no sound, saw no movement, no one on the bed. In panic, fearing some trap, they were turning to hurry away when a servant of the empress stopped them. He pointed to a man lying asleep upon the floor, protected only by a panther's skin and a scarlet blanket. In a few moments, struck and tortured, pierced by swords, his cry of "Mother of God, help me!" answered by the mocking voice of John, the emperor Nicephorus Phocas died.

So John Tzimisces in 969 gained rule in the East as emperor; he held it until 976. But before Polyeuctus, patriarch of Constantinople, would crown him, John was forced to submit to penance; he declared in his anxiety that not he, but Theophano, had plotted the crime. Polyeuctus could not pass over murder and high treason in silence; yet, he had been no friend of Nicephorus, and John Tzimisces was promising to support his wishes in regard to the Church. Charge of the killing of her husband was brought against the empress, as due to her ambition, and Polyeuctus drove her from the imperial palace to exile on an island. During Christmastide of this same year John received from him solemn coronation in Constantinople.

By 970 Otto I had had enough of campaign in southern Italy. His ally, Pandulf Ironhead, had been captured by the Greeks and held in prison at Constantinople. There, after the death of Nicephorus, he was trying to persuade the Emperor John Tzimisces that alliance with the king of Germany was a better policy than war. Finally John released him and Pandulf went back to discuss peace with Otto. In 971 Gero, archbishop of Cologne, was sent to Constantinople; on his return after long parley and negotiation he brought with him a Byzantine princess as bride for Otto II. Her origin has been disputed in much learned argument. With Thietmar and George Ostrogorsky let us call her here a kinswoman of John Tzimisces; she was not "born to the purple," as one of the Macedonian imperial line of the East. But the offer was accepted, and with all pomp and magnificence the marriage was celebrated on April 14, 972. Her name, also, was Theophano, and she was to play an important part in German affairs; at this time she was only sixteen years of age, and she delighted all whom she met in Rome.

Alliance, then, had after some sort been brought about between Germany and Constantinople. Pandulf Ironhead was lord of Capua, Benevento, and Spoleto; through him, as vassal of Otto, the German king held some small influence south of Rome. But Apulia and Calabria remained under the control of the Byzantine Empire.

In August Otto determined to go back to Germany. Much had happened during his absence to depress him. His mother Matilda and his son, William, archbishop of Mainz, had died during these six years. There was trouble in the government. Otto's own duchy of Saxony was said to be restless, in discontented mood. The king had been away too long, occupied with another country, men were complaining, neglectful of his own.

France, in spite of many minor quarrels and conflicts between its own nobles, had been in general at peace with Germany since 954. At Eastertide 965 when Otto had been in his own kingdom, he had gathered his family and his friends at Cologne and had openly made known his friendship with Lothair. But after the death of Bruno in this year and that of Gerberga in 969, the king of France acted on his own initiative, eager to increase his power. Already in 965, when he was twenty-five years of age and Arnulf the Great, count of Flanders, died, Lothair, overlord of Flanders, invaded the land and occupied Artois. In 966 he furthered his ambition by marrying Emma, a daughter (by her first husband, Italy's king, Lothar) of that Adelaide who was now the queen and empress of Otto I.

Time was running out for this Otto of Germany. He kept Easter in March 973 at his well-loved Quedlinburg palace, surrounded by his friends. Ascension Day found him at Merseburg, grieving over the death of Herman Billung who had worked so faithfully as duke of Saxony under the king and as count on the German border. Hermann's son, Bernard, followed him as duke in this same year. Early in May the emperor went to Memleben, where his father, Henry the Fowler, had died amid the Harz Mountains. On the next morning, May 7, he rose very early, as usual, heard nocturns and matins, rested a while, returned to church for Mass, and then gave alms to the poor before his frugal breakfast. At dinner, his friends told afterward, he was cheerful, even gay. During vespers they suddenly saw that he was ill. It was his last hour. He asked for a priest, who gave him viaticum, and then "with great tranquility and no lament he committed his soul into the care of the Creator of all."

His people, Widukind the Saxon wrote, when they heard of his death, "gave him praise and thanks. He had been to them as a father; he had freed them from their enemies; he had conquered the pride of Hungarians, Saracens, Danes and Slavs; he had made Italy subject to his rule; he had destroyed pagan shrines of dwellers on their borders and had put in their place Christian churches and priests."

He was laid to rest in his cathedral of Magdeburg in Saxony on the river Elbe, some months after his sixtieth birthday.

What had this Otto I, to whom history has given the name of "the Great," accomplished in his sixty years? He had brought his kingdom of Germany into a power acknowledged by his own dukes and by the rulers of Western Europe. Over France, brother-in-law of both Louis IV, d'Outremer, and of Hugh, duke of the Franks, he had thrown his influence; his first marriage, with Edith, sister of King Athelstan of Wessex, was to leave its traces and its memories among English men. In Lotharingia, that middle land between France and Germany, he had held his own; he had subjected the king of Burgundy to his control; he had gained the crown of Lombard Italy in the teeth of plotting and ambition from Burgundy and from his own duchies of Bavaria and Swabia; over the kingdom of Germany, including the duchy of Lotharingia, over the kingdoms of Burgundy and of Lombard Italy, he had cast his title of emperor in the West.

Yet, his empire was not one which looked back in its shaping to that of ancient Rome; Otto the First had not been brought up to revere and hold in mind classical imperial tradition. Nor was it that of the Charlemagne whose memory and working, secular and Christian, he so deeply admired. It was far more limited in extent. Otto did not reign as king over the Western Franks, of France; his power in Italy was confined to its northern and central land; the Byzantine emperors held their claim to the south. His rule was centered in Germany, and for Germany's ordered standing, peace, prestige, and authority he worked and fought, both as king and emperor. For this cause, ambitious to be held ruler of a power in no way inferior to that of Byzantium, but fearing opposition from Byzantine pride in Italy, he extended German conquest over the lands north and east of his kingdom; he proved to civilized Europe his might and his skill in battle, by freeing this Europe from the terror of Hungarian advance. At Quedlinburg during Eastertide of 973 envoys came from Hungarians, Slavs, Bulgarians, Danes, and Greeks; there came, too, the dukes of Bohemia and of Poland. All came to assure him of their friendship and respect.

He worked for the Christian faith wherever he ruled or conquered. He built and endowed churches; constantly he issued acts in favor of monasteries or convents. He founded in 948 two bishoprics, one at Havelberg, another at Brandenburg, for his mission to the heathen Slavs. Work for the conversion of the peoples in the northern regions of the Elbe, carried on from the archbishopric of Hamburg-Bremen, was furthered by the establishing of a see at Oldenburg on the Baltic. His content was great when in 962 Pope John XII granted his petition that the abbey of Magdeburg on the Elbe in Saxony, founded by this same Otto in 937, should be made into a seat for an archbishop. For years episcopal jealousy hindered progress here. Then at a council held in Ravenna during April 967 Pope John XIII confirmed this decree, declaring that "our son Otto, most august among Emperors, third in honor after Constantine, has highly exalted the Church of Rome: Rome, chief city of all the world." On October 18, 968, this pope did more for Magdeburg; he directed that Magdeburg as archsee, from that year under the rule of Adalbert as metropolitan, should hold authority over five suffragan bishoprics: Havelberg and Brandenburg, both formerly under the jurisdiction of Mainz; Merseburg; Meissen; and Zeitz.

Adalbert is of interest in another way; he gives us a connection of Otto the Great with Russia. Educated and professed as monk in the abbey of St. Maximin at Trier, he had been chosen by Otto and by William, metropolitan of Mainz, as missionary bishop for Kiev. Envoys in 959 had reached Otto from Olga, widow of Igor, duke of Kiev, and regent for her son, Svyatoslav, praying him to send a bishop from Germany to her and her people. She herself had recently received Christian baptism, in Constantinople, we may believe; in 957 she had visited Constantinople, welcomed with much ceremony, as the Emperor Constantine Porphyrogenitus himself tells us. She was eager for good intent toward Kiev from both the Byzantine court and Otto, king of Germany. On his side Otto was delighted to grant her request, for he saw here further hope of extending his influence eastward.

In 961 Adalbert arrived; but he soon saw that episcopal work in Kiev was beyond his power. Olga had been succeeded as ruler by her son, and Svyatoslav had no desire for the progress of Christianity in his land. In 962 the missionary bishop was forced to return to Germany.

As archbishop of Magdeburg, Adalbert, at Christmastide 968, duly consecrated bishops for Merseburg, Meissen, and Zeitz; at Merseburg, we may note, Otto fulfilled the vow made by him on the Lechfeld in 955. We have already seen Adalbert as author, in his "Continuation of the Chronicle of Regino of Prüm."

The course of conversion to the Christian faith in Poland during the reign of Otto I deserves special notice. Sometime in the period

964-66 Miesko I, the first duke of the Poles in historical record, married Dubravka, daughter of Boleslav I, duke of Bohemia. Christianity had by this time reached Bohemia; Dubravka was a devoted member of the Church, and in 966 her husband, Duke Miesko, was himself baptized.

This alliance of Poland with Bohemia through his marriage, and the fact that his own conversion and that of many of his people came, not from Germany, but from Bohemia, brought distinct comfort to Miesko. He was thinking not only of his country's religion but also of its political standing. Since 963 Miesko had recognized the imperial authority of Otto I as emperor in the West, and he desired his protection; but not at the price of Poland's independence. He had therefore been seriously worried by the bull in which Pope John XII in 962, grateful for Otto's aid in Italy, had allowed Germany and its ruler the creation of an archbishopric at Magdeburg. According to this, it seemed to Miesko, the pope was giving to the archbishop of Magdeburg and his suffragans religious authority, and to the emperor political power, over all the Slavonic tribes dwelling north and east of the Elbe. The words of the bull declared this; it was a menace and an affront to Poland.

The menace grew stronger when in 968 Adalbert was raised by Pope John XIII to be primate of Germany. John XIII, however, did not always bow to Otto in gratitude and anxiety to please. With his consent and his authority, by this same year, we may believe, by 968, Miesko had won consecration of a bishop for Poland. The name of this bishop was Jordan; his seat was at Poznán; he was a missionary father in God for the whole of Poland; his see was Polish and independent of Germany.

At the end of the reign of Otto I, Duke Miesko very possibly was once more seeking papal support as defense against this emperor. Miesko was still nominally loyal to him; he was even paying tribute. But in 973, after Hodo, margrave of the eastern Saxon border, had dared of his own accord to invade Miesko's territory and battle had been fought, Otto called both men into meeting with himself and bade them promise to keep the peace. Then, so tradition tells, in guarantee of his promise, Miesko entrusted his son, Boleslav, later on to be known as Boleslav Chrobry, the Brave, to the German crown as hostage. He also, as we are told, whether truly or not, took the precaution of placing him under papal protection. Boleslav was seven years old, at the age when the long hair of a Polish prince was ceremonially cut short, and now a lock of his hair was sent to the pope, Benedict VI. Reception of this gift symbolized adoption of its giver into permanent care of the Holy See.

In Denmark the Christian Church had gained adherents long before the reign of Otto the Great; in 935 the archbishop of Hamburg-Bremen was continuing there the labor of Anskar in the ninth century. Perhaps about 965 we may date the conversion of Harald Bluetooth, king of Denmark and son of the pagan Gorm. Widukind, who was living at the time, has left us a story at any rate. At a banquet in the Danish court, he tells, a dispute arose between Danes who believed that Christ was but one god among other, even greater gods, and a Danish priest, Poppo, who held firmly the Catholic doctrine of the Holy Trinity. King Harald at the time refused to state his own position, but on the next day he invited the priest to prove, if he could, the validity of his creed through the ordeal of redhot iron. Poppo cheerfully consented, and endured until Harald ordered him to drop the burning metal. There on the spot the king decreed that in Danish land Christ was to be worshipped as in very truth its God; pagan idols were to be cast aside, and Christian priests were to receive due honor.

Over the Holy See in Rome Otto held a firm hand, both of support and decision, to the day of his death. Pope John XIII died in September 972, and the emperor named as his successor Benedict VI, a cardinal-deacon of Rome. He was not consecrated until January 19, 973, and his appointing aroused keen feeling of opposition in the city.

Much had this Otto done, hard had he labored, to ensure peace and settlement in the troubled land of Italy. Yet, resentment continued to the last. In 966 Benedict of Mount Soracte had ended his *Chronicle* with a cry of anguish: "Woe unto thee, O Rome, captured by a Saxon king, thy people slain with the sword, thy glory brought to nought!"

Even among his own German people the authority of Otto the Great did not equal the autocratic will brought to bear by Charlemagne upon his Frankish nobles. The dukes of Otto were feudal lords, masters of their own subjects, freely dispensing land on tenure, supported in turn by their vassals and tenants. Here the emperor showed wisdom; he sought to rule through, rather than over, the supporters of his throne, spiritual and secular. Far less wise was the missionary campaign carried on in his reign and in that of his son, Otto the Second; their missionaries toiled not only for the victory of

the Christian faith among the Slavonic peoples but for the power of
the German monarch over and among them. The tribes who dwelt
around the Elbe and the Oder were determined to resist this imperial
yoke; constantly, year after year, they strove to keep the independence which their fathers had known, fighting against emperor,
against count of the border, against bishop or priest who in making
them baptized Christians would bring them into subjection to the
German will.

2

The son whom late in 955 his queen and empress-to-be, Adelaide,
had borne to Otto the First was now but seventeen. In his few years
he had received abounding honor: crowned king when only five
years old, emperor of the West at twelve, joined to a Byzantine bride
at sixteen. Brilliance of early fortune was to distort the vision of his
mind.

He reigned for ten years and seven months: a short little man,
who had none of his father's genius for conquest or government but
much of his energy and his determined will. In this second Otto the
will was bold and impetuous, refusing guidance from wiser and
surer sources, following its own judgment or the advice of men more
ambitious for themselves than for their emperor. Otto had given his
son an education far better than his own; from his mother he had
learned to revere the Church and to uphold its houses of religion.
From the monasteries of Germany and Italy he was, indeed, to draw
no little support. Two archbishops had directed his early training:
his uncle, Bruno of Cologne, and his half-brother, William of Mainz.
Now both were dead, and from 973 the young emperor was to move
back and forth between the varied desires of two women: the Empress Adelaide and the Empress Theophano.

His reign was beset by storm; four campaigns troubled Germany in
the years 974-80.

Resentment ripened again into rebellion among the dukes of his
land. The House of Bavaria at this time was of marked power. Its
duke was now that Henry known as "the Quarreler," by this time a
young man of intense ambition; his sister, Hedwig, was wife of
Burchard III, duke of Swabia; together their united houses made
strong alliance.

To strength they added cunning craft. When, in July 973, Ulrich,
bishop of Augsburg in Swabia, died, leaving a vacancy of high im-

portance, both Henry and Hedwig were extremely eager that one of their house, another Henry, should succeed him and thus augment their influence. This was finally brought about by dishonest stratagem on their part and against the wish of both the emperor and the Swabian people.

They paid the penalty. The following November saw the death of Duke Burchard; promptly the governing of his duchy was granted by the emperor to an Otto who was grandson of Otto the Great by his first marriage, son of that Liudolf who had risen against his father in 953.

Immediately, Henry of Bavaria and his sister, the widowed duchess, broke out in anger. Why had Swabia been given to this Otto, son of a rebel? Why not to Henry of Bavaria himself? Or why not to whatever lord Hedwig might shortly elect to end her widowhood? She would gladly see herself once more duchess of Swabia.

To Henry's wrath Boleslav II, duke of Bohemia since his father's death in 967, lent keen encouragement; so did Miesko, duke of the Poles. Soon Henry received envoys from his king-emperor; Otto II was calling him to court for explanation of his conduct. The duke of Bavaria judged it wise to obey the command; he made a very bad attempt at defense and was sent by Otto into captivity at Ingelheim. Then during the next year came the turn of Bohemia; the emperor ordered his army to invade, to ravage and plunder its land.

The year 976 found Otto at open war with the duke of Bavaria, Henry the Quarreler. Henry escaped from his prison and returned to Bavaria; Otto marched for Bavaria's capital city of Regensburg; he heard a gathering of German bishops in his camp before the city declare sentence of excommunication passed upon the duke; he seized Regensburg by force of battle; Duke Henry fled for refuge to Bohemia. The emperor declared him deprived of his duchy, and its rule awarded to Otto, son of Liudolf, from this time duke both of Swabia and of Bavaria; Duke Otto had been vigorously loyal to the crown of Germany. We may note that the land of Bavaria's duchy as awarded to him was smaller in extent than it had been under Henry the Quarreler; Carinthia, a land bordering upon Bavaria, was now separated from it to become a distinct duchy, governed by a nephew of Duke Arnulf of Bavaria named Henry the Younger.

Once again the emperor ordered his army to invade Bohemia; but this time he met with disaster. Thietmar tells the story. Otto's soldiers were awaiting the arrival of a large auxiliary force of Bavarians; these, indeed, were already on their way. But on their

march, they pitched camp near Pilsen and were caught unawares. Word had reached Duke Boleslav's troops that men of Bavaria were careless, that they kept little guard against attack. One fine evening the Bavarians were enjoying their leisure, bathing near the meadows around their tents, when the Bohemian enemy swept down, took all completely by surprise and killed right and left. The news of his severe loss compelled Otto to abandon the campaign.

In 977 Henry the Quarreler was joined in rebellion by two other nobles of high standing: Henry the Younger, who rose against his king in spite of the gift of his duchy of Carinthia, and Henry, bishop of Augsburg since 973, ever conscious of his king's disapproval of his appointment to that see. The struggle which followed is known as the "War of the Three Henries."

By the end of 978 all three had surrendered. Henry the Quarreler and Henry of Augsburg were both in exile, the Quarreler under charge of Folcmar, bishop of Utrecht, and the other in the keeping of the abbot of Werden on the Ruhr; only, however, in his case, for three months of captivity. Henry the Younger had lost his duchy of Carinthia; it had passed to another Otto, son of Conrad the Red. There was peace for the time between Germany and Bohemia; at Easter 978 Boleslav II had visited the emperor to pay him all courtesy and homage. The rebellion had cost Germany four years of effort.

The effort had been interrupted in 974 by a rising which had driven Otto into war with Denmark; the Danes under King Harald Bluetooth had invaded the German March. This trouble had not lasted long. The emperor had destroyed part of the Danish fortification (the Danewirk); he had built a stronghold for the protection of his own realm and had sent the invaders hurrying back to their own land.

Third, the same year had seen Otto II marching into Lotharingia to put down revolt of its chieftains, inspired by two brothers, Reginar IV and Lambert. Their father, Reginar III, had been sent into exile by Bruno, Lotharingia's duke, for rebellion against his rule, and the family estate had been forfeited in punishment; the brothers were now striving to regain this inheritance. The emperor advanced upon Boussu, their fortress near Saint-Ghislain in Belgium, destroyed it and seized its defenders; but those who had led them, Reginar and Lambert, escaped in safety to France. Later on they fought him again in battle for their desire; finally in 977 Otto yielded them their heritage in Hainaut and they were content.

Of greater interest is the picture given us by history of the relations of Otto II with Lothair, king of France from 954 to 986. Lothair's ambition since the death, in 965, of his uncle, Bruno, duke of Lotharingia, had been that of his Carolingian predecessors, to see Lotharingia under his crown. For this end he and his brother Charles had encouraged the revolt of Reginar and Lambert against Germany. In 977, however, a violent quarrel broke out between the royal brothers of France. Rumor told that Emma, queen of Lothair, had been guilty of adultery, and pointed to Ascelin, bishop of Laon, as her lover. No source for this accusation was openly named. But here and there it was traced to Charles; men knew well that he held no liking for his sister-in-law. In his wrath Charles left France for Germany, where Otto, its king, promptly handed to him rule of Lower Lotharingia, one of the two divisions, Upper and Lower, into which Lotharingia had been divided for administration when Bruno governed it as duke.

This naturally in its turn aroused anger in Lothair and his nobles. In 978 he crossed the border into Lotharingia and took the road to Aachen. Its king was in residence there at the time with his queen, Theophano, who was awaiting the birth of a child. With great reluctance he decided that he must flee, and secretly by night he set out with his wife for Cologne. Lothair seized Aachen, plundered the palace built by Charlemagne, and even, to signify his triumph over Germany, turned around in reverse the great bronze eagle which stood with outstretched wings upon its roof. Then, his pride satisfied, he marched back to France.

Otto II did not allow this insult to remain unmarked. With the enthusiastic cooperation of his subjects he gathered an army, which his chroniclers described as huge, and led it through Lothair's kingdom by way of Reims, Laon, and Soissons, plundering secular lands and castles as he went, but in reverence sparing churches and abbeys, already robbed of treasure by Northmen and Hungarians. Soon he was in Paris, encamped on the height of Montmartre. Revenge he now held attained, and before he left the city he proclaimed his presence far and near. He gathered all the clergy and singers in his army together into one great choir on this height and ordered them to awake the echoes of Paris with one long, loud burst of "Alleluia!"

Then he retreated, and Lothair caught up with him on the Aisne, to drive by the terror of his army's sudden appearing German baggage and porters into its flooded stream. Soon both kings realized that nothing was to be gained by this duel of two countries; in 980 Otto II and Lothair met at Margut-sur-Chiers, near Sedan and the river Meuse, which in German thought was the boundary between their kingdoms. There Lothair agreed to keep the peace and to leave Lotharingia in Otto's hands; Otto on his side promised aid to this cousin of his against his enemies in France.

Now at last, as his father had done before him, Otto the Second could turn his mind to Italy. The situation there threatened danger to his empire. From a fortified position, won in Sicily, Saracens were invading Apulia and Calabria; even the Byzantine forces, themselves hostile to Otto, could not put an end to Saracen plundering and ravage. It was time, the emperor held, to march out boldly for defense and for conquest; the more boldly since a son and heir had been born to him in the summer of this year.

By November 980, he was on his way through the Alps. At the end of December or early in January 981 he presided over a crowded audience gathered in Ravenna to hear a debate on questions of philosophy between Gerbert, scholar, teacher of the liberal arts, secretary to Archbishop Adalbero at Reims, and Otrich, until 978 head of the cathedral school of Magdeburg. It lasted nearly a whole day, and Otto only ended it when the listeners were growing weary of this strain upon their wits.

Eastertide 981 found the emperor in Rome, face to face with problem and peril. On the political side the death of Pandulf Ironhead in this year caused unrest and quarrel throughout central Italy; the Saracens, too, were as great a menace as ever.

As evil, also, had been the recent history of the Church in Rome, only too similar to that of the past. At the beginning of the reign of Otto II Rome's secular nobles had risen afresh to dominate the city under one Crescentius, member of a powerful family and "son of Theodora." Very possibly this Theodora was of the family of that Theophylact who had seized rule over Rome in the earlier years of the century.

In the summer of 974 Crescentius had ordered his men to force their way into the Lateran, to capture the pope, Benedict VI (consecrated in January 973 with the consent of the Emperor Otto I) and to thrust him into the dungeon of Sant'Angelo. In his place the people of Rome, led by Crescentius, had elected as pope a deacon

named Franco, a Roman by birth and prominent in opposition to
the imperial crown. He was known as Boniface VII.

Word of this had quickly reached Otto II in Germany; in angry
haste he had despatched to Rome his envoy, Count Sicco, with full
authority to act. Franco, *alias* Pope Boniface VII, had treated his
coming with defiance; in July 974 he had ordered a hireling—a priest
it was said—to strangle in Sant'Angelo the captive Benedict VI. This
murder was long remembered; in 991 Arnulf, bishop of Orléans, ad-
dressing a council of bishops at Verzy, near Reims, held up before
them in bitter words "Boniface, an horrendous monster, surpassing
all mortal men in iniquity, red with the blood of the pope who ruled
before him." But Count Sicco was no coward; he had swiftly brought
affairs in Rome under control. The same year, 974, had seen not only
the consecration of another Roman, the bishop of Sutri in the province of Viterbo, central Italy, as Pope Benedict VII but the damnation of Boniface VII—known also as Maleficius—by a synod at
Rome. He had fled to Constantinople, where he continued to plan
evil designs.

With Pope Benedict VII, the emperor now worked in Italy during 981-82, urged on by his mother, Adelaide, for the benefit of the
Church; of its clergy and, more especially, of its monks and their
cloisters, now in sore need. At the same time he was preparing his
campaign against the Saracens, while friends and counselors who
had Germany's cause at heart tried in vain to point out its danger.
At the moment the secular aims of Crescentius were arrested. Then
news came again that the Byzantine Greeks were fighting in Calabria, advancing to hold its land against the Saracens. The emperor
called men from Bavaria and Swabia to reinforce his army.

At last, in March 982, with Otto, ruler of both these duchies, he
marched to Tarentum, then occupied by the Greeks, and after a
brief siege he captured the city.

Doubtless this conflict in southern Italy prompted a new move
of diplomatic policy on his part. From Tarentum, during this same
month of March 982, he issued a decree in favor of the church at
Cremona, and signed it as "Otto II, Romanorum Imperator," "Emperor of the Romans."

The Byzantine emperor, John Tzimisces, we remember as a
usurper, even though Otto had married one related to him. But now
for some six years he had been dead, and his successor, Basil II, was
no ruler from without. He held a surer tradition by his birth; he be-

longed to the Macedonian line of the Byzantine Empire. Now Otto II was all the more determined to defend his imperial title in Italy. Basil II would not aid him against the Saracens; the Byzantine emperor was now his enemy. Therefore, by this new title Otto was asserting in more definite form his claim to imperial dignity in the West.

Early in July his army won a marked advantage over the Saracens on Calabria's east coast, killing and wounding right and left; he devoutly hoped that this victory would prove decisive.

It was not so. The enemy rallied and came back in mid-July 982 to defeat him entirely on the Capo delle Colonne near Cotrone, in a disaster which was to bring ruin, lasting and tragic. Now his fighters fled in all directions; Henry, bishop of Augsburg, taken prisoner or, more probably, killed on the field of battle, was only one of the many men of note who were lost. Otto himself narrowly escaped capture.

Word of his failure and flight quickly reached many peoples, moving some to grief and deep anxiety, others to wild joy. Among the Slavs of the Elbe and Oder rivers new resolve at once sprang up; here was a splendid chance to cast off German dominion, to be free again, to yield hated tribute no longer. They rose during 983 in force to destroy German workings in their lands, political and missionary alike. They overran much of the district around Magdeburg; the sees of Brandenburg and Havelberg they wiped from the earth; they undid the labor of Otto the Great, and they utterly refused its renewing.

The Danes also seized their opportunity. Again they invaded the German march, to capture the stronghold built by Otto II in 974 and to kill men of its garrison. Bernard I, however, who in 973 had succeeded Hermann Billung as duke of Saxony and count of the border, put an end to their advance.

But nobles, both German and Italian, were now thoroughly alarmed; they realized the danger threatening Germany and the empire. At their stern request Otto called a council, to meet in May 983 at Verona.

Much was done, during its sittings or shortly afterward, for the administration of Germany. The duchies of Bavaria and Swabia were without a ruler; Duke Otto, who governed them both, had died as he was traveling from Italy's scene of disaster to his German home. Otto, son of Conrad the Red, was deposed by the emperor from the rule of Carinthia, for no fault of his, it would seem, possibly through the will of the Empress Adelaide; Otto III was to restore him to his office in 995.

Three replacements filled the vacancies. The duchies of Bavaria and Carinthia, the latter for the second time, were assigned to Henry the Younger, now forgiven his rebellion of 978; Swabia went to Conrad of Franconia, a nephew of Hermann, formerly its duke.

One declaration, naturally expected, found its place at Verona; the emperor's little son, born in 980, was now made known as king of Germany in union with his father.

The ordinances of 983 did little for Otto II; the end of his reign was at hand. Late in the year he was not only exhausted but seriously ill, probably through malaria. The historian Richer declared that, suffering from indigestion and "melancholic humor," he sought remedy in aloes; the dose was too great and led to fatal complications. On December 7, 983, twenty-eight years old, the emperor died at Rome, and there he was buried, in the entrance to St. Peter's. One of his last acts had appointed a pope to follow Benedict VII, who had died shortly before. The man chosen had served Otto in many ways, as Peter, bishop of Pavia, and as archchancellor of the kingdom of Italy; he was consecrated now as Pope John XIV.

This second of the Ottonian emperors left no record of greatness as his father, Otto I, had done, nor of interest equal to that of his son, Otto III. In Germany he had put down rebellion; in Rome, "emperor of the Romans," he had won control through another man's skill and power; in southern Italy his ambition had spread tragedy far and wide. The Ottonian empire still lived, but it had fallen upon cold and dismal days.

CHAPTER FIVE

Summer, 983-1002
Otto III

1

ONCE AGAIN, in 983, a little boy sat on the throne of Germany; Otto III was three and a half years old. His right to this throne had been openly declared seven months before at the Diet of Verona; he was crowned king of Germany on Christmas Day 983 at Aachen by John, archbishop of Ravenna, and Willigis, archbishop of Mainz. His title as king of Italy might be considered acknowledged by the presence and solemn act of John of Ravenna; but years in plenty were to pass before the people of Italy held it valid and true.

The ceremony was hardly over when word arrived of his father's sudden death. It could not have come at a worse moment; the Slavs were still raging in a tumult of revolt. After long deliberation the nobles of Germany, assembled in council, decided that Otto's mother, Theophano, should administer political affairs in the kingdom during her son's minority; her shrewd skill and intimate knowledge were openly admitted, and her Byzantine birth gave her influence in regard to Constantinople. At her side stood Archbishop Willigis and Hildibald, bishop of Worms, for support and counsel.

Nevertheless, as was to be expected, many German fighting men looked in discontent upon a woman in charge of Germany's government; two women, in fact, for Otto's grandmother, the Empress Adelaide, still held power at court. Moreover, Theophano was Greek, and, as Thietmar observed, a German looked with suspicion upon a Greek, however able in mind. Twelve years must pass before the child king could rule independently; meanwhile disorder and destruction on German borders, together with Italy's problems, both for pope and for people, called for a warrior and a statesman in command.

The man desired by these rebels appeared. Late in 983 Henry the Quarreler, a prisoner since 978, was released by his keeper, the bishop of Utrecht, known now as Poppo, now as Folcmar. Whatever his name, the bishop, like Henry himself, saw in this kinsman of Otto III the only proper guardian of the realm. To Henry's side now rallied important prelates of Germany: Egbert, archbishop of Trier; Gisler, archbishop of Magdeburg; and Dietrich, bishop of Metz; the Slavs also joined the movement. Against Henry resistance was led by Willigis and by Bernard, duke of Saxony.

Soon word spread that Henry had captured the royal child Otto himself, with the aid of Archbishop Warin of Cologne, Otto's guardian. In March 984 at Magdeburg Henry claimed not only to be protector of the crown; he declared that the crown was his by right. A week later, at Quedlinburg where he was spending Easter, he was hailed as king; among those who swore to give him service were Miesko I, duke of the Poles, and Boleslav II, duke of Bohemia.

Then loyalty hurried to the rescue, threatening war, and Henry at an assembly in Bürstadt, near Worms, was forced to give his oath to Willigis and to Conrad, duke of Swabia, that he would restore the little king to them and to his mother. He did so on June 29, 984, at Rohr, near Meiningen. The Empresses Theophano and Adelaide had journeyed from Italy to assume responsible government.

For a while Henry remained quiet. But he was still rebellious. Had not his duchy of Bavaria, taken from him in 976, in 983 been granted to Henry the Younger? Toward the end of 984 he was striking a bargain for mutual aid with Lothair, king of France. Lothair, also, had hoped to see himself established as protector of the German crown. Was he not a nephew of Otto the Great? He was, indeed, of Carolingian descent, and he was still longing to see Lotharingia under his rule. So great was this desire that he even offered to support Henry's ambition to be king of Germany if Henry in return would fight to win Lotharingia for France.

Henry agreed. The two conspirators, each leading a strong army, planned to meet on February 1, 985, at Breisach on the Rhine for the march upon Lotharingia.

But Breisach lay in Germany, and Henry, "Quarreler" though he was, did not relish the prospect of being held a traitor to his country by appearing in alliance of war with a king of France on German land. Lothair arrived at Breisach; his partner was not there and he decided to act alone. Lotharingians, always ready to welcome the crown of France, joined him, and he marched forward to capture

Verdun in their land. But some Lotharingian nobles were loyal to
Germany and in their wrath they recaptured part of it. Lothair per-
sisted; in March 985 the city was once more his, and so it remained
as long as he lived.

In this year, very probably at the end of June, Henry the Quarreler made his submission. At Frankfurt, so the annals of Quedling-
burg tell, before the child sovereign, in the presence of his mother,
Theophano, of his grandmother, Adelaide, and of his aunt, Matilda,
abbess of Quedlinburg, the pretender to Germany's throne humbly
acknowledged his offenses and was forgiven. In the hope of permanent peace the duchy of Bavaria was now restored to him; Henry
the Younger from this time held only Carinthia's duchy.

The relief was great. In April 986 the royal court of Germany
kept Easter at Quedlinburg with ceremony of feast which recalled
the coronation banquet of Otto the Great at Aachen. Once more four
dukes of Germany served the table of their king, now nearly six
years old: Henry of Bavaria, Conrad of Swabia, Henry the Younger
of Carinthia, Bernard of Saxony. Also Miesko of the Poles and Boleslav II of Bohemia were there, once again allies of Germany's lawful crown.

Yet, Otto III as a child was growing up amid constant assault from
without. Continually the Slavs were burning and killing within the
borderland. In 985 his army went out against them; in 986, if record
be true, he himself rode with his soldiers in his country's defense,
and then received the homage of the Polish Miesko. We read that
the duke gave the boy many gifts, and among them a camel. At last
in 987 the Slavs were subdued for the time, and the fortresses, once
owned by Germany on the river Elbe and destroyed in the great
rising of 983, were now rebuilt.

In June 991 the kingdom was in mourning; the Empress Theophano, who had presided over German policy for her son so ably
since 984, had died at Nymwegen in the Netherlands, where the
court was staying. She was buried at Cologne, in that same monastery of St. Pantaleon where Bruno, brother of Otto I, had been laid
to rest. As the boy king was still but eleven years old, Adelaide, his
grandmother, now acted as administrator. But her power had never
been that of Theophano in matters political; her thought dwelt continually on the care and support of churches and abbeys.

Encouraged by the news, various enemies descended upon Germany. In this same year Henry of Bavaria drove back Hungarian invaders, quiet since 955. The Northmen from Scandinavia came to

plunder. Slavonic raiders, assisted by a Saxon traitor, Kizo, seized Brandenburg and ravaged the land far and wide. In 992, at the age of twelve, King Otto was once more on campaign, still supported by Duke Henry of Bavaria, true to his vow of loyalty. Duke Miesko I, with his wife, made about this time a "donation" of Poland to the Holy See at Rome, hoping thus to assure its independence of secular dominion, especially of Germany. Shortly afterward he died; his son, Boleslav the Brave, allied himself with the German crown and fought for its protection against the Scandinavian pirates. In 993 Kizo yielded his obedience and the city of Brandenburg to Otto as his king.

This year, 993, brought other worries to Germany: blight, famine, and pestilence. The annals of Hildesheim give a vivid description of its summer and autumn: "From the Nativity of Saint John the Baptist" (June 24) "until the ninth of November there were drought and intense heat; unnumbered crops did not ripen at the proper season because of the blazing sun. There followed extreme cold and great fall of snow, with outbreak of plague that destroyed far and wide both man and beast. The Saxons marched three times against the Slavs but did nothing; the Slavs harassed Saxony day after day in raids and robbery."

Battle against Northmen continued in 994; in 995 Otto and Boleslav II of Bohemia won success against the Slavonic Obodrites who had rushed down from the Elbe and the Baltic Sea. The success, however, was only for the moment.

In the same year Henry the Quarreler of Bavaria went to stay at the guesthouse of Gandersheim Abbey, lying in the valley of the Gande below the Harz Mountains; his sister Gerberga had ruled its community since about 957. There sudden illness came upon him and he died, bidding his son Henry, now in 995 to become duke of Bavaria and in 1002 to gain the crown of Germany as Henry II: "Never shall you resist the king, your lord; deeply I repent that ever I did this." At Gandersheim he was buried, near its altar of the holy cross.

995 also saw Otto III governing his realm in his own right, no longer a child in the eyes of law, free from regency and guardianship. It will be well to look at him for a moment.

German and Greek blood both ran in his veins. As German he had inherited ambition for conquest, for rule, for dominion, from his grandfather, Otto the Great, from his father, Otto the Second. From childhood he had lived with war. As one of Greek parentage he had been well and thoroughly introduced to Greek culture, its

literature and its art. John of Piacenza, himself a Greek from southern Italy, had been his teacher here. But, above all, his mother, the
Byzantine Theophano, had nourished his native impulse of delight
in things artistic, lovely, human and humane. Otto the Great had received scant knowledge in learning; Otto the Second had fared somewhat better; this third of the Ottonian line was receiving as a boy,
and as a young man was to welcome with a passion of eagerness, all
the knowledge, of letters, arts, mathematics, and science, which the
men around him could offer in that age.

It is not surprising that in 995 John, archbishop of Piacenza, and
Bernward, bishop of Würzburg, set out for Constantinople as delegates from the German court, commanded to undertake negotiation
with the emperor in the East, Basil II, for a marriage of this Otto III
with a Byzantine princess of the Greek Imperial House.

2

Early in 996 Otto did, so Thietmar records, what he had long
wanted to do. He traveled across the mountains to Italy. The journey was not prompted by pleasure alone; in Rome trouble was rising high, and his presence there was needed.

History in Rome had been marked by crisis ever since Otto had
been declared king in 983. John XIV had then been pope. The following year, in 984, a Crescentius once again had risen to dominate
Roman politics and people. This was not "the son of Theodora." He
had died, and his epitaph told that he had spent his last days in the
monastery of Saint Alexius on the Aventine doing penance for his
sins.

It was his son, Crescentius II Nomentanus, who was now to rule
in Rome, and in his turn to urge forward its citizens. With demo-
cratic fervor they had hastened to follow his lead when he had decided to call back from Constantinople that Franco, "the horrendous
monster," elected ten years before as Pope Boniface VII and driven
from Rome by Count Sicco in the name of Otto the Second.

Franco had speedily returned to the city, perhaps aided by
Basil II, keen to promote strife in the West during the minority of
its king. Once more as Boniface VII he had sat in the Holy See. In
April 984 he had seized John XIV, had thrown him into the prison of
Sant'Angelo, and had held him there four months. In August Pope
John had died, either through slow starvation or through a quick
dose of poison.

For eleven months Boniface had continued to act as pope. Then he, too, had met his death, in July 985; rumor told that by poison he had ended his own life. "So hated was he that after he died men cut and pierced his body with spears, then dragged it, stripped and naked, by the feet to the Campus Martius and threw it to the ground before the "Horse of Constantine" in front of the Lateran. There it lay, alone and neglected, until early on the next morning some of the clergy of Rome saw it as they were passing by and in mercy carried it away for burial."

The *Book of the Popes* told this story. It also told that in 985 a pope, Roman by birth, had been elected and consecrated as John XV. This John XV was still pope in 996, the year in which Otto the Third was crossing the Alps on his journey to Rome. Crescentius II was also in action. During the years 985 to 995 he had used his power with some restraint; we read of no quarrel between him and the Empress Theophano when, as guardian of the crowns of Germany and Italy, she had come to Rome, to stay from late in 989 until the spring of 990 and to charm both nobles and people by her diplomatic grace. She had powerful friends in Italy; Easter of 991 had found her keeping joyful feast at Quedlinburg in the German court with two of them: Hugh, marquis of Tuscany, and John, archbishop of Piacenza.

Yet, throughout these years there had always been a strain of rivalry, even if subdued, between the secular and the spiritual elements in Rome. In 995 Crescentius II suddenly had resolved to grasp control over the Holy See. So bitterly had he attacked the pope that John XV had been forced to leave the city and to send an urgent call for help to Otto III in Germany. The appeal had come at the right moment; the king was now of age, and rebels on his borders were comparatively quiet. In the spring of 996 he set out, and by Easter he was in Pavia.

As he journeyed, messengers had met him; Crescentius had shown signs of relenting. He had even allowed John XV to return to Rome; but the pope, worn out by distress, was now dead. The authority of Otto was recognized; both the clergy of Rome and Crescentius himself were asking that he name John's successor. In answer Otto requested the election of a chaplain of his court, Bruno. The nomination was significant. Bruno was young; he was energetic, able, and well trained in learning, secular and ecclesiastical; he was German by birth; and, finally, he was of Germany's royal house: a son of Otto, duke of Carinthia and count of the march of Verona; and a cousin of King Otto III himself.

Church and people in Rome assented to the choice; Bruno was

escorted from Germany to Rome by Willigis of Mainz and Hildibald of Worms. At the beginning of May he was consecrated in St. Peter's as Pope Gregory V; on May 21, Ascension Day, Pope Gregory anointed and crowned Otto there as emperor of the West.

A few days later the emperor, now acknowledged as king of Italy as well as of Germany, assembled a council at Rome to deal with the tyrant Crescentius. He was condemned and sentenced to exile; but through petition of the pope, quick to show mercy in the joy of recent events, his sentence was remitted.

Gregory V was twenty-four years old and the emperor was but fifteen. Yet, already in the mind of Otto III a vision of the future was rising. Three times during his short life he crossed the Alps to stay in Rome. He entered its churches, he looked upon its ruins; the churches told him of martyrs and saints in Christian history, the ruins recalled the glory of ancient Rome, of republic and of empire. Even now he saw power shared by a German emperor and a German pope: one in their reverence for Rome, extending hand in hand authority, spiritual and political, over Germany, over Italy, over a world both civilized and barbarian. Otto the First had bound together Germany and Italy in the repute and title of empire; he had fought and planned to raise that title in the West to the dignity of Byzantium. Otto the Second in his ambition to extend and to win further recognition for his imperial standing had declared himself emperor of the Romans, and in so doing he had ruined much of the work of Otto the Great.

Now this grandson of Otto the Great dreamed of building anew, and won support from nobles of Italy, especially from the Tuscan Count Hugh. Already in 996 Otto's diplomas placed in solemn succession and in significant order the peoples whom he governed: Romans, Franconians, Bavarians, Saxons, Alsatians, Swabians, Lotharingians. His empire, in his thought, was to last down the years to come; he placed the citizens of Cremona under "the imperial protection of ourself and our successors."

3

But also in other ways the months in Rome during 996 were to influence the mind and spirit of the young ruler. This influence was to come to him from three men. To learn something of their lives and character we shall have to retrace for a while the course of the tenth century's history.

One of them was Adalbert, bishop of Prague in Bohemia, in this year, 996, about forty years old. Two things brought emperor and bishop together; Adalbert's love of learning was only surpassed by his fervent hope to make known the Christian faith to the multitudes still pagan. Born of a noble house in Bohemia, he had been sent at the age of sixteen to study in the cathedral school of Magdeburg, Germany, under its head, Otrich. There he stayed niие years. In 981 another Adalbert, archbishop of Magdeburg, died and Otrich was elected by Magdeburg's clergy as their primate. Archbishop Adalbert had never cared for Otrich and had utterly rejected all and every thought that Otrich might follow him in office. Gisler, bishop of Merseburg, gained the vacant see; now both Otrich and the younger Adalbert left Magdeburg. In the same year, 981, this Adalbert was ordained subdeacon at Prague. Under Otto I, in 973, Prague had received an episcopal seat, though it did not gain its first bishop, Dethmar, until the reign of Otto II; in 983 Adalbert became the second, by will of its people and by action of Otto II as emperor.

Until 989 he worked hard as father and guide of his diocese. Then he left for Rome. A longing for a strictly ascetic and a contemplative life had gradually brought him to hope that perhaps this, together with carrying the Gospel to the heathen in wilder districts, might be his vocation. But the real and immediate reason for his departure was a bitter lack of harmony between himself as bishop and the leading laymen of his charge, especially Duke Boleslav II of Bohemia. All around him he saw sin and disorder: bigamy, negligent priests living with women, wedded or unwed, Christian prisoners sold for money to Jews, captives whom in no way he could free. Moreover, was not the duke an enemy of the Poles, a Christian people, and carrying on negotiations with the Slavonic Liutici, still firmly pagan?

For some time Adalbert was happy in Rome. Then, while trying to decide his future, he resolved to seek help by that common resource of medieval souls in trouble, a pilgrimage. Perhaps his stay in Rome had prompted this. From Pope John XV he obtained permission to leave Rome for Jerusalem; the Empress Theophano, who was in Italy at the time, warmly encouraged him to go. On his way south he stayed to rest with the brethren of Monte Cassino, and their abbot found him a most congenial companion. "Why wander on pilgrimage?" he asked as he talked with Adalbert. "Why not stay here with us, enter our community and follow in the steps of Saint Benedict? We need a bishop!"

But Adalbert now was wholly uncertain of his future. Should he return to pastoral work as bishop among sinners in the world, or enter the solitary life of contemplation, or vow obedience to Benedictine rule? He decided to travel on and to ask advice of Saint Nilus the hermit.

Saint Nilus also was to leave his mark upon this time, as another counselor of the Emperor Otto III and as a monk of importance in the history of Greek solitaries in southern Italy. He was himself of Greek origin, though at this moment he was grateful for hospitality given him by Latin brethren. The Benedictines of Monte Cassino had allowed him and his followers to settle at Valleluce, on land near their own abbey, and there the Greeks had built a monastery of rude hut-like cells, surrounding a chapel in the midst, and had dedicated all in honor of Saint Michael. Many of their own people and tongue were coming to join them in their hermit life; Nilus was known far and wide through his strictly ascetic adherence to Greek monastic custom.

Again Adalbert felt a new attraction. Here was a saint who surely would lead him in the path of true holiness. But Nilus sorrowfully said that this could not be. He himself, the abbot of Valleluce, was a foreigner, a Greek in the eyes of Latin Benedictine monks; the land on which Saint Michael's stood belonged to Monte Cassino; the generosity of its Latin brethren was not his to offer to one who came from Rome. Far better for Adalbert to return to Rome, Nilus declared, with a letter from him to Leo, abbot of its Benedictine monastery of Saints Boniface and Alexius.

Adalbert did as he was advised to do. He returned to Rome, "mistress of cities and head of the world," as his biographer, John Canaparius, held her. He was received with all hospitality in the cloister and in 990 after due proving he was clothed with monastic habit. The joy was great; but it did not last. Duke Boleslav II of Bohemia, together with Willigis, archbishop of Mainz, under whose authority the see of Prague lay, in 992 petitioned Pope John XV to send him back. The see was without a bishop and its people had promised to amend their ways.

The bishop went his way to Prague in due obedience, and for some time things seemed to prosper there. Then the old difficulties rose again, and again he despaired of lasting success among hindrances many and insurmountable. Once more in 995 he made for Rome and its monastery, "as a storm-tossed ship coming into the haven where it would be." To the pope, John XV, he told all his troubles and gained permission to stay, for the present.

There in 996 the fifteen-year-old emperor found him. They talked long and often together; Adalbert well understood the struggle of a young man called to rule various and different peoples, to conquer and convert the heathen barbarians, one who longed for leisure and peace among his books, for debate with learned scholars. Perhaps there was other difficulty. It may be true, as tradition has suggested, that in his love of beauty and aesthetic delight Otto was now and then to feel within himself the power of sexual temptation, possibly to yield for the moment to this, to recover, and to repent. At any rate, already at this time the seeds of ascetic penance and self-denial were also lying imbedded in his character; in the summer of 996 Adalbert brought them into active life. The *Life of Adalbert* by John Canaparius tells us that "the Emperor often spoke with him and held him his familiar friend, gladly listening to his words, whatever he said."

As strong, however, as either Adalbert or Nilus in influence upon this emperor's life and character was a man of France: Gerbert, the source of knowledge and inspiration, Otto's teacher, guide, and support.

Gerbert was born some time between 940 and 945, of humble parents living in Auvergne; he was sent for his training during boyhood and youth to its abbey of Saint-Géraud at Aurillac. About 967, when he was in his twenties, Borrell, a Spanish duke, visited Aurillac and was persuaded by its teachers to take this very promising young man with him for further study in Catalan Spain. Gerbert had already absorbed much of Latin classical and early medieval humanism; in Spain he was introduced to research in science and mathematics and to Arab learning under the skilled leadership of Hatto, bishop of Vich in Catalonia.

Three years later Bishop Hatto and Duke Borrell invited Gerbert to travel in their company to Rome. In Rome he was given audience by the pope, then John XIII, who was much impressed by their conversation and suggested that he might be of service to King Otto I, at that time in the city. Gerbert told the king that, as Pope John had said, he did feel at home in mathematics, but that now he was very anxious to study logic. Nevertheless, for some months he remained in Ravenna and in Rome, teaching mathematics at the royal court.

Then Gerann, archdeacon of Reims and a noted professor of logic, arrived in Italy. Otto the Great was at Rome; Gerann had been sent to him as legate from King Lothair of France. Naturally Gerbert seized his opportunity to learn, with so much enthusiasm that Gerann carried him to France when, in 972, he returned to Reims. At Reims Gerbert made brilliant progress in philosophy; so brilliant that Adalbero, archbishop of Reims, made him head of its cathedral school. Pupils came to him from all directions.

Already during his stay of 871-72 in Italy Gerbert had talked with Otto II, then a boy of sixteen. We have also seen him in Ravenna at the turn of the year, 980-81, arguing in the presence of this same Otto II, now sole king of Germany and emperor, against Otrich, recently head of the school of Magdeburg. The debate once ended, Otto in keen admiration could not forget Gerbert's skill; full of eagerness to hold this scholar of France in Italy, the emperor at last won his consent to assume rule of the monastery of Bobbio amid the Apennine mountains. Probably the year 982 saw Gerbert installed there as abbot.

This act of Otto II turned Gerbert into a firm supporter of the crown of Germany, sworn to faithful service. He did not, it is true, remain long at Bobbio, however much he delighted in its library. Its finances were in disorder; its monks, miserable through cold and hunger, were in no state to keep the rule; Italy itself was racked by enemies from without and robbers from within. By January 984 he was back at Reims, directing its school and working as secretary for Archbishop Adalbero.

Adalbero was also a friend of Germany, and from Reims both he and Gerbert gave all possible aid to the Empress Theophano, against Henry the Quarreler and against King Lothair of France, so zealously trying to recover the duchy of Lotharingia. The archbishop, born of a noble Lotharingian family, wanted his native land to remain in German keeping. Early in 984 Gerbert wrote, in Adalbero's name, a letter to Willigis, archbishop of Mainz; "Loyal affection, and the many favors shown us by the Ottos, forbid us to oppose the son of the Emperor" (the little king, Otto III); "we have induced our kings" (Lothair and his son Louis V, co-kings of France) "to give him aid." He had also declared the same in a letter to Notker, bishop of Liège: "My faithful adherence to our emperor's son [Otto III] is strong because of the many good deeds done for me by Otto [Otto II]." April 985 found him upholding in a letter to friends the most powerful noble in France, Hugh Capet, son of Hugh the Great and duke of the Franks: "Lothair is king of France only in name; Hugh, not indeed in name, but in act and working. If you had sought his friendship and had allied his son [Robert] with the emperor's son [Otto III], you would not now be holding the kings of France as your enemies."

On May 11, 985, Gerbert and his archbishop had reason to be grateful to Duke Hugh Capet. Adalbero had been summoned by King Lothair to trial for high treason against the throne of France. A council of leading men was assembled at Compiègne for this purpose, and Hugh marched there with his soldiers to scatter them in complete disorder.

On March 2, 986, Lothair died, and his son, already crowned seven years before, now became sole sovereign in France. He was only nineteen, weak in body and unstable in spirit; more than ever, Adalbero of Reims and his secretary Gerbert looked for support to Duke Hugh and to Germany.

Louis V, however, as his father before him, was of Carolingian blood and ambitious to regain Lotharingia. He detested both Adalbero and Gerbert, as friends of the German crown. Shortly before the Council of Compiègne met in 985 Gerbert had written in confidence to the Empress Theophano: "You know that the kings of France look upon me with no favoring eyes, because I am faithful to you and my views differ from theirs. I am, too, greatly attached to Adalbero, archbishop of Reims, whom they also accuse of deep disloyalty. Things have gone so far that now it is not a matter of casting him out from his see, an evil which we could endure. They are striving for his very lifeblood; and I am in this together with him as one driving him on against the royal will." So angry was this young Louis that he marched against Reims with an army. Before its gates he sent word to its archbishop: Would he stand battle or would he defend himself before his judges in trial, for treason against the king's majesty? Adalbero chose trial, and once more a council of nobles was called to meet at Compiègne, on May 18, 987. Once again Adalbero escaped penalty, this time through the death of King Louis V a few days later. He had gone off to hunt in forest land and his foot slipped as he rode.

Louis left no son, and the heir by right of birth was his uncle, Charles, duke of Lower Lotharingia; Charles also claimed right of succession through his Carolingian descent. He tried hard to win support from Adalbero of Reims, now of marked power in current politics. To no purpose; Adalbero denounced him and upheld Hugh

Capet. At Noyon, on July 3, 987, Hugh was crowned king of France; the following December his son, Robert, was crowned as co-ruler at Orléans. The Carolingian line of France had come to its end.

But Charles, duke of Lower Lotharingia, was planning his revenge. He decided to make for Laon; the city was of high importance to the kings of France. In 988 he captured it, and in spite of repeated efforts by Hugh and Robert, aided by both Adalbero and Gerbert, he was still in possession of Laon when the archbishop of Reims died, in January 989.

Some two months later King Hugh appointed as head of the see one Arnulf, an illegitimate son of Lothair. The decision caused Gerbert deep disappointment; he had hoped for his own election as archbishop. He wrote to Remi, a monk of Trier: "My father, Adalbero of blessed memory, was so sure a source of equilibrium to me in things pertaining to eternal life that now he has returned whence he came I feel the world slipping back into its original chaos. I say nothing of myself, threatened by a thousand deaths ever since Father Adalbero, with all the clergy and all the bishops and some knights, marked me out as his successor." To a friend living in the German kingdom he declared: "To no other man at any time have I sworn homage save to the Emperor Otto, sacred in remembrance." Here the reference is, of course, to Otto the Second.

But tragedy hitherto undreamed of was yet to fall in this year to Gerbert's lot. He had carried on his work at Reims, teaching its students and writing letters for Archbishop Arnulf as he had done for Adalbero; he had even himself announced Arnulf's election, formally and with words of praise, in a letter to the Church at large. Just before his consecrating in March 989 as archbishop of Reims, Arnulf had sworn allegiance to the kings of France, Hugh and Robert; in his secret mind, however, he preferred his own uncle, Charles of Lower Lotharingia. Were they not both Carolingians, hostile to these new kings of another line?

Soon feeling led to action. In the deep silence of a night of August or September 989, by order of Archbishop Arnulf the gates of Reims were opened to admit Charles and his army. But the archbishop's treachery was carefully hidden. He posed as enemy of Charles and falsely was announced his "prisoner"; with equal pretence Charles in later time made known Arnulf's "escape." The city was plundered and the two conspirators remained firm allies.

Gerbert remained at Reims, in misery. Late in 989 he wrote

again to Remi of Trier: "Through most grievous and constant troubles I fell sick during that pestilential autumn of 988 and nearly lost my life. Then there came upon me an assault of evil fortune, taking from me through those robbers who laid waste Reims all that once had been given. I weep for the capture of my friends; I wonder with worry that never ceases whether I ought to leave here? Our land is in so great sorrow; fear and trembling surround these walls. Starvation threatens our citizens; the clergy, monastic and secular, dread desolation to come. Pray for us!"

He did not only stay; he continued to act as secretary to Arnulf, tortured by a sense of guilt. Arnulf and Duke Charles compelled him; he himself believed that Reims needed his care. At last the situation became unbearable, and he fled to shelter with Hugh, king of France. "Now I am staying at the royal Court," he wrote in 990 to the archbishop of Trier; "and I say the words of life together with the priests of God. No longer for love of Charles or of Arnulf will I let myself be made accomplice of the Devil in crying lies against the truth."

King Hugh Capet appealed to the pope, John XV, for support in this time of trouble at Reims. "Arnulf," he wrote, "was adopted by us as a son and was given free gift of the metropolitan see of Reims. He swore homage to us in a statement, written and signed; he read it aloud, he confirmed it, he had it witnessed. He compelled his soldiers and all his people to swear constant loyalty to us, if ever he should fall into enemy hands. Now, contrary to all this, he has given over the clergy and people under his charge to the keeping of those who rob and hold them prisoners."

No answer came from the pope. But in Holy Week, March 991, by treachery of Ascelin, bishop of Laon, Duke Charles and Arnulf were both delivered captive into Hugh's power. In June the great Council of Verzy, near Reims, was assembled by both kings of France in its church of Saint-Basle for the trial of Arnulf, accused by them of treason against the crown. The director of proceedings during this council was another Arnulf, bishop of Orléans, and Gerbert himself made the record of its action which is still ours to read. From the moment when Adalger, priest of Reims, confessed that from his archbishop, Arnulf, he had received the keys of the city and that at Arnulf's order he had unlocked its gates, to the climax when Arnulf, prostrate before his kings, confessed his crime and with his own consent was deposed from his see, the debate grew more and more intense and grim. Adalger was finally forbidden to administer the sacraments of the Church and ordered to fulfill heavy penance; in the place of Arnulf, Gerbert was elected archbishop of Reims.

The honor, once so eagerly desired, was to bring him no joy; he was to spend the next six years in struggling to hold his cathedral. His struggle was made more bitter, more fierce by other happenings at the Council of Verzy. Into the ears of the assembled prelates Arnulf of Orléans had hurled virulent accusation against the popes of Rome themselves: John XII, "a traitor, wallowing in lust"; Leo VIII, "the neophyte"; Boniface VII, "the monster." "Why, most reverend Fathers," he had cried aloud, "through what fault can it have come to pass that the head of the Churches of God, raised on high, crowned with glory and honor, has been cast down to the depths, defaced by ignominy and shame? Ours, ours is this sin, ours the betrayal of our faith; we look to ourselves, not to Jesus Christ!"

There followed a bitter feud between the papacy and the bishops of France, largely concerned with the deposition of Arnulf and with Gerbert's appointing to Reims, deeds which the Holy See held illegal. In 992 John XV sent Leo, abbot of the monastery of Saints Boniface and Alexius at Rome, to act as papal legate for the settling of the quarrel. Leo called the bishops of France to meet him at Aachen and they did not come. The pope summoned them to Rome and they did not obey. In 993 or 994 they gathered in council at Chelles, near Meaux. If our only account of this meeting, given by the historian Richer, is true in detail, they were in fiery mood. King Robert Capet was presiding; Gerbert was present, together with the archbishops of Sens, Tours, and Bourges. There they affirmed: "That if aught should be put forward by the pope of Rome contrary to the decrees of the fathers of the Church, it shall be held null and void, according to the words of the apostle: *Shun utterly a heretic and him who follows not the Church.* Another resolve ordered: "That the deposing of Arnulf and the promotion of Gerbert be ratified in permanence, as has been determined according to canon law: *The ordinance of a Provincial Synod shall not be set aside without due and proper cause.*

At a third meeting, of June 2, 995, at Mouzon, near Reims, the legate Leo appealed to German and Lotharingian bishops. Kings Hugh and Robert had forbidden those of France to appear; among them only Gerbert arrived, as archbishop of the diocese of Reims and as pleader for his cause. This assembly decided to propitiate Pope John XV for the time being by an agreement, forced upon Gerbert, that he refrain from celebrating Mass until the first of July.

On that day another council was held, it would seem at Reims, in the abbey of Saint-Remi. Its debate brought no deciding of the dispute, and Gerbert remained in anguish of mind.

To the day of his death, in March 996, Pope John XV refused to approve the election of Gerbert in place of Arnulf; the bishops of France, he maintained, had acted without the due consent of the Holy See. At last Gerbert decided to go to Rome and to lay his problem before the head of the Church. When he arrived, in 996, Gregory V sat as pope, and Gerbert hoped with all eagerness for his support. He gained nothing. Gregory V was indeed closely allied with Gerbert's friend, the Emperor Otto III, but he was nevertheless a ruler of independent mind. In this very year of his elevation to the papacy he had consecrated at Rome with his own hands one Erluin as bishop of Cambrai, a suffragan see in the archdiocese of Reims; "since, because of the dissension between Arnulf, archbishop of Reims, and Gerbert, invader of that archbishopric, Erluin could not canonically be consecrated at Reims."

Of these three men who influenced the life of Otto III as emperor— Adalbert of Prague, Nilus of Valleluce, and Gerbert of Reims—Otto, then, met two, Adalbert and Gerbert, when he was in Italy during the summer of 996. Both of them, and also the emperor himself, left Italy before autumn ended.

In a synod, called at Rome by Pope Gregory, a request for Adalbert's recall had again been put forward by the archbishop of Mainz, and it had gained general support. Willing or unwilling, since his people of Prague desired his rule as their father in God, Adalbert was to return to his see in Bohemia. Soon he was in Germany, at Mainz, where he conferred with Archbishop Willigis and awaited Prague's decision. But before he had once more said goodbye to his fellow monks in the cloister of Saints Boniface and Alexius on the Aventine, he had sought private word with the pope. "In Prague," he had said, "I shall do no good to its people and I shall harm my own soul. If they declare themselves ready to hear my voice, then truly I shall be theirs in life and in death. But if they do not want me, Father, of your apostolic goodness let me go forth to teach barbarian and foreign tribes who know not the word of God!" Pope Gregory had not found heart to resist his appeal.

It was still summer in 996 when the emperor wrote to this cousin of his that the climate of Italy was undermining his health; he would have to leave for Germany. There was also political need for his return there; the Slavs were still invading from their land of the Elbe. The pope heard the news with deep distress; Crescentius the Second had made evil answer to papal clemency earlier in the year. He was now again spreading fear throughout Rome, and Gregory sent word to Otto, imploring him to stay. We have the emperor's reply, written just before he began his journey home: "I am indeed so very sorry that I cannot do as you ask. I feel all sympathy for you; but Nature, who governs all things by her own law, in her own contrary fashion is stirring up enmity between the peculiarities of the Italian air and my body. And I leave with you for comfort and support the foremost men of Italy: Hugh of Tuscany, ever faithful to us, and Conrad, Count of Spoleto and Camerino's Prefect."

His health, nevertheless, may not have been Otto's only reason for leaving Italy. The bishops of its Church do not seem to have given him eager welcome, eager though he himself was to do all in his power for its clergy, its monks and its abbeys. At any rate he set out for Germany, for Mainz, where again he talked happily day and night with Adalbert. From Mainz he went to Aachen, where he placed precious relics brought from Italy to honor the royal chapel of Saint Mary.

Gerbert left for France, and arrived there in time to hear of the death of its king, Hugh Capet, in October 996 and to witness the assumption of sole rule by his son, Robert II, "the Pious." Robert had once been a pupil of Gerbert at Reims. Soon, at the beginning of 997, through act of this new king, the bond between them broke. In his nineteenth year, about 991, when Robert was already co-king with his father, he had caused great scandal by divorcing his wife, Suzanne, daughter of the Italian King Berengar of Ivrea and his wife Willa. Some years later he was passionately in love with Bertha, widow of Odo, count of Chartres. He was utterly determined to marry her, and marry her he did, in 996 or 997. This aroused new disturbance; the Church declared the union illegal. Bertha was a cousin of Robert; worse still, she had already several children by her first marriage, and Robert, her new husband, was godfather of one of them. Therefore, the bishops of France decided that the two "coparents" were united in a relationship which forbade the sacrament of holy matrimony; Gerbert refused to approve the marriage and Robert became his enemy.

Even more serious for Gerbert were events in Italy. Pope Gregory was at last driven into exile, in 997, by Crescentius Nomentanus and found refuge at Pavia. There on February 7 he presided over a synod of bishops, among whom not one of France, not even Gerbert, was present. Three decrees were approved and issued:

First: That all bishops of the West who had taken part in the deposing of Arnulf from the archbishopric of Reims and had refused to obey the call to attend at Pavia, be forthwith suspended from episcopal function.

Second: That King Robert of France be summoned to account for his "incestuous marriage." Should he refuse, he would meet excommunication.

Third: "By common consent of the brethren we have separated Crescentius, invader and plunderer of the holy Church of Rome, from all the fellowship of the faithful."

We learn of these proceedings from a letter written by Pope Gregory to Willigis of Mainz.

Gerbert, therefore, as one of those active at Saint-Basle in deposing Arnulf, could no longer act as archbishop in his cathedral of Reims. The situation was impossible; he fell sick in mind and in body. Before the spring of 997 was over he gave up the struggle; he fled from France to the imperial court of Otto III in Germany. He found enthusiastic welcome. "You received me with joy," he wrote a little later to Adalbero, bishop of Metz; "me, delivered by grace of God from unjust persecution by my brethren. You grieved that you had not been with me in my perils." So, in more vivid detail, he told Adelaide, queen-dowager of France, widow of Hugh Capet: "Not only the knights of France but even the clergy joined together against me; not one of them would eat with me or attend my Mass."

4

The emperor was still in Aachen, and from this time his story is linked with that of Gerbert. At the moment Otto needed his sympathy; word arrived that Adalbert on April 23 of this year had been murdered by the savage Prussians who lived on the borders of Poland and Russia. The bishop after much travail had found his reward; Thietmar wrote that "Otto offered praise to God for giving him in these days of anxiety so victorious a martyr for his support." Future time knew him as Saint Adalbert.

Otto was in truth anxious; his mind was torn between fear for Germany and fear for Rome. The Slavs were now laying waste land around the towns of Bardowiek and Lüneberg, in the Bardengau. In

July he marched out on campaign, much to Gerbert's distress: "I cannot bear your absence, now that you are so far away; and the bare report that you have done splendidly, as you always do, has brought me not one spark of relief."

From Italy came message of crisis acute and immediate, involving the Papal See. The Romans heartily disliked Gregory V as an alien from Germany; with satisfaction and content they had seen him driven from Rome. In the early spring of 997 a new turn of events was caused by the arrival in the city of John, archbishop of Piacenza, coming back from Constantinople and his negotiation in regard to a bride "born to the purple" for Otto III.

This John, known as John Philagathos, Greek by birth, was a native of Rossano in Calabria, southern Italy. Otto the Second had given him rule over the famous monastery of Nonantola, declaring that after long and intense search this John alone had been found worthy to be its abbot: a man of all prudence, of shining holiness, a scholar skilled in Greek learning. Otto III was his godson; he had also been his pupil as a boy. In 988 John had been elected to the see of Piacenza, which in his honor had then been raised from a simple episcopal seat to an archbishopric. He had worked with the empress-guardian, Theophano, during her stay of 989-90 at Rome; Thietmar called him her "dear companion."

With him as he traveled he brought a companion, a special envoy sent by the emperor of the East, Basil II, to state the view taken by Constantinople concerning the proposed marriage.

The envoy's name was Leo. Happily we have a number of letters written by him during his stay in Italy. They have been published by Alcibiades Sakellion and interpreted for us by Percy Ernst Schramm; much light is thrown by them upon Leo's character and doings.

As a Greek he loved the Byzantine Empire and Basil II in his ambitious mind as heartily as he hated the Romans in Italy, and he had made zealous use of his journey from Constantinople with John Philagathos. His great desire was that Basil, as ruler of the true Roman Empire, should hold power over Rome in the West, and he had thought busily on his way, searching for means by which he could promote this. Was not his companion on this journey himself a Greek? Was he not also an archbishop in Italy, one of repute both in East and West, one who—as Leo easily could see—was as ambitious as he himself? Why, then, should not this John Philagathos sit in the seat of St. Peter at Rome, to serve the interests of Constantinople, instead of that cousin and friend of Otto III? Why should Crescentius II not be friend of the pope at Rome, instead of his oppressor? True, Leo himself had no love for Philagathos. But he could use him as a tool for the glory of the Eastern emperor, and for his, Leo's, good in the end, he hoped. Meanwhile, he would work secretly, with great caution; he would allow the elevation of Philagathos to be looked upon, not as his work, but as an act of force suddenly brought about by Crescentius.

John Philagathos yielded to Leo's secret persuasion; so did Crescentius II. In or about the month of May 997 Philagathos was declared Pope John XVI by Crescentius II, with the consent and acclamation of Rome's citizens. Gregory V was still an exile when Leo wrote privately to a man whom he could trust, a courtier of the palace in Constantinople:

"I can see you laughing in derision as you hear from me that we have made Philagathos pope at Rome. In the future you may weep. But for the present, laugh and rejoice and fare well and think of me. Rome has need of a man strong and shrewd of mind: qualities of which, as you know, our great and majestic emperor possesses more than those who reigned before him."

Leo, however, was not entirely free from fear. There was always the thought that Basil II might not, after all, approve this sudden upheaval, that possibly it might be traced to his own influence. Besides, as he wrote to another friend: "Rome does have a Pope in Gregory, even though he has been banished by force and necessity. Gregory may seize this foul carpetbagger Philagathos and work hot vengeance upon him. If the Basileus receives my service generously, it will be well. But should he be displeased, what should I say?"

Troubled as he was by a call from Gregory, entreating him to return to Rome, Otto could not leave Saxony at the mercy of Slavonic invaders; it was not until late in the summer of 997 that he could see his victory won. Now Leo was on his way to Aachen to carry out his diplomatic mission. As Otto knew nothing of Leo's vital part in the overthrowing of Pope Gregory, he received this ambassador with goodwill, and negotiation concerning a Byzantine bride proceeded in peace. Leo's travel to Aachen and back, with his stay there, occupied the months of August, September, and October.

The year was nearing its close when at last the emperor felt it possible to start for Italy. Affairs of his German kingdom were placed for the duration of his absence in the capable hands of his aunt, Matilda, abbess of Quedlinburg. In March 998 he was in Rome; but the man whom he was seeking, Pope John XVI, had fled. For long this rival pope had known that he was facing disaster; his friend and his fellow countryman, Saint Nilus, also born in Rossano of southern Italy, had warned him well. After twenty-five years of strenuous life at Valleluce near Monte Cassino, Nilus had founded about 995 a new monastery in the bleak solitude of Serperi, on a point running into the Gulf of Gaeta. From there he had written to Philagathos, imploring him to forsake human pomp and pride for the seclusion and happiness of prayer. John had already sent answer that he was ready to do so, when he was caught by Otto's sudden arrival. He fled, but was speedily captured and dragged out from the tower in which he was hiding. The hideous story of his fate comes to us in relentless detail from Leo himself; he wrote it about the time of May 998 to a friend of name unknown:

"Now you are going to laugh, a big, broad laugh, my dear heart and soul, you who have never done evil to any one, the very man for doing good to all. That Philagathos who, to put it briefly, never had his equal, whose mouth was full of cursing and bitterness, of blasphemy and knavery and abuse, that pope stained with blood, arrogant and supercilious—O God! O Justice! O Sun!—has fallen, caught hand and foot! And why shouldn't I tell you, brother, openly how he fell?

"Well, first, the Church of the West dealt him anathema; then his eyes were gouged out; third, his nose, and, fourth, his lip, and fifth, that tongue of his which prattled so many and such unspeakable words, one by one, were all cut from his face. Item six: he rode like a conqueror in procession, grave and solemn on a miserable little donkey, hanging on to its tail; a piece of old hide from some animal covered his head, with the beast's own head sticking up on top. Item seven: he was brought to trial and condemned. Then they put on him the priestly vestments, back to front, the wrong way round; and then they stripped them off again. After this he was pulled along the church, right through it, and out by the front portico to the court of the fountain. Finally, for his refreshment, they threw him into prison.

"So now I have told you, my brother, you who think as I do, all that happened to the wretched Philagathos, not adding, not hiding anything. But I also warn all men not to dare to do what he dared. Justice does not sleep. Fare you well; pray for me always and keep me in mind. It would be good to see you soon, happy and prosperous."

One man pleaded for Philagathos: Nilus of Serperi who had warned him. Nilus was old, nearly ninety, and he was keeping fast, for it was time of Lent. But painfully on horseback he rode to Rome, to pray the emperor and the pope that this victim of brutal punishment, now almost dead, might be handed over to his care. He asked in vain. From the records it may well seem true that the mutilation and the mockery were due either to order of Pope Gregory, now again in Rome and overcome by wrath at the insult to the Holy See, or to impulse of soldiers and people of Rome, fearing that Otto would forgive Philagathos and send him away unharmed. It would also seem possible that Nilus arrived in Rome after the maiming of Philagathos; that Gregory then gave immediate command, without the emperor's knowledge, for the degrading of his prisoner in that public procession; and that Nilus then turned away in anger, despairing of mercy at his hands.

Yet, without sight, unable to speak, defaced and deposed, John Philagathos lived on into the eleventh century, at Rome and in his native Greek-Italian land of the south.

In terror the second Crescentius had also hurried to find shelter, within Rome's fortress of Sant'Angelo. When Easter week was over, during April 998, the emperor ordered Ekkehard, margrave of Meissen, to attack it by siege. The siege did not last long. At Otto's word, quickly given, the lord of Rome was executed in sight of all the spectators crowding around; his headless body was left hanging on the Monte Mario as a lesson to all.

In the autumn Leo, now staying in southern Italy, wrote to his friends of the Byzantine Empire in a sardonic temper of mind. To one: "I was traveling in Frankish land the whole of August, September, and October 997; back to Italy for November and December, and for January 998. Then I was four months in Rome, and I saw what I saw. But God kept me without harm, and unsuspected in regard to all that I had planned." To another: "Your writing was to me like rain upon the thirsty earth; it cheered me up; it made me forget painful experience and the men I have been with these last two years." To a third: "My plans have not gone forward as I had hoped myself, but as God, good and mighty and all-wise, has ruled; not, I tell you, as either I or any one else had expected!"

The Emperor Otto and Gregory V had long since been welcomed with exultation in Rome after their return to extinguish the power of Crescentius: a statement which no doubt should be read as meaning that Otto's friends set the example and the fickle but shrewd multitude followed it. Certainly intense indignation blazed out against the intruder into the Holy See. Thietmar wrote of Philagathos in his *Chronicle* as "no shepherd, but a wolf, a minister of Satan, who received office in the Church not for ruling but for plunder. Drunken with the Devil's poison of avarice, he raised himself to the seat of blessed Peter, there to fornicate rather than revere." Thietmar was a loyal German and as such resented any action against the king of Germany; the Romans had no lasting love for foreign rulers, German or Greek.

But the triumph of these two German rulers was celebrated by another and a very different Leo, who in 999 was made bishop of Vercelli and was to share greatly in Otto's imperial service and aims. Now he wrote rhythmic verse in honor of Otto and Gregory; a song of joy over the punishment of a sinner, over the renewing of Church and empire through the united power of Otto as emperor and of Gregory as pope. Antioch, old in time, Leo told his world, reveres in all things this pope; Alexandria, ancient in days, with anxious haste runs to his side; the Churches of all the earth look to him as head. From ironclad Babylon to golden Greece men fear and bow to Otto's will. Through all lands, throughout Christendom, may these two shining lights, emperor and pope, banish darkness from human hearts, the one by the might of his sword, the other by the ringing sound of his words!

Of importance also in these verses was a mention of Gerbert. We last saw Gerbert a fugitive in Germany at the court of the emperor, who in delight over this companionship of culture gave to the archbishop an estate at Sasbach, perhaps in the region of the Rhine. Gerbert was not slow to write in gratitude: "Magnificently for my magnificence have you granted to me this magnificent Sasbach, and so your Gerbert dedicates himself eternally to your eternal rule."

After a while for some obscure reason Gerbert lost part of this gift, and his happiness turned sour. "Would that it had never been mine," he now wrote, "to receive from your generous hand those things bestowed so splendidly, or, once received, to lose them in so great bewilderment! What am I to think?" He reminded Otto of all that he, Gerbert, had done for the Ottonian House: "Through three generations, for you, for your father, for your grandfather, amid enemies and battle I have shown utter faithfulness; for your safety I have thrust my own self, whatever that may be worth, face to face against raging kings and furious peoples. Through places impassable

and desert, through inrush and onrush of brigands, by hunger and
thirst, by bitter cold and surging heat tortured and broken, in so
many storms I have stood firm, choosing rather to die than to see
the son of Caesar no emperor, but a captive. Emperor to my joy have
I seen him; may it be mine to rejoice unto the last, and with you to
end my days in peace!"

Reply came quickly. Otto called Gerbert to his side, to remain
in permanence with him, not as a fugitive but as an honored teacher
and guide, in things intellectual, spiritual, and political. Gerbert's
happiness was intense as he wrote: "I obey, Caesar, your imperial
will in this; yes, in all things, whatsoever your divine majesty shall
decree. For I cannot be lacking in reverence, I who see nothing
sweeter in human life than your imperial power."

5

Gerbert was now well on in his fifties; Otto was but seventeen. But
the older man was to foster in his pupil a vision already lying half-
awakened within him: of dominion of empire, of authority of the
Church, leading and governing together in the service of God and
man a fellowship of peoples, a commonwealth of nations, East and
West, ever spreading outward. While Gerbert in the winter of 997
was on his way from Germany to work with the young emperor in
Italy from the year 998, he wrote out for Otto a treatise long and
carefully studied: *Libellus de rationali et ratione uti:* "On the Rea-
sonable and On Reasoning." Its preface shows clearly his desire in
regard to Otto's imperial rule:

"Now that good health has been restored to me, with thought
for things both public and private in my mind as I travel toward
Italy, your inseparable companion in all deference as long as life
shall last, I tell briefly what I have conceived in my thought. This
is my aim and hope: that Italy shall not keep her sacred palace slow
and hesitant, and that Greece shall not proudly deem herself sole
possessor of Imperial policy and Roman power. Ours, ours is the
Roman Empire! Italy, fertile in fruits, Lotharingia and Germany,
abounding in armed men, give us their strength; nor will the Slavic
lands fail our cause! Ours, above all, are you, Caesar, emperor and
majesty of Rome, born of the noblest blood of Greece, you who sur-
pass the Greeks in imperial dominion; you who rule the Romans by
right of inheritance, who excel both Greeks and Romans in intellect
and eloquence!"

Once in Italy, in the spring of 998, Gerbert heard news of importance from France: the archbishop's seat at Reims had been restored to Arnulf by the supreme will of the pope.

This extraordinary act had been brought about by the mediation of Abbo, since 988 head of the Benedictine monastery of Fleury-sur-Loire in France.

It sprang from the vehement eagerness of Robert II, king of France, to escape excommunication for his "incestous marriage" with Bertha and, even more vehement, to win papal consent for this union. Perhaps, he thought and hoped, this would be given by Gregory V if he, Robert, by royal order were to set free Arnulf, since 991 prisoner of the crown of France, and to bring about his restoration at Reims. In 997 Abbo was starting for Italy, anxious to gain privilege for Fleury from the pope; at the request of his king he undertook the business of discussion with Rome in regard to the royal "queen."

Pope Gregory V, however, was not in Rome when Abbo arrived there during September 997; Gregory did not return until Otto III brought him back early in 998. So the abbot of Fleury set out in search; "through deep valleys and across precipitous mountains" he went, and at last found the holy father in the region of Spoleto. Privileges and presents were freely given him for his cloister. We learn of his experience in regard to the royal commission from a letter written by him to the pope soon after his return to France: "Venerable Father, I conveyed your views to King Robert faithfully and simply, as you bade me, fearing no enmity from the king through loyalty to you; I added nothing, cut out nothing, changed nothing. Sure evidence of this lies in the fact that Arnulf, freed from captivity, is now archbishop of Reims."

Nevertheless, in 998 Robert was banned from communion with the Church. For years he remained stubborn, and hoped that Bertha would bear him a son. She did not. Early in the eleventh century he cast her off and made his peace with Rome by lawful marriage with another. His title of "the Pious" is due to his biographer, Helgaud, not to truth.

Gerbert no longer laid claims to Reims. In April 998 the emperor appointed him archbishop of Ravenna. This was the most important episcopal office under the papal see in Italy and one closely connected with its working. Had not Leo of Vercelli foretold that Gerbert would by his wisdom support the imperial crown? The next year, 999, saw in February the death of Gregory V, and in April the consecration at Rome of Archbishop Gerbert as Pope Sylvester II.

The name signified, of course, the bond between pope and emperor; as Sylvester the first had guided the Emperor Constantine in the fourth century, so would Sylvester the second guide Otto in the tenth.

Yet, as the bond between these two powers grew closer, it became clear that Otto's life was to see constant conflict between various elements striving for mastery within his body, mind, and spirit. His health, especially in the Italian climate, gave lasting concern to his friends. It had to bear the burden of his triple heritage, from Germany, Italy, and Greece; of his imperial ambition, of his mission to the heathen, of the ascetic ideal quickened in him by Adalbert and Nilus, hermits of the solitude.

Inner striving fought with outer in the struggle. He delighted in discussing with Sylvester problems of history, of mathematics and science, of philosophy, drawn from the writings of Plato, of Cicero, of Boethius. As "emperor of the Romans" he now was established in a palace on the Aventine, magnificent, beautifully constructed and adorned. He longed to restore the ways of ancient Rome; he gave Byzantine titles to his ministers; he dined alone at a high table, fashioned in a semicircle; as Thietmar remarks, "raised above the nobles of his court," who held varying opinions concerning this novelty.

Policy of empire had called for change in administration. Through the death in 998 of Hildibald of Worms, chancellor of Germany, his office had been given by Otto to Heribert, already chancellor of Italy. One man thus held government in both countries and bound them together by his passing to and fro across the Alps; the more closely when in 999 Heribert also became archbishop of Cologne.

Political aim also was sending the emperor early in 999 on a journey to the south of Italy, for the maintaining of control over his vassal lords in Capua and Benevento and Naples.

On his way he visited the shrine of Saint Michael the Archangel at Monte Gargano in Apulia. It was a pilgrimage of penance and he walked barefoot in shame, thinking of the tortured John Philagathos. As he traveled back to Rome he turned aside to ask a blessing from Saint Nilus at Serperi. The monastery lay low beneath him when he first caught sight of it from the distant hill. "Look," he called to those behind him, "the tents of Israel in the wilderness! Here are they who dwell not, but only pass upon their road." To Nilus he said: "Ask of me as of your son whatsoever you will and with all gladness it shall be given you." But the old man replied: "Nothing do I ask from your majesty but the saving of your own soul; for though you are emperor, yet die you will as a mortal man, to stand before the judgment-seat of God and render account of what you have done, good or evil." With tears in his eyes the emperor placed his crown in the hands of the saint, knelt for his blessing, and turned to march for Rome.

Germany, he knew, was anxious to see him back again. Yet, he felt that first he must draw the Slavonic peoples into closer connection with his empire. He would journey to Poland, on pilgrimage to the grave of his beloved friend and counselor, Adalbert of Prague, at Gnesen (Gniezno); and thus he hoped to deepen both there and in Bohemia a fellowship with himself in loyalty to the Holy See.

Christmas 999 he kept in Ravenna; in the New Year, 1000, he passed through Germany. February found him in Regensburg, where its bishop, Gebhard, gave him splendid welcome; "with greater honor no Emperor will ever depart from Rome or return to it," are Thietmar's proud words. Then he went toward the Polish border, from Meissen to Eilau, near Sprottau, where again there was enthusiastic greeting, this time from Boleslav Chrobry, the Brave, duke of the Poles, who escorted him to Gnesen. Barefoot the emperor walked humbly into the city, to receive reverent salutation from its officials, including Unger, then bishop of Poznán, and to kneel in prayer before Adalbert's tomb.

Administrative action followed religious in Poland's honoring. Otto raised Gnesen to the dignity of a metropolitan see and named Gaudentius, half-brother of Saint Adalbert, as its first archbishop; under him three suffragans were to hold episcopal authority, at Kolberg, Breslau, and Cracow. There was, indeed, some hesitation in the Church with regard to this; Thietmar wryly remarked: "I hope that it was legally correct; the bishop who ruled there had not given his consent." But there is no doubt that the pope had done so before Otto left Italy.

Duke Boleslav offered rich gifts to the emperor, with a body-guard of three hundred men in shining armor. He even accompanied his royal guest as he returned to Germany, which Otto reached in time to keep Holy Week at Magdeburg. The year was still 1000, and with the thought of his pilgrimage in his mind Otto was describing himself in his imperial diplomas as "Otto the Third, servant of Jesus Christ and emperor of the Romans." So had the missionary author of the epistle to the Romans.

The expedition to Poland had given deep content to both emperor and duke. Otto had allied Poland to himself in Christian rule; henceforth he could rely upon Polish aid against invading rebels. Boleslav rejoiced to see free and independent administration granted to state and Church within his land. Had he not heard himself now declared in most honorable promotion "a brother of Imperial Rome, a friend of the Roman people?"

German nobles of that empire did not share his joy; among them resentment was rising. "God have mercy on the emperor," wrote the German Thietmar, "for conferring lordly rank upon a man bound by necessity to render tribute to his imperial power."

April found him in Aachen, "a city which he willed to prefer before all others after Rome"; it was the city of the Emperor Charlemagne. Here young Otto, longing for inspiration and encouragement, dared an act which the annalist of Hildesheim was to declare "against holy religion and destined to bring upon its doer vengeance for evermore." According to the story given in the *Chronicon Novaliciense* by a count of Lomello, who with two bishops was attending the emperor, he entered the church of Saint Mary at Aachen and sought out the place where Charles the Great had been laid to rest. The grave was opened, and, so we are told, the figure of Charlemagne was discovered, sitting upon a throne as in life, a crown of gold upon his head and a sceptre in his hand. All those present fell on their knees in reverence. Critics have widely debated the question of truth in this report. Thietmar adds, with greater probability, that Otto took away for his own keeping a golden cross which hung around the neck of Charles, and part of the vestments in which the dead had been clothed.

In the autumn of 1000 Sylvester II fervently rejoiced in his emperor's return to Rome; once more there was active trouble in Italy. Already in June the pope had sent off "reliable information," as he called it, to Otto concerning an outbreak of rebellion at Orte, near Rome; swords had been drawn and he himself had been forced to find refuge. Was he not, like Gregory V, unpopular, as a man born outside Italy? Nor was the influence of Crescentius II dead in Rome; the year in anxiety and apprehension drew to its end, and its successor opened under no happier auspices. It began with a synod, assembled in January at Rome, for discussion of the grievous and long-continued controversy between Bernward, bishop of Hildesheim in Germany, and his metropolitan, Willigis of Mainz. This we shall notice when we come to the history of the abbey of Gandersheim, around which the dispute raged.

Even in these uneasy times missionary work went forward. This same month of January 1001 saw Otto taking, in a diploma issued in favor of Bernward and his see of Hildesheim, the title of "Otto the Third, Roman, Saxon, and Italian, servant of the apostles, by gift of God august emperor of the Roman world." By the apostles were primarily meant, of course, Saints Peter and Paul; Otto was trying to follow Peter in working for the Church at Rome and throughout his world, Paul in spreading the Christian faith.

Ambassadors, in the years 1000 and 1001, came and went between Rome and Vladimir, Christian duke of Kiev in Russia. Hungary received Christianity during the rule of its Duke Geiza, very possibly baptized or confirmed by Adalbert of Prague. Bruno of Querfurt, who was a younger contemporary of Adalbert and wrote his *Life*, told that this bishop sent missionaries to the Hungarians and went to them himself: "he turned them only too little from their error, but he did cast over them a shadow of Christianity."

Not deeply, it is true, did the Christian doctrine take root in Hungary of Geiza's time. In 997 he died and his son, Waic or Vyak, baptized in the name of Stephen, succeeded him as duke. It was he who firmly established Christianity in his land; constantly he worked to found, to build, or to restore episcopal sees, churches, and abbeys for his people. With him in this endeavor stood his wife, Gisela, a sister of that Henry, duke of Bavaria, who was to become king of Germany in 1002.

This relationship with Germany brought Duke Stephen into close contact with the Emperor Otto III, then eagerly hoping to see Hungary, with Poland and Bohemia, united in harmony, Christian and secular, under the leadership of the Roman Empire and the Holy See. Tradition tells that in 1000 or 1001 Duke Stephen received a royal crown and a Christian blessing from Otto and Pope Sylvester. Later years revered him as saint.

6

We are now in the last year of Otto's reign and it was sad. While prelates of Italy and Germany were trying to settle dispute in synod at Rome during January 1001, they heard that the citizens of Tivoli, close to Rome, had broken out in revolt against the emperor. Otto determined to lay siege to its walls with all the power he held; the pope himself went with Bernward of Hildesheim to give warning of this purpose. The men of Tivoli hesitated, realized the danger, and decided to yield. Pardon was allowed them upon their solemn oath to live henceforth in loyalty and peace.

But rebellion left Tivoli only to rise in Rome, wrathful at this meek surrender to an emperor who sat aloof in his pride, issuing his august decrees. Tivoli was held in no affection by Rome even before this time. Now day by day armed men marched in constantly increasing force through Rome's streets and squares, until the emperor's palace was threatened by their mass and he was driven to seek safety in that same Sant'Angelo which had held his enemy, Crescentius.

But he did not lose courage. On its tower he appeared, to rebuke and to reproach the multitude swarming over the open space far below:

"Hear and consider the words of your father," he called to his angry people; "lay them to heart! Are you in truth my own Romans? For your sake I have left my fatherland and my family. Through love of you I have cast aside the Saxons and all the Germans, my own blood; I have brought you to the furthest parts of our empire, where your fathers when they held the world under their rule never set foot. And this I have done that I might spread abroad your name and your glory to the ends of the earth! You I have adopted as sons, you I have preferred before all! For your sake I have brought upon myself ill will and hatred from all others. And now in return you have cast away your Father, you have killed my friends, you have shut me out. But you cannot shut me out. Never will I let you escape from my love; for as my sons I hold you fast within my heart."

The words moved those who listened and they gave over to the emperor two of the chief conspirators in the tumult. This milder mood did not last long; the stubborn hostility of Roman nobles, once let loose, would not hear of submission or quiet. Otto could do no more. On February 16 he and the pope, by the aid of Hugh, marquis of Tuscany, and Henry, duke of Bavaria, managed to escape on the road to Ravenna. Thietmar now wrote bitter words: "The emperor held every region, Roman and Lombard, in loyal adherence to his crown; except only Rome, which he loved and cherished above all."

At Ravenna's monastery of Sant'Apollinare in Classe Otto, struggling under his wrath at Rome's enmity and his despair of attaining his dream of empire, spent the early spring of 1001 in supplication to Heaven for the future and in penance for the past. Beyond the city stretched its dark and lonely salt marshes, dotted here and there with huts of solitaries, dedicated to prayer. Among them were friends of the emperor; above all, Saint Romuald, founder of monasteries. He was living at Pereum in this fenland, and Otto often talked with him, listening to his eager words on the joy and comfort of the monastic life in retreat from the world. As the weeks passed by, one after another, the young exile, sick and weary, haunted by a sense of failure, for a moment yielded to this earnest persuasion. He pledged his word in Romuald's presence: in three years' time, after he once had brought his empire again into due order, he would abandon his throne; he would take upon himself the life and the habit of religion.

He did not keep his word. Two forces rose to arrest this moment of desolation: the vision of world-wide Christendom which in union with the See of Peter he, as head of the Roman Empire of the West, might bring nearer to reality, and, in a lower key, refusal to leave the Roman people unconquered, defiant of his rule. Romuald listened and replied: "If you go to Rome, you will see Ravenna no more."

Four acts now marked this reawakening of political energy in Otto's mind. He journeyed secretly by night to talk with the doge of Venice in that city and stayed with him two days; he called for fresh troops from Germany; he sent Arnulf, archbishop of Milan, on another errand to Constantinople in quest of a Byzantine bride; he marched back toward Rome.

In June 1001 he was before its gates. Then, in spite of all his brave determination, hope again died down. His force was not equal to the labor of a siege; there was nothing for him but to return northward again in retreat. His misery was increased without measure by messengers who brought word of another rising, in his own German land, of dukes and counts, even of the bishops who in long tradition had supported his Saxon House. The rebels had turned to Henry, duke of Bavaria, for leadership. "But he, remembering the counsel of his father, Henry the Quarreler, had always since this father's death in 995 been loyal to the German crown and now he refused treachery."

Beneath all these troubles Otto's health gave way. He spent Christmas of 1001 at Todi, in Umbria; then again he marched for Rome. On his way, at Paterno, overlooked by Mount Soracte, fever seized him and in a few days he was dead. It was January 23 or 24, 1002; both days are given in varying authorities. The city to which he marched was only some thirty miles away; the German reinforcements were even now hastening to join his camp. Shortly after Otto died Arnulf of Milan docked at Bari in the south, bringing with him a bride from Constantinople's imperial line. She stayed a little while and then returned to her home.

Otto was only twenty-one. As he had wished, his body was carried across the Alps, escorted by Heribert, archbishop of Cologne, and buried in the church of Saint Mary the Virgin at Aachen. It was Easter Day. "May all the faithful pray for God's mercy on his soul," wrote Thietmar, who had disapproved of his imperial pride in Rome and in the Slavic lands; "for he worked with all his might for the renewing of our Church."

But even as those who bore him marched upon their way through northern Italy, its citizens were stirring in revolt, led by Arduin of Ivrea, who in February was declared Italy's king. The vision of Otto III had faded and the summer of his dream was over; his youth had not the power, the skill, the experience to carry it from the ideal into reality. His hope of renewal through bond between Church and empire, through the union of peoples, Christian and civilized—Italian, German, Slavic—under the twofold protection and charge of emperor and pope, was to become a memory in men's minds. How it would have fared had he lived we cannot tell. He sorely needed guidance, and the sharer of his vision, Pope Sylvester II, was to die very soon, in May 1003. He had his weaknesses, in plenty. If we may believe St. Peter Damian in his *De Principis Officio,* this Emperor Otto was not always loyal, even to a firm friend. We are told here that when in his own last days he heard of the death of that Hugh, marquis of Tuscany, who had enabled him to escape from Rome in February 1001, he burst out in a glad cry from the hundred and twenty-third Psalm, prompted by jealousy long nursed: "The noose is broken and we are free!"

Yet, it is well to think of him as one who struggled with rebellion, with war in all the lands of his empire, with opposition from his nobles and his people, with counterclaims of desire within himself, to gain the end which he believed would be for the glory of God and the good of man.

There remain two questions. First: Which did this Otto hold as center and mainspring of his empire—Germany or Italy?

The question in his case concedes two answers. The Germans had complained that he neglected his own land for Italy; yet, he had refused in 997 to leave Germany in order to defend Italy in her peril. Gerbert had written to him in the summer of 997: "If we leave the Slavs alone, I am afraid; if we do not go to Italy, I am full of fear." The emperor had stood firm. Germany was the land of his grandfather, Otto the Great, who had won the imperial crown which he wore; it had seen and sustained the long struggle of this crown's holding. It was the land of Charlemagne, himself emperor over the West, and Aachen was the city from which Charlemagne, like Otto the Great, had marched to Rome.

Yet, this third Otto again and again in his declarations had placed Rome before Germany, before Aachen. He saw Rome as the center of imperial sovereignty from the days of Charlemagne to his own. He had firmly determined to rule within its walls against Roman nobles, against German rebels, in his last months, when he was desperate, sick, and nearing death.

Second: What was the relationship between empire and papacy under Otto III? Light is thrown upon this question by a diploma—DO III, 389—which the emperor issued in 1001, it would seem. It was written for him by Leo of Vercelli and its opening words were bold: "We declare that Rome is the head of the world, that the Roman Church is the mother of all Churches." The thought was that of other men of this time, including him who during the tenth century poured out his feeling in that interesting document, the *Libellus de Imperatoria Potestate in Urbe Roma.*

But in the diploma of 1001 there followed a bitter attack upon popes of former years. Had they not seized for their own profit possessions of the Holy See, and, too, of the empire itself? Had they not thrown the blame for this robbery upon the imperial crown? Finally, after condemning the "Donation of Constantine" as a forgery, Otto had declared: "Scorning fictitious precepts and imaginary records, of our generosity we give to holy Peter what is in truth ours; we do not give him what is really his, under the *appearance* of its being ours. Even as for love of Peter we have chosen our lord and teacher Sylvester, and by will of God have appointed and created him our most serene pope, so for love of this same Lord Pope Sylvester we now confer upon holy Peter from our own property these gifts, that our teacher may offer them to our Saint Peter, prince of the apostles."

The offering was of interest for two reasons. First: it consisted of eight counties, named collectively the Pentapolis, a region of special relationship with the papacy. Second: the former pope, Gregory, cousin and friend of Otto III, had keenly desired that these counties should be handed over to his keeping as head of the Holy See. Otto had refused to do this; in a letter of 996 to Gregory V he had written that he was placing them—"a source of dispute"—in charge of his imperial legate, the count of Spoleto.

As Catholic Christian and as emperor Otto III looked to the pope
with all reverence for the fulfilling of those responsibilities and
duties, for the exercise of those rights, which belonged to his office;
as a man he asked Sylvester for teaching, for inspiration, for guidance. Together Otto saw them marching; in this march Rome and
Germany would share: Rome, head of his empire; Germany, land of
that empire's birth. Yet, the emperor always held sacred to himself
his divine right of independence; it was he who under God appointed
the pope.

Part Two

The Tenth Century in Its Harvest

CHAPTER SIX

The Harvest in History, Chronicle, and Story

1

CHURCHMEN of the tenth century have, for our reading, handed down records of its events in a form usually restricted to bare outline and only now and then carrying some substance of detail. Such are the annals of Prüm, Quedlinburg, Hildesheim, and many other monasteries, and they are of great importance for the specialist. But perhaps the general reader will prefer the more varied color of general histories, of *Lives* of statesmen and of saints who left their mark upon this time.

Among famous abbeys in the tenth century was that of Corvey in Saxony, near Höxter and on the river Weser. It was a daughter house of Corbie on the Somme, and as a "New Corbie" it had been founded in 822 for the enlightenment and, especially, the conversion to the Christian faith of ignorant and heathen men, both in Saxony and in the lands stretching northwards. During the Carolingian ninth century it had developed its own school of culture and scholarship. Saint Anskar in his earlier days had come there from Corbie to teach its novices; Paschasius Radbert had meditated there on the doctrine of the Eucharist.

About 941, when Folcmar was its abbot, a youth of some fifteen years, named Widukind, entered its gates as postulant and remained to make his profession as monk. He was Saxon by birth and belonged probably to one of Saxony's aristocratic families. With his monastic training went study of texts sacred and secular. He read constantly the Vulgate Bible, and learned histories and legends of holy men; especially the facts concerning Martin of Tours as told by Sulpicius

Severus, and the legend of Saint Vitus, patron of Corvey. We now think of this saint as giving his name to a "dance"; in reality medieval men called to him for aid against the torture of this malaise. Widukind thought of him, also quite without foundation, as a martyr of the fourth century under the Emperor Diocletian in Rome. But he knew very well that what men held to be his "relics" had been brought to Corvey in 836 and had ever since been revered there as treasure of great price. Widukind's secular reading included books of classic and later Latin: Caesar, Cicero, Livy, Virgil, Ovid, Lucan; the *History of the Goths* by Jordanes, the *Church History of the English People* by Bede, the *History of the Lombards* by Paul the Deacon.

At last our young student felt a longing to write something of his own, and he began, as was natural, with homage to saints. He composed a *Passion* of Saint Thecla in verse, and a *Life* of the hermit Paul of Thebes in a mixture of verse and prose. We need not regret that these two endeavors are lost; they were but a dutiful offering to religion. Time went on, and in his thirties a far more exciting venture offered itself. As he described it: "After the first of my works, in which I told the triumphs of soldiers of the Most High Lord, let no one be surprised that I want to put into writing the deeds of our own princes. In my former work I paid, so far as I was able, my debt to my monastic calling. Now I do not refuse to labor with all my power for my own race and people."

These, in translation from their Latin, are the opening words of the three books of the *Saxon History* which were to increase greatly the renown of Corvey as a home of literary men and to give permanence to the name of their author. From boyhood Widukind had watched the rise of Saxony. When he was about eight years old he had heard that a Saxon king, Henry the First, had won great victory over the invaders, Slavs and Hungarians, who brought terror to his land; then, later on, from 955 onwards, Otto was raising the crown of Saxony to heroic greatness of peace and power, in not only his own but in other realms. Widukind's soul was afire with pride; he would put all his learning, all his energy, into a record of the Saxon people which should live and be worthy of their deeds.

The first book tells of the origin of the Saxons, in legend and tradition of folklore: "Some say that they trace their descent from Danes and Northmen; others, as I heard some one tell when I was a boy, from the Greeks, those survivors of the army of Alexander the Great who after his death were scattered throughout the world. At any rate, they came of a race ancient and noble."

With the Franks, according to this tale, the Saxons lived in harmony of friendship. Charles the Great, "partly by kind persuasion, partly by force of war," brought them from error to the way of truth; "thus Franks and Saxons were made brothers and, as it were, one race." Then rapidly we reach Liudolf and his successors, founders of the duchy of Saxony; the coming of the Hungarians, aided by the Slavs; the failure of a Franconian army to crush Saxony by conquest; and, finally, the yielding of the German throne by a Franconian to a Saxon king, Henry the First, in 919.

Henceforth Saxony held the crown. Civil wars ceased; the Hungarians were driven to offer truce; the presence, we find, of relics of holy Vitus in Saxony brought lasting peace to Henry, and the story of Vitus, complete and enriched by the martyr's own words, into Widukind's narrative. Far more interesting is his account of Henry's shrewd device for the years of Hungarian truce: "Of the soldiers drawn from peasant folk living on the land, every ninth man he ordered to fortify and protect city walls, to make and defend dwellings for his eight fellows; under his care and guard was to be kept a third part of all the produce of his city. The other eight were to sow, to reap, to harvest and to store the fruits of the fields for the ninth and for themselves."

Then came the victory over the Hungarians at "Riade" in 933, and as father of his fatherland, as "emperor," Henry was hailed by his army. "Wherefore the chieftains of other countries came to him, longing to hold firm faith with so great, with such a man." A great man he was in every sense to Widukind: "His girth of body was in all keeping with his royal dignity. He outdid all in rivalry of sport; in hunting he would capture at one meet forty or more head of wild game. Merry he was at feasts; but he lost none of his kingly command."

Last of all he conquered the Danes: "and when he had overcome all the peoples around, he purposed to set out for Rome and could not, seized by sickness."

Books II and III tell of the progress of Otto the Great in his will to succeed, from his coronation in 936 to his defeat of the Hungarians on the Lechfeld in 955. Then "legates came to him from the Romans and the Greeks and the Saracens, bearing gifts: vessels of gold and silver and bronze, curiously engraved in differing patterns; vessels of glass and ivory; rugs of every shape and sort; balsam, pigments and paints in endless kind; animals never before seen by Saxon eyes, lions, and camels, apes and ostriches; for in Otto every Christian everywhere saw the vision of his holdings and his hopes."

The work, which continued its story until the death of Otto the Great in 973, has many faults. It suffers from revision, from insertion, from addition of supplementary material, from lack of order. It yields a multitude of errors. In places it is obscure; its form, as we have it, is disturbed by traces of its first draft of Saxon history, which ended with the year 958. Sometimes its author, struggling for expression, borrows some unfamiliar word from his native medieval German. Only one official document is given: a letter of Otto I written in 968. Fictitious speeches abound, with echoes of Widukind's Latin reading; the whole *History* is soaked in the rhetoric of Sallust. Each book has its preface, in each case a dedication and a poem of praise for the young Matilda, born in 955 to Otto and his queen, Adelaide; as a child of eleven years she became abbess of Quedlinburg's monastic house.

Worse still, Widukind does not look beyond his own land and its rulers in any but a passing glance, and this too often malicious. He does not even write as monk or churchman. "Grievous persecution of monks has arisen," he declares, "since some bishops judged it better to have a few really good religious in monasteries than many who are negligent. If I mistake not, they forgot the words of the householder who forbade his servants to gather up the tares in his field, ordering that both tares and wheat should grow together until harvest."

No mention is made of the founding of Magdeburg's archbishopric in the years 962 to 968, of the establishing of sees for the conversion of the Slavs, at Merseburg, Meissen, and Zeitz. Italian history is scarcely noticed; the popes themselves are only present incidentally. To this German monk, William of Mainz and Bruno of Cologne are each only a *pontifex summus*. Even the imperial crowning of Otto I in 962 at Rome finds no place; although in two passages—one of them written by Otto I himself—that of his son, Otto II, does occur. Far more often than for Henry the Fowler, the word "emperor," *Imperator,* is used to describe Otto the First; but it merely points to a ruler acclaimed by his army as conqueror, acknowledged by men of foreign lands as holder of power strong and wide. Only at the very end of this *History* does Otto appear as "emperor of the Romans": another touch of pride, no record of an event.

Nevertheless, we owe much to Widukind. He has given us a narrative vivid and appealing, filled now with incidents more or less important described to him by reliable authority, now with his own memories of past and present: wheat amid the straw of legend and myth. From beginning to end it is quickened by the energy of one who in his cloister had discovered a task of deep meaning for himself and for his fellow men; his pages reflect the joy of struggle, the thrill of advance, the vigor of life.

Very different from this Widukind was another well-known recorder of German history of the tenth century, Thietmar of Merseburg. Widukind hid personal details concerning his life; Thietmar talked in familiar ease with his reader: of his own doings, of his family, of his friends among prelates and statesmen, those in office high or humble. He was connected in one way or another with almost every noble house in Germany. His father, Sigfrid, was hereditary count of Walbeck on the Aller; his mother, Cunigunde, belonged to the line of the counts of Stade, near Hamburg. Two of his brothers, Sigfrid and Bruno, ruled at different times the monastery of St. John at Magdeburg; Sigfrid was afterward bishop of Münster, and Bruno, of the see of Verden. Thietmar himself in 1009 was consecrated for that of Merseburg, since 1004 restored to new life and service; he held it until his death in 1018.

In his *Chronicle* he tells us that he was born on July 25, 975, that he was baptized and confirmed by Hildiward, bishop of Halberstadt. His earliest training he received at Quedlinburg from his great-aunt Emnilde; and there, as Robert Holtzmann suggests, at the age of eight he may well have heard Henry of Bavaria acclaimed as king by his supporters during Eastertide 984 in their rising against the little Otto III and his mother, Theophano. He must surely have been present when Theophano and her royal son kept Easter of 986 at Quedlinburg, rejoicing with their court in the restoration of peace.

The next year saw Thietmar at Magdeburg, learning his lessons under Abbot Rikdag of its monastery of St. John; in 990 he was transferred by his father to Magdeburg's Cathedral School. There he remained a long time, while first Gisler and then Tagino held rule as archbishop. Tagino was his firm friend, and from him he received ordination as priest at Allstedt in 1004. It was also through Tagino's recommending that in 1009 as bishop of Merseburg Thietmar followed Wigbert, who in 1004 had been the first bishop to hold its see after its suppression had been ended by Henry II, successor in 1002 of Otto III upon the throne of Germany.

Thietmar, therefore, was well equipped to write his work, his *Chronicle*. He had received an excellent education at Magdeburg; he knew his Latin classics well. He could gain information from innumerable sources, very largely through conversations with his friends and acquaintances. His view was broad, and included not only Germany, but France, Italy, and, especially, the Slavonic peoples on the Elbe and the Oder. His passion for completeness led him to put down everything experienced by himself, everything gathered from without, in a record spiced with words taken from his reading, ancient and medieval. Much he borrowed from the annals of Quedlinburg and of Hildesheim. Altogether he has given us a mixed story of bishoprics and battles; of birth, love, and death; of miracles and visions; of things weighty and things trifling; of incidents personal or public in their interest. His Latin is both easy and difficult to read. Anecdotes abound, told in popular style; many statements are written in plain language. But the order is highly irregular; the dates do not follow in proper sequence, and not seldom the statements are incorrect.

The whole narrative sheds its light on the history of western Europe from 919, when Henry the Fowler began to rule Germany, until 1018, the year of its writer's death, when Henry II had been king for sixteen years and, since February 1014, emperor of the West. Lines of hexameter verse adorn its pages at intervals, in its prefaces, the first of which dedicates the work to Thietmar's brother, Sigfrid. Division is made very neatly into eight books. As the first tells of the time of Henry I and the second of that of Otto the Great, and, therefore, both draw largely upon Widukind's *History of Saxony*, and as books five to eight all deal with the reign of Henry II, we will look here at the third and fourth, which describe respectively the doings of men and women who lived under Otto II and Otto III. Thietmar was writing early in the eleventh century, writing not in a straight course from beginning to end, but in bits and pieces as these came to him, going back often to insert passages which he thought it worth while to add. This, of course, makes for obscurity and for trouble in folllowing the line of events.

Naturally he has much to say concerning Merseburg, his own see. In the time of Henry the Fowler, Merseburg had been a town on the Saale in Saxony, fortified for the land's protection against Slavonic invaders from the north. Otto the Great, we remember, had founded there in 968 a bishopric as a center for mission to those same heathen Slavs; Boso (968-70) was its first bishop. Thietmar describes him as a monk of St. Emmeram's abbey near Regensburg, most zealous in

work for the unconverted, translating Latin words of the liturgy into
Slavonic language and trying to teach his heathen to sing the Kyrie
Eleison. But they laughed in mockery, wilfully choosing to misinter-
pret its chant.

In 971 Boso was succeeded by Gisler. Merseburg was no
wealthy see, and in 974 Otto II endowed it with monastic and
civilian property, eager to help its bishop.

Seven years later this Otto was in Rome, busy with plans for his
intervention in southern Italy. With him at Rome were two men:
Otrich, who had left his position as head of the school of Magdeburg
to be near the emperor, and Gisler himself, present for the same
reason.

Thietmar tells with bitterness his story of the fate now to fall
upon Merseburg. Adalbert, archbishop of Magdeburg, had died in
June of this year, 981, and its clergy had elected Otrich as his
successor. They knew well that Otto II had declared in a diploma of
979 that no king, no imperial power, under pain of anathema, could
interfere with their freedom of choice. They therefore, in all confidence, had sent Ekkehard the Red, now director of their school, with
other brethren of Magdeburg's chapter to obtain from the emperor
at Rome the customary confirming of election.

Whether Thietmar's view on matters from this point is fully true
or not we do not know. According to him, Otrich and the envoys
from Magdeburg, in their anxiety to win approval, asked Gisler, as
one who had great influence, to seek private audience with Otto and
to intercede for their cause. Gisler readily promised to do his best.
He did indeed whisper their wish secretly into the emperor's ear, and
then promptly dropped upon his knees and implored him to give the
archbishop's seat of Magdeburg to him himself, Gisler of Merseburg.
Had he not worked long and laboriously in the service of the German
crown? Otto granted his prayer and Gisler went forth in well-
concealed joy, to find Otrich and his supporters waiting outside the
imperial chamber. "How did it go?" eagerly they asked. "Scarcely
could I get what I wanted," was his ambiguous reply. Then he
promptly bribed all Italy's leading judges, and especially those of
Rome—"to whom all things are always for sale"—to favor his own
election by all possible means. After this, to make matters even more
certain, he went to ask help from Pope Benedict VII himself.

A synod was assembled in September 981, and Gisler was declared archbishop of Magdeburg on his plea that he had been robbed
of firm and rightful possession of his own diocese by Hildiward,

bishop of Halberstadt. Since, however, men knew him to be bishop of Merseburg and canon law forbade transference of a prelate from one episcopal see to another, it was decided that the bishopric of Merseburg should be suppressed. Its lands were portioned out, shared among the sees of Meissen, Zeitz, and Magdeburg itself. Gisler, Thietmar observes, in the words of St. John's Gospel, "was no shepherd, but an hireling." "He arrived at Magdeburg on November 30," the *Chronicle* goes on to say, "accompanied by Dietrich, bishop of Metz. Dietrich was a friend of the emperor, very dear to him, and corrupt in his morals. He gained one thousand talents of gold and silver from Archbishop Gisler for casting shadow over the truth. To this same Dietrich some one said one day: 'May God satisfy you in the future, since all of us cannot do so here with gold!' "

Gisler, then, attained his ambition and "the properties of the church of Merseburg were divided up, just like a clan of Slavs accused of crime, sold and scattered here and there!"

The next king of Germany, however, Otto III, had no reason to love this archbishop; in 984 Gisler was on the side of the rebel Henry of Bavaria. Later on the *Chronicle* tells us that Otto, as man and king in his own right, was "always lamenting the destruction of Merseburg and resolutely planning its renewal." Did not Saint Laurence himself, patron of Merseburg, appear to the king in the dead of night, to declare: "The loss which now is on your mind was brought to pass by your own father, seduced by the persuading of that man who has by his sin brought strife upon a multitude of Christ's elect"?

In 997 Otto and Pope Gregory V were working hard for Merseburg's renewal. At a synod held in Pavia it was ordered that "Gisler, who contrary to canon law has left his own see and invaded another, be called to Rome to explain his act, under penalty of suspension from his priestly office, should he fail to appear." Again in the winter of 998-99 decree was passed in the emperor's presence at a general council in Rome that Gisler be summoned to judgment on a charge of "ambition and avarice." So, once again, in the spring of 1000, after Otto had returned from Gnesen in Poland, the accused, who hitherto had done nothing, now, pleading illness, sent the provost of Magdeburg to act for him in his defense. Again trial was postponed, to take place at Aachen in Germany. But nothing was decided, and, as Thietmar puts it, "all was left until God in His goodness deigned to end the matter in these, our days": that is, in 1004.

Yet, Gisler had some virtue; he fought bravely with his fellow bishops in the wars against the Slavs. Thietmar again and again dwells on the horror of battle, especially during the great rising of 982-83. His father, Sigfrid, he writes, had warning of what was to come when a voice rang through his ears as he slept: "Now shall the prophecy be fulfilled: *God sendeth rain on the just and the unjust.*" The storm struck Havelberg on June 29, 983, when the rebels destroyed its cathedral. On July 2 they rushed into Brandenburg. Folcmar, its bishop, fled before them, and the relics of Dodilo, once also ruler of its see, and three years before, in 980, strangled to death by these same Slavs, were now dragged from their resting-place, thrown to the jaws of savage dogs, then cast back into the grave. Mistui, chieftain of the Slavonic Obodrites, burned Hamburg, robbed it of treasure, and—so Thietmar tells—was only put to flight by a vision from Heaven.

Perhaps the most interesting story of fighting by Thietmar's family meets us in 994, when Germany was invaded by the Northmen of Scandinavia. His uncles, Henry, Udo, and Sigfrid, marching on campaign, ran up against the pirates plundering the land, on June 23, and struggled with all their might to resist capture. With no success; Udo was killed, Henry and Sigfrid were both caught and held. Quickly Bernard, duke of Saxony, who was himself leading his men in battle near by, sent envoys to negotiate ransom. "How generous at this crisis were King Otto and all our Christian friends!" Thietmar writes; "I have no words which can describe it! My mother in her terrible distress for her brothers gave every penny she had or could raise anywhere."

The Slavs demanded not only ransom but hostages, members of the family, as its guarantee. Henry had a son who readily offered himself and departed. Sigfrid had no such fortune; he sent word to Thietmar's mother, Cunigunde, begging her to hand over one of hers, either Sigfrid or Thietmar himself. Sigfrid was a student at Magdeburg under Abbot Rikdag, who firmly refused to let him go. "He has been delivered into my charge by God," said Rikdag, "and I have no choice." Only Thietmar was free and able to help his uncle. He was also at Magdeburg, but in its cathedral school. Without delay he went, only stopping to change his student's clerical gown for a lay suit of clothing, as proper "for a hostage staying with pirates."

But that same day Uncle Sigfrid, having seen his guards fast asleep, "those greedy hounds," after a banquet of rich food and heady wine, provided by his friends, managed to escape his prison. He arrived home safely, to hear fearful news. The pirates, enraged at the loss of so valuable a captive, had taken their revenge in hideous mutilation of his nephew, Henry's son, and, with him, of all the hostages in their keeping. Thietmar, who was well on his way to meet, no doubt, the same fate, thought it sensible to turn round and make for Magdeburg while he still could.

The *Chronicle* criticizes where it will, and even the royal house of the Ottos. Thietmar takes leave of Otto the Second thus: "Mindful of human fate and as one myself greatly in need of mercy, I implore the Lord of heaven and earth that, whatever sin this Otto did against my church, He of His grace will forgive." Of the battle near Cotrone on July 13, 982, he declares: "Only God knows the names of the countless men who fell." But he tells a marvelous tale concerning the rescue of this Otto after the terrible defeat. The emperor, according to this story, in his flight reached the shore and saw in the distance a Greek ship. Could he swim out to reach it? Quickly a loyal Jew standing near, named Calonimus, offered him his horse. On it Otto rode the waves to the ship; its captain refused to take him on board. Back to the shore the emperor went, and found his Jewish friend intensely worried for his "dear lord"; Saracen fighters were riding up fast in pursuit. Again Otto leaped upon the horse; through the sea he made for a second ship, in sight some way off. He gained it, and as he came near he was recognized by a man of Slavonic race, known as Zolunta, who persuaded the captain to take this fugitive on board and to give him rest on his bed. "Who is he?" said the captain, and soon Otto was obliged to make himself known. But, so the story goes, he added a few details thought up for the moment. "Please let us go to Rossano," he pleaded, "where my wife is awaiting me. From Rossano I will take all my treasure—treasure greater than I could possibly tell you—and then we will all go on to Byzantium to your emperor, my dear brother, who, I am sure, will help me in my need!"

The captain was delighted; day and night he hurried his ship toward Rossano. When it drew near Otto sent Zolunta ahead to summon his empress, Theophano, with Dietrich, bishop of Metz, and many mules, laden with money, it was supposed.

Soon the ship arrived; the crew cast anchor; Dietrich came aboard with a small escort. Suddenly, from the bow the emperor leaped into the sea, trusting his muscles and his skill in swimming to get him to land. One of the Greeks caught his sleeve and tried to stop him, but at once fell back dead, pierced by the sword of one of Dietrich's men. Those of the crew who were near fled to the other side of the ship, while the emperor's friends escaped to join him, safe and sound upon the beach.

Otto, it is also told by Thietmar, tried hard to keep his promise and to reward the Greeks most generously; but they speedily set off for their own country, full of fear and suspicion. Great joy welcomed the emperor; his friends had been afraid that he, too, was among the dead on the field of Colonne.

Of the third Otto Thietmar tells: "Long had he yearned for Italy." He himself, however, had no warm feeling for that land. "Its climate and the character of its people," he observes, "are not like ours in Germany. Many—the tragedy of it!—are the snares in the land of Rome and Lombardy. Little love meets those who come there; everything necessary for the guest must be bought by money, and to his undoing; many die there of poisoned drink."

Nevertheless, he can give praise with equal sincerity. He can say of Otto III that in the years following 996 "he ruled his empire in the manner of his forebears, overcoming his youth by his character and diligence." He praises German prelates and nobles, William of Mainz and Ulrich of Augsburg with others, and tells of the victory of Adalbert of Prague over death. Very moving are the words which he, German as he was, attributes to Pope Benedict V, banished from Italy by Otto the Great to die in exile at Hamburg: "Here will my frail body find release, and then all this region will be laid waste by the swords of the heathen and left to wild beasts for their habitation. Not before the translation of my relics will it see lasting quiet. But when I rest at home, whensoever that shall be, I hope that through my apostolic intercession the pagans will no longer trouble it."

A chaplain of Otto III, named Razo, brought the relics back to Rome. In 999 he gained nomination from the emperor as bishop of Worms while lying sick in bed, and he died before he could be consecrated. Thietmar highly disapproved of this untimely appointing.

He can criticize himself as bitterly as any other man. "Since I became a shepherd of souls," he tells his reader, "only in words have I taught my people, not by example. Outwardly I have appeared good, but my inner self I have violated by most evil thoughts; conceived in impurity, I have rolled in vice as a hog in the mire. You may say, 'A bad recommending!' But I tell you that it is true; I know none worse than myself." The words do not seem wholly born of the common medieval habit of apology.

There is, indeed, other trouble. He sees himself as he is: "a little man, my left jaw and cheek constantly swollen through ulcerous inflammation; a man comic to look upon, my nose broken when I was a boy. I would not mind all this, if only I were somewhat bright and beautiful within."

We turn from this to see him bending over the eight scribes who wrote down his words as he spoke, or copied them from his rough draft; sitting as he toiled to correct their manuscript; doing his best as bishop, as soldier, as historian, for his Church and for his king, for the Saxony which he loved so well. To him, as to Widukind, Otto the Great was "the glory of Italy, and Saxony's salvation"; under him Germany knew "a golden age."

From historians of Germany of the tenth century we come to historians of France. Two of these will be remembered by all; both were connected with that famous see of Reims for which in the ninth century Hincmar and Fulk had done so much. Two long-lasting struggles racked the church of Reims during the tenth; Flodoard of Reims is our source for the first, and Richer of Reims for the second.

Flodoard, a native of France, educated in the cathedral school of Reims, was a little over thirty years old when trouble broke out. He was a canon of the cathedral; as such he spent most of his active life in Reims, writing down in his spare hours day by day a record of events, for the greater part events in France, but also in Germany and Italy. Thus, he produced his annals, a work dry and bare, but of immense use to later time. Its course runs from 919 to 966, and includes matter drawn from archives, which very probably Flodoard himself had kept; from the minutes of councils which he had attended; from news concerning leading men and women; from rumors and reports of every kind, including miracles and strange phenomena of nature. In 963, as he himself tells us, "broken by age and worn out by sickness," he resigned his office as canon, to live on in retirement, perhaps in some monastery, still continuing his record, until his death in 966 brought it suddenly to an end.

The annals, then, give us the facts. But for interest of detailed and literary writing we must turn to his *History of the Church of Reims*, written in four books, of which the fourth deals with our period.

The tenth century opens here for Flodoard with the assassination of Fulk, archbishop of Reims, in 900 by men in the service of Count Baldwin II, the Bald, of Flanders. The count was very angry because King Charles the Simple of France had taken away from him, on a charge of disloyalty, his holding of the abbey of Saint-Vaast, Arras, and had granted it to Archbishop Fulk. Such conduct could not be endured. Fulk imprudently traveled with but a very small retinue as escort to confer with King Charles; he was caught and killed.

The next two archbishops of Reims were Hervé (900-922) and Séulf (922-25). Séulf was anxious to please that all-too-ambitious count, Herbert of Vermandois, and one unhappy day he solemnly promised that Herbert should hold the privilege of nominating his successor in the see. Shortly afterward, in 925, Séulf died; rumor had it that Herbert had conveniently poisoned him. At any rate, in this same year the count marched upon Reims and boldly announced to its clergy and people that he was nominating as its archbishop his son Hugh, not yet five years old. A deputy would act for him until he reached due age.

Herbert of Vermandois, however, judged it prudent to dispatch envoys to Rome, asking papal assent for his proceeding. In 926 this assent was given by Pope John X, with the provision that Reims during Hugh's minority should be governed by Abbo, bishop of Soissons, one of the envoys. Soissons was a suffragan see in the archdiocese of Reims. Two years later, having heard that Pope John was in prison, the count dismissed Abbo and gave acting power in Reims to one Odalric, bishop of Aix-en-Provence, who had fled from invading pirates and was without a seat. Meanwhile Herbert was using for his own ends the monies due to the clerics of Reims. "I had taken no part in the election of his son," Flodoard writes, "and he deprived me, with some others, of the benefices which former archbishops had granted us. He gave them to whom he would."

The king of France was now Raoul; fierce enmity raged between him and Count Herbert, largely in connection with Reims. In 931 the king sent order to that city that its clerics elect in regular and proper manner a permanent metropolitan. Their answer declared that this was impossible, since not only they, but Raoul himself, had allowed the count's nomination of his son, Hugh of Vermandois. Quickly Raoul gathered his most forceful allies, marched to Reims and laid siege to its walls; after three weeks of assault he gained entry, dismissed the deputy, Odalric, and appointed as permanent ruler of the see, one Artaud, a monk of the abbey of Saint-Remi at Reims. Artaud was consecrated archbishop and in 933 received the pallium, symbol of his high office, from Pope John XI, under order of the pope's brother, Alberic, who at the time was holding the holy father in prison.

Three years later, in 936, at Laon we find Archbishop Artaud crowning Raoul's successor, Louis d'Outremer, as King Louis IV of France; in 939 he was excommunicating Herbert of Vermandois for plundering property of the church of Reims. The following year Herbert, who was in hot rebellion against Louis IV, led his men against Reims and its archbishop, who had not only condemned him but was a firm supporter of Louis and his throne. Within a week the city yielded, and Artaud, either through strong persuasion of its clergy or in sheer terror, departed to live as abbot of the monastery of Saint-Basle at Verzy, near Reims: a concession made by his conqueror.

Count Herbert felt sure that Flodoard, canon of Reims, had secretly been aiding Artaud; in anger he took from him another benefice. The canon finally decided that he had better leave Reims for a while; he would journey as pilgrim to the tomb of holy Martin at Tours. It was a fact, he admitted to himself, that he had not openly supported Hugh; "I did not know," he tells, "whether it was God's will that he should be our archbishop." Herbert accused him of planning to get away in order to injure the House of Vermandois; for five months he held Flodoard under some kind of restraint within Reims, and not until Holy Week 941 did he restore his liberty to come and go.

By this time the count of Vermandois, supported by Hugh, duke of the Franks, had determined upon definite action. His son Hugh was twenty years old; fifteen years had passed since he had been nominated archbishop. Much of this time he had spent in study at Auxerre under its bishop, who had ordained his deacon; in 940 he had received office as priest from Guy, bishop of Soissons.

Now in 941 Duke Hugh and Count Herbert summoned the bishops and lesser clergy of the archdiocese of Reims to meet in the church of Saints Crispin and Crispinian at Soissons. Flodoard came there, with Hugh of Vermandois; so did Artaud from his place of exile. There he was publicly called upon to abdicate his seat as archbishop of Reims; publicly he not only refused but threatened excommunication for any suffragan of his great diocese who should dare to nominate for his place another man while he still lived.

The Council of Soissons declared that Reims could not be returned to Artaud; by violence he had been installed and of his own free will he had resigned its see. In a burst of joy the duke of the Franks took the unwilling Flodoard by the hand and with a smile promised that young Hugh would be to him a gracious prelate; holding and benefice were promptly restored him or given in new donation.

Members of the council as promptly took the road to Reims, and there Hugh of Vermandois was consecrated archbishop in this year, 941; in 942 Pope Stephen VIII sent him the pallium as assurance of his standing.

The next year Herbert, his father, died. Then Artaud left the abbey of Saint-Basle, to plead with Louis IV of France. Would the king help him to regain his see? Louis gave his promise, and in 945 he did make an attempt, sending soldiers who plundered buildings near Reims and burned outlying fields. But all this came to nothing in the end, and this very year Louis d'Outremer was captured by pirates from the Scandinavian North who handed him over to his enemy, duke Hugh of the Franks.

Not long, however, was the king of France held a captive. By the aid of Otto I of Germany, who could not bear to see his brother-in-law thus humiliated, Louis was set free. Through his sister Gerberga's entreaty Otto was also induced to invade France, and with Louis in 946 he bore down upon Reims. Archbishop Hugh, seeing that the city could not hold out, asked his friends what he should do and was advised rather to leave at once than wait to be rudely banished. After the third day of siege he left; the two kings entered, Artaud was at once enthroned, and Robert, archbishop of Trier, with Frederick, archbishop of Mainz, had the pleasure of leading him again to his cathedral chair.

Yet, even now, the struggle was not over; there was still need to maintain and support Artaud in his see. At Verdun in 947 a synod declared his right; in 948 another, assembled at Mouzon on the Meuse, did the same. Hugh of Vermandois appeared at neither. To the Council of Mouzon he sent a letter, saying that it had been procured in his support by a cleric from Pope Agapetus II at Rome. It was read aloud, and answer was made by the bishops: that a papal mandate concerning the conflict of Reims had already reached Archbishops Frederick of Mainz and Robert of Trier; it was neither right nor proper for this council to set aside this mandate because of a letter received from a cleric designing evil against Archbishop Artaud. The process of decision had been begun in a legal manner; let it be fulfilled in canonical obedience. Decision gave Artaud due right as metropolitan of Reims; Hugh of Vermandois, absent from two synods, would be held excommunicate until a council should meet for final judgment on August 1, 948.

Before that day Artaud himself wrote to Pope Agapetus a long letter of complaint; the pope sent off a legate, Marinus, to Otto I in Germany, requesting him to call a general synod for the settling of this quarrel. He also ordered influential bishops of France and Germany to attend. The synod opened its meetings at Ingelheim in Germany, not on the first of August but on the seventh day of June. Flodoard was present as supporter of Artaud.

All those who now gathered in assembly, including Louis, king of France, and Otto, king of Germany, heard the papal legate himself move that just judgment be passed against Hugh of Vermandois as in truth the guilty offender in the case. Sentence of anathema and of exile was then pronounced upon him. As "an invader of the see of Reims" he was cast out from the Church of Christ; only by appointed penance, exacted and fulfilled, could he hope to be forgiven. In 949 this "damnation of bishop Hugh" was confirmed by Agapetus in St. Peter's at Rome. Henceforth Artaud sat in rule over his archdiocese; he lived to crown Lothair, son of Louis IV, in 954 as king of France.

He died in 961, and then, according to the historian Richer, Hugh of Vermandois once more claimed the see of Reims. He was rejected, and Odalrich, a candidate supported by Bruno of Cologne, was consecrated as its archbishop in 962. Flodoard, who also stood firmly on the side of Odalrich, tells us that Hugh by this time had met a second condemnation, from Pope John XII, successor of Agapetus, in a decree issued at Pavia. Richer adds that a few days after hearing of his final condemnation he died at Meaux, "crushed by vexation."

Devoted to the writing of annals and chronicle as Flodoard undoubtedly was, he also had ambition to rank among the poets of his century. Between the years 936 and 939, while the Holy See was held by Leo VII, he made a pilgrimage to Rome and met with kindly welcome from the pope. In gratitude he gave him fervent praise amid the course of a long poem entitled "On the Triumphs of Christ in Italy." Unhappily Leo was under the hand of Alberic, then master of Rome; Alberic had raised him to papal rule. His character was blameless; but his rule left little legacy of good.

There could not be a greater contrast to Flodoard than Richer, born in the mid-tenth century, a devoted pupil of Gerbert in the cathedral school of Reims and a monk in its abbey of Saint-Remi. It was Gerbert who gave Richer his enthusiasm for learning; in his *Histories of France* we find a detailed picture of Gerbert as teacher and scholar, with a full account of his memorable debate against Otrich of Magdeburg at Ravenna shortly after Christmas 980.

But Richer was neither accurate nor independent. His *Histories* begin with the year 888 and follow Flodoard as a source from 919 until 966. He was a painter of pictures rather than historian; he enlivened his descriptions of battles, councils, conferences, of the characters and lives of his heroes and his villains, with every color which his imagination could invent or his memory could recall: fictitious speeches, fabulous numbers, startling qualities of mind, unusual physical details. Like Widukind he held Sallust his model. Especially he loved to pore over treatises on medicine; from these he drew horrors to deepen the anguish of his tales of disease and death.

It is he, then, who illustrates for us in vivid words the treachery and its outcome, the trial and the deposing of Arnulf, enthroned as archbishop of Reims in 989, degraded by his fellow prelates with his own tragic consent in 991, restored in 998.

Here Richer ends his *Histories*. Gerbert is still "archbishop of Reims" in his preface, although in notes added in the last pages we are told that "Gerbert receives from Otto the bishopric of Ravenna" and that "Pope Gregory permits to Arnulf exercise of episcopal function until formal judgment shall decide whether by right of law he shall hold or lose the same."

Two more of Richer's narratives we may recall here. The first, flavored by his fancy but at least based upon truth, is the story of Ascelin (also known as Adalbero), bishop of Laon, and his betrayal of his guests, Charles, duke of Lower Lotharingia, and this Archbishop Arnulf, on Sunday and Monday of Holy Week 991.

A double motive induced Ascelin's action. He was eager to deliver his king, Hugh Capet of France, from the menace facing him in Duke Charles and in Arnulf, who had secretly opened for Charles the gates of Reims in the late summer of 989. Second, the bishop hated both men. Had not Charles captured Laon itself in 988? Had not Hugh Capet repeatedly tried to recapture it, in vain? Had not Charles held Ascelin himself captive, and had not he, the bishop of Laon, been driven to escape by a rope let down from the window of his prison? And had not King Hugh made Arnulf archbishop of Reims, and Arnulf secretly was a traitor? He was still at large, unpunished; Ascelin determined that he would bring about the capture of both duke and archbishop and hand them over to the king of France. And, third, was not this Hugh Capet ready enough to reward any man who would thus support his royal throne?

Accordingly, Ascelin pretended friendship for both Charles and Arnulf; when he felt that this policy of pretence had made sufficient progress he offered them hospitality under his roof. Richer tells the story of their stay as he heard it and as he imagined it. One night, when the bishop was gaily enjoying his evening meal with his guests, Charles fell silent, deep in thought; then, holding out a cup of wine into which he had broken bread, he gave it to his host, saying: "In obedience to the custom of the Church today you have blessed branches of palm, you have sanctified your people with holy benediction and have given to us the Eucharist, caring naught for the scandals whispered against you by those who declare you treacherous. The Passion of our Lord Jesus Christ is drawing near; I offer to you for your honor this cup of gold with its wine and broken bread. Drink of this cup, as a sign of your firm and proven faith. But if verily you have no mind to keep faith, then touch not the cup, lest in dreadful sight you appear a second Judas!"

"I will receive this cup," answered Ascelin, "and freely will I drink." "Add," said Charles, "*And I will keep faith.*" Ascelin drank, and said: "Keep faith I will, or may I die with Judas!" And many other such oaths he swore as they dined.

They night drew on, "witness of tragedy and betrayal to come." While his guests slept, Ascelin took away the swords and armor lying on their beds and hid them carefully. He sent off on an errand the innocent guard who was keeping watch at their door; the errand was important, the bishop said, and he himself would stand as sentinel. Charles and Arnulf peacefully remained oblivious of all, of Ascelin waiting in the doorway, his sword beneath his cloak, of soldiers ready to spring at their master's word. Morning dawned at last, and his men quietly entered the room. Charles and Arnulf suddenly awoke and sprang to their feet. The duke cried: "What do you here at this time of day?"

Ascelin answered: "You took me from the city of Laon and drove me into exile; now you, too, shall be driven forth, but with fortune of a different sort. I, exiled though I was, remained my own master; you shall be bound under another man's power." Struggle they did, duke and archbishop, with all their strength; but they were seized and held to await the meeting with Hugh Capet, the king they had defied.

Richer had good reason if he lacked truth of detail in telling this story. Two weeks before its barbarous events took place he had started out from Reims on his way to Chartres; a cleric of Chartres had a book by Hippocrates, he had learned, and he wanted at all cost to read it. Hippocrates would tell him of medicine and natural science. He could think of nothing more delightful.

But the costs of that journey needed no imagination; they were real and they were endless. With two companions he rode from the walls of Reims: a knight from Chartres and his own servant, who carried the baggage on the third horse in line. Their path wound here and there through the woods; they lost their way and wasted much time in finding it; evening came on and rain poured down. For long the packhorse had been stumbling, going from trot to walk, from walk to crawl; suddenly it stopped, sank down and died, six miles from Meaux, their stopping-place for the night. It was too much for the servant. He was not used to traveling, and now he sat down beside the horse and declared he could do no more. By this time the rain was falling in floods and the road was invisible.

But Richer was going to get that book, and, as usual, Heaven helped the brave. He left the servant where he sat, telling him to be sure not to fall asleep, and to watch for passers-by who might come to the rescue. Then with the knight from Chartres he picked his way to Meaux in the darkness of night, guiding his horse as best he could. Just outside the city a bridge crossed its river; the bridge was full of holes, lying in wait to trip up the horses, and there was no boat. So very haltingly they walked over, stopping as they went to cover the holes with pieces of wood or some part of the knight's armor, a shield or breastplate.

In Meaux Richer found welcome in a hospitable monastery; he sent back his friend from Chartres, an energetic and experienced traveler, as he carefully tells us, with the two horses to rescue the servingman. Of course the rider again lost his way, but finally about midnight he came upon the poor creature, crying for help.

Richer himself, as he also tells, spent a terrible night, tortured by anxiety. But with the first break of day the rescued and his rescuer arrived, hungry, tired to death, but safe. All, including the horses, had a hearty breakfast; then Richer and his friend rode on to Chartres and, once there, sent back an escort to bring the servant to its house.

Now the story ends: "All my worries banished, I eagerly fell to study of the *Aphorisms* of Hippocrates in the home of the reverend Heribrand, a man as generous as he is learned. But as it only held diagnosis of diseases and this simple fare did not satisfy my curious mind, I asked him to lend me the *Concordance of Hippocrates, of Galen and of Soranus.* There I found what I wanted; the secrets of pharmacy, of botany and of surgery could not escape one who was as skilled as the author of that book."

When, finally, we look at Italy, we find perhaps the most remarkable production of historical writing in the West of this period. It comes from Liutprand of Cremona, whose work is entirely needful for the understanding of tenth century politics; his name has already appeared eighteen times in this book.

Here we have a character of violent contrasts: a scholar of culture deep and broad, skilled in languages and letters of antiquity, Greek and Latin, and in those of his day, Italian and German; a traveler who knew well not only his own Italy, but the kingdom of Germany and the empire of the East. His eyes and ears took in all that he saw and heard, down to the smallest details, and his mind handed on these details to his active conceiving.

For Liutprand, the cultured scholar, was equally a man of his world, who knew well and enjoyed the lust and lewdness of tenth century Rome and Pavia. Priest and bishop he became, mainly because the Church offered the clearest paths to his ambition. He was a man of hot and surging passion; fervently he loved, and more fervently he hated. His wit was quick, his sarcasm and satire were exquisitely barbed; he delighted to pour out all in lasciviousness and wicked tales upon the heads of those who had displeased him or treated him ill. The very motives which brought into being his three works were mixed. He would entertain and divert weary men; he would give his readers a trustworthy record of events; he would serve his emperor and the officials of the court of Western Rome and Pavia, especially in opposing the claims of the empire of the East. He would reward his friends and punish his enemies. He would make known in full extent his familiarity with ancient classics; with words rare and exotic; with kings and their realms; and, too, not for the sake of the Church whose bishop he was, but for his own laudation, he would fill his pages with argument of Biblical and theological display.

His works, then, are as mixed as the character of their writer: narratives which reveal, now the serious historian, now the imaginative artist, and now the temperamental man.

He was born about 920, probably in royal Pavia itself, of an aristocratic family well acquainted with the court; from the age of about six years he knew Hugh of Arles as king in Italy. He grew up with immense pride in his Lombard birth. Men of Rome to him were "ignorant, cowardly, greedy, liars, full of vice"; and, indeed, it was during his boyhood that Marozia held her notorious power in the Eternal City. As a child he saw his father set out for Constantinople, sent on a diplomatic mission by King Hugh to Romanus I Lecapenus, then ruling in the East for the Emperor Constantine VII Porphyrogenitus. The king wished to announce his recent crowning in 926 as ruler of Italy, and to the Byzantine emperor his envoy carried rich presents. Among these, Liutprand tells us, were two dogs, of a breed unknown in Greek circles. Unfortunately they rushed toward the enthroned Romanus in a wild endeavor to tear him to pieces; "because of his Greek widely flowing robe they saw in him no man, but some sort of monster." Nevertheless, Liutprand's father was received with high honor. Had he not on his journey encountered and conquered a band of Slavs, rebels against the empire of the East? And was not this ambassador at the moment handing over two of these wretches, chieftains and alive at that, to meet the will of the emperor himself?

Soon after his return to Pavia this head of Liutprand's family died, and his widow married a second time. His stepfather was to be of great influence in the son's training. With earnest desire that his new charge should be well educated he presented him at King Hugh's court in Pavia, and there as an eager pupil the boy imbibed all the culture it could give him, including its enjoyment of worldly and immoral life. The king was especially kind, attracted by Liutprand's ear for music and his clear treble voice; as an angel he sang in choir.

Thus he grew up, and in due time he was ordained deacon at Pavia. In 942 his stepfather, as one "trustworthy, a man of dignity and full of wisdom," was dispatched by King Hugh on another embassy to Constantinople.

Meanwhile, as we have seen, the course of Italian history had been changing. Young Alberic II had become master of Rome and Hugh held but the empty title of royalty, try as he might to overcome his rival. In his turn Berengar II of Ivrea began secretly to work against the unhappy king, and—so Liutprand declares—Hugh in retaliation plotted to put out his eyes. But in 945 Berengar, "marquis in name, was in truth king in power." Hugh stood finally defeated, and Liutprand's parents hurried to commend their son to the new ruler by "immense offering of gifts." Their advance bore fruit; Liutprand, known as a young man of marked shrewdness, ability, and diplomatic skill, endowed with promise of wealth, became confidential secretary to Berengar at his court.

Long he served this ruler. In 949 Hugh was dead in exile, Berengar was still firmly established as Italy's regent, while Lothar, son of Hugh and once his fellow king, was a mere figurehead. In the East, Romanus Lecapenus had departed this life, deposed and banished; from Constantinople the Emperor Constantine VII, now reigning alone and anxious to hear news of doings in Italy, had sent an envoy to gain information. As he looked around for a suitable messenger to speed reply to the Eastern court, the "king" of Italy thought of Liutprand. His thought was much encouraged when he discovered that Liutprand's stepfather was entirely willing to pay all expenses incurred by the visit, in return for the young man's chance to improve his Greek in Greek land. Berengar was noted for keeping a tight hand on the royal purse.

Liutprand in 949 went on his way; but this choice of envoy brought trouble in its wake. Berengar's position, indeed, was strengthened by the death of Lothar in 950; yet, the ambassador's feeling for his sovereign changed for the worse soon after his return. Loyalty yielded to resentment, and resentment ripened into hatred. We do not know the final and definite cause of this quarrel; we may believe that the mean, grasping Berengar was no hero to a lover of letters, luxury, liberal spending, and lively fellowship.

At last, about 955, Liutprand could endure no longer. He left Italy for the German court of Otto I, and from the day he arrived there he offered all his endowment, of whatever kind, material and mental, to the service of this patron. The king rewarded him well; early in 962 he appears in record as bishop of Cremona in northern Italy. As such he was present in St. Peter's at the imperial coronation of 962; in 963 Otto sent him with Landward, bishop of Minden on the Weser, from Saxony to answer accusations made against him as emperor by Pope John XII. Toward the end of this year we have seen him taking a prominent part in the synod gathered at Rome for the deposing of Pope John and the election of his successor, Leo VIII,

The year 964 saw Berengar II, captive of the Emperor Otto, exiled to Germany for the short remnant of his life. There, in Germany, we find once more Liutprand in 965; it was he who upon the death of Leo VIII set out again for Rome, this time with Otger, bishop of Speyer, to preside over the election of the imperial nominee, the bishop of Narni, as Pope John XIII. In 967 he was present in synod at Ravenna. The next year Otto sent him as ambassador to Constantinople, charged to redeem the failure of Dominic of Venice to negotiate a marriage for the royal heir with a Byzantine princess of the Imperial House. The emperor of the East, since 963 Nicephorus II Phocas, was no more ready to yield to Liutprand than he had been to Dominic. His bitter experience is described in hot wrath by Liutprand's own hand. It was one of his last acts; in 970 he was disappearing from public life and in 973 his successor held Cremona's episcopal seat.

Early in 956, shortly after he had fled for refuge in Germany, Liutprand had met there an envoy to Otto's court from the Omayyad Caliph Abd-ar-Rahman III, who ruled in Spain from 912 until 961. The envoy's name was Recemund, and he was bishop of Elvira, a town near or upon the site of the present Granada and famous for the synod which in 305 forbade marriage to the higher clergy of the Church. Liutprand enjoyed talking with this Spanish ecclesiastic, and when Recemund asked him to write, for his information, a history of Europe—that is, of Italy, Germany, and Byzantium—during the last seventy years, he willingly consented. He knew all three lands and their people. Two years passed, however, before in Frankfurt he began to write, and he was still writing after Otto's coronation in 962. The work was never finished.

Already in its preface he made clear to Recemund his keen desire to produce an entertaining story. "Why have I not written before? Here is one reason. Envious and arrogant men, who, as said Boethius, have a shred of the robe of Philosophy and think they have it all, will of course attack my book in the words of Terence: 'Nothing will be said here which has not been said before.' Well, perhaps these gentlemen, tired of struggling through Cicero's complicated periods, will at least be amused by my trifles!"

The course of this work of Liutprand, divided for us into five books and part of a sixth, runs in the West from the reigns of King Arnulf in Germany and of King Eudes in France, from the struggle for kingship between Guy of Spoleto and Berengar I in Italy, and in the East from the rule of the Emperor Basil I (867-86). Papal history begins with the "Council of the Corpse of Formosus" in January 897. Then its writer continues to reflect events and characters, with truth, bias, imagination, wry mirth, praise, and searing denunciation, until its actual framing ends for us in 949-50; its words, however, rage with the wrath of later years. No touch of lurid color is allowed to escape the reader's eye, authentic or not. The defeat in Italy of King Arnulf during 896 was brought about, Liutprand believed, through a cup of poison, offered by the widow of Guy of Spoleto (here wrongly called "wife"); the German king died "tormented by tiny worms which men call lice, swarming beyond any doctor's power to drive away." Lambert, emperor and king in Italy, here, as in the Appendix to the *Chronicon* of the *Monumenta Novaliciensia,* died "more probably" of no accident in hunting but at the hand of Hugh of Milan, seeking revenge for his father's execution. The murder of Berengar I in 924 claims six chapters, including much Ciceronian language and a poem in glyconic verse. Verse, this time hexameter, also pictures for us the hideous burning of Pavia and the slaughter of its citizens by the Hungarians in the same year, while Rudolf, lately elected Italy's king, was absent in Burgundy. Hugh of Arles is declared a king "endowed with knowledge, boldness and shrewd skill, devoted to God and those who follow holy religion, careful for the poor, eager to aid the churches, one who loved in all honor clergy, monks and philosophers. Yet, these virtues he defiled by his wanton pursuit of women." In addition to Hugh's two wives, Bertha of Swabia, and Marozia, who is roundly denounced:

> What profit, cursed one, to ruin a noble man,
> Through fearful sin to toil, athirst to seem a queen?
> To thee, by God's avenging will, is lost great Rome!

our chronicler gives him "many mistresses, three of whom he adored above all with most shameful passion: Pezola, Roza, and Stephanie." They were known, we are told, by the Roman people as Venus, Juno, and Semele, and they bore children; but no one knew to what father, for they each had more lovers than one.

In writing the first three books Liutprand drew upon oral tradition as source, both from men who gave him known facts, and from popular gossip. From Book IV onward to the fragment of Book VI he was able to use his own experience. Already at the beginning of Book III he had given his work its title: *Antapodosis,* in its double meaning of revenge and reward. The shafts of revenge were hurled against Berengar II of Ivrea and his queen: "The aim of this work is to relate the doings of that Berengar who at this moment is not ruling as a king in Italy but as a tyrant; and of his wife, Willa, who through *her* limitless tyranny is a second Jezebel, and through her insatiable greed for plunder is rightly called a Lamia, a sucker of blood." "Long I served Berengar faithfully," Liutprand laments in Book V, "and I met a reward which—oh! the pain of it! I shall describe in due course. Truly this return from him would almost drive me to despair if it did not give me so many comrades in misery! Those words of Job just fit him: 'The wings of the ostrich are like the wings of the hawk and the heron. When the time comes she lifts her wings on high and scorns the horse and its rider.' While Hugh and Lothar, his son, were still ours, that great voracious ostrich was not indeed good, but only seemed so. For when they departed ar d all men pushed Berengar forward to pride of rule, how he lifted up his wings and how he made mockery of us all I tell not so much with words as with sighs and groans!"

Willa is described here as "a true wife for Berengar; through her acts men have come to realize that her mother was *not* the most evil of all women!" Salacious story accuses the queen of adultery, lying, intent to murder, and witchcraft. Anecdote equally unsavory is told of her mother. The very Alpine mountain across which Berengar of Ivrea and his wife hurried to Hermann of Swabia in 941 from the menace of King Hugh suffers malediction in prose and in verse:

> Thou knavish Avian Mount, unworthy of such name,
> That givest life to pest thou couldst destroy!
> What can I say but bid God's lightning burn
> And rend thee into chaos for all time!

True, however to the second interpretation of its title, the *Antapodosis* was also written as a return of gratitude to those, saints and men of secular note, who had aided and encouraged its author.

The little which is ours of Book VI tells of Liutprand's trials during some six months, in 949-50, at Constantinople as envoy to the Emperor Constantine VII Porphyrogenitus. The mission was a formal

exchange of courtesy but apparently gave King Berengar's repre-
sentative little content. He begins his narrative with caustic words:
"It were better for me to write tragedy than history, were it not that
the Lord has prepared a table in my sight against those who trouble
me."

Yet, there was interest for him, and there is for us, in the details
of diplomatic etiquette and court procedure, costly, curious, and
childish, but contrived with all care and thought at Constantinople
under Constantine VII. This same emperor ordered the compiling
under his own eyes of the great *Book of Ceremonies of the Byzantine
Court,* and he was determined that practice should follow precept.
"We have thought it needful," his preface declares, "with assiduous
care to gather in this work from many sources the records of older
time, the reports of eyewitnesses, and our own knowledge of the
ritual followed in our court; to put all this evidence before the eyes
of all; to hand down the customs of our fathers, now fallen into neglect, and to commend them to posterity; thus, plucking as it were
flowers from the meadows, to add these to the splendor of our empire for its inestimable honor; and, finally, to place this work as a
clear and newly polished mirror in the midst of our royal palace,
that through it the things proper for our Imperial sovereignty and
meet for those who hold office in our imperial realm may be made
known to all, and the reins of power be handled in due order and
beauty of seemliness."

The Byzantine emperor held himself heir of ancient Rome, head
of the Roman Empire and of the Christian Church; and his court,
he willed, must act in keeping with his magnificent claim.

Liutprand, then, pictures here what he saw, or believed that
he saw, when in September 949 he was presented to Constantine in
his palace. In front of the imperial throne stood a tree of bronze,
covered with gold; on its branches were many birds of various sort,
also made of gilded bronze, singing each in the manner of its kind.
Lions of enormous size, carved either in bronze or in wood, but in
either case covered with gold, stood as if on guard by the throne,
lashing the ground with their tails and sending out deep roars from
open mouths and quivering tongues. All this he surveyed and heard
quite calmly; he had learned all about this show, he remarks, before he arrived. Three times he bowed low before the emperor, and
when for the third time he raised his head he saw that his imperial
majesty, whose seat had been of moderate height, had not only risen
to the ceiling of the hall of audience but was sitting there in entirely

different robes. At this distance conversation was not easy, and it was only one of the officials of the palace who talked with the visitor.

Three days later he was invited to dine in state with his host. All the dishes were of gold, and at dessert vessels of fruit were carried in, so heavy that they had to be swung on to the table by pulley ropes hanging from the palace roof. Machinery, Liutprand observed, was in general use for the emperor's service. Gymnastic entertainment was provided after the banquet, and this did arouse him from disdain to high respect, even to thrill of astonishment. He was far less pleased when at a later time by his own wish he was allowed to watch the ceremony of dealing out reward in money, given according to custom just before the joyful "Festival of Palms" to those who served the emperor. So long was the line and huge the amount distributed, that when Constantine asked him how he liked the scene he answered: "Truly it would please me if it did me any good; just as the vision of Lazarus in joy would have pleased the tortured Dives, had it been his to share. Since it was not, I ask you, how could it please him?" The emperor, somewhat embarrassed, hurried to make his guest a liberal present, and Liutprand's envy melted away in satisfaction.

From this frankly outspoken history, spiced with Greek words, varied by verses in many meters, we come to a serious and formal document, a record of the rule of Otto I from 960 to 964. It was drawn up, we may think, in the first place for private recognition by the emperor in the West, and given afterwards to the world at large. As this *Liber de Rebus Gestis Ottonis,* Liutprand's *History of Otto,* has been used repeatedly in these pages, we will only note here that its writer was as fervent in praise of Otto as he was in hatred of Berengar.

His third work, which gives the story of his journey to Constantinople in 968 to win a promise from Nicephorus Phocas of a Byzantine princess as bride for young Otto II, is full of vitriolic insult, of abuse levied against almost everyone whom he encountered there. Doubtless as a firm supporter of Otto the Great's empire of the West he resented what he held as the arrogance of the East. Yet, behind this, as he traveled homewards after four long months of waiting, from June the fourth, when he arrived in Constantinople, until October the second, when he left "that city, once so rich and flourishing, now famished, perjured, deceitful, crafty, rapacious, avaricious and vainglorious," there lay other springs of rancor. They rose in him nonetheless fiercely because they came in part from his own fault. He was returning to his emperor to add another failure to that of Dominic; he had been deeply offended by the lack of understanding of his own high importance, disdainful of Constantinople's wealth and its parade; and within his own mind he knew that had he been more tolerant, more patient, more diplomatic, indeed, things might perhaps have turned out differently. Hence a torrent of invective.

His lodging, he wrote in this account to Otto, kept out neither cold nor heat, and there he stayed imprisoned by armed warders who allowed none of his staff to go out and no visitors to come in. Water for their use had to be bought by them at a price and the Greek wine was undrinkable. The officer in charge of hospitality was like no man on earth; possibly you might find his fellow in hell. Whatever injury, robbery, expense, grievance, or misery he could think up, that he dealt us, Liutprand declares, and all, one after another, in a cresting flood: "Not during one hundred and twenty days did he let one of them slip by without giving us cause to suffer and lament."

The logothete—imperial minister appointed to communicate with the envoys—insisted upon insulting Otto by speaking of him not as "emperor" but as merely "king." After a few days this official conducted Liutprand to the audience-chamber of Nicephorus: "a man," he writes, "of pigmy size, his cheeks creased with fat, his eyes tiny as a mole's, his beard short, spreading and thick, mottled with gray, his head covered with a dense mass of hair, stiff as a boar's bristles, his skin black as an Ethiopian's: in short, 'a man whom you would not care to meet in the dead of night.' ... His words were insolent; he was cunning as a fox, and Ulysses himself could not beat him in perjury and lies."

This first cheerful impression is heightened for the reader by the words in which, according to Liutprand, the emperor addressed Otto's ambassador:

"It had been Our duty, nay rather, Our desire, to bid you welcome with all courtesy and honor. This, however, the evil conduct of your lord does not now permit: he who in most hostile invasion has claimed Rome for himself, has seized land from Berengar and Adalbert by force, against law and sacred right, has killed Roman men by the sword and on the gallows, has sent them into exile and has endeavored to subdue the cities of Our empire to his rule by slaughter and by fire. Furthermore, since his wicked attempt did him no good, now under the guise of peace he sends you here, aider and abettor of his malice, to spy out Our land!"

Nevertheless, protocol required that Liutprand be invited to a banquet, and the guest continues his story: "The emperor did not consider me worthy of a place above any of his nobles, and so I sat fifteen seats away from him, where the table was bare, without a cloth. Not a soul among my companions was at the dinner, or even entered the banqueting hall. The food was foul and stinking enough, soused in oil like a drunkard's mess and sprinkled wtih some horrible fishy liquid. He asked me many questions concerning your power, your reign, and your fighting men, and I gave him correct and truthful answers. "You are telling lies," he said. "The soldiers of your lord know nothing of horsemanship; they are unskilled in fighting on foot; the size of their shields, the heaviness of their breastplates, the length of their swords, the weight of their helmets do not allow them to offer battle either on horse or on the ground." Then, with a mocking smile: "It is gluttony," he went on, "the cramming of their stomachs, which hinders them; their stomach is God Himself to them; their boldness is but drink, intoxication is their courage, for them fasting breeds lasciviousness and sobriety springs from fear. Your lord has no force of ships upon the sea. Courage on the sea is mine alone! I shall attack him with my fleet; in war I shall destroy his cities along the coast; I shall reduce to ashes his cities on the rivers! How, tell me, with his scant resource will he resist me, even on land? His son was with him, his wife was with him, Saxons, Swabians, Bavarians, Italians, all were at his side and they could not even capture that one little town of Bari!"

It is not surprising to find the answers of Liutprand equally venomous. Stoutly, as this dialogue between East and West continues, he prophesies that "the lion and his cub, father and son, Otto and Otto, together will one day exterminate that wild ass of the forest, Nicephorus." When the Greeks ask him: "Tell us, does your most reverend lord wish to confirm friendship with our emperor by treaty of marriage?" he replies: "When I came here, he did! But now that I have been hanging around here so long and he has heard nothing from me—the shame of it!—he thinks of me as your prisoner, bound in chains! And so all his heart is boiling with wrath within him, as a lioness robbed of her young, and he only longs for sharp revenge. He loathes the very thought of marriage!"

Just before he left that "hated lodging" in Constantinople, Liutprand wrote verses of farewell upon its wall and its table of wood. They began:

> Argolicûm non tuta fides; procul esto, Latine,
> Credere, nec mentem verbis adhibere memento!

> "Trust not the Greeks; nor, thou of Latin birth,
> Believe or give thy hearing to their words!"

2

We turn from chronicles and histories to the *Lives* of men who took a leading part in events of this tenth century, *Lives* written either during its course or shortly afterward. Three of these are of special interest: that of Bruno, archbishop of Cologne, by Ruotger; of Ulrich, bishop of Augsburg, by Gerhard; and of Bernward, bishop of Hildesheim, by Thangmar.

In the *Life* of Bruno, written by a friend who knew him intimately, there is constant witness to his loyal support of the German crown. With equal skill and energy he guided his bishops, priests, and people as archbishop of Cologne and at the same time disciplined his unruly subjects and defended his land of Lotharingia as its secular duke. He was seen, now at councils of the Church, firmly declaring his will, now fighting in the ranks with his men against barbarian invaders of his duchy. He was a monk of strictly ascetic practice, working hard in the cause of monastic reform; he was a student, scholar, and teacher, absorbed in his books whenever he had a moment to spare.

He was born in 925, when his father, King Henry the Fowler, was gaining comparative peace for his people; at the time, indeed, when Lotharingia was ceded to his rule. From without, the Hungarians were still raiding German land, but in 926 Henry was to gain his welcome truce. At the age of four this, his youngest son, was sent off to Utrecht, to learn his early lessons under its bishop, Baldric. The see of Utrecht was subject to the authority of the archbishop of Cologne in Lotharingia; Baldric was a kinsman of Gilbert, governor of that duchy, and Gilbert had lately become Bruno's brother-in-law through his marriage with King Henry's daughter Gerberga. It may well be, also, that Henry had sent the boy to Baldric as one who was doing excellent work in Utrecht. He had found it devastated by the Northmen and had been busy, not only in rebuilding its city and cathedral, but in making them centers of culture both intellectual and spiritual.

At Utrecht Bruno stayed some nine years, delighting in his Latin, especially in the verses of Prudentius, learning elementary Greek, mathematics, and philosophy.

He was about fourteen years old when his brother Otto, now king of Germany, called him back to the royal court; the Lotharingians, led by Duke Gilbert, had risen in rebellion. But he continued his study of history, oratory, drama; we read that Terence fascinated him in his varied use of meter, rhythm, and language. Learned men often sought refuge under King Otto I from barbarian invasion of their lands; among them was an Irish bishop, Israel by name, who was glad to teach in return for a home. As usual, the court was continually moving from one city to another, and with it young Bruno traveled, "carrying his box of books with him as an ark of the Lord."

As he grew older, he received his place also in politics, if we may trust the evidence of diplomas; and in the life of the Church. At any rate, we find him signing his name on September 25, 940, as "royal secretary," acting for Frederick, archchaplain of Otto; on June 23, 942, he is mentioned as "deacon"; in the annals of Flodoard, under the date 947, when he was at most only twenty-two, he appears as "abbot," attending with Israel the council gathered at Verdun in Lotharingia to support Artaud as archbishop of Reims.

In tradition Bruno is said to have ruled several monasteries; of these we only know by name that of Lorsch, near Worms. In one and the same year, 953, he became archbishop of Cologne on the death of its metropolitan, Wikfried, and also duke of Lotharingia through the deposing of Conrad the Red, its duke from 944 to 953.

The *Life*, then, is filled with the story of his determined will to conquer the disobedient, to execute justice, to care for the oppressed, to minister to the needy, to rule with all vigor and to sympathize in all sincerity. But now and then its author leaves Bruno to throw light on the character of other men as he sees them. In describing the siege of Mainz during 953 he turns to its archbishop, Frederick: "Some praised to the skies his innocence; others, and these the conspirators, boasted that they relied in all things on his aid." Conrad is roundly accused by Ruotger: "He left nothing untried which he could devise for breaking up the concord brought about in Lotharingia by the wisdom of its leader." Most people, Ruotger reports here, believed that Conrad was inspired by hatred of Bruno. He invaded Metz and threatened even Cologne. In 954 the Hungarians came marching into Bruno's duchy, "induced by wicked citizens," and, we read, Conrad fought against Germany with them. On the side of Bruno, however, was marching Reginar III, count of Hainaut in Lotharingia. "None among the enemy watched so eagerly for death and ruin as Bruno did for the safety of his people; I myself, Ruotger, have seen him, not only reading, giving counsel, disputing and debating, but even standing in the line of battle. Some people, ignorant of the divine will, have asked why one who had received the charge of souls as pastor should enter upon politics and perils of war? If they have any sense, they will see that the answer lies in the good that Bruno did as protector and teacher of the Lotharingians, and the way in which they responded by their loyalty to his rule."

It was at Bruno's suggestion, we are told, that Otto sent his son Liudolf in 956 to defend the Lombard realm of Italy. The next year saw this archbishop and duke no longer allied with Count Reginar III, but at war against him before Cambrai. In 959 Bruno was with Queen Gerberga and her sons in France, trying to settle hot dispute within the royal family. From France he hurried back to Lotharingia, to struggle against another revolt, this time led by one Immo who had been his faithful minister.

At last, in 959, he decided, for the sake of peace, to divide his duchy into two parts, Upper and Lower Lotharingia, and to place each under a governor acting on his own authority, subject only to Bruno in matters of supreme importance. Ruotger thinks of him as both "archbishop" and "archduke."

His work for his duchy never was allowed to interfere with his duty as archbishop. He found time to adorn his cathedral at Cologne, to establish Cologne's church of Saint Pantaleon, to build or repair many others. Relics of saints were his great joy; he gathered them from many sources. Now and then he was with his family; in May 965 he kept Pentecost at Cologne, happy in the return of his brother Otto, now king and emperor, from Italy. With him, their host, were his mother, Queen Matilda; his sister, Queen Gerberga; his nephews, King Lothair of France and Charles of Lotharingia, with Otto II, nine years old.

It was his last great happiness. In the autumn of the same year, as he was once more returning from France, he was taken ill and forced to enter the hospital at Reims. There he lingered ten days, reading alone, sometimes talking a little while with his friends, bishops of France. On the eleventh of October 965, he died.

Ruotger wrote this *Life* during the years 967-69 at the request of Folcmar, successor of Bruno at Cologne. He was a cleric of its cathedral, perhaps a monk of that church of Saint Pantaleon which his archbishop had loved so well, in which this Bruno was buried. His work gives a reliable picture of his hero, though it has to be completed by details gathered elsewhere. We must admit, also, that he could see nothing amiss either in Otto the Great or in his saintly brother.

When we compare his conception of history and the form in which it should be written with that of historians proper such as Widukind and Thietmar, we see that he, too, bears the mark of the tenth century. His placing of Otto I as "Imperator" is somewhat higher than that of Widukind; to Ruotger before 962 Otto was "Imperator" in the sense of a great ruler; after his imperial crowning in Rome he was invested with dignity that has something of the majestic, as "Caesar Augustus." Yet, neither the thought of imperial Rome nor of the Carolingian Empire caused Ruotger to count Otto as successor of their rulers. Nor does the dignity of Ruotger's "Caesar Augustus" approach the adulation of Thietmar.

Here, also, we find the influence of Sallust; here, also, are invented speeches. Here Duke Bruno reproaches his rebel nephew Liudolf, whom Otto has declared heir of his crown: "Think! Who has exalted you so greatly? Who has brought all the nobles of this realm of Germany to swear to you their oath of loyalty? Why did he this? That you should prove ungrateful? That you should learn to be a traitor? Truly those men are imbecile who try in this way to mislead you!" To Bruno himself his brother Otto, the king, can say: "In you priestly religion and royal firmness unite their strength."

It is the thought of Ruotger that speaks here, and it speaks truly. To him Bruno lives on for his German people: "Men visit constantly his grave; they remind one another eagerly of what he did, what he taught, how he lived, how he died. Now they pray for him, now they ask him of his charity to pray for them. They seek no miracles. They think back over his years; they feel sure that from him some great thing will come, for them or for their children. For, as they were moved to the heart while he was among them, so now that he has gone, for him they give praise and glory to God."

Bruno's contemporary, Ulrich, bishop of Augsburg, resembled him in his threefold vocation: as prelate of the Church, as statesman devoted to the Ottonian House, and as soldier defending its realm. But he was no scholar; action, practical and successful, was his joy.

He was a faithful pastor, in private life as in public. He prayed and fasted with the same zeal with which he ruled his household, cared for the sick and poor, journeyed on visitations to his churches and abbeys. Yet, he never forgot his noble ancestors, the pomp and ceremony due to him as prelate, the seemly architecture proper for the cathedral in which he held his seat. He loved to entertain in his episcopal residence, to welcome guests in multitude and to feast them splendidly. His courage in these critical days was in keeping with his magnificence as host; he risked his life gladly for his people, his city, and his king.

And so, twenty years after he died, in February 993, the story of his life was read aloud before a great synod, meeting in Rome, and the pope, John XV, proclaimed him saint of the Catholic Church. The papal bull which he issued is the first formal record which we possess of a canonization by the Holy See.

The *Life* is also of importance in other respects, both for literature and for history. Augsburg was in the duchy of Swabia, situated at the confluence of the rivers Lech and Wertach; Ulrich was born in Swabia about 890, of a family related to its ducal house. But Swabian men of this time, even the aristocratic and better educated, were not known for their literary productions. It is, then, the more remarkable that we have here a work by a contemporary of Ulrich, written in this tenth century by Gerhard, provost of Ulrich's cathedral of Saint Mary. In Ulrich's later years the two, provost and bishop, constantly met one another to talk and discuss; it was Gerhard who aided Ulrich in his old age and was with him when he died. And, therefore, we possess a full record of these years. Sometimes it is obscure; now and again it carries strange and rare words; its German-speaking author was not entirely at home with his Latin. Ulrich traveled to Italy; but we learn from Gerhard scarcely anything of Italian history in his days. We may be grateful for what he tells us concerning Germany.

As a boy Ulrich was sent to the monastic school of Saint-Gall, that abbey near the Boden See, renowned for its teaching in this earlier medieval age. He learned quickly and remembered what he learned; he showed promise of monastic calling; when he reached the moment prescribed by the Rule, Saint-Gall's brethren were more than willing that he should enter their community. But courteously he declined their suggestion. He returned to Augsburg and was invited by Adalbero, then its bishop, to take some part in the administration of his household and diocese; there he worked with enthusiasm and gained high praise. In 909 Adalbero died and was succeeded as bishop by one Hiltin. This election by no means suited the ideas of young Ulrich; "Hiltin," Gerhard tells us, "was not the kind of distinguished and noble prelate under whom Ulrich wished to serve."

For the next fourteen years he lived at home. His mother was now a widow, and he spent his time taking care of the family estate and looking after her. "Was that not ordered in the fifth commandment?" he retorted to those who wondered at his comfortable and undistinguished life.

He was in his early thirties when Hiltin departed this earth. Promptly his kinsman, Duke Burchard II of Swabia, and other relatives approached the king, then Henry the Fowler, to ask that by his royal nomination this young man might be the next bishop of Augsburg. Henry was anxious to conciliate Duke Burchard so far as his crown would allow. He consented, and in December 923 Ulrich received the see.

He faced a hard and difficult charge. Under Hiltin Hungarian invaders had ravaged Augsburg and had set fire to its cathedral. Ulrich not only watched over its rebuilding but saw that was done with due attention to the beauty of architecture, from the roof to the crypt.

Now and again he journeyed to visit King Henry's court and to discuss problems of state with him and his ministers. Regularly his comfortable carriage was seen rolling along the rough roads of his diocese, escorted by lackeys who rode before and behind, to right and left, as he went to make his inspection of churches and abbeys under his rule. With him he took some one of his chaplains, or a layman of dignity and experience, that he might talk over problems, ecclesiastical or secular. Time must not be lost. He pleaded that the privacy of a carriage saved him from useless chatting with people on the way, that he had to have time for chanting his office with one of his priests.

So thirty years passed and Ulrich grew prosperous, into a prelate of importance in Germany. Then in 953 Liudolf, Swabia's own duke, rose in rebellion against his father, Germany's king, Otto I, and his uncle, Henry, duke of Bavaria. Bavarians themselves in great number supported this rising. So did Arnulf, count Palatine, son of Arnulf "the Bad," angry because his hereditary claim had been passed over in favor of Henry. In this crisis Ulrich decided that it was for him to prove his loyalty by action; he left his carriage at home and rode on horseback to fight for Otto in Bavaria. There he stood with his king until December 953 when Otto left Regensburg and its siege for Saxony.

Meanwhile Bavarian rebels had entered Swabia, to work ravage and ruin upon Ulrich's episcopal city. When he saw it again, in January 954, it was torn and broken beyond belief, deserted and silent, partly through treachery, partly through the wounding and death of its people. Ulrich was forced to take refuge in a battered castle outside Augsburg; he repaired and strengthened this miserable shelter as far as he could, while his followers held out, half-starved, in huts and outhouses around him. For week after week they waited, shivering in the bitter cold of winter; their only hope of rescue lay in Dietbold, brother of Ulrich, and his friend Adalbert, described as count of Marchthal: both Swabians, both horrified at their duke's action.

Worse was yet to come. An army of Bavarian rebels marched to camp near Augsburg; from it came messengers of Count Arnulf, ordering Ulrich to surrender or pay the penalty. The bishop defiantly refused, and prepared to die bravely. Then, on February 6, 954, Dietbold and Adalbert swept down upon Arnulf's men, took their camp by surprise and won victory, at the cost of Adalbert's life.

In the spring of this year Otto was once more at Regensburg, besieging its walls, and Liudolf was riding from Regensburg, now in misery of famine, to seek aid for its citizens from his Swabian duchy. Otto followed him with his own army, and soon the troops of the two enemies, father and son, were facing one another, ready to rush into battle. Just at this moment two bishops of Swabia, Ulrich of Augsburg and Hartbert of Chur, came up in hot hurry to implore, to command Liudolf to end this folly of destruction. Their words prevailed. Truce was made and on June 16 the Council of Langenzenn met for debate.

As we have seen, Liudolf changed his mind; he would not yield, and the siege of Regensburg was renewed by Otto's decision to end this struggle. In July the Count Palatine, Arnulf, was killed by a fall from his horse near the city's gates. Two days went by before this was made known to Otto and his men, encamped outside the walls, by a woman who in agony of hunger had slipped unnoticed through those gates to beg mercy from her king.

The winter of 954 also saw Liudolf at last a penitent, forgiven but deprived of his duchy. Not until the following spring did Duke Henry once more hold Bavaria, and Ulrich his seat at Augsburg, in freedom from the menace of civil war.

Yet, the most vivid picture of Ulrich as warrior-bishop comes to us from this same year 955, the year of Hungarian invasion of Swabia. Near his city of Augsburg the Hungarians burned the church dedicated to holy Afra of the fourth century—once a common prostitute, then a convert to Christianity, martyr for her faith, and finally Patron Saint of Augsburg. In August they battered the city's ramparts, at that time low and without towers of defense; they rushed to and fro outside, shooting their arrows, hurling missiles and flaming torches to set fire within. In the midst of his people sat Ulrich on his horse to cheer and urge them on. He wore no armor; arrayed in full pontifical splendor he presided over the battle, calm and confident. When darkness fell, he was still there, driving on his fellow citizens to repair damage done, to pray with him for the Lord of Heaven to come swiftly to their aid. At dawn on the morrow he said matins and Mass, before the sun rose; encouraged by his call his men stood their ground, so firmly that among the enemy loud threats were heard, driving the disheartened forward to the fight. Suddenly above the tumult a voice rang clear; Berthold, a rebel against King Otto, like his father, the Count Palatine Arnulf, had ridden in all haste to the Hungarian host outside Augsburg. "King Otto himself," he cried, "is on his way with a multitude of men!" At once the Hungarian commander, Bulksu, gave order to sound the trumpet for recall. His barbarian besiegers quickly left the city walls to rush against the forces of Germany, now seen advancing in the distance.

The battle ended in the victory won by Otto in August 955 on the bank of the river Lech. Until evening he pursued the fleeing enemy; then he came into Augsburg and spent the night with its bishop, trying to comfort him in his grief at the loss of his brother Dietbold, killed as he fought.

Along the riverside Ulrich walked next day, searching amid the carnage of battle for the bodies of both his brother Dietbold and his nephew Reginbald. They were found, and brought to Augsburg for burial. Then with his flock he set to work, and hard they all toiled, until churches and houses were rebuilt, ruined fields were reseeded and planted anew, until, so far as might be, the blight of war was swept away.

Three times this bishop, who delighted in travel when peace and quiet allowed it, crossed the border into Italy; on his second visit he was graciously received by Alberic, master of the Roman people; on the third in 971, when he was an old man, he met the emperor, Otto the Great, in Ravenna.

The meeting was to have serious result. It began with joy. Otto was so glad to see his friend of Augsburg that he hurried out from his chamber, one shoe on, the other shoe off. Long they talked. Ulrich spoke of his weariness, of the burden of age; he had passed his eightieth year and he was anxious to secure an able successor for his see. Would Otto, he asked, name Adalbero, his, Ulrich's nephew, as administrator of secular affairs in the diocese of Augsburg as long as he himself should live, and after his death present him for consecration as bishop in his place? He would so happily now hand over to Adalbero the financial and other business which could be carried on under a layman's charge.

The king gave his consent, and soon Adalbero was lay administrator for Augsburg's cathedral and diocese. His confidence in his power was not wanting; soon he felt so sure of his position that on ceremonial occasions he was even seen carrying in his hands the episcopal staff of office.

This soon aroused resentment, so keen that a synod was called at Ingelheim in September 972 to debate the matter. As Ulrich's voice had failed in recent years and he could not address the judges in his defense, he was represented by his provost, Gerhard. The bishop was told that he was setting a bad example; other aged prelates had nephews to whom they would willingly hand over problems of secular duties. In the end, upon his promise that he would again assume all responsibility in his episcopal rule and would hold this as long as his strength would allow, he was not only forgiven for Adalbero's presumption, but also received solemn assurance that this nephew should succeed him in Augsburg.

This never was fulfilled. Shortly afterward Adalbero suddenly died, and his death was followed on July 4 of this year 973 by that of Ulrich himself.

Thangmar, who wrote the *Life* of Bernward, bishop of Hildesheim in Saxony, was the ideal man for his task. Saxon himself, he taught Bernward as boy and youth; he was continually at his side during Bernward's years as bishop, and he acted for him in times of anxiety and crisis. In the preface to his work he writes: "No aim, no endeavor in all his life, could escape my mind; I knew it all to the full."

Thangmar was a priest of the cathedral of Hildesheim and a teacher in its school. He tells us in regard to this pupil of his, born about 960, grandson of a Count Palatine in Saxony: "I found him of extraordinary intelligence; he would sit at the back of the room, listening with all eagerness; then, happy in his understanding, he would explain secretly to other boys what he had learned from me." Later on, when Bernward was older: "I used to take him with me when I went around the diocese on errands for the bishop. Often all day long we would read as we rode, or amuse ourselves by making up verses in meter, or argue with one another some tricky point of rhetoric or dialectical debate. In his shy fashion but with quick understanding and real knowledge he would put before me questions of philosophy, quite difficult to answer. He was clever also in handiwork; he learned the arts of script and illumination, of designing, of building in wood, stone, and metal."

From Hildesheim, Bernward went for further training at Mainz under its archbishop, Willigis, who ordained him deacon and priest. For a while he felt it his business to take care of his grandfather; in 987, after the count's death, he was called to court by the Empress Theophano and soon found himself teaching King Otto III, then about seven years old. The two became close friends, especially after the death of Theophano in 991. Then, when Gerdag, bishop of Hildesheim, died in December 992, Bernward was quickly elected to succeed him; on January 15, 993, he was consecrated by Willigis.

Now he, like others in Saxony, lived in fear of Slavonic or Scandinavian invaders of his diocese. He built a fortress on the Aller for its protection; he stationed soldiers to guard its frontiers and surrounded their stations with deeply dug moats. He thought also of comfort for his people. Clusters of houses soon appeared, surrounded by gardens in which their proud tenants grew vegetables and fruits. The houses he made attractive by his own designs in stone and tiling of varied color, patterned after mosaic fashion.

Often he was with the royal family. It was Bernward whom Matilda, aunt of Otto III, abbess of Quedlinburg and regent for Germany, called to her bedside as she drew near to death; it was Bernward who stood with Otto outside Tivoli in January 1001 and bade him press on its siege with stringent assault. It was Bernward, also, who when Tivoli had surrendered, ministered to Otto's soldiers and with them faced the angry Romans at his emperor's side, the Holy Lance itself in his hand. Only when Otto had left Rome and was on his way to retreat in Ravenna did the bishop say farewell, on February 20, 1001, and turn to go back to his German diocese.

There remains the story of the long dispute between Bernward and Willigis concerning rule over the famous convent of Gandersheim. This story, it would seem, was written separately by Thangmar and subsequently inserted as part of this *Life* of Bernward; the whole work was finished before 1030.

The abbey of Gandersheim was situated in Lower Saxony, not far from Brunswick, on the bank of the brook Gande from which it took its name. It was on the border between the dioceses of Hildesheim and Mainz, and therefore its rule rested on a question of geography. This point should be kept in mind, since Thangmar, honest as he was, could see nothing against Bernward's claim; we have no defence of Willigis in our records.

The Liudolf of earlier time, called in tradition the first "duke" of Saxony, had founded this house for nuns in 852; his daughter Hathumod was its first abbess. He chose its site with a view to protection against barbarian assault; it stood in the midst of dense forest and swampy fenland. For many years it remained under the authority of Hildesheim's see.

Then, in 987, when Otto III was king of Germany and one Osdag, bishop of Hildesheim from 985 to 989, was about to receive Otto's sister, Sophia, into religious life within Gandersheim's walls, rebellion suddenly broke out. Sophia was nine years old; from Thangmar we infer that both as child and grown woman she was always firmly determined to get what she wanted, whatever the cost. So now she protested to her family that no bishop, not even the bishop of Hildesheim, would be a proper person to act on this occasion. Was she not a royal princess of Germany? Who should veil her except Willigis, archbishop of Mainz? Invitation was sent him; he not only gave her his promise but also informed Osdag that he intended to officiate.

On October 18, Saint Luke's Day, a multitude assembled in Gandersheim's church. Sophia's mother and brother, the Empress Theophano and King Otto III, with the bishops of Paderborn, Minden, and Worms, were present, together with very many guests; a number of other young girls were also to be received. All were conscious that trouble was brewing and most were distressed for the bishop; but through reverence for Willigis, metropolitan of Mainz, they were afraid to show their feelings. It was finally agreed that the archbishop should sing the Mass at the high altar, that both prelates should veil Princess Sophia, and that Osdag should do the same for those of lesser rank in the world. It was an unheard-of thing, Thangmar declared in anger, that two bishops, each arrayed in full pontifical splendor, should sit side by side together as officiants on this solemn day.

But neither Thangmar nor anyone save Osdag himself knew the mind of the bishop of Hildesheim on this day. When the time for the veiling came, instead of waiting for Willigis to begin the ritual, Osdag quickly rose from his chair. Standing before the altar, he asked, first the king, as sponsor for Sophia, and then the others who were answering for their candidates, whether in very truth they gave consent. All, not knowing what else to do in their astonishment, declared their will; and then Osdag inquired of the princess and of all those waiting to be received, whether here and now they professed their faithful obedience to him as bishop of Hildesheim and to his successors in the see. Sophia was furious, but she could not disrupt the ceremony. Nor could any of her fellow postulants. It was clear that Osdag was ready to risk his deposing in his determination to uphold his right, as he saw it. For some reason, hidden in the mind of Archbishop Willigis, proceedings were allowed to reach their end in peace and every one went home with apparent goodwill.

Outwardly this peace lasted for years; Willigis made no move of censure against the see of Hildesheim. Yet, as Thangmar remarks, "the tares of falsehood were destroying this rising harvest of charity." They were working within the abbey of Gandersheim to drain away its once ascetic life. The nuns grew careless, irreverent, and irresponsible, the more so since their abbess Gerberga, daughter of Henry, duke of Bavaria, and his wife Judith, was now old and infirm. Sophia once more led rebellion; she even left the convent for a while, entirely against its rule, to pour out complaint in the ears of the archbishop of Mainz.

Then came another crisis, in the year 1000, when the nun, once Princess Sophia, was twenty-two years old and Bernward was bishop of Hildesheim. A new church, built by the effort of Gerberga, was ready for consecration. She was too ill to attend, and, therefore, she requested Sophia to represent her. At once Sophia as deputy invited

Willigis to officiate, while at the same time Gerberga as abbess called to Bernward. Both promised their service, and the ceremony was arranged for Holy Cross Day, the fourteenth of September.

At the last moment the archbishop sent word that he had been obliged to change the date, and that he would carry out the consecration on September 21, Feast of Saint Matthew. Bernward without delay replied that the later date was impossible for him; he had to be at the royal court on important business.

So Bernward, bishop of Hildesheim, decided to arrive as officiant on September 14. He found nothing prepared for his coming except entire refusal of Gandersheim's nuns to cooperate, urged on by Sophia in this move. The bishop chanted the Mass of the Feast, preached a sermon which was constantly interrupted by whispered insult, and went home.

On September 21, Archbishop Willigis, with Duke Bernard of Saxony and a large congregation, was at Gandersheim for the consecrating. He, too, was unable to act. Before the ritual could begin, so vehement a protest was voiced by Ekkehard, bishop of Schleswig and a great friend of Bernward, that Willigis was forced to declare the ceremony postponed until November 28, when a synod would meet to judge this quarrel.

Soon Bernward could endure no longer. The Emperor Otto III was in Rome; to Rome he would go. On November 2, weeks before the synod was to assemble, he set out with Thangmar; by the fourth of January 1001, he was in the city, greeted with all warmth of welcome.

In Germany the synod met on November 28, 1000, as announced, and at Gandersheim, with the archbishop of Mainz in the chair. Once again Ekkehard opened action with a blast of rebuke. Ordered by Willigis to be silent, he retorted: "My diocese of Schleswig has been laid waste by Slavonic barbarians; my city is deserted; my church is desolate. I have no longer a seat as bishop, and therefore I now serve the church of Hildesheim. With all my will, with all my power, I support this holy place!"

In Bernward's absence the synod refused to make decision; nothing was declared except that letters must be dispatched both to Bernward and to the emperor in Italy. When Otto heard from Bernward of all that had happened he was greatly vexed; by the advice of Henry, duke of Bavaria, he summoned a council of bishops to meet on January 13, 1001, in Rome's church of Saint Sebastian. They came from Italy and from Germany; Duke Henry was there, and a multitude of abbots, priests, and deacons. Bernward stated his case, and the vote was given in his favor. At the end Pope Sylvester II solemnly gave judgment: "By apostolic authority we do demolish, destroy and annul all that has been devised and declared by Archbishop Willigis and his associates in the diocese of our brother and fellow bishop, Bernward. Then, turning to Bernward himself, he added: "The holding of charge of the abbey of Gandersheim with its adjacent buildings and bounds I renew and confirm herewith for you, in right of authority; and in the names of holy Peter and Paul, I forbid that any one oppose this right, save as canon law may allow."

It was then announced that another synod would convene in June at Pöhlde in Germany, and that the Saxon Frederick, cardinal-priest of Rome, would attend as papal legate.

At Pöhlde, in the diocese of Mainz, Frederick duly appeared on June 22, robed in full ceremonial array. With all respect Bernward and many others welcomed him. But there were not wanting those who scorned his presence and his words; Saxon nobles and bishops were now irritated, even angry, at the long absence of their king in Italy. A letter from Pope Sylvester was read aloud, rebuking the acts of the archbishop of Mainz. Lievizo, archbishop of Hamburg-Bremen, had just risen to move that the synod declare decision, when the assembly was thrown into sudden disorder and panic by a rush through the doors of armed soldiers, men in the service of Willigis. At last, after repeated calls for order, Frederick and Bernward brought the tumult under control; those present, they announced, including Archbishop Willigis, were to leave the hall in quiet and meet again on the morrow.

But on June 23 Willigis did not appear; during the night he had secretly left Pöhlde. In silence the members of the synod now heard the papal legate pronounce Willigis suspended from all episcopal function until he should come for judgment before the pope himself; the bishops now present, he commanded, were to gather again in assembly, this time in Rome at Christmastide.

Christmas 1001 found Otto III still in Italy, at Todi in Umbria. His strength was now failing and it was felt necessary that the renewed meeting of the synod should take place there instead of at Rome. Nothing meanwhile had been done in Germany concerning Gandersheim except some vague discussion in August at Frankfurt. On December 27 the synod of Todi opened session; Bernward of Hildesheim, exhausted by the long and confused dispute, was unable to leave Germany and Thangmar acted for his bishop.

Once again the issue was left undetermined. Revolt by this time had broken out in Germany; it was thought unwise to provoke the wrath of Willigis and his powerful friends against the emperor in this anxious time. Was he not at this very moment on his way to put down rebellion in Rome?

And so the question of episcopal authority over Gandersheim remained unanswered until 1007, when the convent church built by Gerberga was finally consecrated in the presence of Henry, once duke of Bavaria, now king of Germany as Henry II. Both Bernward and Willigis took part in the ceremony, and in the same year, perhaps on the same day, January 5, the archbishop of Mainz renounced all right of jurisdiction over this abbey of nuns. For the future it would lie in the hands of Bernward and the bishops who would follow him in Hildesheim's seat of rule.

3

Lastly we will think for a moment of men who fled from the civilized world to live as hermits and as missionaries among the heathen.

Monastic reform was now seeking to replace disorder throughout Europe of the West. In Italy two separate currents were mingled in this reform: one of Greek asceticism and one of Latin reason. Those dedicated to this twofold course had but four desires: religious custom, vows, and habit; contemplation of God in solitude; the converting by words, spoken or written, of those who knew not the Catholic faith; absolute self-denial, ending, if God so willed, in the joy of martyrdom.

Tradition traces to a disciple named Bartholomew the *Life* of Saint Nilus, born about 910 at Rossano in Calabria, southern Italy, to aristocratic parents of Greek origin who trained him well in things sacred and literary. Story, possibly but not certainly true, tells that in his youth he succumbed to feminine charm "as a stricken deer," and that he married. At any rate he lived to find a more abiding attraction in religion. With stern striving after his ideal he worked here and there; now in community with his brethren, now in solitude, hidden in a cavern dedicated to Saint Michael the Archangel, now retreating before the Saracens who raided the country around him. For a while at the monastery of Sant'Adriano, founded by his own labor near Rossano, he taught any who came to him; at last, at the age of sixty, unable to find peace for others or for himself through the Saracen assault, he asked and received welcome from the Latin Benedictines of Monte Cassino in Campania.

We have already seen him in later days: about eighty years old, giving advice to Adalbert of Prague at Valleluce; at Rome in 998 pleading with Otto III; warning this same emperor at Serperi in 999. After Otto's death, when he was past ninety, he left Serperi and built the abbey of Grottaferrata, thirteen miles from Rome. He died in 1004 or 1005, and at Grottaferrata his memory is still revered on his feast day, September 26.

Nilus was only one of many Greek monks who in Italian land were following the example of Saint Basil. Another hermit whom we have noticed is Saint Romuald of Ravenna; his connection with Otto III is told in his *Life*, written about 1042 by Saint Peter Damian of the same city.

We may place the birth of Romuald about 951; his father, Sergius, was devoted to the luxuries of this world and well able to indulge in them. Romuald, therefore, was also gay and careless in his youth, though now and then he found himself longing for better things. He was just over twenty years old when a violent quarrel between Sergius and a rival of his in business affairs caused the rival's death. This murder, as he held it, caused Romuald so great a shock, and the greater shock since his father seemed quite indifferent to its tragedy, that he decided penance must be done in atonement. Sergius would hear nothing of penance. His son, then, as the next male member of the family, felt bound in conscience to assume responsibility; vicarious penance was often carried out in these times. For this purpose he entered the monastery of Sant'Apollinare in Classe near his home, satisfied his conscience by hard living, and then surprised himself by praying for admission as novice. Its community was also doubtful concerning this serious but wealthy young man; only the express order of the archbishop of Ravenna induced consent. It should be observed that the brethren of Sant'Apollinare were just then distinctly lax in regard to their rule, which was strict; when three years had come and gone they so heartily detested Romuald, steadily increasing in grace and fervor, that they decided to throw him out of their highest window.

Fortunately, he heard what they were planning; about 974 he fled for refuge to the hermitage of Marinus, a solitary, living near Venice. Marinus certainly was not lacking in discipline; he was so disgusted at Romuald's ignorance of what he himself considered proper austerity that he was constantly beating his young novice on the head with his staff. At last Romuald, who had been trying as best he could to practice patience, burst out with a prayer: "Master, would you please for the future do it on the other side? I am getting quite deaf in my left ear!"

He did not stay long with this hermit. In 978 we find him leaving for the south of France, where he studied the *Institutes* and *Conferences* of Cassian for ten years under Saint Michael's monks of Cuxa in the Pyrenees. Then he returned to wander from place to place in Italy: now in a cell of Bagno di Romagna on the river Savio; now not far from Florence; now in the Umbrian Apennines, near Gubbio and Sassoferrato; now, from 993 onward, on the "island of Pereum," or in swamps and lagoons bordering on the Valli di Comacchio and the Adriatic Sea, north of Ravenna. The marshland was haunted by fever; foul stench arose from its murky ponds; monks who dwelt within it gave day and night to prayer, hunger, and suffering without end.

Sometimes Romuald left his retreat to take part in what was going on in the world outside. In 998 he was bidding Otto III and his friend Tammo, brother of Bernward of Hildesheim, to do heavy penance for their treatment of Crescentius. This second Crescentius, besieged in Sant'Angelo by Tammo and the emperor, had only consented to come out of its fortress after they had promised him life and safety in return for surrender; he had come out, and at once he had been killed. It was Romuald, then, who sent Otto in 999 on pilgrimage to Monte Gargano for what he had done to John Philagathos and to Crescentius Nomentanus.

It was also in the last years of the tenth century—the exact dates are disputed—that the emperor during a visit to Ravenna asked Romuald to accept election as abbot of Sant'Apollinare. Under pressure he yielded. But after a short tenure of office he threw down his staff before the emperor and the archbishop of Ravenna, refusing any longer to rule his monks. They did not know what monastic life meant, he declared, not as he understood it.

We see him next recovering from critical illness at Monte Cassino, under the care of a monk named Benedict. In January 1001 he was with Otto during the rising of Tivoli's citizens; together with Bernward of Hildesheim he persuaded them to sue for peace. In December of this year, when the emperor was failing in hope and health, Romuald left Ravenna for Istria, that peninsula which skirts the Adriatic from the Gulf of Trieste to the Gulf of Kvarner and is now largely under Yugoslavian control. A little later in the eleventh century he founded near Arezzo the hermit order of Camaldoli with which his name is still closely bound.

A third counselor of Otto III, Adalbert, bishop of Prague, we have already seen leaving his diocese in misery through his people's immoral and irregular lives. But that is only part of the trouble; a deeper cause of anxiety lay in the politics of Bohemia. Its land was under the control of two families of ducal rank: the Slavniks and the Prszemyslides. The future bishop, son of the head of the Slavnik clan, was brought up at their family estate of Libice in eastern Bohemia. The priest who baptized him gave his name as Vojtiekh; at his confirmation this was changed to Adalbert. Of the two ducal clans the Prszemyslides held greater power; Boleslav II, duke of Bohemia from 967 until 999, belonged to their house. The Slavniks, it is true, were content to acknowledge the Prszemyslide leadership; yet, there was constant feeling of hostility between the two families, originating for the greater part in Prszemyslide ambition.

In 981, the year in which Adalbert left Magdeburg for Prague, his father died, and Adalbert's eldest brother became head of the Slavnik House. Adalbert as subdeacon in Prague was a cheerful and lighthearted youth, about twenty-five years old, delighting in human joys of social life. His bishop we have seen as Dethmar, and it was in January 982, when Adalbert stood by Dethmar's bedside as he lay dying, that his character radically changed. The bishop of Prague died mourning with bitter regret what he called his lax and worldly years on earth. We have no reason to think this accusation true; but the shock of hearing it from his deeply revered pastor made young Adalbert think hard.

He thought the more when in 983 election to the see of Prague fell upon him himself. He could not refuse. Otto II in Adalbert's presence confirmed the election at Verona in June 983 and saw him consecrated, also in Italy, by Willigis, archbishop of Mainz, the same month.

Once back in Prague, Adalbert did his utmost for his people. But always there was resistance; supporters of the Prszemyslide faction resented rebuke by this son of the rival house. About 989 he left for Rome.

From 993 until 995 he was again in Prague, recalled to his see in a moment of reconciliation by the Prszemyslide Duke Boleslav himself. Then tragedy, born of political discord, drove him out once more. A woman, wife of an enthusiastic follower of the Prszemyslides, was publicly accused at Prague of adultery, and, too, with a cleric as her partner in sin. Hunted by indignant relatives of her Prszemyslide husband, she fled for refuge to her Slavnik bishop,

Adalbert, who in hope that he might bring her to penitence gave her sanctuary in a convent church near his own house. The church was firmly locked and the key given by Adalbert to its sacristan. Soon an armed band of Prszemyslides broke into the episcopal residence. Adalbert met them with dignity and calm: "If you are seeking me," he said, "here I am." The answer was shrewd in its evil: "Doubtless you hope to die a martyr at our hands! Not so! If you do not quickly deliver to us that harlot woman, we shall give you more than death; the wives and children of your family shall atone for your crime!" The bishop, of course, firmly refused; it was the sacristan who in terror yielded up the key. The woman was found and killed; Adalbert drove her executioners from the communion of the Church and for his courage was forced to leave the city.

The Prszemyslides again vowed vengeance, and they carried out their vow. At Rome Adalbert heard the terrible story. On September 27, 995, four of his brothers with their families, servants and farm laborers, were peacefully making ready for the festival of their national hero, Saint Wenceslas, on the next day. They had no thought of trouble; the eldest brother, head of the Slavniks, had just made a pact of peace with the Prszemyslide House. Without warning, men of this house suddenly rushed upon the workers, busy in their preparations at Libice. All did their best to resist the attack, but in vain. For three days it lasted, while Bohemia outside this family estate was holding holiday. The Slavnik castle was seized, and all who could, ran for shelter in its church. The four brothers, after pledge had been given that the lives of all would be spared, came out from the sanctuary with their wives and children. All were killed; only the eldest brother, who was absent in the service of Otto III, the half-brother, Gaudentius, and Adalbert himself, lived to represent the Slavnik ducal line.

Adalbert was filled with horror and grief. In 996 he left Rome for Germany; soon the word came that Prague's duke and people no longer wanted him. It was more than welcome; he had Pope Gregory's permission to go forth as missionary bishop to wild and barbarous men, and go he would.

In the spring of 997 he was at Gdansk (Danzig) on the Baltic; then he journeyed on by boat to labor among the Prussians in that region, near Baltiysk (Pillau). There early on the morning of Saint George's Day, as he was reading his office on the shore after Mass, he was struck down by a man named Sikko, one of a band of eight natives of the country who resented his presence, declaring him a spy. They cut off his head, to exhibit as proof of their deed, and threw his body into the running tide. The head was rescued by a devoted friend and the body was cast up on Polish land after drifting for six days; both were carried with all honor by Duke Boleslav of the Poles to Gniezno for burial.

Three narratives tell of Adalbert. One, the *Passion of Adalbert*, probably the oldest of the three, describes his death; it was written soon after this occurred, by a man who knew Poland and Bohemia well. The other two are records of the bishop's life. One of them comes from John Canaparius, a contemporary and a friend of Adalbert: a monk, indeed, in that abbey of Saints Boniface and Alexius where Adalbert had followed religious rule. Canaparius, like Adalbert, was a loyal admirer of Otto III. Here he writes of him: "When the king of the Franks came to Rome, his years, advanced beyond boyhood, and his character, more mature than his age, called forth from him the dignity of emperor. Rome, head of the world, and in name mistress of cities, alone makes kings into emperors. Since she cherishes in her heart a prince of saints, she has the right of her own will to enthrone a prince over lands of this earth."

The second of these *Lives* of Adalbert was written by one who needs more words than Canaparius for due description. He was another Bruno, distinguished as Bruno of Querfurt, since his father owned the estate of Querfurt in Saxony. He, too, was a pupil at the school of Magdeburg, but long after Adalbert. About 997, when he was in his early twenties, he left for the court of Otto III, who was then in Germany; for a while he acted as chaplain there. The following year he was with Otto in Rome; but before long he, as so many others, forsook the world for monastic round of discipline among the religious of Saints Boniface and Alexius. His name in religion was Boniface.

Probably late in 1000, while he was in Rome, he came under the influence of Romuald. Early in 1001 we find him with Romuald in the marshland near Ravenna, talking of his hope for mission work with two of its hermits. One, originally from Benevento, was that Benedict who had nursed Romuald at Monte Cassino. The other was named John, one "who hid his austerity behind a cheerful countenance. His face was covered with sores which long ago had taken from him the sight of one eye." So Bruno tells us.

The three were all longing for a call to serve among heathen

barbarians, and when, as it seems, a call did come from Duke Boleslav the Brave, of Poland, for laborers to work in its wilds, they at
once offered themselves. It was soon decided that Benedict and John
should go straight to Poland, build a monastery where it might best
be placed, and begin to learn the Slavic language; Bruno was to go
to Rome to ask formal permission from Pope Sylvester II for their
undertaking.

In 1001 Benedict and John safely arrived and began their work,
to the great satisfaction of the duke, who settled them near Gnesen.
Before long they were joined in the hermitage by two Polish men,
who, as time went on, made profession as monks under the names of
Isaac and Matthew; a lay brother, Christian, served the community
as cook.

Then two troubles began to worry these zealous laborers in the
field. Henry II, who had succeeded the third Otto as king of Germany, was a man of high character. His devotion to the Church was
deep; his aim was bold; he was to wield power far and wide; before
his death he was to be hailed as saint. But he did not share the vision
of Otto III and Pope Sylvester. Duke Boleslav of the Poles decided
that Henry, loyal Churchman though he was, kept clearly in mind
his own ambition for his realm of Germany. Boleslav, therefore,
determined that he on his side would endeavor to extend his power
over the Slavonic peoples. He proceeded to take possession of
Slavonic lands and hoped that Henry would look on this act with
tolerance.

He did not, and in 1003 Duke Boleslav marched upon Bohemia,
now under an inefficient and worthless ruler whom German menace
had reduced to a state of inferiority—Boleslav III, called Rufus, the
Red. By March Boleslav of Poland had blinded and sent into exile
this Boleslav the Red and had seized from Germany control over
Bohemia by a determined attack.

Benedict and John were much distressed by this change from
alliance to enmity toward the German crown on the part of Poland's
duke. They were also worried by the continued absence of Bruno;
they had no papal authorizing for their mission. To no purpose
Benedict, provided with money by the duke, started out in search of
their missing brother; the fact of war made traveling impossible. He
returned his gift to Boleslav after reaching Prague, where the Polish
duke was now master, and then wearily made his way home.

Far greater evil was in store. News of that gift of money had
come to the ears of greedy thieves. On the dark night of November

10-11, 1003, when the five hermits—Benedict, John, Isaac, Matthew, Christian—had chanted the office for the vigil of their patron, Saint Martin, these robbers, led by a man who had once been a servant in the house, crept into the dormitory where they lay asleep. Startled by a sound, John awoke to see this leader, candle in one hand, axe in the other, standing in the doorway. "Friend," cried the monk in Polish words, "what do you here, with that axe?" "At the order of the Duke Boleslav of the Poles," was the answer, "to seize you without mercy." John, who knew nothing of fear, laughed in scorn. "That," he retorted, "never did our good duke say! Why such a silly lie, my son?" "We are here to kill," snapped the murderer, and struck. "God help you and us," John called aloud, and died. In a moment Benedict and Isaac also were killed. Matthew ran from the room to get help, only to meet his fate just outside the chapel; finally the fifth brother, Christian, who slept in another place, was added to the dead.

The thieves, angry at finding no money, tore to pieces a precious missal which Otto III had given to the hermitage. Next day, neighbors, wondering at the absence of sound and signs of life, entered the house and found the five bodies; on November 13 they were reverently laid to rest, the monks in their own chapel and Christian, the lay brother, in the cloister outside. Later on, however, his relics were placed by the side of those whom he had served.

Bruno of Querfurt, the only survivor, gained his desire. In 1004, at Merseburg by the archbishop of Magdeburg, Tagino, he himself was consecrated archbishop for missionary service among the Slavs. From 1005 he was for a while with King Stephen of Hungary; then he was in Russia, in Kiev with Duke Vladimir. In 1007 he was teaching and ministering in Poland, with the aid of its Duke Boleslav. The archbishop was deeply troubled by the conflict between the Polish duke and King Henry of Germany; this was destroying, he felt, the vision of Christian fellowship among nations seen and held in mind by Otto III and Pope Sylvester. In the winter of 1007-8 this Bruno of Querfurt wrote a letter to the king which we still can read.

"Is it well," he pleads here, "O king, to war upon a Christian and to ally yourself with a pagan people? What has the Holy Lance in common with the banners of demons?" (Henry had sought support from heathen Slavs.) Then: "Were it not better to hold Boleslav of Poland as your friend, and with him to receive tribute from the heathen and bring them to the holy faith of Christ? Beware, O King, beware lest you do all things with power and none with mercy!

"Duke Boleslav now is hindered from helping me in my work by this war which you, an able and intelligent ruler, have forced upon him. He has no time, no power, to further my mission. The Slavs are worshippers of idols; and, yet, God cannot turn your heart, king though you are, to fight and conquer them in glorious battle for Christianity. Does not the Gospel bid us *compel* men to enter?"

In 1009 Bruno left Poland and went to try to convert the Prussians, as Adalbert, always his hero and ideal, had done. Like him, he found among them a martyr's death. With eighteen companions on March 9 of this year he fell before a pagan axe, and once again Boleslav of the Poles honored a martyr by burial in Poland.

To this Bruno of Querfurt we owe not only his *Life of Adalbert*, but a *Life of the Five Martyr Brothers*, written by him in 1008.

CHAPTER SEVEN

The Harvest in Religion

1

In the tenth century we have seen men dedicated to religion in Italy and in Slavonic lands; we shall consider here those who worked during these years to bring new life to monasteries and monks of France and Germany.

Invasion by the Northmen from Scandinavia during the ninth century, by Hungarians during the tenth, had left the monasteries of Western Europe in grievous disorder. Buildings had suffered robbery and ruin; communities had fled hither and thither, seeking refuge; property and income had been lost. Those abbeys which still survived had in many cases passed under the control of lay lords, granted to them by will and favor of their king. There they either declared themselves lay abbots or held the abbots proper and their communities in subjection, seizing monastic revenues. Monks, therefore, in many cloisters either lived in misery and want, or decided to break their vows and seek happier conditions in the world outside. In 909 a council of bishops, meeting at Trosly in the diocese of Soissons, France, heard the prevailing tragedy of religion summed up in these words:

"Concerning, not the standing, but the fall of our monasteries, what we ought to say, how to act, we really do not know. For the multitude of our crimes and the judgment coming upon us from the house of the Lord, our abbeys have been burned and destroyed by the heathen, plundered of their possessions, reduced almost to nothing. And if in some of them there seems still to remain a few traces of outward form, within them no customs of regular discipline now abide. Communities of monks or canons or nuns, they have no proper and lawful director in charge; against all authority of the Church they are subject to rulers who are not of their household, who come from the world without. Through poverty, through malice, and especially through this enormity of directors unfit to hold office, our religious are living in irregular manner, forgetful of their profession, occupied in worldly business. And more. In monasteries dedicated to God and holy Religion, lay abbots are living with their wives, their sons and their daughters, their armored guards and their dogs!"

Yet, as ever, the Catholic faith had still its witnesses. Among them was a young man, Berno, born to parents of noble rank in Burgundy of the mid-ninth century, who as he grew up felt within him a longing for religion, monastic religion in some real sense, different from that of the lax and dissolute monks or canons whom he saw or of whom he heard. Such discipline, he was told, was in practice at Autun, some sixty miles southwest of Dijon, in its abbey of Saint-Martin. To Autun he went, and there he stayed. There he learned, indeed, strictness of rule, learned it so well that he went out from Autun to found through his own resources a new monastery of St. Peter at Gigny in the Jura Mountains, near Lons-le-Saunier. At Gigny he was abbot, and from Gigny he went on to establish monastic custom with all zeal at the "little cell" of Baume-les-Messieurs in its neighborhood.

His enthusiasm found support from both the king of Burgundy, Rudolf I, and from the Holy See itself. Across the Alps he hastened to Rome, and in 894 he won from Pope Formosus acts of privilege for the communities of Gigny and of Baume: promise of papal protection from interference by anyone from outside, exemption from tax and tithing, and freedom for their monks upon his death to elect whom they would as their abbot.

The rule followed in Gigny and in Baume was austere; it came from two founders of monastic discipline, both of the name of Benedict. One, of course, was St. Benedict of Nursia in Italy, who, with the aid of earlier patterns of religious living, had given to the West its great Benedictine rule and had administered its course at Monte Cassino in the sixth century. The other was St. Benedict of Aniane, a monastery in Languedoc, southeastern France. He was friend and counselor of the Frankish emperor, Louis the Pious, who in his ninth century founded for Benedict's rule the abbey of Kornelimünster on the river Inde near Aachen. In and from this cloister Benedict endeavored with all diligence to govern monasteries of the empire in the West, on the basis of the rule of Monte

Cassino but with some changes, judged by him suitable for his time.

We learn of his monastic pattern from his biographer, Ardo, a monk who knew him well. Constant prayer, silence, and solitude, marked the hours of day and night, which held not only the full round of office from nocturns to compline, but also the *trina oratio,* the triple chanting of the fifteen gradual psalms. To these customs in regard to prayer were added others concerning clothing, food, travel, sleep, conversation. All monastic communities in the realm of Louis the Pious were ordered to follow this mode of life in common; one rule was to prevail.

To monks who had fallen into disrespect of discipline, the legislation drawn up by Benedict of Aniane, though confirmed and imposed at a council in Aachen during 817, was anything but welcome. It is not surprising that after his death in 821 his work also died away.

Berno, then, restored it in some degree at Gigny and Baume. His labor was immense and unending. But so was his energy; men in France began to take notice of the movement toward reform. Among them was William, duke of Aquitaine and count of Auvergne. He was a loyal member of the Church and he was wealthy; the hardships and the irregularities of monastic brethren had reached his ears, and his conscience was uneasy. At last he called Berno from Baume to his castle and opened to him his troubled mind. What could he do? Berno did not hesitate. "Give me your land of Cluny," he promptly answered, "and the buildings which stand upon it; with God's help I will see to the rest." The duke pulled a wry face; Cluny was his favorite hunting lodge. "Monks," said Berno, "are better than dogs; they can pray for your soul." The matter was settled.

On September 11, 910, Duke William signed at Bourges his charter of gift of Cluny, "eager to take thought for the salvation of his soul." "For love of God," he declared, "I hand over to the holy Apostles Peter and Paul from my own domain the estate of Cluny on the river Grosne, with its chapel of Saint Mary, Mother of God, and Saint Peter, and all pertaining to it: buildings, fields, meadows and vineyards, woods and streams, mills and all revenues, land cultivated and uncultivated, situated in the neighborhood of Mâcon."

There, in southern Burgundy, for the joy of hunting Duke William had often stayed in his "villa": a simple country chalet lying in a vale protected by hills both from winds and cold and from the world of men. Now Berno gathered in its rude enclosure those who willed to follow Benedictine rule. He himself was their abbot during the first years; after his death, election, as at Baume, was to be in their own hands. So Duke William had directed; to the see of holy Peter he had entrusted them for their protection and to it every five years they were to render ten pieces of gold. No man, however, neither lay noble nor bishop, was to invade their property of Cluny or to assume authority within their walls. Day by day they were to offer of their charity to the poor, of their hospitality to strangers and pilgrims.

Only twelve men, we are told by Rodulf (Raoul) Glaber, historian of France in the tenth century, came to Cluny as postulants in its earliest days. Seven years later, in 917, Ebbo I, founder of the noble House of Déols, close to Châteauroux on the river Indre in the province of Berry, gave to Cluny the abbey of Bourg-Dieu; his charter of gift almost exactly followed that of Duke William. Other monasteries were also yielded to Berno's direction as abbot; among them that of Saint-Martin, Massay, in the diocese of Bourges, capital of Berry, and, in 921, that of Saint-Pierre, Souvigny, in the same region.

The chapel of St. Peter still served the community at Cluny; but while Berno was abbot its monks were raising their own church (Cluny I).

The dates of tenure of abbacy in Cluny are variously given by our authorities, probably because a coadjutor or an "heir" was apt to be appointed by its first abbots. This they did, either because they were troubled by old age and sickness, or because they were anxious to maintain in constant, unfailing control the command over their abbey's members and resources: a hint of days to come. In 927 Berno died and was buried in Cluny's church behind its altar of Saint Benedict. During his last months he had written out his desire for his monks in his "Testament," leaving the direction of Gigny and Baume to his nephew Wido, and that of Cluny, Massay, and Bourg-Dieu (Déols) to Odo, one of the monks of Cluny since 910, trained at Baume.

2

From 927 until 942 under this second abbot, Odo, whose appointment received due approval from the community, Cluny rose gradually to power and influence both in and outside France. He was a man of determined will and wide view in regard to monastic reform.

John of Salerno, Italy, his friend and disciple in Cluny, wrote a *Life* of this father abbot; in spite of John's passion for digressions, visions, and all kinds of anecdotes, his almost total disregard of chronological order, we learn much from him concerning Cluny and other abbeys of the time.

Odo, like his predecessor, was the son of a man aristocratic by birth and education. Abbo was his name; he was distinguished in political circles of Aquitaine, his native land, and he was devoted to religion. In one of his stories John tells on the authority of Odo himself that his father once came very quietly into his nursery when he was a little child, lifted him from his bed and, holding him high, dedicated him for life to Saint Martin, "jewel among priests." The boy grew up strong and muscular, a joy to look upon. Abbo changed his mind in regard to this son's future years; perhaps he might, after all, serve the Lord as a soldier? Was not Saint Martin himself a soldier before he was consecrated bishop of Tours? So he sent Odo to learn the duties of a page in the household of William of Aquitaine and after some years saw him leave it, partly because of stubborn sickness, partly through longing for exercise of mind and spirit rather than of body. At nineteen this Odo was a cleric at Saint Martin's, Tours, then served by canons. There in the midst of many duties he found time for the reading which he loved, not only of books sacred and theological, but also of the secular and pagan. One day, as he sat absorbed in Virgil, a vision—so he often used to tell—rose before him, of a bowl, lovely in artistic form but full of venomous serpents within. There was death in heathen charm.

He turned from Virgil to study the Vulgate and the writings of the fathers of the Church; here he came upon the rule of Saint Benedict of Nursia and read that the monks of Monte Cassino slept all night in their clothes. For three years, according to John of Salerno, Odo lay in bed fully dressed night after night: "not yet a monk but bearing the mild monastic yoke."

From Tours he went to Paris, to grasp knowledge of philosophy and the liberal arts in eager discussion with the famous Carolingian scholar, Remigius of Auxerre, who died about 908. Back in Tours, his repute for learning encouraged his fellow canons to ask him to sum up in one volume the very lengthy lectures of Saint Gregory the Great on the Book of Job, known as his *Moralia;* naturally Odo replied with firmness that this was impossible for any man. Vehement argument followed on both sides, until at last the saint himself decided the matter; he appeared to Odo in a vision of the night, handed to him his own pen and told him to go ahead. So tradition has it. At any rate Odo's work is still ours to read, if we will, in thirty-five books, more than four hundred columns of the *Patrologia Latina.*

For the writer of this précis the result to be expected happened; he fell in love with the Benedictine rule followed by Gregory as monk and abbot. With a friend, Adhegrin, he set out from Tours to seek it, and found it in Burgundy, at Baume-les-Messieurs; there they both received the monastic habit. Adhegrin lived for three years at Baume, an anchorite in his cell; Odo was first a lay brother, then a priest of its community and head of its school.

The monks of Cluny at this time lived simply but in no extreme asceticism. They wore a woolen habit with sleeves and belt; over this they put a long sleeveless garment, the scapular, falling to the ankles and provided with a hood. A cloak for the shoulders, leggings, and shoes were added; in the winter stouter shoes were worn and gloves of sheepskin. Once a week, on Saturday, the brethren washed their shoes. Cleanliness was also encouraged by a double portion of clothing, for wash and wear.

In spring and summer, from Easter until Holy Cross Day, September 14, the monastery provided two meals daily: dinner at noon and *collatio,* a light supper, in the evening, shortly before bedtime. The same custom held its course throughout the year on Sundays and greater feasts. From September 14 until Easter only one meal appeared, in the early afternoon; on days of stricter fast it was postponed until the evening. Meat was forbidden, except for the sick; eggs and fish, cheese and vegetables grown in the monastery garden were served, not all on one day, but in varying succession, and in limited amounts; bread, however, could be had in plenty. There was also an allowance of wine.

Silence from talk was rarely broken, and only by express permission. Day and night, as prescribed by Benedictine rule, chanting of psalms and reading of lessons in the monastic hours went on; even during their working in the house or in its fields those who knew their psalms well were bidden to say them quietly. Manual labor, carried on regularly at Monte Cassino, found its own place among Cluniac monks of the tenth century. Yet, even at this early period of growth the transference of monks from household work to prayer and study was beginning. Schools were being formed for the instruction of boys and youths dedicated to the cloister; writing, of essays dealing with theological philosophy, of biography, and of verse came from Cluny's cells.

One of Odo's first acts as abbot was the dedication of its church, Cluny I; he also added to its buildings later on as need arose, for the care of the sick, of visitors, and of pilgrims.

Four matters of importance marked his rule. One was papal recognition and support. In 928 Pope John X commended Cluny to Raoul, king of France, ordering that property in Gigny, bestowed by Berno upon Cluny and seized by Wido as abbot of Gigny, should be at once restored. Three years later, in 931, John XI at Odo's petition confirmed for the monastery its liberty, properties, and privilege; in 938 Leo VII did the same "for the love of our sons, King Hugh and his son Lothar, who, as we have heard, hold this place in deep reverence and regard."

Second, Odo preached and practiced Benedictine precepts; John of Salerno relates many stories of his abbot's zeal. His kindness to the poor was unending. Constantly he gave a beggar twice as much as he asked; John, as prior, dared to tell him to his face that this extravagance was not fair to the community. "Silence!" snapped Odo, "you speak for your own undoing." Often, however, he pointed his rebuke with a tale. Charity, he said with pride and pleasure, found its reward for a young monk who in the dark of a winter's night on his way to matins saw a poor wretch lying half-naked at the church door and promptly stripped his own cloak from his shoulders. After matins, chilled to the bone, he crept into bed; suddenly he saw lying on the coverlet a gift of pure gold. "The blind and the lame of this world," Odo assured his sons in religion, "will in the hereafter be guardians of Paradise, and, if you thrust them from your doors, some day they may shut fast its gates against you!"

Feasting on meat he attacked with two terrible examples of monks who sinned while visiting their relatives—an indulgence allowed now and then in Cluny. One of these sinners ordered his family to serve him meat and wine; for years and years without end, he said, he had lived on fish and he was sick of it. The other cried: "No fish, but fowl for me!" And when his family said in astonishment: "Is fowl permitted you, Father?" he retorted: "Fowl is not flesh-meat; fowl and fish have the same origin and making, as our hymn declares!" Certainly, according to the first chapter of Genesis, God bade the waters bring forth abundantly on the same day both fish and fowl, and many from the sixth century onward cheerfully served chicken on days of abstinence. But Odo did not see the matter in this light; both of these erring brothers in his story died, choking as they ate.

John delighted in these anecdotes. "Our father," he wrote in his *Life* of Odo, "was full of joy, and sometimes he made us laugh aloud as we talked. Then he would remind us of holy Benedict's words: "It is the fool who lifts up his voice in laughter!"

The abbot was as keen on study and reading for his monks as he was on charity and fasting. There was one of them who spent most of his time in lamenting his sins; day and night he was praying the Lord for mercy and forgiveness. The quick eye of Odo noted this and he sent for him. "Why are you not at your work of teaching and learning with your brothers?" he asked. The monk confessed his misery and received a stern rebuke for such constant dwelling on his own small self.

The third labor of Odo was concerned with reform of monasteries in France and in Italy; for this purpose he was frequently on the road. Among these abbeys Fleury-sur-Loire in France cost him much struggle and effort; it was an ancient house, and in its church, so men believed, were lying the relics of Saint Benedict of Nursia himself, translated from Monte Cassino after a Lombard raid.

In the ninth century Fleury's monks had fled here and there before the Northmen, and when at length they had returned to their cloister, they found both it and their own life in hopeless confusion. For years this continued, as in so many other monasteries. At last, about 930, a lay noble of France, Count Elisiard, asked his king, then Raoul, for the gift of this unsettled house; he would try to bring it into due order. His petition was granted, and he begged Cluny's abbot to take it in charge. Odo could not refuse; together they set out for Fleury. Its community was in no mood for discipline; when they heard that Odo was arriving, they at once prepared to keep him out. Some of them, sword in hand, stood firmly in front of the abbey; others climbed to its roof, ready to hurl rocks and stones upon "this enemy." As Odo drew near he was met by determined denial: "To no one of another congregation is it permitted at any time to hold authority in this place." The abbot answered with all calm: "I have come in peace, hoping to offend no one, to hurt no one, but to change the disturbed into due form." For three days argument went to and fro, while Fleury's monks threatened to call upon King Raoul for protection, even to murder Odo outright if he did not at once depart. Throughout this attack Odo remained resolute. Directly he was sure that further talk would be of no use, he came toward the rebels, riding upon an ass, like the Christ entering Jerusalem. Behind him ran bishops and counts of his company, shouting: "Father, are you bent on death? Don't you see that they will kill you?"

The enemy could not face this courage; some of them had once known Odo as friend. They surrendered, and in their relief they received him now within their gates quietly enough.

So it happened elsewhere. Adelaide, the duchess of Burgundy, already in 929 had asked Odo to restore regular customs to the abbey of Romainmôtier in the Swiss canton of Vaud, near Vallorbe. Its church still holds work of the tenth century. On monasteries at Limoges, Sens, Clermont, and Tours his influence was soon at work, together with that of Saint-Géraud of Aurillac, where later on Gerbert was to learn his early lessons. Counts and dukes yielded to his ruling the houses of religion which they had held by feudal gift; communities of their own accord asked for his direction; bishops, priests, and laymen, noble and simple, came to live in Cluny or in one of the abbeys which Odo had reformed.

In 936 he was called to Rome, then in a state of crisis. Alberic, son of Marozia, was master of the city; Hugh, king of Italy and stepfather of Alberic, was besieging its walls. Pope John XI had recently died; his successor, Leo VII (936-39), summoned Odo in hope of peace. Odo came and did all that he could, "going back and forth, in and out of the city, trying to calm the fury of the king and to protect Rome from so dreadful an assault." But he does not seem to have won the success for which he labored. Liutprand of Cremona relates that King Hugh offered Alberic marriage with his daughter Alda in a false pretence of friendship; Alberic married her, but neither man ceased plotting and warring against the other.

Yet, in another undertaking Odo and Alberic worked together with better result. Hugh, abbot from 997 until 1038 of the monastery of Farfa in Sabine territory near Rome, wrote in his *Destructio Monasterii Farfensis:* "Alberic, glorious prince of the Romans, longed so greatly to restore the monasteries in his land to regular course, lost to them through Saracen invasion, that he called Odo to come to Italy for this purpose and made him archmandrite in rule over all the abbeys round about Rome. He gave Odo his own house on the Aventine for a cloister; it still stands there in honor of Saint Mary." Thus were reformed the monasteries of Saint Paul, of Saint Laurence, and of Saint Agnes-Outside-the-Walls, as well as Saint Benedict's abbey of Monte Cassino and many others.

These words make joyful reading; but we may perhaps question the title "Archmandrite" here.

Odo did all that he could to gain restoration for Farfa's abbey, but he was not able to make it endure; we learn from the same *Destruction of Farfa* that struggle was going on there before Odo became abbot of Cluny and that it continued long after he died.

The story of Farfa, then, also deserves a few words of detail. Toward the end of the ninth century it held as abbot one Peter: "in all kinds of wealth it had not its like in the realm of Italy, excepting only the monastery of Nonantula."

In their greed Saracen robbers swept down again and again to seize its stronghold. For seven years Peter and his monks bravely resisted; then in despair he was forced to bid them yield. He divided into three parts his community, and its few possessions in this barren time, then sent these divisions on their three different ways, to Rome, to Rieti, and to the county of Fermo. Farfa's treasure of high price he buried deep within its darkness; he left its buildings deserted and empty. At once the Saracens marched in. Barbarians though they were, they recognized with awe the power and beauty of their form and moulding; they did not destroy them. Their ruin was to come from Christian men, who one night, in dire need of shelter, crept inside and lighted a fire for their comfort. By accident it spread, and the trespassers left in panic; nothing was discovered until the flames were beyond control and Farfa's abbey was a wreck.

Years later, when Peter was dead, one of his successors as abbot led some of the monks back again. Between 930 and 936 under his direction they rebuilt and furnished the house.

As at Fleury, here also disorder of matter had bred disorder of mind and soul. Evil was hard at work in the reconsecrated monastery. Before long two of its members, Campo and Hildebrand, ambitious for power, longing for comfort and release from control, decided to dare all, even death. They offered their abbot the cup of fellowship; in the cup was poison and joyfully they saw him die. Amid the tumult which followed they made themselves masters of the abbey, of its dependencies and its revenues; henceforward they lived in luxury, in dissipation and in vice, with companions whom they chose, with women on whom they lavished gifts from their spoils.

This to Alberic was unbearable, and he descended upon Farfa with a heavy hand. He sent there men whom he could trust to order stern reform, and the rebels nearly murdered them one night as they lay asleep in bed. In rage at this insult and crime Alberic raised a force, drove Campo from the abbey and gave it to the rule of one named Dagibert. The date of this upheaval was about 947. Campo took refuge at Rieti; Hildebrand, conveniently absent, found delight from this moment in robbing monasteries, homes over which Alberic had no power of control.

For five years Dagibert survived, fighting to establish order in Farfa. Then its monks killed him, too, by poison. Alberic died; abbot succeeded abbot, and each one failed to rule, leaving his community in disorder. Robbery, indulgence, luxury, taking of wives by "monks" who spent most of their time in absences from the cloister, decay of Farfa's buildings, lack of postulants—these were the steps which led down to the abbey's destruction. It was not until later, in the eleventh century, that Italy and Otto III saw Farfa rising in Cluniac practice, in regular custom under that Abbot Hugh who told the story of its ruin. All the years of his abbacy Hugh sorrowed bitterly over that sin of simony which had brought him his sacred office; but he united reform at Farfa with his repentance.

We return to earlier years and to Odo, abbot of Cluny. In 939 he was on another visit to Italy, once more called to try to make peace between Alberic and King Hugh. A third journey is mentioned by Flodoard in his annals against the year 942; it was prompted by the same trouble. In the autumn on his way back Odo was seized by serious illness and lay helpless for a while at Tours. There on the Octave of Martinmas he died, and was buried in its abbey of Saint-Julien, a monastery which he himself had reformed.

The fourth picture of Odo shows him as a writer of books. We have already seen him summing up at Tours the *Morals* of Saint Gregory the Great. While he was at Baume, the bishop of Limoges, Turpio, who ordained him priest, had asked him to put together from patristic teaching a treatise which might bring comfort to the many men distressed and bewildered by evil in France and Germany under Charles the Simple and Louis the Child. After long hesitation he had produced two books; then request had been made for a third. Thus we possess, in nearly one hundred and twenty columns of Migne's *Patrologia*, his work called *Collationes*, "Conferences," a name borrowed from Cassian.

More interesting are seven books of hexameter verse, written by him under the name of *Occupatio* when he was abbot of Cluny. From the first book, which deals with the creation and the fall of the angels, the work goes on to tell of the creation and the fall of Man, of his expulsion from paradise, of the growth of wickedness in the world, of the flood, of Sodom and Gomorrha, and of Man's corrupted nature. The patriarchs of the Old Testament then appear, and the prophecy of redemption to come. In the fifth book one reads of Christ Incarnate upon earth; in the sixth of His Passion, Resurrection and Ascension, of the growth of the Christian Church. The seventh book gives a meaning to the whole narrative. The end of our world is approaching, and it is foul with sin: with pride, selfishness, simony, avarice, immorality. Indeed, Odo urges, it is high time for those deep in slumber to awake, before grace is no longer theirs to gain.

Now and then the poem rises to vividness of description, as its editor, Antonius Swoboda, has remarked. There are Adam and Eve, living in the joy of innocence; no fear, no anxiety do they know, but happiness fills all. There is Adam in the misery of exile, toiling to plough the earth, now persevering amid his tears, now sitting down in despair as he thinks of the troubled future which awaits his children. But his deepest anguish lies in the loss of the sense of the presence of God:

> To know God, to hold Him, this is in sum the highest good,
> To lose Him, than that there can in truth be nothing worse.

So, Odo bids, let each man, while still he may, make it his work, his occupation, both to know and to use well whatever power he has, committing himself and his talent to the Christ and to His holy Mother.

We have a second *Life* of this Odo of Cluny, written in the twelfth century by Nalgod, one of Cluny's monks, at the prayer of his brethren that he revise and bring some order into John's confused ramblings. His work is far more brief and does show respect for chronology; it adds practically nothing to our knowledge.

3

The third abbot of Cluny was Aymard, who held office from 942 until 954. Saint Odilo, Cluny's abbot long afterward, wrote of him as "a son of blessed simplicity and innocence." He by no means had the keenness and spirit of enterprise which had marked Odo in matters spiritual and intellectual; comparatively few monasteries were re-formed under his direction. But, as Odilo acknowledged, he did much in business temporal and economic to increase material bless-ings for his community, especially by acquisition of land. Through his devotion to Benedictine rule he won the support of two kings for the abbey: Conrad the Peaceful, king in Burgundy, and Louis IV, d'Outremer, king in France. In 949 at his petition Pope Agapetus II confirmed Cluny's privileges of tenure, of papal protection, and aid.

After twelve years of administration Aymard's sight failed; then with all humility and goodwill he gave Majolus, one of his monks, responsibility for Cluny's directing. Majolus was Cluny's abbot for forty years, from 954 until 994. Of him we also have two *Lives*. One, written by Syrus, monk of Cluny, after the death of Majolus, is a tale swollen into three books by bursts of praise, stories of miracles, leg-end, and verse; it yields, nevertheless, a good deal of authentic in-formation. Abridgments of the work were made by Adelbald, a monk of Lérins, and by the Nalgod who cut down John's *Life* of Odo.

The other *Life* of Majolus came from Odilo, his successor as abbot; in a preface he told of the thought which induced him to be-gin its work. On a night in 1033 he was lying in bed at the abbey of Romainmôtier, deeply worried by the troubles of his time and un-able to sleep. It was the eve of the solemn commemoration of Ma-jolus and to him he sent a prayer for help. Then there came to him many memories and he decided to write them down; they might give some guidance to men bewildered by the eleventh century's turmoil. His narrative, however, like that of Syrus, dwells far too long on the virtue of its subject.

Majolus was born about 910 in Provence of distinguished and noble parentage on either side. He received an excellent education and all care from both father and mother; but both died while he was still young, leaving him an ample heritage. Neither land nor money was of interest to his mind; he wanted to study and to work for the Church. Off he went to Mâcon in Burgundy, where he was ordained priest, taught for a while, and was appointed archdeacon. He spent some time in reading philosophy at Lyon, famous for its school. Back at Mâcon, he worked for its people until 943, under constant terror of the Saracens; there, so Syrus states, he received a call to consecration as bishop of Besançon.

Again his thoughts were tending in another direction. As we know, Mâcon was near Cluny, and often he had visited its monks; the vision of monastic reform in France and Italy, as carried out by

Odo, strongly appealed to him. He entered the cloister; in time he was bound to it by vows of profession; then he went forth to do all in his power.

In 949 we find him in Rome, very probably sent there by Abbot Aymard to obtain that privilege for Cluny from Pope Agapetus II. On the return journey one of his companions fell sick and after three days of illness was healed by Majolus' ministry; the news immensely increased Cluny's respect for this brother-priest. His work for sick souls was to bring him even higher honor: "If he did not raise men from the dead," wrote Odilo in his *Life* of Majolus, "there are other miracles, more powerful, more famous, brought to pass through him by the Lord. The restoring of souls to eternal life is a far greater and more splendid thing than the raising of bodies which will return to the bitterness and the perils of existence on this earth."

Under its fourth abbot, Cluny rose yet higher in range of influence and power. In France, King Lothair, son of Louis d'Outremer, and, later on, King Hugh of the House of Capet, with his brother Henry, duke of Burgundy, all gave support; so, in Burgundy of the Jura, did King Conrad and his wife Matilda. In Germany, Otto the Great, his empress, Adelaide, and her mother, Bertha, delighted in the friendship of Majolus. During this Otto's reign Pope John XIII wrote to the bishops of France, ordering them to protect Cluny under Abbot Majolus, to excommunicate with all severity any who should attempt impious interference. Otto the Second in 974, after the murder of Pope Benedict VI, earnestly asked Majolus to follow him in the Holy See, and met with refusal. So, at least, we are told. The pope elected was Benedict VII; in 978 he donated to Cluny the island of Lérins off the Mediterranean coast near Cannes.

Indirectly and by accident Majolus did much for France. As he was on his way home to Cluny from Rome in July 972, Saracen robbers from Garde-Freinet in Provence fell upon his escort to kill and to capture; the abbot himself, as chief prize, was held for ransom. When his monks at Cluny heard of this, in their horror they quickly sent the sum demanded, a huge amount. Majolus, then, was set free; but the nobles of Provence could bear robbery and murder no longer. Led by Count William, in 973 they attacked and destroyed Saracen headquarters at Garde-Freinet; at last their land rested from its fear.

Reform was also set on foot by him for abbeys in France and in Italy. Among those of France were Marmoutier, Saint-Pierre at Sens, Saint-

Germain at Auxerre, Saint-Denis on the outskirts of Paris. In Italy he brought new order to the monastery of Saint Paul, once reformed by Odo, now again fallen into negligence, to Ravenna's abbey of Sant'Apollinare in Classe which Otto III was to know so well, and to that of San Pietro in Ciel d'Oro of Pavia.

Nor should we forget the connection of Majolus with that famous reformer of the eleventh century, Saint William of Dijon, who lived from 962 until 1031. It was Majolus who gave him his life's ambition. William was born at a castle near Novara, north Italy; it stood in the center of the lake of San Giuglio, and within it at this time were not only his parents but also Willa, wife of Berengar II, king of Italy. All were under siege by order of Otto I, lately crowned emperor of the West and determined to make the realm of Lombard Italy his own. Soon all surrendered, and the imperial conqueror graciously consented to name the baby; his empress, Adelaide, was godmother at William's baptism.

We learn these details from Rodulf Glaber, who knew William well and was to write his *Life*. The child grew up in a religious house near Vercelli; there he was professed as monk and there he heard of Cluny. He longed to visit this famous abbey, and about 987 his longing found content. Cluny's Abbot Majolus came to visit William's monastery, and when he left it, he took the young monk with him to France; William was then about twenty-five years of age. Majolus quickly recognized his promise of genius; in 988 he ordered him to go with some of Cluny's brethren to the abbey of Saint-Saturnin, on the Rhône near Avignon, for its restoring to regular custom. The work prospered, and when Bruno, bishop of Langres, asked Majolus to undertake reform at Dijon in its house of Saint-Bénigne, William in 989 was sent there for the purpose. In 990 the same Bruno gave him office both as priest and as abbot of Saint-Bénigne.

From that time life, spiritual, intellectual, and artistic, rose to all energy in this monastery of Dijon. A school was founded; a new church, Romanesque in architecture, was built and became the wonder of France. From Dijon reform under Abbot William's direction spread far and wide, in Burgundy, in Lotharingia, in Italy; Rodulf Glaber declared in the third book of his *Histories* that "through renewing of churches the whole world glowed with light."

Lastly, one thinks of the growth of architecture at Cluny. During the tenure of Abbot Aymard decision had been made to raise another church for the abbey, Cluny II; under Abbot Majolus it was built, and in 981 it received dedication.

In the spring of 994 Majolus was again traveling. He was now old and frail, but his king, Hugh Capet, had begged him to revive Benedictine life in the abbey of Saint-Denis. On his way he remained a while with the monks of Souvigny, near Moulins. Illness, sudden and severe, fell upon him as he was leaving them; soon, with the words: *Domine, dilexi decorem domus tuae et locum habitationis gloriae tuae:* "Lord, I have loved the beauty of thy house, and the place where thy glory dwelleth," with his hand raised in blessing, he died in peace. It was the eleventh of May. Saint Odilo, now following him as abbot, held that in serenity and charm, in grace of every movement, in dignity and noble bearing, "Majolus was the most beautiful of all mortal men."

In the time of Odo and Majolus the abbeys which came under their direction might, indeed, be made priories or cells of Cluny; yet influence rather than subjection was their aim. It was during the eleventh century that a decisive change was taking place under the rule of Saint Odilo, who held this rule until 1049; it reached maturity under Saint Hugh, abbot from 1049 until 1109. Then Cluny's abbot gradually became the ruling power over its houses of every degree, bound together in one body, looking for direction to Cluny, receiving authority from its head.

Centralization of Cluniac abbeys did not develop unopposed. Abbo, head of Fleury's monastery from 998 onwards, wrote, courteously enough, to Odilo himself, "Father of Cluniac monks": "On a journey to the Basque country I happened to call at the abbey of Saint Cyprian on the outskirts of Poitiers. I found it subject to your authority, though I believed it ours." There follows a protest concerning resentful talk, current against monks. None, however, felt more resentment than bishops of France, and of all perhaps the most bitter was that Ascelin, or Adalbero, who was bishop of Laon from 977 to 1030. Early in the eleventh century he poured out his grievance in satiric verse addressed to Robert II, the Pious, his king. Did not Robert, he charged, prefer as bishops Cluniac monks? Was he not working for Cluny? And was not Odilo "king" of Cluny's martial host?

l. 145: "A thousand thousand monks are on the march";
l. 156: "Odilo, head of his army, sends us now to thee;
l. 157: his warrior line salutes thee, Lord of monks";
l. 171: "How changed is churchly order in thy realm!"

The name of Abbot Odilo reminds us of his *Life* of the Empress Adelaide, second wife of Otto the Great, mother of Otto the Second, grandmother of Otto the Third, and, with her daughter-in-law, Theophano, active in governing the realm of Germany.

How did these two women regard each other and their common responsibility? What do we know about the relationship between this Lady Adelaide and her royal son and grandson?

The elder empress, as described, and truly, by Odilo, her fervent admirer and friend, was a woman ever busy in works of charity for all whom she found in want, continually building or endowing churches and abbeys through her own resources or, during her regency, through those of the royal and national chest. She was not only intensely devout; she was given to intense emotion, a woman of firm will, whose generosity, we may think, sometimes conquered her discretion and skill in matters political.

Theophano, the daughter-in-law who owed to her respect and submission, had not only received intellectual training from her childhood but was marked by an extraordinary quickness to understand, control, and manage men and affairs of government, of diplomatic intrigue and correspondence. She had the advantage of experience both Byzantine and German; she was excellently educated, a lover of the beautiful and the luxurious, of her world and of her Church.

Naturally the two Empresses found it hard to work together for their kingdom and empire; of course Odilo's sympathy was with Adelaide. Evil tongues, he declares, sowed discord between her and her two nearest kin, Theophano and the second Otto, her own son; she suffered in all patience until at last, unable to bear the trial, with dignity she retired from the court (to Germany's sorrow, Odilo adds) and went to live with her brother, Conrad the Peaceful, in Burgundy. Two years later Odilo pictures this Otto crushed in penitence, sending envoys to Conrad and to Majolus, abbot of Cluny, begging their aid in reconciling him with his mother. This happy event came about at Pavia in December 980 when the Empress Adelaide "generously forgave him."

In 991, however, when both empresses were at work on the boy king, Otto III, eleven years old, we find Theophano in Abbot Odilo's story declaring: "If I live out another year, Adelaide shall *not* dominate this whole world!" Four weeks after this foolish outburst, Odilo continues, Theophano was in truth dead. Henceforward all was well: "This third Otto was entirely correct in his bearing toward his Regent grandmother; and so by her merits and diligence he gained Imperial rule as Emperor of Rome." We know that he wrote in warm appreciation to thank her for all that she had done for him.

Nevertheless, Thietmar in his Chronicle tells that in the same year, 991, which saw his mother's death the Empress Adelaide went to Otto's side to comfort him by sharing his sorrow. With motherly care she stayed with him, so long that "led astray by advice from his bad young friends, he told her to depart; and sorrowfully she did."

4

The second great rising of monastic reform in the tenth century was seen in the region of the Meuse, the Moselle, and the Rhine: that is, in Flanders and in Lower and Upper Lotharingia. It was prompted in part by two lay nobles: Gilbert, duke of Lotharingia, and Arnulf, count of Flanders; it was encouraged by bishops; it was put into action by two monks: Gerard of Brogne and John of Gorze.

This movement shared in common with Cluny customs of prayer, normal in religion; ascetic practice; love of culture, of writing and study. It, also, sprang from the miseries within and without which marked the ninth and the tenth centuries, together with a deep realization of the degraded state of abbeys held under lay tenure.

Yet, it is important to note that the movement was in its rise wholly independent of Cluniac working, and was so regarded by those in secular authority, whether emperor, king, duke, or count. Its aims, the point of view of its leaders, were very different from those of Cluny. It held no controlling impulse toward one body, one head, one way of monastic life.

Second, while Cluny and its dependencies from the beginning gained freedom from external authority, secular and episcopal, the monks of Lotharingia were guided and assisted by their bishops; these bishops had frequently been pupils in monastic schools and therefore looked with affection upon their former teachers. Many daughter-houses of Gorze in Germany, moreover, were "royal" abbeys, under the authority of their king, Otto, in regard to their secular affairs. Others looked to some duke or lesser noble of the land as their lord and patron so far as the things of this world were concerned. In either case the royal or noble patron held the right to appoint a steward charged by him to superintend and carry out the financial and economic business of the abbey or abbeys under his special protection.

Third, Lotharingian reform rose from the need of individual men, longing for solitude, for life far from the turmoil of the world, even while they held it good to share this life in common as cenobites. The current of ascetic ideal ran far deeper here on the whole than in Cluniac monasteries.

In Belgium, near Namur, there is a little town, now Saint-Gérard, once called Brogne, on the edge of the forest of Marlagne. Upon its site once lay a country estate belonging to a young man, Gerard, marked not only by wealth but by a keen desire to share it with others. On this land of his he built a small chapel and clergy house, dedicated to St. Peter; for their service he gathered priests of canonical but not monastic calling. It was about the year 914; Europe was distracted by Hungarian invasion.

In spite of difficulties in travel, Gerard eventually decided that he must set forth to seek some blessed relic of a saint for the honor of his chapel. At the abbey of Saint-Denis to his delight he was given a treasure: the bones in almost perfect preservation of Eugenius, a holy man of Toledo, Spain. From the bishop of Liège he obtained necessary permission to keep his prize, and with much ceremony he saw it deposited at Brogne. About 919 a monastery was rising there. As years went on Benedictine monks replaced canons; Gerard, himself dedicated to the life of religion, became their abbot.

For a while in Brogne he was happy and content, in round of prayer, in solitude, in contemplation. But not for all time. The repute of Brogne's abbot had spread; during 934 at a meeting in Dinant on the Meuse, Gilbert, duke of Lotharingia, pleaded for his help. One of a number of monasteries held by him as lay owner was in great need of reform; it was now a house of canons, and they were living in reckless disorder and negligence. Ambitious and disloyal to secular government Gilbert certainly was, but he meant to have due order in his own possessions and he revered his Church. This particular monastery had been founded in the seventh century by Ghislain, a hermit of the forest land in Hainaut; there, at Ursidongue, "the bear's den," he had prayed and tended his community, and there after his death he was revered as saint.

Gerard could but consent; he brought this abbey of Saint-Ghislain into regular discipline and made it a house under Benedictine rule.

During the years 937-44, by request of Arnulf, count of Flanders, Gerard was doing even more important work in two abbeys of Ghent: one, of Saint-Bavon, at the meeting of the river Escaut with the Lys, the other, of Saint-Pierre, on the Mont-Blandin.

Missionary campaign, also of the seventh century, had been carried on in the region of the Escaut, Scarpe, and Lys, by a bishop born in France, known in the tenth century as Saint Amand. It was he who had founded in Ghent its house of religion dedicated to St. Peter. The abbey of Saint Bavon was in all probability not of his making; but Bavon, once a sinner of dissolute life, then a saint, had left to it his renown for holiness and his name. He had been converted by Amand and was one of his most fervent disciples.

In both cloisters Amand had gathered Benedictine monks; but while the years rolled on, monks had gradually given place to canons, abbots to lay owners, and thus both communities became highly irregular in their way of living. Early in the ninth century the Emperor Louis the Pious had handed them over, with their revenues and properties, to his friend and counselor, Einhard, and Einhard, lay abbot though he was, had treated his canons well in material matters. Then the Scandinavian pirates had descended to raid and rob; for many years the brethren were either fugitives from their home or were living wretchedly within desolate walls.

At last Count Arnulf, their patron in the tenth century, "awoke from sleep," as he himself confessed, and realized that something must done. It was a bishop, Transmar, ruler of the see of Noyon-Tournai from 937 until 951, who begged him to put into proper working the abbey of Saint-Bavon. In 937 its reform was begun, and in 941 Arnulf declared his resolution to restore Benedictine customs and decent living to that of St. Peter.

At Ghent Gerard, then, was busy from 937 until 944. That year found him in northern France, in the Pas-de-Calais, a region held in possession by the counts of Flanders; Arnulf had again sought his aid, this time for his abbey of Saint-Bertin. About the beginning of the eighth century Bertin, a native of France, had been abbot of this house, then called by the name of Sithiu; in the tenth century it bore his own. Here Gerard met rebellion, fierce and persistent; the monastery still held monks, but they would not obey their rule. At last he was forced to send them away and to call others in their place; then from St. Peter's, Ghent, he called its monk Womar for their direction.

Some years later Womar returned to Ghent, and Gerard, also, returned to lead his communities at Ghent and at Brogne. He had given the care of Saint-Bertin to his nephew, Wido.

From this time the history of this abbey is somewhat tragic.

Wido was young, inclined to make light of things; soon he was deposed from the abbot's chair and Count Arnulf asked that a nephew of his own, Hildebrand, might be appointed. Until 954 all went well; then Arnulf declared his need of this skilled and efficient Hildebrand for reform elsewhere, and he was replaced by one Regenold. Conscientious and diligent Regenold certainly was, but the brethren of Saint-Bertin cared little for him; they were not sorry when in 961 he was struck by leprosy and forced to resign. To their great satisfaction Hildebrand was recalled.

Eight years before, in 953, Gerard had retired from his abbacy in Ghent to live and work in Brogne; there he had died on October 3, 959. Never did he try in any way to make either himself as abbot, or Brogne as abbey, head or center of the monasteries which he reformed.

We learn of John of Gorze, of his efforts and adventures in trying to become a monk, and of the monastery which he and his companions founded in Upper Lotharingia, from his *Life*, written, though not finished, by John, abbot of the Lotharingian house of Saint-Arnoul at Metz.

He was born at Vandières, a village on the Meuse near both Metz and Toul. His parents were of middle class in social rank but of substantial means, and his early lessons came from his father, who was devoted to this son, one of three. Later, in school at Metz, he learned little. His idle ways, however, soon ended; he was still in his teens when his father died and his mother, much younger than her husband, promptly married again. The man of her choice cared little for his stepsons, and John found himself working hard in the fields to provide for their home.

Religion was already active in his life. He obtained employment on the side as caretaker of St. Peter's church at Metz and of others in the region of Toul; Berner, a deacon of Toul, taught him a little theology, a little grammar from Donatus. But it was a young girl, a student in Metz, who first opened his eyes to the ascetic life in practice; by accident he learned that she was wearing a hair shirt. "What on earth is that horrid thing?" he asked. "Don't you know," was her quick reply, "that we shouldn't live for this world and its vanities?"

John thought this over very seriously. Should a faithful but frail Christian woman be able to do more in denial of comfort than a strong Christian man?

He set to work, reading sermons, annals of saints, church history, missals; he listened to monastic office in one or another abbey; he began to think of monastic life for himself. But where in his present world was the kind of religious community which he saw in his reading? Wherever he looked—the time was early in the tenth century—he could find none in his neighborhood that resembled it. Other young men joined him in his search; especially Rotland, head of the School of Chant in St. Stephen's, Metz, and Warinbert, a priest of St. Saviour's in the same city.

Then it occurred to him that solitude might do more for his desire than talking with friends. He heard of one Humbert, said to be living a saintly life as hermit at Verdun. With him he spent a few days, then went off to find another solitary in the forest of the Argonne. His name was Lambert, and he was nearly killing himself by starvation. John, indeed, admired that; but the holy man was so ignorant, so uncouth! Did a monk have to be uneducated, un-civilized? This Lambert was practically naked; one measure of meat, with a few vegetables soaked in water, lasted him for a month or more and often he fasted for days at a time. Kindly people sought John out, bringing gifts; they said he was a fool to stay with that madman. Why not go as pilgrim to Rome and learn sense from those who really understood monastic customs?

John went, with Warinbert and a friend of his, Bernacer. The journey was long and difficult; but they reached Italy and visited famous places: the sanctuary of St. Michael the Archangel at Monte Gargano, and Monte Cassino, with its abbey of St. Benedict.

Back again and settled to ponder his experiences, he met one who was to influence all his future: Einold, archdeacon of Toul. Einold for three years had been trying out his own vocation, enclosed in a cell built into the wall of Toul's cathedral; his bishop, Gozlin, in sympathy was supplying his few needs. Finally he had left Toul to find deeper quiet with Humbert of Verdun in a lonely spot across the river Moselle. Humbert told Einold about John of Vandières, and the three discussed in all earnestness their problem; so often that at last it reached the ears of Adalbero I, bishop of Metz from 929 to 962. Adalbero was concerned far more with politics than with ascetic life, but he did feel interest in these undaunted seekers after religion. He called in the provost of his cathedral and asked him if he could think of any site suitable for a cloister. As they talked, Lambert, the provost, mentioned Gorze, near Metz, and the name brought a vivid memory to this bishop. Gorze lay in the vale of a little river from which it drew its name; it was a place of silence, remote from the world, and Nature had given it beauty and charm. Adalbero had visited it long before, for it held the shrine of Gorgonius, a saint of the fourth century; monks in time past had served it well and pilgrims had flocked there to pray. But when Adalbero saw it he was struck by horror and pity; the abbey was run down and filthy; animals had polluted its sanctuary, and it held a mere scattering of monks, ragged, hungry, and miserable. Then and there Adalbero knelt to vow that if ever he were called to minister in the diocese he would rescue Gorze from its dishonoring.

It was now possessed by yet a third Lambert—Saint Lambert of the seventh century was patron of Liège in the tenth, and his name was frequently given by parents to their sons. This third Lambert was a man of fierce and grasping temper; he held Gorze in feudal tenure, granted by Adalbero himself. Bernacer begged for its transfer, and, thus entreated, Adalbero remembered his vow; with all confidence he faced Lambert's wrath and gained from him Gorze for Einold and his friends.

Then, when Henry the Fowler was ruling Lotharingia, in 933, Einold, John, and Bernacer, with five others, began to restore its abbey and their own new life within it. Adalbero received them into monastic enclosure; Einold was elected abbot, and the others promised to follow him in his administration of Benedictine rule. John's mother came to live near them, to care for food and household; gradually men, more and more of them, came to enlarge the community.

During the same year, 933, this same bishop gave them their charter of foundation, which bore record of the abbey's original founding by Chrodegang, bishop of Metz from 742 until 766. It restored to Gorze all the properties which Adalbero could offer; some part, however, was under dispute of ownership and much was in poor condition. At first these novices and their abbot fared badly enough, and John, who was made cellarer and provider of daily meals, had a difficult time.

But a long effort gained its reward. Bishops, of Trier, Toul, and Liège, in days to come called from Gorze monks to reform other centers of religion: Saint-Maximin, Trier; Saint-Èvre, Toul; Saint-Arnoul, Metz; Moyenmoutier in the Vosges; Stavelot-Malmedy in the Ardennes. At Gorze was trained the Irish-Scottish Maccalan who was to become abbot of Waulsort in Dinant on the Meuse where Duke Gilbert had once pleaded with Gerard of Brogne.

In 960 John succeeded Einold as abbot; the work of these two leaders, one after another, lasted more than forty years, from 933 until 974. Sigebert of Gembloux, in writing of Guibert, monk at Gorze, describes its influence in these words: "No man believed that he had caught the first touch of conversion to monastic life, had he not received initiation at Gorze. Here was milk for the suckling babe, solid bread for the mature."

CHAPTER EIGHT

The Harvest in Verse

1

THREE POINTS of interest may be noted here. First: verse of the ninth century passes into that of the tenth, of the tenth into that of the eleventh, and often critics have disputed the dates of poems; Second: in regard to external form, secular poetry is found now and then in a form usually associated with the religious and liturgical; Third: poetry in the tenth century pays its own tribute to the men and the events of its age.

We begin with religious verse; and, therefore, as basis for its writing in the tenth century we will look first at the community of Saint-Gall in Swabia, famous for learning and for literature. During the eight hundreds its abbots Grimald and Hartmut were training a native of Swabia itself, young Notker "the Stammerer," whose years were to run from about 840 to 912. The later ninth century found in him a great teacher and a poet, exchanging his views on verse and art of various kinds not only with his friends Ratpert and Tutilo but also with his pupils, Salamo the Third and Salamo's brother Waldo. We still have letters and poems sent to and fro by the teacher and these two brothers whom he was trying to drive along the path of religion and hard study. They were aristocratic in descent; both their great-uncle (Salamo I) and their uncle (Salamo II) were bishops of Constance, and Notker was ambitious for their future. When at last they left Saint-Gall for visits to friends in palace or court, ecclesiastic or secular, he continued his urging.

He wrote in eager Latin prose to beg them to follow discipline rather than indulge in foolhardy experiment. So long they had been nourished by the solid food of his instruction! Yet, though they were now of mature age, they were still not masters of grammar and rhetoric, not at home in geography, astronomy, or problems of the

law and prophets! "Away with this sloth; make ready your questions!
Otherwise I shall neither write nor aid you any more until I goad you
into answering me. I beseech you, by our affection of old, pay heed
to your books, that your kinsfolk may see you ordained priests and
you may minister in God's service before all the multitude of
people! . . . Return now to the monastery if you want me as your
friend. If you don't, well, then go off to see the land you will inherit;
divide it up with your kindred; get you to farming; build houses; go
hunting! But should you care to see Saint-Gall and me, know that I
have no greater joy than to serve you; I pray for you always more
than myself. O! if only I might see you both!"

In 884 Salamo III was ordained deacon; the following year his name
appeared as acting chancellor at the court of Charles the Fat. But he
did not stay there long. He knew quite well that Charles was
doomed, and he had his own ambition. It was not that which Notker
had in mind for him: a life devoted to prayer, ministry to other men,
and study. He did, indeed, desire monastic profession in Saint-Gall;
but it was because he hoped, thanks to his own ability and the
reputation of his relatives, that he would one day reach a high place
in Church and state as bishop of Constance.

Soon he was a priest, and Notker was writing verse to him, in a
prayer that he keep his soul free from evil. The hands which touched
holy things, the eyes which looked toward Heaven, the tongue which
sang of God, the ears which listened to words so solemn, the nose
which breathed in the air of eternity, they must not suffer defilement
of this world.

At length sorrow came upon this earnest counselor, and Notker
was writing his verse to beg Salamo to return to Saint-Gall:

> Brother, remember now the brother of thy heart,
>   Come back, if now thou canst; I long for thee.
> Dost thou refuse? Against thy will thou shalt be drawn,
>   And forced desire shall forfeit its reward.
> Art thou unwilling? Neither the raging Rhine
>   Nor wave-tossed shore nor forest's shuddering depths
> Shall call thee back from me; follow I will throughout
>   To bind thee fast with rope, thou runaway.
> Awake and watching, conquering night and day alike,
>   I taught thee, with no thought of drink or food.

All things I laid aside to serve thine own desire;
   Now I am scorned, another is thy friend!
Yet wheresoe'er thou goest, by whatsoever chance,
   May God go with thee, blessing all thy days.

Salamo, also, was a poet and in the tenth century, as we shall see hereafter. Meanwhile fortune was with him. Just at this time Charles the Fat was deposed in favor of Arnulf. Charles had been king of Swabia before he became king of Germany and emperor; the monks of Saint-Gall, then, held him in deep honor and affection and this deposing of their patron aroused serious discontent. Their abbot even made himself a party to revolt against Arnulf. The new king promptly retaliated in 890 by driving him from office; Saint-Gall was a royal monastery under the protection and the will of the German crown. On the other hand, Salamo had speedily offered support to Arnulf; the same year saw him not only abbot of Saint-Gall but bishop of Constance as well.

His future career only needs a few words here. As we have seen, he fought for political power of the Church as opposed to the rising domination of secular "dukes" in the various German lands. From 909 onward under Louis the Child, and under Conrad I until 918, he was chancellor of Germany. Upon the death of King Conrad he lost his holding of political authority; in January 920 he died.

Another of Notker's pupils was Hartman, who was to be abbot of Saint-Gall after Salamo's death. To him, also, Notker sent lines of poetry, bidding him tell in verse of the life of Gall, the abbey's founder and patron:

Sing thou the deeds of blessed Gall,
Sing and make dulcet melody,
Himself Christ lays on thee this task,
   Seize it with joy.

Should weariness cause thee to slip,
Quickly I speed, quickly to aid.
Thy youthful feet myself will guide
   In modest way.

Later on, Notker writes again:

Dear son, why silent lies thy tongue,
Nor speeds with joy its praise of Gall,
His life and wealth made thee true man,
   Was it in vain?

> What use to spend, bent over books,
> The little space of our short life,
> To break and mortify one's health,
>   And nothing dare?

And Hartman answers:

> A mighty bull thou longest
> To yoke with tender calf,
> And mellow wine to flavor
> With vintage rarely new!

Nevertheless, he carried out his task, and we still have part of a *Life* of Gall, written as dialogue between Notker, Ratpert, and young Hartman.

More important, however, for us is Notker's connection with the history of the sequence, and for this we must go back to his own younger years. The "prose" or "sequence" was a kind of hymn, but not a hymn proper. It was sung after the gradual and the alleluia, between the epistle and the gospel at Masses of the Church, except on days of fast and penitence. Originally the final *a* of the alleluia was prolonged in a melody of music, the jubilus; as time went on, words were set in keeping with this melody, and the "prose" was born.

The place and date of the rise of this "prose" or sequence in Western Europe has been widely discussed and disputed. Had Amalar of Metz, who did his work on the ritual of the Mass and offices of the Church from about 823 to 833, knowledge of its development? We do not know. Wolfram von den Steinen places its birth at the earliest about 830, and its first growth in Western Europe he gives to Lotharingia, Flanders, France, and Champagne: the regions of the Moselle, the Meuse, the Scheldt, and the Somme.

The sequence as it developed differed from a hymn in that a typical form consisted of a line or lines of introduction, a coda or conclusion, and between these a number of double strophes. Each pair, strophe and counterstrophe, tended toward equality in number of lines; and, also, in number of syllables in corresponding lines. To take one instance: if a strophe held four lines of six, three, seven, six syllables respectively, its counterstrophe would tend to follow suit. Irregularities, however, naturally occurred. The number of strophes was chosen at their writer's will, and they were sung alternately, first the strophe and then the counterstrophe, by a choir of men and a second choir of boys. All, we may think, joined in singing the introduction and the coda. At times neither introduction nor coda appeared. The prose in which the sequence was written held rhythmic character; often its lines ended uniformly in *a*. But this practice was by no means universal; nor did the *a* ending of rhyme always spring from the alleluia after the gradual.

Sequences, in fact, both in the earlier and in the later times of their history, differed often from one another in detail. Among the comparatively small number which critics place in the earlier years, there is one especially appealing: the *Stans a longe,* written before or about 850. It tells of the publican, in words which follow the story of St. Luke's Gospel.

At an early time, we may think, but we do not know exactly when, the composing of sequences reached Italy.

About 860 Germany was introduced to this fascinating composition, and here for the first time we stand on firm and solid ground, provided for us by Notker of Saint-Gall in Swabia. Notker was then a young monk, reading with all diligence liturgical and literary texts under Saint-Gall's famous teacher, Iso. Verse and music were already his great interests, and he was wishing very hard that he could keep in memory the notes of the music of the jubilus, as yet unaccompanied by words in Saint-Gall. One day, he tells us, a priest from France arrived at the abbey for a brief stay. He had lived in northwest France, at its monastery of Jumièges. But after a while the Danish invaders had destroyed its buildings, and its monks had been forced to seek refuge elsewhere. With him this priest had brought a copy of the antiphonary of Jumièges, a collection of the antiphons which had been sung at its abbey before its community had fled. Notker to his delight gained permission to study this book, and, of course, found in it a number of melodies in music. He also found what he had not been expecting: "some verses" written as a setting of words to one of these. Unhappily the writing here was faded and indistinct, and Notker was greatly distressed. But this did not stop him from trying at once to follow this model, to set words himself in harmony with the music of a jubilus. Long and hard he worked, and finally he managed to produce what seemed to him a rhythmic prose setting. This he promptly carried to Iso and asked for criticism. Iso already knew something about the rise and composition of the sequence, born some thirty years before; Notker, as he admitted, knew nothing. The master gave him due praise for his ambition; but he pointed out that in his ignorance Notker had broken the rule which governed the composing, not of all, but of the best of the sequences already written: "Each note of music must have its own syllable of text."

From this moment Notker toiled, writing sequence after sequence for more than twenty years. The boys of Saint-Gall sang them in choir. At last, about 885, when he was in his mid-forties, he ventured to send a number of them, bound together with a letter of dedication in what he called his *Book of Hymns,* to Liutward, bishop of Vercelli and confidential minister of Charles the Fat, the king of Germany and emperor. It is from that letter of dedication that we learn of Notker's experience.

Thus sequences became known and were composed in Germany, as well as in Italy and France. They were governed both by tradition and by circumstance, together with the art and the will of their individual authors; sometimes, when voices were lacking, they were composed without counterstrophes, and were sung by one choir instead of by two.

2

We come now to those sequences which critics have assigned to years near or of the tenth century, to look at a few selected from many, written for various seasons of the Church's calendar. They are given here in the Latin, in a rough translation, or in brief description of their content.

First Sunday in Advent. Title: Salus aeterna.
    c. 900. Anonymous.
Lines 14ff.:

> Quae fuerant perdita
> omnia
> salvasti terrea,
>
> Ferens mundo gaudia.
>
> Tu animas et corpora
> nostra, Christe, expia,
>
> Ut possideas lucida
> nosmet habitacula.

Adventu primo justifica,

In secundo nosque libera.

Ut, cum facta
luce magna

judicabis omnia,

Compti stola
incorrupta,
nosmet tua

Subsequamur mox vestigia
quocumque visa.

Things now lost beyond all hope,
all and each,
Thou hast saved on this earth,

Bearing the world gifts of joy.

For these our souls and bodies, too,
we pray, Christ, make atonement,

That Thou mayst hold fast, clear and pure,
us ourselves Thy dwellingplace.

By the First Advent justify us,

In the Second unchain and free us.

That when in midst
of that great light

Thou shalt be Judge of all things,

Arrayed in robes
unstained, unspoiled,
we, too, ourselves

May follow straight upon Thy footprints
wheresoever seen.

Christmas. Title: Eia recolamus laudibus

Date, place, and author's identity are all disputed. The date has
been suggested as early tenth century, as before or about 900; the

author has been held to be Notker of Saint-Gall and, also, left anonymous. Possibly sung in Saint-Gall.

Eia, recolamus laudibus piis digna

Huius diei carmina,
   in qua nobis lux oritur gratissima,

Noctis interit nebula,
   pereunt nostri criminis umbracula.

Hodie saeculo
   maris stella
      est enixa
         novae salutis gaudia;

Quem tremunt barathra,
   Mors cruenta
      pavet ipsa
         a quo peribit mortua.

Gemit capta pestis antiqua;
   coluber lividus perdit spolia;

Homo lapsus, ovis abducta,
   revocatur ad aeterna gaudia.

Gaudent in hac die agmina
   angelorum caelestia,

Quia erat drachma decima
   perdita et est inventa.

O culpa nimium beata,
   qua redempta Natura!

Deus qui creavit omnia
   nascitur ex femina. . . .

Lo, now let us recall worthy of faithful praise

The songs of this our day of feast,
   in which again for us there dawns that light most blest.

Now dies the deep dark cloud of night,
   the shadows of our sinfulness now fade away.

Today in this our world,
  the Star of sea
    brought forth in birth
      for us a new salvation's joy.

Before Him trembles very hell;
  bloodthirsty Death
    now fears that One
      through whom it shall be lost and dead.

Captive now wails our ruin of old,
  the envious serpent loses now its prey;

And fallen Man, the sheep once ravished,
  now is recalled home, to everlasting joy.

Today armies rejoice, marching lines,
  of angels in high Heaven's light,

Because that silver piece, the tenth,
  once lost, now once again is found.

O blessèd fault, blessed beyond word,
  by which all Nature was redeemed,

God, Maker of all things that are,
  is born of woman today!

The days of Epiphanytide go quickly by, and Septuagesima approaches. From Septuagesima Sunday until Easter, for nine weeks, the alleluia, cry of gladness, will not be heard in the Church's liturgy. And therefore the choirs bid it farewell in a song of praise. This was a custom in vogue long before the tenth century, seen in a sequence of the ninth which is still remembered: *Alleluia: dulce carmen.* In its third strophe it reminds us:

> Alleluia non meremur * nunc perenne psallere;
> Alleluia nos reatus * cogit intermittere;
> tempus instat, quo peracta * lugeamus crimina.

Alleluia now we may not * sing on earth for evermore;
Alleluia guilt of evil * now compels us to forego;
time approaches when as sinners * our offences we must mourn.

Another sequence, of the tenth century, was chanted in the days before Septuagesima as the same giving of goodbye. But, since its

words were so full of the gladness of praise, it was often reserved for
Sundays in ferial seasons, and, indeed, its title describes its use as
Diebus Dominicis. We may well believe, however, that farewell on
Septuagesima Sunday did not forbid choirs to sing their joy in its
sound.

*Septuagesima Sunday. Title: The Alleluiatic Sequence: Diebus
Dominicis: Cantemus cuncti melodum.*
        Early tenth century. Sung in Swabia.
Lines 17ff.:

> Nubium cursus,
> ventorum volatus,
> fulgurum coruscatio
> et tonitruum sonitus,
> dulce consonent simul
> *Alleluia!*
>
> Fluctus et undae,
> imber et procellae,
> tempestas et serenitas,
> cauma, gelu, nix, pruinae,
> saltus, nemora pangant
> *Alleluia!*
>
> Hinc, variae volucres,
> Creatorem
> laudibus concinite cum
> *Alleluia!*
>
> Ast illinc respondeant
> voces altae
> diversarum bestiarum
> *Alleluia!*
>
> Istinc montium
> celsi vertices sonent
> *Alleluia!*
>
> Illinc vallium
> profunditates saltent
> *Alleluia!*
>
> Tu quoque, maris
> jubilans abysse, dic
> *Alleluia!*

Nec non terrarum
molis immensitates:
Alleluia!

Nunc omne genus
humanum laudans exsultet
Alleluia!

Clouds in their courses,
winds speeding in their flight,
lightning flickering and flashing,
thunder pealing and reechoing,
let all sound in harmony
Alleluia!

Rolling seas and waves
rain and surging storms,
tempest and calm day,
heat, ice, snow, hoar-frost,
forest and glades, sing
Alleluia!

From hence, all ye birds,
the Lord who made you
praise in concert of
Alleluia!

From thence, let reply
the full-throated voice
of beasts of the field,
Alleluia!

Now here, all the mountains
shall call from their height,
Alleluia!

And there, too, the valleys
From their depths shall cry
Alleluia! . . .

At last the nine weeks are over and the *Alleluia* rings out again at
Eastertide. In one Easter sequence, coming about 900 and from
an anonymous poet, the first choir represents Man on earth and the
second the *Alleluia* itself, as a living spirit. Man chants his question:
"Whence comest thou once again to our fatherland, bringing to all

the world new tidings of joy?" And the *Alleluia* answers: "An angel has told me of holy wonder touching the Christ, that He who rules the stars in Heaven has risen from the dead. Therefore, flying through the winds in joy have I come back to His household, to tell you that the Old Law is void and gone; the New Grace reigns on earth. Give thanks, ye servants of God with clear voice, and now together with me keep holy Easter! Christ is our Peace."

Many sequences of the tenth century gave honor to saints of the Church: Mary, Virgin Mother; Stephen, proto-martyr; the Holy Innocents; Margaret of Antioch; Maurice of Valais; Martin; Gall and Othmar of Notker's own abbey. To Ekkehard I (c. 910-73), dean of Saint-Gall, have been attributed sequences in memory of St. Bene-dict, St. Columban of Luxeuil, and that St. Afra whom we have met in connection with Ulrich of Augsburg.

3

Next are short poems secular in aim or character but loosely connected with religion. Here verse by one Eugenius Vulgarius is of interest.

From 897 onward the see of St. Peter had been troubled alternately by stern condemnation of Formosus and by equally stern ratifying of his acts, as pope succeeded pope. In January 897 Stephen VI had thrown scorn on these acts; at the end of 897 Theodore II had approved them; John IX, a friend of Formosus, in 898 had done the same; Sergius III, pope from 904 to 911, declared the opposite; ordinations, he decreed, carried out by Formosus were invalid, and those on whom he had laid his hands were still but laymen. Eugenius Vulgarius, a man of learning, well-read in Latin classics, was then living in or near Naples; he had himself received priesthood from Formosus. About 907 he wrote a pamphlet in defense of this pope, now dead since 896, and he renewed his act by another writing of the same sort, cast in dialogue form.

Sergius in wrath called him to account; even, it would seem, sentenced him to monastic prison. The offender promptly changed his mind. Papal order was now summoning him to Rome itself. In abject terror he begged to be allowed to live, forgotten and forgiven, in his tiny cell of southern Italy; in fulsome flattery he wrote verses, praising Sergius literally to the skies. Under the guidance of this pope, Vulgarius declared, shall "Golden Rome" rejoice in glory. As another Troy it rises from destruction, rises high to the stars. The world knows no equal to Sergius; none may approach him in renown.

So terrified of Sergius was our learned scholar that, possibly from Monte Cassino's walls, he wrote in hope of support to Theodora, that senatrix of Rome whom Liutprand of Cremona was to describe as "a shameless harlot." Eugenius Vulgarius declared her a "most pious and venerable lady, beloved of God." "The fragrance of your religion," he continued, "is sensed everywhere; we have heard from very many lips of your holy life and conversation, and we give thanks with spiritual joy that God has placed you as a lamp to light the ways of men in this present age."

Doubtless both Vulgarius and Liutprand were guilty of exaggeration; but, we may think, Vulgarius sinned more deeply against truth.

For date of the well-known *O Roma nobilis,* the ninth, tenth, and eleventh centuries have been suggested; for place of origin, Verona in northern Italy and some monastery in the vicinity of Monte Cassino, or Monte Cassino itself. The little work was long described as a pilgrim song. Now, however, it is rather a poem in praise of Saints Peter and Paul or of the city of Rome, the dwelling of the saints. Its author remains anonymous. It begins with Rome:

> O Roma nobilis, orbis et domina,
> cunctarum urbium excellentissima,
> roseo martyrum sanguine rubea,
> albis et virginum liliis candida;
> salutem dicimus tibi per omnia,
> te benedicimus—salve per saecula!

O Rome, noble art thou and of the world ruler,
of all other cities in glory exceeding;
with the blood of the martyrs roseate and red,
radiant in white with the lilies of virgins;
All hail to thee sing we for ever and ever;
thee we bless, mayst thou prosper, for all time to come.

Placed with this greeting, as of about the year 900, is a cry of the people of Modena, then harried by the Hungarians who were sweeping through northern Italy, to Christ and His glorious Mother that they keep safe its walls. With this petition is joined an urgent prayer to the young fighters in Modena that they hold constant watch. It is a song of four divisions, each with six iambic lines. A reason for placing it about 900 is that Hungarian invasion of Italy finds a date in that year. The *Continuation* of the *Annals of Fulda* even declares with horror against the twenty-fourth of September: "Meanwhile the Avari who are called Hungarians so devastated all Italy that, when very many bishops had been killed, the Italians marched out against the enemy and in one battle there fell of the defenders twenty thousand men." Another exaggeration; but it reveals the fear of Modena.

From these short poems, written in passionate earnestness, we come to others, eccentric, burlesque, heroic, and epic.

In 913 Hatto I died, archbishop of Mainz, a man of immense energy, deep thought and subtle skill, a leader in German politics under Arnulf and Louis the Child, prominent among Germany's nobles and bishops. Ordinary folk suspected his sharp mind; Liutprand, as we can well understand, accused him "of all kinds of deceit and trickery."

But Hatto had, in a poet of celebrated scholarship and circumstance, a devoted admirer who composed in his honor one of the most extraordinary concoctions of the early Middle Ages. Hatto, it would seem, was bald, and to him this poet Hucbald, a monk of Saint Amand's abbey, lying between the river Scarpe and the little stream of Elnon in Belgium, dedicated some hundred and forty-six hexameter verses, in defense, in fervent praise, of baldheaded men. Every word in these verses from start to finish begins with the letter c, also in honor of *calvus*, the bald.

A preface asks plaintively: "If the dactylic Muses keep silence, who, pray, will write songs for the bald? Who, I ask, will stop the mouths of barking dogs, full of mockery against the bald?"

To become bald, indeed, Hucbald believes, is a sign of glory for him who thus wins a crown of dedication from the hand of Christ Himself. It is the baldheaded man who chants the liturgy, who inscribes canon law, who as monk builds his cell, who as priest gives to Christ's guests the Host at the altar, who as bishop blesses the holy oils.

Nor are laymen less fortunate in their shining heads: scholars, poets, lawyers, judges who condemn the criminal; "Beware, barbarian blasphemers, blindly belittling brothers bald!" Among these bald brothers, experts in medicine and surgery specially find notice.

Can they not deal with anything, from a cold in the head to cancer, from blindness to cerebral hemorrhage, from a stomachache to a complete breakdown?

Burlesque is shown in a tale drawn from folklore, contained in a manuscript of *The Cambridge Songs,* a manuscript made in the eleventh century and preserved in the Library of the University of Cambridge. Many of the poems in this collection were composed in the tenth; we may perhaps date our tale about the year 1000. Our tale is named the *Modus Liebinc,* from the music to which its verses were set, but it is more commonly known as "Das Schneekind, The Snow-Child."

Its anonymous author was undoubtedly a master of form who understood well the Latin sequence of his time, the late tenth century. Here we have five pairs of strophes and counterstrophes, with a conclusion, or coda. The pairs of strophes differ in length— seven, eleven, fourteen, eight lines; but each strophe has the same number of lines as its fellow, and each corresponding line in both strophes has the same number of syllables. Here is the first pair in the Latin, which throughout the poem is amazingly simple and easy to understand:

Strophe:
> Advertite,
> omnes populi,
> ridiculum
> et audite, quomodo
> Suevum mulier
> et ipse illam
> defraudaret.

Counterstrophe:
> Constantiae
> civis Suevulus
> trans aequora
> gazam portans navibus
> domi coniugem
> lascivam nimis
> relinquebat.

It tells of a man of Constance in Swabia, and it is wryly malicious; the Swabians were held in Germany to be people of doubtful character and little learning. He departs from his home on a voyage across the sea, carrying merchandise for trade, and he leaves behind him a wife of easy virtue. Hardly has he sailed when a storm blows up at sea, and after many perils he is cast upon an unknown shore, to find his way as best he can.

Meanwhile his wife, entirely forgetful of her husband, is enjoying herself with music and men; before long she finds that she is pregnant, and "in due course she bears an undue son."

Two years go by, and suddenly the exile is back from his wanderings. His faithless wife, taken by surprise, feigns joy and they embrace. Joy turns to fear when her husband sees the little boy at her side. "Tell me straight," he orders, "whose son is this, or there will be an end of you!" The woman hesitates, searching wildly for words, and then answers: "Dear husband, once, as I was walking in our mountains, I was thirsty and I quenched my thirst with snow. The snow it was that did it, woe is me! Through it I grew heavy with child and bore this boy!"

Five years or more pass on, and again the man of Constance decides to travel; this time he takes with him the child, now some six years old. Across the sea they go. In a foreign land he sells the boy to a merchant for a hundred pounds, and then returns home, happy and rich:

> And entering his home,
> these words spoke to his spouse:
> "Now be not distressed, wife,
> not distressed, my dear one,
> that your own son I have lost,
> whom not even you
> more indeed than I
> truly did love.
>
> For a tempest arose,
> the winds in their fury
> upon shoals and quicksands
> drove us, oh! so weary!
> And grievously all of us
> were burned by the sun.
> But he, your snow-child,
> melted away!

So did the Swabian deceive his faithless wife, and so did deceit meet deceit; for that child to whom snow gave birth, quite properly sun melted away.

Our next poem is also a fantasy, and also comes from the *Cambridge Songs;* it has been assigned variously to the tenth and the eleventh centuries, but it may well find place in the tenth as one concerning Heriger, archbishop of Mainz from 913 until 927. Heriger did not lack ability and influence, but history does not know him as it knows other prelates of Mainz: Hatto, Frederic, William, and Willigis. We think of him above all as the archbishop from whose hands Henry the Fowler in 919 refused consecration to the kingship of Germany. Nor does history know the name of his poet.

Here Heriger is said to have met a "prophet" who declared to him that he had been caught downward to see Hell and upward to dwell awhile in Heaven. Hell he described as covered by dense forest. With a laugh Heriger remarked: "Of course I want to send my swineherd there to feed my lean pigs!"

In Heaven the false "prophet" said he saw Christ feasting with His saints; John the Baptist was serving the wine, and Peter was head cook. "That was wise of Christ," said Heriger; "for John never drank wine. But you are lying when you call Peter head cook; he is doorkeeper of highest Heaven! How did God treat you? Where did you sit, and what did you have to eat?" "In a corner I stole a bit of meat, ate it up, and vanished." At this the archbishop in high wrath ordered the liar to be tied to a stake and soundly flogged: "If Christ invites you to His table in Heaven see to it that you don't act the filthy thief!"

Here again an artist was at work. The lines are each divided into two parts of from five to six syllables, usually five, and the last syllable of the first part rhymes with the last of the second, as:

Qui ad infernum * se dixit raptum.

There were originally twelve stanzas of three lines each, but one (concerning St. Peter) is now missing.

In the second half of the tenth century one Letald, a monk of Micy near Orléans and the river Loire in France, produced a short poem of heroic style. Folklore was its source, and it told of a fisherman of English race and home. Written in hexameter verse, it shows here and there that "leonine" internal rhyme which in early medieval days was softening the masculine virtue of the meter: the rhyming of the syllable at the caesura with the final syllable of the line; for example, line 11:

Robustas animis gaudentesque edidit armis

It is a story of horrific adventure and mischance. Letald says that he heard it from "a venerable old man," and that not even were Pindar or Homer himself by his side could he do it justice.

At the beginning a few verses describe the English, a people of fair hue, sturdy and warlike, who live in a region of mild climate and fertile vegetation, whose harsh tongues were taught by holy Gregory to sing the songs of Christ. "Within," as the poem's hero is called, was a fisherman, and he lived at Rochester, on the river Medway in Kent. Well skilled he was in his art, and day by day eagerly he hunted sea and stream.

One morning, then, he set out at dawn in his boat, carrying with him nets, kindling to make a fire, food and drink for his enjoyment, and his faithful double axe. Gaily he sped along, cutting the waves, looking ahead to find some quiet spot where he might anchor and cast his net.

He found it, and for a while rocked in peace. Then suddenly from the depths of the sea rose up an enormous fish, a monster "that could gulp down whole cities in its hellish gorge." In terror Within made for the shore. But his hands shook, he lost his breath, and he could only stay tossing in the waves, helplessly awaiting his doom. On came the whale with open jaws; in a moment it had swallowed whole both man and boat.

Through the sea the monster swam, while Within, boiling hot in his prison but otherwise unharmed, slowly came to himself. What should he do? He had no idea. Then in his boat he caught sight of the kindling, and hope awakened. He would light a fire and destroy the beast. The kindling was gathered, all the fuel he could find was piled upon it, cables and oars and pieces of wood, and the fire caught.

Up it flamed, clearing the darkness; smoke rolled from the mouth, eyes, and ears of the whale. Tearing through the water it tried savagely to escape this torture. Now it leaped above the waves, now it dived below. Its prisoner beat and hammered with all his might upon its mass, stomach, ribs, and heart. At last his courage found reward; the monster screamed aloud twice with dreadful cry, and died. The victim had slain its victor.

Five days and four nights Within floated in its dead body, roasting its meat and sleeping when he could. Scarcely could he hope to live, but bravely he endured. Then by a miracle he felt that he was being washed up on shore. It was the shore of Rochester itself, his home; but that he could not know.

In immense surprise Rochester's citizens flocked down to see this sight. They fastened ropes around the mass and with great effort pulled it to dry land, never dreaming of what its dark hollow held. But its captive gathered voice and called for help. Naturally all who heard fled in panic: women with their day's work in their hands, men young or bent with age. Rochester's bishop ordered his clergy and layfolk to the cathedral; there he prayed the Lord that this lurking evil, "this demon which has brought ghostly menace to our shore, do us no harm." Relics of the saints and holy water were promptly brought forward for the defense.

In solemn procession the bishop led his clergy to the water's edge. There he cried aloud: "If aught of evil thou art, threatening us, the men of Rochester, declare thy name and thy nature!"

"Within I am," cried the prisoner, "caught by the Furies and plunged into these depths! O my citizens, hurry to my rescue!"

All labored and hacked until they broke up the monstrous prize. The remains were distributed in due portion, the greater portion to the bishop, much to his priests, and the rest to his faithful flock. Within gave all who saw him stumbling forth a shock of fear and pity. His head was completely bald, his fingers were stripped of their nails, his eyelids drooped down over his eyes, and he was blind. Yet, with great ovation he was greeted and with a roaring of questions in voices loud and shrill. Soon his friends led him to his own cottage and left him to the care of his wife, who had wildly sought him up and down. The poem ends happily: "He lived to regain his own old comely self."

4

A longer poem of heroic-epic character calls for notice, not only on account of its own importance but because its dating has been in dispute.

The *Waltharius,* of about 1450 Latin hexameters, was long held an epic of the tenth century, a work of Ekkehard I, dean of Saint-Gall, who lived from about 910 to 973. This belief rose from a statement by Ekkehard IV (c.980-1060), a monk of Saint-Gall, where he earned fame as author of the *Casus Sancti Galli,* which gave vivid pictures, true and imagined, of Notker the Stammerer, of Ratpert and Tutilo. In this he declared (SS II, 118) that Ekkehard I as a boy had written a *Life* of Waltharius, and that because of its many faults, he, Ekkehard IV, had been bidden by Aribo, archbishop of Mainz, in the eleventh century, to revise the whole.

The poem, however, shows intimate knowledge of Latin writers:
classical—Virgil, Ovid, Statius; and early medieval—Boethius, Venantius Fortunatus, Valerius Flaccus, Corippus, among others. It is
well written, and it enjoyed high repute during the later Middle
Ages. The *Waltharius,* which is ours today to read, was not written
by an ignorant boy.

It was written, we may think, in the later ninth century, about
880-90. This belief rests on its intimate connection with poetry of that
century, on its verbal reminiscences, on its language and style, on
the technique of its verse. There is evidence, also, that early writers
of the tenth century looked back to it. Its author was one Gerald,
who wrote both the Prologue and the epic poem which follows.
Their separation in the volumes of the *Poetae Latini Medii Aevi*
(prologue: V, ii, p. 407; poem: VI, i, pp. 1 ff.) has been supported by
the fact that the prologue is written in heavy and labored style, the
poem in far simpler, in lively narrative. This difference in style has
been explained by Otto Schumann as caused by a differing attitude
of the one and the same poet to different parts of his work; he felt
weighed down by responsibility and a sense of unworthiness in the
prologue of dedication, but he enjoyed with delight his art of telling
a vivid story. Gerald, it would seem, was Bavarian by birth and
dedicated his poem to Erchambald, bishop of Eichstätt, Bavaria,
from 884 to 912.

Once again folklore is found; here it is German and Old English,
springing from olden time. The tale is of so deep interest that, in
spite of its date as given here, it may be worth while to describe
briefly its course. It was at any rate read by many in the tenth
century.

Its action opens in the time of Attila, that hero of German
history and saga who in the fifth century was troubling Western
Europe. From the Franks, we read, their King Gibich sent one of his
nobles, Hagen, to Attila as hostage, with promise and, indeed,
yielding of tribute in return for peace. King Hereric of Burgundy
likewise gained peace from Attila by surrendering his daughter, an
only child, Hildegund; King Alfere did the same for his Aquitanian
people by handing over his son Walther.

These three hostages were but children at the time; they grew
up in Pannonia, Attila's land. At last, when he had reached youth,
Hagen contrived his escape and safely reached his Frankish people.
Among them, upon Gibich's death his son, Gunther, succeeded him
as king. But Walther and Hildegund stayed on together at Attila's

court. In infancy their royal parents had arranged betrothal between them, and now, having reached age of decision, they truly fell in love. As the years went on, Walther was known through all Pannonia as a warrior, strong and skilled to fight.

King Gunther of the Franks was very different in character from his father. Above all, he loved treasure of wealth, and he could not bear the thought of that tribute which Attila year by year was exacting from the Franks. He refused to pay, and Attila sent Walther with an army to force him into compliance. Walther won a great victory, which left the king full of resentful humiliation.

At last Walther and his Hildegund, like Hagen, grew weary of exile from home. By stealth and much cunning they also escaped, and they made their way safely until they approached Frankish land and crossed the Rhine. Then by accident King Gunther heard of their coming. Hope at once filled his covetous heart; surely Walther must be bringing back to him treasure sent by the Franks to Attila in return for a treaty of peace?

Soon, with Hagen and eleven other warriors, chosen from his most valiant wielders of sword and battle-axe, he was riding out in search. The two, Frankish king and Aquitanian prince, met in a wild and narrow pass amid the Vosges mountains. Hagen, who loved Walther, once his fellow hostage, begged his lord and king to keep the peace, and Walther himself at once promised to yield treasure on his own account, if only Gunther would forget tribute paid to Attila. Not through his own desire, he pleaded, had that tribute been exacted!

But there was no peace; King Gunther was determined to recover lost wealth. One after another, eleven of his fighting men marched forward to match strength and skill against Walther the Aquitanian, only to fall dead at his hands, thus forced into defense. Of the Frankish band only the king and Hagen now stood facing him; and Hagen refused to go forward. His own nephew lay among the fallen and his bitterness was great; he himself, he declared, was no man to carry on this fearful duel of arms. In vain Gunther urged and prayed him to do battle for the Frankish crown; night fell as they contended, and only the morrow's chance could decide, for life or death. Hagen drew apart with his king to hide while darkness lasted, and by the side of Hildegund as she slept Walther knelt in prayer, offering to Heaven thanksgiving for his own life, and petition for the dead.

At dawn, man and girl, seeing no sign of the enemy, together started once more on their journey to Walther's home. They had hardly covered a mile before they saw Gunther and Hagen riding in pursuit. Once face to face, in a fury of rage, Gunther demanded battle. No entreaty, no offer would he wait to hear. The twelfth and last struggle began.

It was still early morning; the three, Walther, Gunther, and Hagen, prince, king, and noble, fought, one against two, for hours and only ceased when all were cruelly wounded; Gunther had lost a leg, Walther his right hand, and Hagen an eye. No more could be done. The poem ends with renewal of friendship between the three, now exhausted, with Gunther and Hagen, supported on horseback, returning to their Frankish land, and Walther on his way with Hildegund to Aquitaine. Their marriage soon was celebrated; King Alfere died not long afterward, and for thirty years Walther, his son and heir, reigned in happiness over the land.

This bare outline gives, of course, no idea of the interest to be drawn from the vivid detail of the narrative in its Latin.

5

We come now to poems which tell of love and springtime, and begin with the *Jam, dulcis amica,* "Invitation to a Loved One," a dialogue between a lover and his desire, found in a manuscript of Vienna assigned to the tenth century. Here the young man prays his love to enter the place he has prepared for her. All is ready; everywhere are flowers, fair and fragrant, and music and song. The table holds its delights; the wine awaits her coming. Yet, what to him are these joys compared with the talk that will follow? What is feasting compared with one's love near to one?

> Come now, my sister, mine own,
> before all, my love alone!
> Light of mine eyes thou, dear heart,
> of my soul the greater part!

Timidly she answers, confessing her awakening to a springtide of passion like to his:

> I was alone in the wood
> and I loved solitude;
> I fled often confusion
> and avoided intrusion.

> Ice and snow now are melting,
> leaf and grass now are greening.
> Sings the nightingale above,
> in heart's hollow burns my love.

Then once again he bids her, Come! He cannot live without her. Why put off what must come in the end?

> Come, fulfill our love today,
> In me nothing gives delay.

The verses, as can be easily seen, hold echoes of the *Song of Solomon,* which also is rightly a dialogue.

Another lay of love from the tenth century is not often read. It has its own charm of a deeply religious nature, and it comes from Ottonian times, though its origin and its author's name are hidden from us:

> Deus amet puellam
> claram et benivolam,
> Deus amet puellam.
>
> Quae sit mente nobilis
> ac amico fidelis,
> Deus amet puellam.
>
> Constans gemmis similis
> atque claris metallis,
> Deus amet puellam.
>
> Candidior nivibus,
> dulcior est et favis,
> Deus amet puellam.
>
> Cedunt illi rosae,
> simul atque liliae,
> Deus amet puellam.
>   . . . .

In the end the lover bids his love goodbye:

> Vale, vale, puella,
> omnium dulcissima,
> Deus amet puellam.

Vale iam per aevum,
Christus sit et tecum,
Deus amet puellam.

Omnes dicant Amen
qui in caelo poscunt requiem,
Deus amet puellam.

God love my maiden!
Fair, with charm laden,
God love my maiden!

In mind wonderful,
To her friend faithful,
God love my maiden!

To true gems akin,
bright as gold within,
God love my maiden!

Clear as snow's white foam,
sweet as honey's comb,
God love my maiden!

To her roses yield,
lilies of the field,
God love my maiden!

. . . .
Farewell, my maiden,
sweetest begotten,
God love my maiden!

Farewell for ever,
Christ be thy keeper,
God love my maiden!

All now Amen cry,
who ask rest on high,
God love my maiden!

A number of poems tell of birds, heralds of summer. The *Vestiunt silvae,* found in a tenth-century manuscript and written in sapphics, gives a spring medley of notes of various kind: of wood pigeon, dove, thrush, blackbird, sparrow, nightingale, hawk, eagle, skylark, swallow, quail, and jackdaw. With the *Jam, dulcis amica* it comes from France or Italy.

Its last lines lead us from birds to the bee:

> Not one from the birds to the bee we liken,
> bearing chastity, similar to no one,
> but her who carried in her womb the Christ Child,
>   pure and unsullied.

From about 900 we have verse in iambic dimeter known as the "Anacreontic Song." It was found together with poetry by Eugenius Vulgarius; but no other reason connects it with him, and we do not know who wrote it. The season once more is spring; the sun is high in the heavens and all the birds are singing. The nightingale, settled on a myrtle with her young ones, bids them listen to her; so will they learn to sing as she does, songs worthy to offer to the Lord God, canticles divine.

As she sings, all the beasts and birds come hurrying from their haunts to listen. Little by little envy rises within them; one after another the birds try their best to conquer her in song. To no purpose; and at last they return homeward defeated. We remember that it was the nightingale who for the lion, king of beasts, sang the Passion of Christ.

Radbod, who died in 917, an exile through the assaults of the Danes, in 899 had been elected bishop of Utrecht; he held its see until he was driven out, early in the tenth century. We have several poems by him; one tells of the swallow which he watched at work in the garden of his home in Utrecht, about 900. Under its roof she built her nest, and Radbod wrote of her doings, even of her thought, in her own name:

> The right is mine to build within God's House,
>   to nurse my young in man's abode.
> To husbandman I come to bring new joy,
>   chattering I cry, "Clear, dig the ground!"

There she stays through summer's sunshine and rain, teaching her brood to fly. When winter brings cold and fog she leaves all, her offspring and her nest, to fly far away to a happier land.

The verses end with her philosophy:

> Ah, Man, while things and reasons thee amaze,
>   scorn not, I plead, thine honor's gift;
> Reason is thine—none have I, not a whit,
>   Death is not thine, but all for me.
> Kinder thy fate, greater than I be thou,
>   faithful to Him who made us all.

In the tenth century, also, a golden oriole delighted a monk who lived in a community of Benedictine order, probably in France. The monk's poem, also in sapphics, pictures the fathers listening to the bird's song, looking at him with wonder, brilliant in his yellow, crimson, and deep blue, as he preens his feathers, turns in the oak-tree, hangs from the bough, flies on the wing, chants his evensong, while they sit at supper in their refectory. When the sun is sinking in the west, he disappears for the night.

6

Lastly, we come to the verse which reflects the history of this age, with its rising of a new vision of Church and state.

In 911 Waldram, monk of Saint-Gall, wrote a song of welcome for Conrad I, who visited the abbey at Christmastide of that year. This gave the monastery great rejoicing, for no king of Germany had come there for over twenty years, since the death of Charles the Fat in 888. Franconia, Waldram declares, has herself come in the person of her Conrad to aid Swabia, and he pleads for Saint-Gall so long neglected by the crown of Germany. There follows a vision of the German king as "monarch," extending his influence over Slavonic people in the East, over lands of the West, Spain and France and Italy, working with the support of his chancellor, Salamo III.

Waldram and his abbey had reason to long for aid. Some years before, about 904, Salamo had written verses to Dado, bishop of Verdun in Lotharingia, lamenting the troubles which pressed so hard upon Germany under its helpless king, Louis the Child. Too great our cause for tears, he writes in his hexameters. From this side and that, tragedy never ceases to strike; Death shows not one, but many faces in our midst. No pity for father, no mercy for mother; the savage spear pierces child before its parents' eyes.

This, of course, recalls the wild invasion of Hungarian riders. But there are quarrels within the German realm itself. All mortal men, Salamo writes, are hurrying to break the law of peace: bishop, count, soldier, men military and civilian alike, town against town, tribe against tribe.

Between 915 and 924 another poet, this time bent on praise, told the deeds of Berengar I of Friuli.

The four sections which make up this work open with a preface, a dialogue in elegiacs between the anonymous author and his book. The writer knows that he is no genius; he fears that his verses will but feed a fire. Well, then, replies the book of his mind, why take the trouble to write? Your work will be of no importance to anyone; writing verse is now the fashion in town and country alike!

No matter, what care I? retorts the poet, and warns the poem, already created in his imagination: "Thou mayst be burned entire, vacuous winds may scatter thee; thy better part shall write, great with love, great in respect!" Of the line of Charlemagne Berengar came, and when Charles the Fat lay dying in exile on January 13, 888, he bequeathed the destiny of his crown to this kinsman of his. Berengar marched to Pavia and was hailed as king of Italy.

At this, Guy, duke of Spoleto, was enraged; from France he entered Italy, and the first two parts of this poem tell of war between the two rivals. The writer is a wholehearted champion of Berengar. He omits disaster; he falsely exaggerates or invents triumph in Berengar's career; he does not scruple to change the course of history. In regard to his verse his model is Virgil, and he follows closely the Virgilian tradition of simile. But he knows well Latin poets and borrows from them where he will.

Part III describes King Arnulf's march to Italy in 894 and his campaign against Guy of Spoleto; the battle of Bergamo and the hanging of Count Ambrose; the death of Guy in this same year, and that of his son and fellow king, Lambert, in 898. Now Berengar stands alone, sole ruler of Italy.

The fourth and last part deals with the second invasion of Italy by Louis of Provence in 905, and his blinding in the church of Verona at the hands of Berengar's nobles. Here Berengar is endowed with warmth of character. In vain he orders his supporters to do no harm to this young Louis, who comes of an aristocratic line and may learn wisdom as his years increase.

The last pages are radiant with a blaze of glory, amid which Berengar is crowned emperor of the West in 915 by Pope John X. It is all here: the welcoming of the king in Rome; his enthusiastic greeting by the pope; the ceremony of coronation and anointing in St. Peter's; the ringing acclamation by the crowds of the city; the multitude of gifts presented by the emperor to the Holy See.

The poet's friends among young men of the future—so he declares—will carry on his work and tell of this emperor's achievements to come. Perhaps they were his pupils in Latin culture. Did he, one wonders, live to hear of his hero's murder in 924?

The *Modus Liebinc*, or "Snow-Child," already noticed, found curious kinship with another poem cast in sequence form, the *Modus Ottinc*. This is a song in praise of the Ottonian kings. Otto I, aided by the courage of Conrad the Red, conquered the Hungarians; Otto II had his virtues, but rarely won a great victory; Otto III could conquer without battle of arms:

> In war mighty,
> in peace potent,
> in either state
> kindly was he;
> amid victories
> happy he was;
> those whom his soldiers' arms
> had not subdued,
> renown of his name
> conquered enough.

The *Ottinc's* Latin text shows the same skill as that of the *Liebinc*. It has been suggested that both were written by the same hand, about 1000; other theory would date the *Ottinc* before Otto III's coronation in 996, as he is not named emperor here. Its source is the *Cambridge Songs*.

Another *Modus*, the *De Heinrico*, comes also from that collection, but it has a more unusual text. The first half of each line is in Latin, the second in Old High German. We will follow here the guidance of Mathilde Uhlirz. The scene shows an audience, given, very probably in September 985, by the little king, Otto III, to Henry, once "the Quarreler," after his reconciliation with the German crown at the Council of Frankfurt in June of that year. He had done homage to his king and had once again received his duchy of Bavaria. As duke, then, he is now receiving audience, and with him Otto is welcoming that fellow rebel, Henry the Younger, duke of Carinthia. After their greeting at the royal throne, king and dukes enter the church near at hand for prayer, and then Otto leads Henry of Bavaria into a council of nobles of the realm and in their presence grants to him "all except the royal power, which Henry does not desire."

As Otto is described here as emperor, this *Modus* must have been written between the year of his coronation, 996, and that of his death, 1002. Madame Uhlirz suggests that, as eleven years, it would seem, had passed, the verses may well have been based on a previous song composed about 985, or even on folksong current at the time.

In the reign of this third Otto, indeed, a new wave of song flowed in Western Europe. In 997 we have seen Abbo of Fleury in Italy, seeking Pope Gregory V at the request of Robert II, king of

France; he was also hoping for Gregory's active influence in inducing Otto to leave Slavonic rebellion on the German border and hurry to the aid of Italy. For this purpose Abbo also wrote to Otto verses in figured form, ingenious and complicated, intertwining in them the words *Otto Caesar* and *Abbo Abba*, "Otto Emperor," "Abbo Abbot," with the prayer, often repeated: "Otto valens Caesar, nostro tu cede coturno"; "Mighty Otto, Emperor, do thou yield to our art!" The Emperor Otto III himself could at times indulge in verse; as in 997, when as a youth of seventeen, he was writing to his master, Gerbert:

> No verses have I ever made,
> Nor ever notice to them paid.
> While, then, I have them now in mind,
> And in them lively solace find,
> As many men as live in Gaul,
> So many songs I'll send for all!

Verse, too, was written by Gerbert: epitaphs for rulers, including the Emperor Otto II and King Lothair of France, and a poem in praise of the philosopher Boethius:

> Tertius Otto sua dignum te iudicat aula,
> aeternumque tui statuit monumenta laboris,
> et bene promeritum meritis exornat honestis.

> Otto the Third doth hold thee worthy of his hall;
> reward for thee, now placed, for ever monument,
> doth honor thee, right truly, with thy true deserts.

Far more interesting is the thought of the streets of Rome, ablaze at night with torches and resounding with song as the great procession in honor of the Assumption of Saint Mary wound its way from the Lateran to the church of Saint-Mary-Major, carrying high her banner's painting. The custom was centuries old. But in August 1000 the Emperor Otto III was either present or near at hand. Some poet, of unknown name, had composed for this year's feast a hymn which united his name with hers:

> Sancta Dei genitrix, Romanam respice plebem,
> Ottonique fave, sancta Dei genitrix!
> Tertius Otto tuae nixus solamine palmae
> praesto sit veniae tertius Otto tuae!
> Hic tibi, si quid habet, devoto pectore praestat,
> spargere non dubitat hic tibi, si quid habet.

Gaudeat omnis homo, quia regnat tertius Otto,
　　illius imperio gaudeat omnis homo!

Holy Mother of God, encourage Rome's people
　　give Otto thine aid, Holy Mother of God!
On thy hand of support he leans, this third Otto,
　　may this, the third Otto, be near to thy grace!
To thee, all he has with devotion he offers,
　　he waits not to give thee whatsoever he has.
May all men rejoice that he reigns, this third Otto,
　　Through rule of his Empire may all men rejoice!

In January 1002 this Otto, with his vision of empire, had passed
away. Another poet, very possibly once more Leo of Vercelli, now,
for those who had loved this young man and had hoped for great
things from his reign, told of their grief in these lines:

Quis dabit aquam capiti?　Quis succurret pauperi?
Quis dabit fontes oculis　lacrimosos populi?
Sufficient quae lacrimae　mala mundi plangere?

Ad triumphum ecclesiae　coepit Otto crescere,
sumpsit Otto imperium,　ut floreret saeculum,
vivo Ottone tertio　salus fuit saeculo.

. . .

Regnorum robur periit,　quando Otto cecidit;
dum Otto noster moritur,　mors in mundo oritur;
mutavit coelum faciem　et terra imaginem.

Plangat ignitus oriens,　crudus ploret occidens,
sit aquilo in cinere,　planctus in meridie,
sit mundus in tristitia;　nostra, fuge, cithara!

Plangat mundus, plangat Roma,　lugeat ecclesia!
Sit nullum Romae canticum,　ululet palatium!
Sub Caesaris absentia　sunt turbata saecula!

Who shall cool the hot brow?　Console the poor now?
Who shall give flow of tears　for our people's fears?
And what tears shall suffice　to mourn the world's vice?

For the joy of religion　grew Otto's ambition,
Otto gained Empire's crown　for the world's renown;
Under Otto the third　no peril was feared.

. . .

Our throne's strength has vanished,   Otto has perished;
Once our king Otto dies,   for us death doth rise;
Heaven changes its face,   grief earth doth deface.

Mourn, fire-kindled, the East,   weep now the raw West!
North sit now in mourning,   South cry its wailing;
The world lie in sadness,   flee now, harp's gladness.

Mourn all men, mourn Rome,   grieve, Church's high dome,
no song give Rome solace,   cry loud the Palace!
Caesar passes from life,   the world falls to strife.

And then, as in duty bound, the poet turned to greet Otto's successor, Henry the Second.

CHAPTER NINE

The Harvest in Drama

1

Before we take a look at the drama of the tenth century, it may be of interest to recall for a moment the history of dramatic action, of action akin to dramatic or classed as dramatic, in the centuries which lay behind it.

We connect early Latin classical drama more especially with comedy, since we have comedies in their fullness by Plautus (died c.184 B.C.) and by Terence (died 159 B.C.), while early Latin tragedies lie in fragments. The Roman people, however, were not in general lovers of serious and literary drama. In 165 B.C., so Terence himself declared, his presentation of the comedy *Hecyra*, "The Mother-in-law," utterly failed; the audience with loud noise streamed away to enjoy the thrilling sight of a man dancing on a tight rope high above them. Again in 160 B.C. he put it on the stage, only to hear a shout that gladiators were coming to give a show and to see everyone get up and dash away in a rush to seize the best places for this far more diverting spectacle.

In the days of the empire, entertainments such as fights to the death by gladiators, struggles of men faced with wild beasts, mimes —hilarious, licentious and obscene—were the joy of the people, gathered in circus or in theatre. Against these delights the Church made constant war. "The theatre," cried Tertullian in the third century, "is the shrine of Venus, and Bacchus is her partner: two diabolical patrons of drunkenness and lust!" On Easter Day 399 John Chrysostom, bishop of Constantinople, stood in his pulpit to denounce his flock for their sin against God and holy Church. "On Good Friday," he stormed, "when your Lord was crucified for all the world, when paradise was opened, when God was reconciled with man and all things were changed, on that Day of Fasting, when it was for you to give thanks in prayer, you, caught by the Devil, went off to the games in the Stadium! Is this to be borne? Is this to be tolerated?" So St. Jerome declared in the West of the fourth century, so St. Augustine and Salvian in the fifth, Alcuin in the eighth, Louis the Pious and Hincmar, archbishop of Reims, in the ninth, rebuking and accusing their light-minded peoples. Of Louis the Pious his biographer, Thegan, wrote: "Never did he raise his voice in laughter when at festive times musicians, jesters, mimic actors, came to the feast in his presence. The people laughed with all their hearts, but he never even showed his shining white teeth in a smile!"

The victory lay finally with the Church. Already in the fifth century Augustine wrote: "Everywhere, in almost all the cities, theatres are falling; falling are the public places, the walls within which demons held their court. And why are they falling, if not through the disappearing of those impious and lascivious uses for which they were built?" Councils, royal and imperial decrees, laid their prohibition upon monks, clergy, and even layfolk, in regard to pleasures barbarous and seductive.

Nevertheless, although the circus, the stadium, and the arena no longer gave their spectacles, their games, and their combats in public, neither pope, bishop, or emperor could put an end to popular entertaining. At gatherings of friends in town and village, at weddings, and upon other special occasions, minor performances were given for the amusement of those whose conscience in no way forbade indulgence of frivolity, flavored with a touch of irreverent fun or boisterous horseplay. We have still two instances of this kind in Latin.

One of them brings forward Terence himself. It is assigned by both Paul de Winterfeld and Max Manitius to the ninth century: a brief composition of six elegiac couplets and fifty-five hexameters.

From the "audience" a voice speaks out, telling the old poet roughly to stop giving his old plays:

> Get out, ancient poet! I care not for your verses,
> Old man, I say, your ancient fables cease!
> I sit here, tired to death, heavy with weariness.
> Are they in verse? I know not. Or in prose?

Terence comes forward on the stage, angry at the insult. "Let the mocker show himself," he shouts, "and get what he deserves!"

The mocker comes, and the quarrel goes on lustily. Terence threatens to knock his critic on the head, and the critic jeers at him:

> Depart, I pray, lest you get the blows you threaten,
> I am still young! Shall I listen to old age?

The little "mime," if we may so call it, is incomplete; it breaks off with a lament from Terence. If only he were young again, what a punishing he would give to this slanderer! We do not know how the quarrel ended; probably Terence retired in defeat.

Our second bit of popular miming had a wide circulation and gained some repute. It is called the *Cena Cypriani,* "The Banquet of Cyprian," and its original composition in prose was falsely attributed to "Saint Cyprian." It is still to be read in the *Patrologia Latina* IV, 925 ff., as a spurious legacy from the pen of Cyprian, bishop of Carthage in the third century. We know neither its date nor its real author's name.

It is actually a pantomime with a multitude of players, drawn from the Old and from the New Testament of the Bible. The scene presents a feast, given by a certain King Johel at Cana of Galilee to celebrate his marriage. All the guests act in keeping with their action or character as seen in the Biblical narrative. Thus, when they assemble for the banquet, Noah takes his seat upon an arca, a chest, Zacchaeus on the branch of a tree, Ruth on some straw, James upon a fishing net, Samson on a pillar. Esau is grumbling, and Job is upset because the only place left for him is in the dirt. Wedding garments are distributed by the king to his guests with equal appropriateness; Daniel receives a robe of tawny-yellow color, Rahab one of scarlet, and so on. After everyone has feasted well, Adam falls asleep, Pilate brings water for the washing of hands, Martha serves it, Simeon gives thanks, Adam offers fruit as a last course, David makes merry music on the harp, and Herodias dances. Just when the feast is ending, word comes to King Johel that treasure of great price has been stolen from the banqueting table. In a passion of anger he orders trial and examination of all who have been present. Zacharias, of course, remains silent, and Peter stoutly denies the charge. Finally the guilt is traced to Achar, son of Carmi, and he is promptly put to death. In pity Mary brings spices for the burial, while Pilate places an inscription over the grave. Then suddenly Sarah, overcome by all that has happened, bursts into laughter, and everyone goes home.

Very probably this farce, with its words gay, ribald, and gross,

was a parody of an earnest instruction written for the newly baptized by Zeno, bishop of Verona from about 362 to 380. His words
describe a banquet given in honor of the new life born for his con-
verts; they hold the same imagination, the same details, here pictured with pious joy. Zeno had many heretics and heathen men to
deal with in northern Italy, and we possess a number of his "Invi-
tations to the font." They are printed in Migne, *PL* XI; the one for
the newly baptized will be found in columns 483 ff.

During the ninth century this satiric story reappeared three
times, in somewhat different versions. Hraban Maur, archbishop of
Mainz from 847 until 856, sent a carefully revised edition during
855 to Lothar II, king of Lotharingia. In a letter accompanying his
gift he wrote. "I think that as you read or listen you will find both
entertainment and instruction in these ancient pages."

At Christmas 875 when Charles the Bald was crowned emperor
of the West by Pope John VIII at Rome and high festival was held,
"The Banquet of Cyprian" was given a public recitation. Bishops of
Italy and ministers of the Frankish court were guests of the emperor,
and a good time was enjoyed by all. Gauderic, bishop of Velletri,
south of Rome, laughed so heartily that he fell from his seat, to the
great surprise of Zacharias, bishop of Anagni, also near Rome, who
maintained a strictly solemn face. Anastasius, papal librarian, a very
learned man among the company, could explain, of course, all the al-
lusions.

Both these renderings followed in general the old original of
"Cyprian." But some months later, in 876, after Formosus in April of
that year had been deprived by John VIII of the see of Porto, John
Hymmonides, a deacon of Rome, known far and wide for his skill in
politics and in literary writings, presented to this Pope John a third
rendering of the *Cena,* flavored with much comment, both gay and
stinging, from his own thought. Most of its lines hold fifteen syllables, rhythmically arranged; actual rhyming often occurs. A prologue
and an epilogue also now appear in this new version, which was
probably given in public during the merriment of Easter. The prologue shows evidence of song and dance, together with satiric jest:

> Quicunque cupitis saltantem me Iohannem cernere
> nunc cantantem auditote, iocantem attendite;
> satyram ludam percurrens divino sub plasmate
> quo Codri findatur venter. Vos, amici, plaudite!

You who long, so gaily dancing me, Johannes, now to see,
listen now to me songs singing, watch me merrily jesting;
play satiric now presenting, a God-given creation,
which would burst the paunch of Codrus! Now, friends,
    your approbation!

Codrus appears in Virgil, Eclogues V, 10, and VII, 22, 29, as a
poet given to envying those better than himself, and therefore as a
fit target for mocking words.

The lines continue with a hope that Pope John will enjoy this
Easter reveling. Reference is made to the performance which cele-
brated the crowning of Charles the Bald, which brought the joy of
Bishop Gauderic and the unmoved silence of Bishop Zacharias. At
Formosus, the condemned bishop, and his friends, John the Deacon
vigorously hurls his scorn.

A dedication to John VIII is written in metrical verse:

Ludere me libuit; ludentem, papa Iohannes,
    accipe; ridere, si placet, ipse potes.
Tristia lassatis dum currunt secula tegnis,
    suscipe de rithmis dogmata grata tibi,
qui laetus poteris spectacula cernere festis,
    iam variis monstris dissimulata nimis.

A play in joy would I write; my playing, Pope John,
    now welcome with laughter; laugh well you can.
While sadly the ages in tired homes are running,
    Receive in my verse the teachings you love.
With joy will this playing delight you on feast-days,
    For plays now are hidden alas! in all vice!

2

From this background we come to the tenth century. People were
still enjoying, in Italy, in France, and in Germany, the same mime
and farce, recited, even acted, at festival times; classical drama was
limited to reading, and to reading by the serious student of meter
and style. We have seen Bruno of Cologne delighting in Terence
during his younger years.

So did others, and among them a nun of this century whose
name is often linked with its drama. Hrotsvitha was born of aristocratic parentage in Saxony about the year 935; when still young, she

was sent for education and training in religion to the Saxon abbey of Gandersheim. There, as she herself tells, she was a pupil of Riccardis, one of its community; she was also taught by Gerberga, daughter of Henry, duke of Bavaria, and of his wife Judith, and therefore a niece of Otto the Great himself. Some time after 854 this teacher of hers, who was a few years younger than Hrotsvitha, was consecrated abbess of Gandersheim as Gerberga II, by Otwin, bishop of Hildersheim, with the ready consent of William, archbishop of Mainz.

Hrotsvitha, duly professed in monastic vows, was a keen student; she gave such leisure as Benedictine rule allowed her to reading both secular and religious works. From every possible source she sought out books, dealing with history and legend, with grammar and with philosophy, books classical and medieval. Among them she came upon the comedies of Terence, and, like Bruno, whom perhaps she met, she zealously studied meter and action in his plays. At last she began to attempt writing in prose and in meter her own compositions, to imagine some "dramatic" plots and scenes in her own mind.

Not yet did she venture to write whole plays. She began her writing with narratives of legends of the Christ and His saints, discovered by her in books and laboriously turned by her pen into hexameter verse. Eight of these stories after long effort lay finished, and timidly she presented them for inspection to her abbess, Gerberga. A preface, written in prose, confesses that often her work will show error in meter and in style. But against one very possible criticism she submits her defense: "If I am blamed in the judgment of some readers, for taking parts of my narrative from apocryphal sources, I plead ignorance. When I first began this writing, I did not realize that my sources might be held doubtful. And when I did see this, I refused to destroy what I had done; perhaps in the future what now seems false may be proved true."

Genuinely humble as Hrotsvitha was, she had a mind of her own. She pictures for her abbess the struggle of this mind: "Secretly, telling no one what I was doing, I have toiled alone; I have been afraid that I might be ordered to stop writing because of my rough and awkward style. Again and again I have torn up my efforts, only to try once more to put together some text with such power as I have, and that is little enough." Her abbess, she gladly acknowledges, has helped her on her way: "Gerberga, to whose authority I am subject, is younger than I; but, naturally, as niece of the emperor, she knows more, and in her generosity she has told me about writings of which I had never heard."

The first poem rests upon the legends of the Christ Child and His Mother, existing as early as the second century in the protevangelium of James, which Hrotsvitha gives as her source, and current in the ninth through the Gospel of the Pseudo-Matthew. Here Hrotsvitha first sounded the note which was to ring through her writings: the virtue of steadfast virginity, pure and undefiled. Veneration of the Mother of God, Ever-Virgin, was very much alive in the tenth century. The story, however, begins with a holy marriage, of Anna with Joachim, and goes on to tell the shame and sorrow of their childlessness: birds and fishes, Anna laments, bear their young by gift of God, but she is barren. Then at last comes the birth of Mary, her dedication to the service of the temple, the decision of its priests that her duty lies in wedlock, the rivalry for her hand among men of the tribe of Judah, and the sign given by Heaven, to Joseph of all men, one already advanced in years and vividly aware of the fact.

The birth of Mary's child is described, and the miracles worked by Him as a little boy, now calming the fear of His parents, now serving their need. The story ends with the conversion from pagan idolatry of Aphrodisius, a mighty ruler in Egypt.

Hrotsvitha's second attempt, verses on the Ascension of the Lord Christ, drawn from a Greek narrative, she tells her readers, found by her in a Latin translation by a certain John, a bishop now unknown by us, calls for no comment here. The next work gives us the legend of Gongolf (Gangulf, Gengulf), said to have been a knight of Germany in the eighth century when Pippin the Short, his friend, was king of the Franks. Gongulf is pictured as young, of noble lineage, handsome, skilled both in fighting on the field of battle and in knowledge of books, a loyal son of the Catholic Church. His wife is also aristocratic and beautiful; he places his happiness in her hands. But the serpent of evil comes stealthily to ruin his hope; one of the men who serve his household falls in love with her and she with him. Word of the treachery of both reaches the knight; he proves it and finds it a true report. His wife he forgives and finds her a home, apart from his. There with her lover she plans her revenge, his death; driven on by her, the man creeps by night into his lord's chamber and strikes him down with the sword. The murderer dies suddenly, punished by Heaven's wrath; the faithless wife, once a noble lady, is doomed to madness and ridicule of the crowd.

Some of this tale was true. Certainly to medieval minds Gongolf was a real figure, revered as saint and martyr in France, Germany, and the Netherlands.

The fourth story holds greater interest, as drawn, not from written source, but from an eyewitness of its scene. It tells of young Pelagius, martyr for his Christian creed in the tenth century.

Spain saw his death. Its land, conquered by the Moors in the eighth century, was ruled in the mid-tenth by the great chieftain Abd-ar-Rahman III, who raised it to splendid renown and wealth. The father of Pelagius, with other nobles of Galicia in northwest Spain, was taken prisoner as a Christian and a rebel by Abd-ar-Rahman. Since he was old and in ill health, Pelagius begged that he might be handed over to the Arab Caliph as hostage in his father's place. After much argument he was allowed to go, and for a while he was kept in prison. Then his handsome face and noble bearing, his natural courtesy and charm, tempted his keeper; Abd-ar-Rahman had a marked weakness in regard to young men of that kind. He brought Pelagius to his court, gave him many gifts, endeavored to enjoy his society, and was promptly repelled. Pelagius would have none of this. The chieftain persevered, and one day received a hard knock on the head. This to the Moor was high treason; the youth, thrown from the city's wall and finally executed by the headsman's axe, in days to come was revered as a martyr by Hrotsvitha and countless others among the faithful.

The four narratives which follow may be summed up in few words. One of them shows Theophilus the Penitent, whose date is unknown and whose life is a romantic legend, recalling that of Faust. A version in Greek was translated into Latin by Deacon Paul of Naples in the ninth century and dedicated to Charles the Bald; this undoubtedly was used by Hrotsvitha.

In the story Theophilus holds an important office of administration in the Church under his bishop. Upon this bishop's death he is eagerly called, both by archbishop and by people, to consecration as his successor. He refuses, declaring himself unworthy, and his persistence in refusing causes resentment; finally the archbishop is persuaded by influential men to deprive him of the office he has held so long in the diocese. This unjust act so upsets the mind of Theophilus that his humility turns sour; in his firm determination to win back influence and position he decides at last to make friends with the Devil, who forces him to deny Christ in a bond written and signed. Satan does his part, and by his evil magic Theophilus rises higher in power and popularity than ever before. But the grace of God is stronger than the Devil; in the end shame and fear of final retribution drive the sinner to seek refuge in a church dedicated to Mary, Mother of God. There in vision night after night she first terrifies him by her very clear picture of his peril, and then, upon his vow of penitence, she pleads for his restoring to Heaven's protection. Open confession of his guilt is followed by his happy death and by thanksgiving for this mercy from all his fellow Christians.

Basilius is another tale of Satan's diabolic cunning. The time is the fourth century and the scene is Caesarea in Cappadocia, Asia Minor, under St. Basil the Great, its bishop. Once again we are faced by unwelcome love. A young serving-man cherishes a passionate desire to possess the daughter of his master, the noble Proterius. In despair of gaining her he seeks advice from one skilled in magic, and soon finds himself invited to a meeting of those who dwell in darkness, presided over by their Prince. There he, too, makes convenant with the Devil, who inspires in the daughter of Proterius a passion for the servant equal to his. This horrifies her father, who has long hoped to place this, his beloved and only child, in a convent under care of the Church. But he hopes in vain; he is forced to witness the marriage. The wife, an innocent girl, knows nothing about the secret league with Satan. One day by accident she learns of it, and in dreadful panic she rushes to her bishop, St. Basil. Will he rescue her husband from Hell? Of course he will, and he does. The sinner repents, the Devil under Basil's menace yields up the charter of agreement, and once again everyone gives praise to God.

The seventh story deals with Dionysius, known as Saint Denis, who, according to St. Gregory of Tours, was sent in the time of the Emperor Decius, in the third century, from Italy to France as missionary to its people; there he became the first bishop of Paris and Patron of the land. He is not to be confused with the "Dionysius the Areopagite" who was converted at Athens by St. Paul (Acts XVII, 34) in the first century. Nor was he the "Pseudo-Dionysius the Areopagite" whose (disputed) date may be about 500 A.D., the author of theological treatises and letters famous in medieval days.

In 835 the Emperor Louis the Pious commanded his arch-chaplain, Hilduin, to compose the *Life of Saint Denis of France*. Unfortunately just at this time the Byzantine emperor, Michael II, sent to Louis a copy of the writings of the "Pseudo-Dionysius," and in his *Life of Saint Denis* Hilduin most grievously mixed up the two men and their doings. So did Hrotsvitha, who dutifully followed Hilduin as her source. We need not trouble ourselves, then, with this part of her work.

Nor need we linger over the verses which told, in her eighth work, the story of St. Agnes the Martyr who would not and could not wed any of the nobles of Rome who sought her. The source of Hrotsvitha here was a *Passion of St. Agnes* falsely attributed to St. Ambrose, printed in the appendix to Migne's edition of his works and in the *Acta Sanctorum,* January II, 352.

3

We now reach Hrotsvitha, composer of six "comedies." The hexameter verse of her legends was thickly adorned with leonine rime; her plays were written in rhythmic prose: sharp, lively, and determined. She was working in the time of John XII, pope from 955 to 964, a ruler declared vain and vicious; in the time of Liutprand of Cremona, teller of salacious tales and gossip, of whose narratives she very probably heard. She did hear, of course, of the mimes and entertainments, lustful and voluptuous, that here and there delighted merrymakers; she wanted, for those who worked hard in convents and monasteries or followed Catholic obedience in the world, some decent and inspiring relaxation for their leisure hours. Why not try, herself, to give it them? She had read Terence long and closely; why not write plays that told in interesting, even comic, dialogue the doings of saints who conquered, and of sinners who repented?

For her six plays, once written and finished, she carefully composed two prefaces. In the first she describes her purpose:

"There are many Catholics—and I cannot entirely clear myself in this respect—who because of the eloquence of a more cultivated style prefer the emptiness of pagan writings to the profit gained from sacred books. There are others, too, who study sacred pages diligently, who for the most part scorn pagan works, yet they are constantly reading the fictions of Terence. Thus, while they feel the charm of his style and enjoy this to the full, they are defiled by acquaintance with execrable evils. It is true that I myself, 'The Strong Voice of Gandersheim' " (an expression explained by Jacob Grimm, page ix, as a Latinizing of her name, Hrotsvith, Old High German Hruodsvind), "have not refused to imitate his style in my writing. But, for the reasons given by me above, I have used those plays of his, plays in which the foul lewdness of lascivious women was pictured, to make known to the world the noble chastity of holy virgins, so far as my small talent allowed. Often I have blushed with shame when I have had to write of the loathsome madness of illicit love and nasty conversations not fit for our hearing. On the other hand, if I omitted all this because of modesty I should not be carrying out my purpose."

The greater and stronger the temptation and assault of evil, she continues, the greater the glory won by resistance, especially when the frail Christian woman overcomes and humiliates the strong, lustful man. Her style, she admits, is naturally far inferior to that of Terence. But that is not really her fault: "I am not such a lover of self that I should hesitate through fear of criticism to use the power which Christ may give me. If my labor pleases anyone I shall be happy; if through rough and rude writing it pleases no one, I am still happy in what I have done."

The second preface is addressed to certain "wise men, cultured and experts in philosophy," who have read her plays and have praised them as worthy and good. She now tells them: "I know clearly that talent has been given me by Heaven. But through lack of constant direction it is untrained; through my own want of energy and perseverance it has lain neglected. And, therefore, to keep God's gift alive in me I have inserted in my work some threads torn from the robe of Philosophy, to light up its dark ignorance by nobler material."

The first play, *Gallicanus*, is in two parts; the time is the fourth century, during the reigns of the Roman Emperors Constantine and Julian. Gallicanus, commander of Constantine's army, is just setting out for campaign against barbarian invaders of the empire; before he leaves he summons up courage to tell the emperor that he is in love with his daughter, the Princess Constantia, and wants to marry her. Constantine, as we know, was a Christian; so was his daughter, so firmly so that she had vowed to remain a virgin, dedicated to prayer. She would rather die, she declares, than marry the heathen Gallicanus. This outright refusal troubles her father, since Gallicanus is a man of high standing in Rome, immensely popular among its citizens. He decides to send with his commander on this campaign two officers, John and Paul, convinced Christians, in the hope that they may win his conversion.

Gallicanus himself has no thought of conversion, in spite of his love. He offers sacrifice to his heathen gods and departs for the field of battle, where he suffers terrible defeat by the enemy, so terrible that only abject surrender is left to him. All his men are in despair.

Firmly John begs his commander, as the one and only hope left, to turn from pagan gods to the Christian faith. Gallicanus yields, and then orders his army to make a final effort. He leads the rush forward; the barbarians are routed; Rome gains a splendid victory, and the invaders not only retreat but solemnly promise permanent tribute. The general, astounded by this miracle, is baptized without delay, and his army returns home in triumph.

In Rome the emperor receives two most unexpected surprises. Not only does he hear that Gallicanus is offering thanks for his success at the altar of St. Peter himself, but the conqueror, already a baptized Christian, has no intention of marrying anyone. He is going off to live a life of Christian charity and goodwill with his friend Hilarinus.

Constantine is delighted that Gallicanus has found conversion. But, though he does not mean to marry Constantia, could he not at least live in the palace, "as it were" a son-in-law of the imperial line? The emperor does not want to lose a good and loyal friend.

But Gallicanus, soldier and determined convert though he is, is yet human and knows human weakness. "It is not well," he replies, "that I should constantly be seeing a girl whom, as you know, I love more than my parents, than my life, and my own soul."

Part II finds Julian the Apostate ruling the empire, and Gallicanus at his good work in Italy. As he is still true to his Christian vow, this pagan emperor orders him into exile; and there he dies, at the hands of heathen men.

Dulcitius, the second play, brings a "comic" touch. Its scene is also laid in the fourth century, but at the time when Diocletian, persecutor of Christians, was emperor. Three young women of high rank in Rome refuse to marry the suitable young nobles whom he has picked out for them or to offer sacrifice to heathen deities before their marriage; like the Princess Constantia, they are dedicated Christians. Their names are Agape, Chionia, and Irene; they are, of course, both beautiful and charming, and now Diocletian orders them to be kept in prison under the governor Dulcitius until they decide to obey his will.

Dulcitius alas! has a weakness for pretty faces and attractive young girls; he hopes to enjoy the company of his captives. His soldiers warn him that he will gain nothing; but he decides to lodge them near his own quarters, in a small room off the prison kitchen where the kitchen pots and pans are kept.

Action then follows thus:

DULCITIUS: What are the prisoners doing at this time of night?

SOLDIERS OF THE GUARD: Singing hymns.

DULCITIUS: Let's go and see.

SOLDIERS: We shall hear their tinkling voices far away.

DULCITIUS: Keep guard with your lanterns before the doors, and I will go in and get my fill of sweet embraces.

SOLDIERS: Go on in; we will wait here.

AGAPE: What is that noise out there?

IRENE: That wretched Dulcitius is coming in.

CHIONIA: God keep us!

AGAPE: Amen.

CHIONIA: What *is* all that crashing of jars and kettles and pans?

IRENE: I'll go and see. Oh, do come here! Look through the chink of the door!

AGAPE: What is it?

IRENE: See there! That fool, that raving idiot! He thinks he has his arms around US!

AGAPE: What is he doing?

IRENE: Petting and pawing the big leather jars on his lap, hugging the pots and pans, giving them sweet kisses!

CHIONIA: What a fool!

IRENE: His face and his hands and his clothes are all filthy; he looks like an Ethiopian, black all over!

AGAPE: Of course he is black; the Devil has got hold of him.

IRENE: There, now he is going out! Let us try and see what happens when the guards see him!

SOLDIERS: Who is this coming out? A lunatic! No, it's the Devil himself! Run for your lives!

DULCITIUS: Where are you running? Halt? Wait for me! Give me a light to my bedroom.

SOLDIERS: It's the voice of the governor, but he looks like the Devil. No, we won't stay, we will hurry off. This nightmare will be the death of us!

DULCITIUS: I shall go straight to the palace and inform the Court of this insult. Doorman, conduct me within; I have secret business with the emperor.

DOORMEN: What is this disgusting, horrible monster, in black rags and ribbons? Let's beat him well and throw him down the steps. We'll take good care he doesn't get inside!

DULCITIUS: Oh! oh! whatever has happened? Am I not dressed splendidly, sparkling from head to toe? Everyone who sees me looks horrified, as if I were some sort of ogre! I will go back to my wife and find out what has happened. Ah! here she is! But her hair is flying wild and all the servants are in tears! What *is* the matter?

WIFE: Oh dear! Dulcitius, what *have* you been doing to yourself? You must be out of your mind! Those Christians have made my husband a sight to laugh at!

DULCITIUS: They must have bewitched me with their magic.

WIFE: The worst of it is that you don't know yourself what they have done to you.

DULCITIUS: Bring out those harlots and stand them up in the marketplace, stark naked. I'll let them know that I, too, can play games with them!

GUARDS: It's no good. Their clothes won't come off; they stick to them like their own skin. The governor has fallen fast asleep. Let's go and tell the emperor all about it.

In the end the three girls, completely defiant against all threatening, are put to death, first the two elder ones and then the youngest, Irene. As she awaits the executioner she remarks to the judge who has condemned her: "The greatest joy is mine and real sorrow will be yours. For your wicked cruelty you will go to hell; but I, I shall receive the martyr's palm of triumph, the virgin's crown!"

More unusual is the third of these compositions, the story of one Callimachus, who is represented as living in the first century of the Roman Empire. He has fallen violently in love with a woman named Drusiana who is not only married, wife of the aristocratic Andronicus, but a baptized Christian and dedicated to rigid rejection of pleasures of the flesh.

All the same, Callimachus tells Drusiana of his yearning, and, of course, receives indignant repulse: he is a panderer, a man lascivious, wanton, without worth, sense, or mind. In spite of these words he continues to plead, until she is so worried, so afraid that in the end she may yield, that she prays Heaven to release her by death. And die she does.

Her husband, crushed by this sudden loss of one whose life he has shared in perfect sympathy, hastens to seek comfort from his friend, Saint John the Apostle. Christian prayer, John reminds him, does more for the departed soul than floods of tears. So they go together on their way to the family tomb.

Before they reach it, however, Callimachus, even more frantic than Andronicus through this destruction of his hope, has been tempted by diabolical suggestion to try to bribe the caretaker of the tomb, one Fortunatus, to bring the body of Drusiana out from its resting-place; dead though she is to this earth, he will yet enjoy that embrace which was not allowed him while she lived. Fortunatus is a man who cares more for money than honor or virtue. He accepts the bribe, and brings out the corpse. Just as he is about to place it in the arms of Callimachus, both men are struck by horror at the sudden appearance of a huge serpent, its venomous jaws wide open, advancing upon them. In a moment both are lying dead on the ground beside Drusiana, Fortunatus through poison of the dragon's fangs, Callimachus through the instant realization of his criminal lust, flashing before his mind as he sees before him the serpent of evil.

Meanwhile, Andronicus and Saint John have also seen a vision. In the path before them as they walk there appears, from nowhere, it seems to them, a young man, so noble, so wonderful, that the apostle is sure he is none but the Lord Christ Himself. He has come, He tells them, that His name may be glorified in the return to life of both Drusiana and "another, who is lying dead near her tomb."

With these words He disappears from their sight, and, entirely mystified, wondering who the other "dead one" can possibly be, they hurry forward.

"What in the name of Christ do I see before me?" cries Saint John as they arrive. "The tomb is open, the body of Drusiana is cast forth, and here, near by, are two corpses, with a serpent coiled around them!"

Andronicus, however, understands at once. The body of his beloved Drusiana by God's grace has not been dishonored; both Callimachus and Fortunatus have been mercifully prevented by death from fulfilling the crime which the lust of the one willed and the greed of the other allowed.

St. John quickly commands the serpent to vanish. Then through prayer to God he causes Callimachus to rise to a new life of penitence, and Drusiana to return to earth and to her sorrowing husband. To Drusiana, by will and authority of Heaven, he entrusts the raising of Fortunatus from the dead. The miracle follows, and Fortunatus, with Callimachus, stands alive once more.

But their future shows no union in spirit. Callimachus promises in all sincerity contrition and amendment. Fortunatus will hear nothing of either; he hates good people and, above all, hates their happiness. At last the apostle, finding him obdurate, pronounces his doom: "Let him die who for envy of another's joy refuses to live. We will go hence in thanksgiving for the penitence of Callimachus, and leave to the Devil his own son." Fortunatus falls promptly to the ground, a corpse once more, and Andronicus, taking his wife by the hand, leads her happily to their home.

The next two plays, Nos. IV and V, both deal with a subject common in the early Middle Ages, the conversion of prostitutes by monks living as hermits in the desert. Here Hrotsvitha was using a Latin version of the *Lives of the Desert Fathers*, translated from the Greek. The fathers described in these two "dramas" may conscientiously be given their place in history; the women whom they brought to penitence exist only in legend.

The first play has as its hero Saint Abraham Kidunaia, variously placed in the fourth and in the sixth century, known for his zealous preaching among the people of Beth-Kidnua, a town near Edessa in Mesopotamia. It was the legend of his penitent, Saint Mary the Harlot, which chiefly gave interest and reverence to his name in Hrotsvitha's tenth century.

An orphan niece, she tells, seven years old, is left to his sole care. How can an elderly hermit, living in the wilds under strict religious rule, bring up a little girl? With a faith and courage which

Hrotsvitha does not find surprising, he decides to dedicate her as bride of Christ her Lord, and to make for her a little cell near his own in the desert, where he may very often visit her, to guide, enhearten and teach this ward of his. The child is readily captivated by the enchanting picture of Heaven held out before her, surely to be hers if she will lead faithfully a hermit's true life on earth. She has not the slightest idea what that life will mean for her, but she yields to Abraham's kindly urging, charmed by the importance given to her name "Mary."

And she shows her own courage. For twenty long years she remains in her cell, following the teaching of Father Abraham, who watches over her with all love and diligence.

Then one day she is found missing; to his horror Abraham finds that she has been seen speaking with a young man clad in monastic habit. No one has heard of this young man; Abraham and his fellow hermits after long search are forced to believe that she has been decoyed away by false promises. Where is she? Finally, a friend, one whom the father can surely trust, offers to seek her in cities and throughout the countryside.

For two years nothing is heard, while Abraham waits, always in hope, day after day. Then the friend returns, with dreadful news: Mary, that niece and "daughter," guarded and dedicated by the old man, is living in a house of prostitutes, a brothel, cherished with wary caution by its keeper, to whom she hands over regularly the money she earns from her "lovers." "*Lovers?* Of *Mary?*" cries Abraham in anguish. "Oh, yes, plenty of them," answers the friend.

Long and earnestly the father hermit ponders over this trouble, and at last he has a plan. He will borrow a horse and a soldier's outfit; in this disguise he will go forth himself into the world as a "lover," resolved at all cost to defeat the Devil who has caught his child. Cramming a cap down on his head that he may not be recognized, and taking with him for his need the one bit of money which he happens to have, he starts out.

He finds the place, secures a lodging as a "customer" in search of pleasure, tips the keeper and gaily makes his request: "Would you ask that very pretty girl whom I saw here just now to have supper with me? I have heard of her charm again and again and I want terribly to meet her."

"An old man like you running after a girl?" replies the owner of the house. But he calls Mary. The sight of her, wanton, tricked out to attract and tempt, nearly breaks Abraham's heart. But bravely he plays his role. Naturally so does she. She throws her arms around this new "lover," and at once feels a strange new fear. Instinct tells her that he is somehow different from the men who come to this place.

Abraham works harder than ever; she must not escape him now. With laughter and seeming good cheer he sups on dishes for many years forbidden him in his hermit's life, then follows her to a private room and shuts the door. At once he turns round to face her and drops all pretence. "Mary," he entreats, "my own adopted daughter, don't you know me?"

The girl bursts into tears in a passion of misery; all that she has hidden deep within her now suddenly rises to the surface. She is lost and ruined; she has no hope of return; she cannot even talk about it, her sin is too horrible. In all tenderness the father does his best to comfort her; all *is* not lost, he says; she can still come back; he will care for her once more. At last she believes it, as she looks at his face; penitent but ready and willing to start again, he brings her home to her cell near him in the desert land.

Very different is the story of the fifth play, the old legend of Saint Thais the Penitent, redeemed by Paphnutius, a monk in Egypt, possibly a bishop in the Upper Thebaid. Several saints of this name are found in Egyptian tradition and it is difficult to know which one to select. But we may believe with some confidence that our Paphnutius lived in the fourth century of St. Anthony and St. Athanasius.

At its beginning this play suffers through insertion by its diligent author of a lengthy extract from the *De Musica* of Boethius: "threads from the robe of Philosophy" which are intended to show forth the harmony of elements within body and soul. These "threads" of learning, placed here to impress the reader, only interrupt his thought. After this break we come to the story and find Thais as an abandoned prostitute, and Paphnutius trying to redeem her with all severity. The terror which his picture of her soul's peril brings upon her certainly does its work; she dismisses all the young men who hover around her, burns all her treasures, and follows the grim and determined saint to a convent of nuns. There he tells her to enter at once "a narrow cell in which she may more freely meditate on her sins." The abbess promptly provides the cell, which has no door, only a little window through which by order of Paphnutius "on approved days at approved hours food is to be given her, sparingly." He continues:: "A grave sin calls for a strong remedy. Enter, Thais, a dwelling well suited for lamenting your crimes."

Thais takes one step forward and then shrinks back: "How small it is! How dark!" she cries. "Hitherto you have wandered where you would," Paphnutius answers; "it is only right that now you be curbed in solitude."

"But—I blush to say it—how dirty, how unbearably foul it will get while I live here, in this one small place!"

The torture of Hell, she is told, is far more fearful than mere passing discomforts here on earth.

Finally she pleads: "Where in this unclean place can I fittingly and purely call upon the name of God's dread majesty?"

"Who are you?" the reply comes quickly, "that you should dare with defiled lips to speak the name of pure divinity?"

The cell is sealed fast and Paphnutius leaves her to silence and the mute cry of her own heart. Three years go by and he does not know whether she has made acceptable offering of repentance to the Lord God or not. Perhaps his brother hermit Anthony can find out for him by prayer? He sets out to visit his brother; then he tells him how he has rescued Thais from a life of sin by pretending to be one of her lovers and that she has consented to do penance in a very tiny cell. Now she has been shut up there for three years and, overjoyed as he is by this willingness on her part, he is a little bit disturbed (*levi tamen conturbor sollicitudine*) lest this long-continued imprisonment may have been too much for her frail body.

Happily during this visit a disciple of Anthony named Paul sees a vision in his sleep: Thais is received with joy into Heaven! At once Paphnutius leaves for her convent and finds her still in her cell, penitent and at peace with her Maker. He now invites her to come out and join the community of nuns; but she asks to stay quietly where she has been so long. "Be bold in the fear of the Lord," he bids her, "and abide in His love; in two weeks you will die and by God's grace pass Heavenward."

Two weeks later this is proved true, and Paphnutius carries out the ritual of her body's laying to rest in earth.

Not every reader knows that Anatole France, when he wrote his famous *Thais*, was familiar not only with its ancient sources but also with this play by Hrotsvitha. Some of his story resembles hers; for him, too, Thais dies a saint. But in his tale, after Paphnutius with praise to God has enclosed the penitent in her cell, he is constantly tempted by the Devil and suffers torture of mind and soul. He practices every kind of austerity; he lives long on top of a pillar and is revered by thousands as a most holy man, worker of miracles. Only a poor fellow of simple mind, Paul, "the Fool," can look at him and tell the truth. "Three demons will seize this man," Paul declares in the presence of the great St. Anthony of the desert; "and their names are Pride, Passion, and Doubt": words which Anthony himself will not deny. In this *Thais* of Anatole France, Paphnutius is indeed with the penitent when she dies. But he is inside her cell, his arms are around her, and he is crying: "I love you, Thais! What care I for God or Heaven? The world, human love, that, that only is real! Oh, Thais, do not die! Come, come with me and let us live and love!"

But Thais does not hear.

The sixth and last play, *Sapientia*, holds little interest; another long extract from Boethius, this time from his *De Arithmetica*, does nothing to enliven it. It is an allegory, presenting Wisdom and her children, Faith, Hope, and Charity. The daughter virtues appear as three little girls, twelve, ten, and eight years old. Cheered and encouraged by their mother, with bold and defiant words they march to death as martyrs in this fable, victims of Hadrian, emperor of Rome in the second century. Wisdom gives their bodies burial in ground three miles outside the city, then gladly finds beside their grave the death for which, as faithful mother if not martyr, she, too, longs.

Nor need we dwell upon two works written by Hrotsvitha during her later years. Here she returned to the hexameter verse of her first labors. One is the *Gesta Ottonis, The Deeds of Otto,* which described what she had gathered concerning the reign of Otto the Great. To him, and to his son, Otto II, she offered separate dedications; she presented both as of imperial rank, which means that she was writing after the coronation of Otto the second as emperor in 967. She also told that the poem, composed by request of Abbess Gerberga, was to be sent for criticism and, she hoped, for approval, to William, archbishop of Mainz, who died in 968. But we do not know the exact date of her own death.

In her preface she laments that she has had no written record to help her, and little enough by word of mouth: "I have worked as one who walks in a wide forest, where every path lies covered deep in snow; no one have I had to guide me while I made my way forward, now wandering in devious paths, now suddenly hitting the trail."

Work hard she undoubtedly did, but the work adds little to our knowledge.

The same is true of her "First Beginnings of the Abbey of

Gandersheim"; in her Latin, *Primordia Coenobii Gandeshemensis.* Here the energy and authority during many years of Oda, co-founder with her husband, Count Liudolf of Saxony, are duly pictured. Visions play a large part in the narrative, which covers the rule, as abbesses in succession, of Oda's three daughters, Hathumod, Gerberga I, and Christina, who died in 919.

Many lines of the *Gesta,* and the ending of the *Primordia,* are lost.

Hrotsvitha, then, knew something of the history of her time; she knew *Lives* and legends of saints; she had read Virgil, Prudentius, Sedulius, and Boethius; she had also read the *Waltharius.* Very possibly she knew in some fashion the work, or knew of the work, of her contemporary, Widukind, who with her admired so fervently Otto the Great. Perhaps she even met him. Her Latin is good, easy to read. Conversation with this shy but resolute nun must have been both pleasant and stimulating. Yet, her plays did not win popularity, though evidence has been offered for knowledge of her work after her death. One manuscript lived on in the Bavarian abbey of St. Emmeram, very probably sent there by Abbess Gerberga II, as daughter of Bavaria's duke. Late in the fifteenth century a German scholar, Conrad Celtes, rediscovered it there and thus paved the way for its copying and editing as *Codex Monacensis,* now in Munich.

4

It is not in the writings of Hrotsvitha of Gandersheim that we see the real drama, or sense of drama, in the tenth century. She was a faithful Benedictine nun, and she loved art for teaching's sake. Her lively conversations may have been read before gatherings of her sisters and their guests. They were not "dramas," and they certainly were not "comedies," even if a small part of the *Dulcitius* may be described as "comic." Hrotsvitha had no idea of the direction, the grouping, and the inspired movement needed by a dramatist who would set a play upon a stage. For this we must turn elsewhere.

First, let us consider in this light the *Ecbasis cuiusdam captivi per tropologiam,* "The Escape of a Certain Captive, Told in Figurative Fashion." It is known as a beast-epic, and its traditional placing has been in the first half of the tenth century, although energetic argument has supported a date in the eleventh. Was the King Conrad mentioned here Conrad I (911-18), or Conrad II, king of Germany (1024-39), and Emperor (1027-39)? Was the king

named Henry here Henry the Fowler (919-36), or Henry III, king
of Germany (1028-56), and emperor (Dec. 25, 1046-56)?

The work is an allegory, described in action by a number of
wild creatures, beasts and birds. Its background is "monastic"; its
timing is in Holy Week, when all religious are looking forward to
Easter; its scene is Lotharingia. Its author, whose name is unknown,
was, we may think, a monk of the Lotharingian diocese of Toul, very
probably belonging to its abbey of Saint-Èvre. He had read Latin
literature, classical, medieval, pagan and Christian; he was moved
to write, according to his tale, by a severe attack of that weariness
and discontent so well pictured by Cassian in the fifth century as
accidie, the "noonday sickness" which assaults those dedicated to
monastic life.

Its verse, Latin hexameter, with much leonine rime, holds two fables,
an outer and an inner one. The outer story tells of a Calf who in his
hot desire to gambol freely where he will slips his halter and runs off
into woods and meadows, only at last to be caught by a Wolf,
hungry for blood. Like Brother Fox and Brother Badger in the old
Irish legend of St. Ciaran the Elder, the Wolf lives under "monastic"
rule; the Calf will make for him a delicious feast after the long fast of
Lent. It is now Easter Eve; tomorrow, after the chanting of Easter
Mass, the Wolf and his friends will gather for the banquet.

Various delicacies for the Easter table are brought as offerings
to the Wolf in his den by the Hedgehog and the Otter. Night comes
on; the Calf, also nurtured in religion, prays the Lord Who created
him to bring rescue in mercy, and then settles down for perhaps his
last sleep on earth. The Wolf's rest is disturbed by a terrible nightmare, and the Otter warns him that if, in defiance of monastic vow,
he sheds the Calf's blood, dreadful things will come upon him.

There is wisdom in this warning. At dawn an army of the Calf's
older friends, oxen and bulls, who have heard of his fate and are
raging with anger against the Wolf, are led to his den by a Dog born
and bred in the region of the Vosges bordering on Lotharingia. As
they approach, the Wolf in panic rushes to escape, calling for aid.
He is terrified that his deadly enemy, the Fox, will join in the assault.

With the Otter and the Hedgehog, his guests, he seeks safety on
a height overlooking his den. His two companions are untouched by
fear, and they ask him why on earth he is afraid of the Fox. The
Wolf tells them, in a story which forms the inner fable. It is a version
of the well-known tale of the Sick Lion.

Once upon a time, in days of spring when monarchs march forth to war, the Lion lay in the forest, tortured by pain. All the beasts of his royal kingdom were called to bring him remedies of every sort, and all came except the Fox. His absence was reported to the Lion by an "ancestor," uncle of the Wolf in the outer fable and royal chamberlain in the Lion's court; he had been appointed for the express purpose of seeking a cure for his sovereign's sickness. The Lion in his wrath ordered the Fox to be hanged by the neck and the Wolf-Chamberlain made ready the gallows.

But a comrade of the Fox, the Panther, ran to find him and to give warning of this decree. In desperation the Fox, who was also "monastic" in profession, turned to prayer, as the Calf had done. But the Fox's prayer was somewhat different. Would the Lord Christ, he entreated, help him to destroy that lying Wolf-Chamberlain? Then with all haste he hurried to the Lion's side. He could offer, he declared, healing entirely sure. The Wolf-Chamberlain must be killed and skinned; he, the Fox, would first rub special ointment, brought by him from India, upon the Lion's aching back and then wrap him for warmth in the Wolf's hide. Soon all would be well. It was done, and in very truth the Lion slowly gained comfort and health.

There rose, however, and there remained, bitter feud between the two families, of the Wolf and the Fox.

The inner fable continues. The Leopard arrived and made plans for a feast of rejoicing; the Fox was honored by the grateful Lion; the Panther, by cunning support of the Fox, his friend, was made heir to the Lion's throne and at once suggested that now had come the time for song. It was Holy Week, and therefore the song was of the Passion of Christ, sung first by the Blackbird and the Nightingale in harmony, then by the Nightingale alone. The Parrot and the Swan came to ask news of the Lion's health.

Joy rose high on Easter morning, when all the creatures of the forest joined in *Salve, festa dies* and assisted at Easter Mass. Breakfast, an occasion of both ceremony and merriment, promptly followed. The Lion now announced the names of those whom he was appointing as his heirs, the future kings of the beasts: first the Panther, then the Fox. The Lion and the Panther granted to the Fox a fortress in feudal tenure, as their vassal.

Now we return to the outer fable, later in time. The scene is again the den of the Wolf, but the Wolf is a nephew of the Wolf-

Chamberlain of the inner story. The same company is gathered in the den. There is the Wolf, rejoicing for two reasons. It is Easter morning and his victim, the Calf, will soon be sacrificed for his pleasure. There is the Otter, once again telling him to set the Calf free. There is the Fox, heaping false flattery upon the Wolf, and secretly hating him with bitter hatred because the feudal fortress which gave the Fox so much pride has been taken from him and given in fief to the Wolf. Did not the Fox cause the death of the Wolf's uncle, once chamberlain to the Lion?

Nor have the angry oxen and the bulls gone back to their fields. Soon, to his delight the Fox sees one of them slowly advancing, head and horns lowered, then rushing upon the Wolf to take him unawares. In a moment the Wolf lies dead; the Calf is safe; peace is restored. The beasts of the fields, waters, and woods leave for home; the Calf runs back to his mother and his stall, delighting in renewal of peace and happiness.

Such is the story. We keep here the traditional date of this *Ecbasis*, in the early tenth century, and we think of it as drama rather than as epic. A very interesting paper by Gustavo Vinay has compared the "drama" of Hrotsvitha with that of our anonymous writer, in these words: "Il senso della scena, il gusto per la varieta e la richezza dello spettaculo è tanto inferiore a quello di cui è ricco lo sconosciuto frate di Toul, la cui opera è veramente la sola compiuta 'commedia' che ci abbia tramandato l'alto Medioevo."

It is pleasant, and very possibly correct, to look upon this work from Toul as written by one who has decided to support Henry the Fowler; one who has grown up in the dark years of Louis the Child and of Conrad I, under whom Lotharingia repeatedly suffered assault; one who is rejoicing for his monastery and for his world in the hope of new life to rise, now that this Henry is king of Germany. So long has sickness been the fate of the land; so long has flattery, so long has disloyalty undermined its rule; so long have violence and war ruined homes, churches, and abbeys, in Lotharingia and in Germany. If the Lion has been sick, so has the Wolf been treacherous. But now the Lion has regained health; the Wolf has met the death which he deserved; the Calf has once more found comfort and security.

So much for politics, with a touch of satire on the one hand, and of encouragement on the other. But the monk of Toul is also a dramatist. He diversifies and enriches his tale with a keen eye for color, for the composition and for the arrangement of his scenes, for the grouping of his actors, for the developing and the interplay of his action. The result is both truly comic and truly serious, as the animals, as the birds, play each their parts. Their director in this masquerade unfolds his themes far more expertly, in far more lively spirit than Hrotsvitha does in her didactic dialogue of virtuous or vicious men and women. There is a lightness, a sense of creative enjoyment in the mind of the writer as he introduces and moves here and there his bird or his beast in this "monastic" picture of field and forest. And there is earnestness as well. From the pain and misery of a troubled world we turn to hear the song of the Passion of Christ which redeems and sets free the world. At last the long Lent is over; it is Easter and the Calf is rescued and restored.

5

More important, however, was the course of medieval drama in the Church of the tenth century. Evidence concerning this has come down to us both in the form of a "trope" and of an acted "play."

A trope was a brief text, set to music, and added as an enrichment to some part of the liturgy of the Church; to the introit, to the kyrie, or to the gloria of the Mass. It might be added as introduction, as insertion, or as ending.

The date and the country of origin are not known in certain fact. Very possibly that antiphonary which a priest of Jumièges in France brought about 860 to young Notker of Saint-Gall in Germany contained tropes as well as sequences; we may well believe that tropes were written in the ninth century in France. It would seem that they were also written during this century in Germany. Ekkehard IV, who wrote in the eleventh a sequel to Ratpert's story of the fortunes and misfortunes of Saint-Gall, states that Tutilo, that genius of the abbey who died about 912, a monk known far and wide for his skill in carving of ivories, in painting, "in music of every kind of pipe and flute," also wrote tropes which were sung to music, and offered them to the Emperor Charles the Fat, deposed in 887. Ekkehard's statement may or may not be correct, but it is of interest.

One of these tropes assigned to Notker by him is still ours to read. It introduced the introit for the third Mass of Christmas Day, the *Missa in die,* and it held dialogue of dramatic character. This

dialogue was sung by two choirs, one querying, the other respond-
ing; the introduction was given by both:

1.   Hodie cantandus est nobis puer,
     quem gignebat ineffabiliter ante tempora pater,
     et eundem sub tempore generavit inclita mater.

2. *Interrogant:*   3. *Respondent:*
    Quis est iste puer,   Hic enim est,
    quem tam magnis praeconiis   quem praesagus et electus
    dignum vociferatis?   symmista Dei ad terras
    Dicite nobis,   venturum praevidens
    ut collaudatores   longe ante praenotavit
    esse possimus.   sicque praedixit:

     Puer natus est nobis et filius datus est nobis . . .

1.   Today shall our choirs tell in song of the Child
     Ineffably before all worlds, not made, of His Father begotten,
     Who, One and the Same, under time was born to His glorious
         Mother.

2. *Question:*   3. *Answer:*
    Who is this little Child   Know, this is He,
    Whom with so great   Whom the prophet,
        proclamation   the elected,
    worthy of honor you cry?   Forerunner of God, to earth
    Tell, tell this to us,   His advent foreseeing,
    that sharers in His praise   long before anticipated,
    we ourselves may be.   and thus did foretell:

     Unto us a Child is born, unto us a Son is given.

We come now to texts of tropes contained in manuscripts of the
tenth century; these were Easter tropes, telling in dramatic form of
the Day of Resurrection.

The earliest in time of these manuscripts, written some years
before or after 930, comes from France, from its abbey of Saint-
Martial at Limoges. Its text runs also in question and answer:

1.   *Question* (by the Angel or Angels at the tomb), sung
     by Choir 1:

                    Quem quaeritis in sepulchro,
                        O christicolae?

> Whom seek ye in the tomb,
> O followers of Christ?

2. *Answer* (by the holy women, the three Marys, visiting the tomb), sung by Choir 2:

> Jesum Nazarenum crucifixum,
> O caelicolae!

> Jesus of Nazareth, crucified,
> O dwellers in Heaven!

3. *Answer* (by the Angel or Angels):

> Non est hic;
> surrexit, sicut praedixerat.
> Ite, nuntiate
> quia surrexit.

> He is not here;
> He has risen, as He had foretold
> Go ye, tell
> that He has risen!

4. *Announcing* (by both choirs):

> Alleluia, resurrexit Dominus,
> hodie resurrexit leo fortis,
> filius Dei.
> Deo gratias, dicite, eia!

> Alleluia, the Lord is risen,
> today has risen the mighty Lion,
> the Son of God!
> Thanks be to God; tell ye this, Alleluia!

Then follows the introit.

Some twenty years later, about 950, is dated a manuscript of Saint-Gall; its message is cast in simpler form:

> Angel:
> > Quem quaeritis in sepulchro,
> > O christicolae?

> The holy women:
> > Jesum Nazarenum crucifixum,
> > O caelicolae!

Angel:

> Non est hic;
> surrexit, sicut praedixerat.
> Ite, nuntiate
> quia surrexit de sepulchro.

Of course the dates of these two manuscripts do not tell us the dates of composition of their texts. We may imagine their composition in the tenth century; but we do not know which was the first to be composed, the simpler one of Saint-Gall, given to us by a later scribe, or the more elaborate one of Saint-Martial, earlier in its script.

We know of at least seven other manuscripts of the *Quem quaeritis*, all written in these same nine hundreds; their texts vary in composition and wording.

From this introduction to the introit of the Mass, the dramatic dialogue, we come to the "Easter Play." The ninth century knew ceremonies honoring feasts of the Church, including Easter; in regard to this feast we possess two sources of importance from the tenth. One of these, from the *Life* of St. Ulrich of Augsburg by Gerhard, tells of the ceremonies connected with Holy Week and Easter Day, as carried out by this bishop himself:

"At dawn on Good Friday he hastened to fulfill his recital of psalms, and then, after Mass and the communion of the people, in the manner customary among us he buried that part of the Body of Christ which remained. . . . On Easter Day, after Prime, he entered the church of Saint Ambrose in which he had placed the Body of Christ and above It had laid a stone for Its covering. There with a few of his clergy he celebrated Mass, and then, bearing in his hands the Body of Christ, escorted by acolytes carrying the Book of the Gospels and wax candles and incense, and by a choir of boys singing hymns, he went forth to the church of Saint John the Baptist."

As we have seen, Saint Ulrich died in 973. About the same time, at some date between 965 and 975, we find action added to words, in instructions for the carrying out of an "Easter Play," written in the *Regularis Concordia*, "The Monastic Concord of the Monks and Nuns of the English Nation." This was a detailed and authoritative setting forth of monastic rules and customs agreed upon for English use by a great assembly of bishops, abbots, and abbesses, at Winchester in England. St. Ethelwold was then bishop of Winchester and St. Dunstan was archbishop of Canterbury. Dunstan guided those who here discussed and decided; very probably Ethelwold drew up into form and wrote out the document. One of the two texts now extant dates from the late tenth century; it is in the British Museum.

The place appointed here for this "Play" was not in the liturgy of the Mass but within the office of nocturns. It was "acted" in this order: On Good Friday, after the ritual of veneration, the cross on the altar of the monastic church was wrapped in a winding sheet and "buried" at this altar in a "sepulchre," a recess hidden by a curtain. From this moment until Easter morning the "Watch over the Cross" was kept by brethren of the community in succession, two or three at a time.

Very early on Easter Day, in the darkness before the dawn, the cross was taken from its "sepulchre" and returned to its customary place upon the altar. The community then began the office of nocturns. During the reading of the third lesson, when it was still dark, four of the monks vested themselves for their acting. One of these, wearing an alb, entered the church very quietly, as though he had some special purpose in mind and was trying to escape notice. He walked, careful to make no sound, to the altar with its "sepulchre," now empty, and there sat down, holding a palm in his hand. All the brethren then, during the third response, saw the three others coming in, clad in long copes and carrying censers. They also walked toward the "sepulchre," slowly and with hesitation, as though they were searching for something.

All this was done in imitation of the angel sitting by the sepulchre, and of the holy women coming with fragrant lotions to find and to anoint the Body of the Lord. When, therefore, the "angel" sitting near the altar saw the three "holy women" as it were wandering about in their search and turning to him for aid, he began with low voice softly to sing his question:

Quem quaeritis?

Whom seek you?

All three "holy women" answered as one:

Jesum Nazarenum!

Jesus of Nazareth!

The "angel" replied:

Non est hic. Surrexit sicut praedixerat.
Ite, nuntiate quia surrexit a mortuis.

He is not here. He has risen as He said.
Go, tell that He has risen from the dead.

At once, following this command, the three "holy women" turned
to face the choir of monks watching them and declared the glad
tidings:

Alleluia. Resurrexit Dominus!

After this, the "angel," who was still sitting by the "sepulchre,"
as though calling them back, said the antiphon:

Venite et videte locum.

Come and see the place.

Then he rose from his seat, raised the curtain which hid the
recess, the "sepulchre," and showed the "women" that it was empty,
that the cross, representing the buried Christ, was no longer there,
but only the linen cloth in which it had been wrapped. When the
three had seen this, they laid down the censers which they were
carrying within the "sepulchre"; then they took the cloth in their
hands and held it out toward the brethren, as though showing them
that the Lord had risen and was no longer buried in its folds. After
this they sang this antiphon:

Surrexit Dominus de sepulchro.

The Lord has risen from the tomb!

Last of all they laid the linen on the altar.
"When this was done the abbot, rejoicing in the victory of our
King, for that He had conquered death and risen again to life, sang
the first notes of the *Te Deum* and all the bells rang out."

From such little beginning were to rise in gradual growth of fame
the medieval miracle plays. We are not to think that this "Play," thus
described in the "Monastic Agreement" drawn up at Winchester between 965 and 975, was confined to England or even original in
England. At one point in the introduction to this Latin document
we are told:
"In due remembrance of the admonitions by which our holy
Patron Gregory zealously guided blessed Augustine, directing him
to introduce customs not only from the churches of Rome but also
of France for the progress of the rude Church in England, the
bishops, abbots, and abbesses who attended this assembly not only

summoned to it monks from the abbey of Saint Benedict at Fleury and from the distinguished monastery which is widely known by the name of Ghent, but also gathered material most sound and good from their honorable customs."

This *Visitatio Sepulchri*, "Visit to the Sepulchre," very possibly was drawn by the assembly of Winchester from the custom and practice of Fleury or of Ghent. And more: the abbey of Saint Benedict at Fleury, or of Saint Peter or of Saint Bavo at Ghent, if indeed one or more of these gave the *Visitatio* to the *Regularis Concordia*, may well have done some borrowing also. Another passage in this Latin document, introducing instructions for the ceremony of the Deposition of the Cross on Good Friday, states that "because on this day we solemnly observe the burial of the Body of our Saviour, if it has seemed good and proper to anyone to follow the example of certain religious men, an example well worth while for the strengthening of faith in people ignorant and untaught, and in the newly baptized, we have thus decreed . . ."

Mention of "people ignorant, untaught, newly baptized" seems hardly in keeping with a congregation of monks. Moreover, we find *sacerdos*, "priest," used at times instead of *abbas*, "abbot," in this document. Perhaps both the *Regularis Concordia* and its source or sources drew matter from a secular use. We may also note that the *Depositio* in Augsburg was of the Host, in Winchester of the cross. Both customs, then, were in practice during this period. On these interesting matters see O. B. Hardison, Jr.

CHAPTER TEN

The Harvest in Art

1

As THIS subject is wide of range and varied in interest, it may be well to restrict our brief glance at it to the realm of Germany. Here, during the earlier part of our period, while Louis the Child and Conrad of Franconia held the throne, architecture was neglected and art of other kind lay dead. With Henry the Fowler building was renewed for purpose of defense against Hungarian assaults. This was the prime motive; but the king, and his dukes with him, for the enhancing of their own power and dignity, added castle to fortress and to castle added church. The feudal lord would entertain his vassals and would worship with his folk in the buildings which marked his high rank. Royal and noble ambition grew infinitely greater when to kingship of Germany was added the imperial crown. With Otto the Great architecture and painting entered life afresh, and the life waxed stronger as the years went on, to reach magnificence and splendor in the tenth century's latter years.

This growth sprang in great measure from religion. Revival of monastic discipline brought need for more churches, for more spacious choirs in which the brethren might recite their office as they increased in number. The ordaining to the priesthood of more and more among the monastic community brought need for more chapels in these churches for the more frequent offering of holy Mass. The gaining of sacred relics, guarded in these chapels, required the opening of passages through the churches, from east to west, from north to south, that countless pilgrims who came to render their devotion and to seek aid in their troubles might find their way from shrine to shrine.

Under the Ottos prelates of the German Church gave freely of their energy and skill in working for the cities in which they dwelt and the buildings in which they prayed. The archbishops of Cologne, Mainz, and Trier were leaders in this activity. Bruno of Cologne, who died in 965 while his brother, Otto I, was king, worked for churches in his city, of St. Andrew, and of St. Pantaleon; he founded a monastery connected with St. Pantaleon and left behind him generous legacy for that church. Archbishop Gero (969-76) followed in the same endeavor. Willigis, archbishop of Mainz, in 975 under Otto II and Theophano began the rebuilding of his cathedral; he saw it consecrated in 1009 and burned to the ground on the same day. Egbert, metropolitan of Trier, never ceased his labor for the beautifying and enrichment of his episcopal seat. Nor did Bernward, bishop of Hildesheim under Otto III and Henry II, his successor on the throne of Germany. In Swabia we have seen its bishop, Ulrich, toiling to rebuild houses and churches in Augsburg after the battle on the Lech in 955. The name of Notker, who ruled the see of Liège under all three Ottos, first, second, and third, has come down to us highly honored for his contribution to his city's defense, health, and religious life. It was said in the eleventh century by one who lived in Liège: "There is scarcely any great or famous work in our city which Notker did not either bring into being or bring to completion. He would seem rather to have made Liège for us than to have ruled it. All has been summed up in a few words of verse: 'Liège, to Christ you owe Notker, all else to Notker himself.'" In the words of Godefroid Kurth: "Monuments religious, monuments secular, works of fortification, works for public service, churches, monasteries, hospices, ramparts, canals, all were of his creation."

Equally striking is the story of Burchard, bishop of Worms from February 1000 until 1025. From his *Life*, written by one who knew him and was himself a priest of Worms, we learn that he was a friend of Otto III, that he was taught and ordained by Willigis of Mainz, and that in 1000 the emperor put forward his name as bishop-elect of Worms. Promptly he was consecrated and then departed for the city, which had suffered much from Hungarian invasion. "He found it destroyed, all but desolate: no home for human beings, but only for wild beasts, especially wolves, who lurked within its ruins. Bulwarks and walls, laid low by brutal storming, yielded easy entrance to prowlers, man or animal. Constantly, so Burchard heard, citizens with their own eyes had seen wolves devouring their sheep and in vain had tried to drive them off. Robbers, also, entered when and where they would. Any attempt at defense was speedily followed by vengeful raid in the dark of night; happy, indeed, was the householder who escaped with his life and only lost his house and all it held. At last in terror the people of Worms left their city to its fate and departed to make for themselves new homes in the country around."

Utter emptiness, then, faced this new bishop of Worms. He recovered from the shock and set to work. In the next five years he slowly rebuilt its walls and then called its inhabitants to live again within them. Trouble and danger still remained; Otto, duke of Carinthia, was holding a castle within Worms. It was well fortified, and he had no desire to see Burchard as bishop controlling the city; for many months he had secretly given aid to those who came to pillage and steal. Nevertheless, in the end Burchard's firm determination won this last battle. He wrecked Otto's castle; he forced him to sue for peace, and in place of the ducal fortress he built a College of St. Peter, a training center for priests. From this time the bishop was not only spiritual but also secular lord in Worms.

On their side the royal and imperial rulers of Germany responded with equal vigor. Was it not the hand of God Himself which had laid upon them their burden? Had not His Spirit held out before their eyes a vision of things changing, of things to come? And so in due reverence they gave constant care to His Church militant on earth. Their records are filled with charters of privilege, of grant, to innumerable sees, monasteries, and convents. They, too, built for the glory of the Lord and the protection of their people. Henry I fortified Merseburg on its hill near the river Saale; he also founded in Quedlinburg a church where he and his queen Matilda should be laid to rest. The queen in 936 founded at Quedlinburg a convent, destined to be of high renown.

In Magdeburg on the Elbe, the great center of defense against Slavs who threatened the German border, and, also, of Christian mission to these same heathen enemies, in 955 their son Otto the First began construction of the cathedral of St. Maurice, strongly fortified, served by zealous priests. From Italy, as Charlemagne had done for Aachen, so he, too, brought marble and porphyry for its enriching. Bishops and abbots were always given warm welcome when they arrived at Aachen, at Magdeburg, at Quedlinburg, to confer with the emperor regarding their needs and his.

Royal princesses gave themselves and all they had to the Church; daughter after daughter of the Ottonian House served as nun and abbess, at Quedlinburg, at Essen, at Gandersheim. Queens offered priceless treasure; especially Matilda, queen of Henry I; Adelaide, second wife of Otto the Great; and Theophano, wife of the second Otto and mother of the third.

2

Under Henry the Fowler architecture was practical in purpose but not artistic. Art in Germany of our period is known either as "Ottonian," a description which, indeed, applies to the years from 960 to 1050, or as "First Romanesque," prevalent during the reigns of the three Ottos. Tradition has declared this "First Romanesque" art subject to various influences, which may be classed under five names: "Late Antique" and "Early Christian," from ancient Rome of about 400 A.D.; "Lombardic," of northern Italy in about 800 A.D.; "Carolingian," from the later eighth and the ninth century; "Byzantine," from both older and more recent times, but especially from contemporary source.

The churches built under the Ottos are marked in history by two characteristics: they may differ in general form, or, alike in this respect, they may vary with regard to particular features, in number, position, or material. Experiment was the fruit of vigorous life, now at last surging through German land.

The Ottonian church, then, might be basilican or it might be cruciform. At the west end one might enter by a wide porch, and then might find before him a forecourt, known as atrium, or a narthex, a wide vestibule. From these he would enter the main building, divided by nave and aisles, perhaps three, perhaps five in number. The nave would be flanked on either side by rounded columns, often alternating with less decorative but sturdy square piers, sometimes one by one, sometimes one pier for every two columns. From these rose arches in arcade succession. Above the arches stood the clerestory, with its windows for the lighting of the church, a lighting extremely dim. The choir might be at the west or at the east end; there might be a double choir, both west and east. Sometimes in a monastic church the choir would be longer than was usual, giving ampler room for the brethren assembled for office. Above the choir in the west might well be found a gallery, probably reserved for the more aristocratic attendance, secular or religious. Apses were commonly seen, at one or at either end of the church. The east end would hold one, or, very probably, three of these semicircular recesses; along their walls would stand "radiating" chapels which held those farsought relics of the saints. So, too, an apse or apses might be found, with chapel or chapels, at the endings of transepts or aisles. The number of chapels in a large church might be seven in all, or even more than this. A passage, called an ambulatory, ran from the transepts and aisles around the apses of the east end, behind the high altar; thus pilgrims could easily reach the chapels for which they were bound.

The roofing of nave and aisles was originally of wood, but in the tenth century it was often constructed in stone vaulting; the danger of fire was ever present. The vaulting was formed either in simple continuous arching, or, especially in the roofing of chapels, it was groined, and the arches met at right angles.

Towers, round, square, or polygonal, were frequently seen. A large church might support six; at west, at east, at the crossing of nave and transepts. Twin towers were favored for both east and west; many held staircases. Belfries often appeared, rounded or square. Along the walls of the church, between the arches of the nave and between the windows of the clerestory, were often seen bands of ornamental decoration, moulded in geometrical design or painted in scenes of Biblical narrative.

Finally, the pilgrim would descend below the church, to find its crypt or crypts, the "hidden" chapels where deeply treasured relics awaited him, enclosed in caskets gleaming through the darkness with gold and precious stones.

Three among Germany's churches of the tenth century merit a word in individual description; all in some way still survive. In Saxony, near the Harz mountains, is the town of Gernrode, where Gero, count and warden of the borderland between the Elbe and the Oder rivers, founded a church in 961. In grief at the loss of his son, Sigfrid, he went as pilgrim to Rome and brought back a decree from Pope John XII for its protection; and, for its honoring, a relic of Cyriacus, a saint now hard to identify. To the church he added a convent of nuns, who elected as their abbess Gero's daughter-in-law, professed in religion after her husband's death. Thietmar, who tells the story, declares that the abbess-elect duly received dedication from the bishop of Halberstadt in whose diocese the convent lay, and that Gero died a happy man. It was the year 965, and his tomb, renovated by modern hands, still remains in his church.

His death delayed for a while the progress of its building; this, however, was continued under Otto II and, later, under the Empress-

Regent Theophano. Much has been done in restoration; but Ottonian working can be discerned in the double choir, the alternating columns and piers, and the lines of galleries above its aisles.

On the outskirts of Quedlinburg there remains an old structure, now only known as a crypt of St. Wipert. Here also may be seen the same alternating columns and piers, with a semicircular apse and an ambulatory.

Perhaps the most interesting of these three churches is that dedicated to St. George in Oberzell, on the island of Reichenau. Witogowo, abbot of Reichenau from 985 to 997, did much work in construction there, as we learn from one Purchard, who proudly described it in the tenth century. He wrote in verse, and his poem is still extant: a dialogue between Reichenau and the poet.

So are the wall paintings, the frescoes along the nave of St. George's church, still clearly present. Their date is disputed, but many critics assign them to the later nine hundreds. In the spandrels between the arches appear the abbots of Reichenau; above them is a band of ornament stretching the length of the wall; and above this can be seen a cycle of scenes of miracles wrought by Christ. Yet higher, there is another band of decoration; and, finally, between the windows under the roof of the church, the apostles look out from their place.

The Christ is vivid in living power, as He heals, in the country of the Gadarenes, the man possessed by evil; as He cures the man suffering from dropsy; as He restores sight to the blind; as He raises from the dead Lazarus, "brother of Mary and Martha," and the little daughter of Jairus, "ruler of the synagogue"; as He stills for His terrified disciples the sudden storm upon the lake.

Other work in fresco from this century survives in the chapel of St. Sylvester at Goldbach, on the shore of the Boden See. Nor should we forget that Otto III called the famous artist "John the Painter" from Italy to adorn for him Aachen's Palace Church. To John's sorrow; *a patriae nido rapuit me tertius Otto,* his lament told, inscribed amidst his painting on the wall: "Otto the Third tore me away from the home of my fatherland."

We turn now from those who built for the glory of God and empire to those who painted its vision on parchment or carved it in relief on panels of ivory. The mind of the rulers and of those who upheld them in Germany at that time is as clear here as in tenth-century verse or chronicle; often, indeed, more clearly revealed. Here the same influences were at work as in its architecture, especially those of Carolingian and of Byzantine artists. Yet, as Wilhelm Köhler has shown, Ottonian art, while it used the tradition of Charlemagne's court and its Ada-Group, a collection of manuscripts connected with some Lady Ada, insecurely thought to be a sister of Charlemagne himself, nevertheless did not adopt that tradition slavishly, but gave it new birth in changing where it willed, to create its own view and styling. The influence of Byzantine art is easy to understand when we remember the new energy which rose during this century in the empire of the East through the Macedonian dynasty; when, also, we think back upon the close connection of Otto II and Otto III with Constantinople through the Empress Theophano.

We will begin with formal documents; and, first, with the charter of privilege, now in the Vatican, by which on February 13, 962, Otto the Great confirmed for John XII and his successors papal possession of papal estates. It is inscribed in minuscule lettering of gold upon purple parchment, with a border of medallions entwined in foliage. Purple, also, was the long document unrolled in St. Peter's at Rome, on April 14, 972, during the marriage ceremony celebrated by Pope John XIII for young Otto II and Theophano. It is now in the Staatsarchiv at Wolfenbüttel, Germany. There it declares the offerings, many and magnificent, made as dowry or "morning-gift" by Otto to his bride: offerings traditionally presented on the morning after the fulfillment of the marriage bond. Lions and bulls fight with one another in the adorning of this roll; medallions enclose little representations of the Christ, His Mother, and His apostles.

From formal charters we pass to manuscripts of the Gospels. In the Pierpont Morgan Library, New York, lie the Gospels of Wernigerode, said to have been prepared in the abbey of Corvey between 950 and 975. Coloring of blue and green here deepens into intense green of foliage; initial words shine brilliant in gold.

Among schools and ateliers those of Reichenau, Cologne, and Trier were now of marked distinction. Probably Reichenau saw the making for one "custos Gero," whom we may believe to have been Gero, archbishop of Cologne from 969 until 976, of a book of pericopes, extracts from the Gospels read or chanted in the liturgy. The Landesbibliothek of Darmstadt holds it, generally known as the *Gero-Codex*. Its artist was under strong Carolingian influence, as can be seen by comparing his painting of the *Majestas Domini*—the Lord Christ enthroned—with that of the Gospels of Lorsch, written and illuminated in the early ninth century. In each manuscript a square border frames a page; within this lies another, a rounded one, intercepted by symbols of the Evangelists: the eagle of St. John, the man for St. Matthew, the lion of St. Mark, the ox of St. Luke. In the midst the Christ sits upon His seat of dominion, His right hand raised in blessing, His left hand holding a Gospel Book.

On another page Gero himself, whom we remember as ambassador of Otto I to Constantinople in connection with the marriage of Otto's son, is offering his codex to St. Peter. The date of the work is given as shortly before 969.

The art of Cologne was distinguished by the *lumen*, the radiance of its coloring. This is marked in another Gospel Book, written late in the tenth century and possessed by a church of Cologne dedicated to St. Gereon, said to be a martyr of Roman days. Once again the Lord is enthroned within a mandorla, an oblong round, holding in one hand the Gospels, the other raised in blessing; above His head two angels with wide-spread wings kneel in adoration. The symbols of the Evangelists are also here, particularly vivid, the lion and the ox intent with wide-open eyes. Below are the prophets: Isaiah, Daniel, Ezekiel, Jeremiah, their hands uplifted toward the Christ. The Four Evangelists, too, have their portraits, as seen by the painter. St. Mark is bowed in writing over his desk-stool; St. Matthew has stopped awhile to meditate, pen in hand; St. Luke, content and happy in his work, is dipping his pen in the ink; St. John in Byzantine fashion is sitting upon an earthen knoll as he writes.

Of equal note, however, is the fame of Trier, of its artists and of its Archbishop Egbert, who during his rule from 977 to 993 so eagerly encouraged its painting and sculpture. About 985 two monks of Reichenau offered him their skill in the *Codex Egberti*, another book of pericopes, now in the Stadtbibliothek at Trier. This was most probably made at Reichenau, although the atelier of Trier may well have had a share in the work. Three hands have been discerned here. One or more of the artists may have gone from Reichenau to study in Trier; or Archbishop Egbert himself may have taught monks of Reichenau during a visit to their island on his way to or from Italy. Influence from the late Roman antique style has been marked, perhaps drawn from the *Quedlinburg Itala* fragment, perhaps from some other manuscript of the late fourth or early fifth century. The *Quedlinburg Itala* was a translation of Old Testament writings; from it, through crass ignorance of its value, only four leaves now remain, in Berlin; they give part of the Four Books of Kings.

The archbishop in pontifical robes looks out sternly from the dedication page, where in deep reverence the two monks, Kerald and Heribert, make their offering. Other pages tell of the life of the Lord Christ on earth. Especially moving is the scene of the Massacre of the Innocent Children. Herod stands at the left in command, urging on his soldiers, who, their spears poised for action, are rushing forward to kill. Two of the infants lie already dead upon the ground, their eyes closed; one is falling headless, his severed head still in the air above him; a spear is driving fast through a fourth. On the right are the mothers. One holds out her hands, imploring the assassins to stop; another, her face torn by agony, clutches her breast; a third covers her face, unable to look or move; a fourth lifts her hands in helpless bewilderment.

Another gift to this archbishop was a Psalter, again executed very probably at Reichenau, possibly at Trier, and now in Cividale, northeastern Italy. Once more Egbert sits in pontifical dignity; but here the bishops who ruled the see of Trier from its foundation also hold each his place. On his throne David the King, against a violet and blue background, is playing upon a harp of gold. Coloring of gold, silver, red, blue, and green are mingled in this book; birds and beasts, never seen on this earth, writhe in gold, entwined with foliage along the borders.

4

The vision of this Ottonian art deepens in its portraits—ideal rather than real—of men of royal and imperial line. Here, from the ending of the tenth century, is one of Henry the Quarreler. It lies in a book containing the monastic rules of St. Benedict and St. Caesarius of Arles, prepared about 990 for the convent of Niedermünster in Regensburg; it is now in the Staatliche Bibliothek, Bamberg. The painting has an air of reality, as showing a man of mature age, "noble and serene," according to its inscription. No sign of claim to a royal crown appears; Henry the Quarreler by this time for five years had been strictly loyal to his king, Otto III.

Reichenau and Trier, as we have seen, were inextricably mingled in their work. Of no man's work can this be more truly said than that of the anonymous *Magister Registri Gregorii*, the "Master of the Gregorian Register," who earned this description as scribe and painter of an illuminated manuscript of the letters of Saint Gregory the Great, pope from 590 to 604. The Master lived in the later years of the tenth century, welcome in both centers of painting and especially admired by Archbishop Egbert. He was one of the great leaders in the progress of Ottonian skill, and he, too, knew the power of the Late Antique, as illustrated by the *Itala* fragment and the *Notitia Dignitatum*, a list of official ministers of the Roman Empire, East and West, drawn up about 410.

It was Egbert who requested from him the making of this text of Pope Gregory's letters, and Egbert who gave it to his cathedral of Trier. Only two leaves and a fragment of text are now left to us, from about the year 983. One of these leaves, now belonging to the Stadtbibliothek, Trier, represents Gregory seated by a desk; his hand rests upon a book placed there. On his right shoulder a dove, symbol of the Holy Spirit, is whispering into his ear; an old story, found by us in chapter 28 of a *Life* of this pope by Paul the Deacon, but very possibly a later insertion, tells that at intervals the dove was silent while Gregory repeated aloud what he had heard. Crouching before a curtain, hidden from the pope, is his secretary and friend Peter, also a deacon; in his right hand Peter holds a pen with which he is boring a hole in the curtain, trying to hear all the sacred words. His left hand grasps the waxen tablet on which he will write them down. The contrast between the faraway look in the eyes of Gregory and the active, eager curiosity of Peter is wonderfully drawn.

The pope faces right, toward the second picture; perhaps the linking of the two scenes as a double and connected imagining was deliberately planned in the Master's mind. Perhaps from this second leaf, united with the first, we may learn something of that vision for the world which was rising at this time.

The inscription describing that second leaf, now in the Musée Condé of Chantilly, near Paris, laments that Otto II has lately died. We have, then, either this Otto II here or an imaginary ideal, intended to represent Otto III, as yet a little child. The emperor, or emperor-to-be, is sitting enthroned under a canopy of green, supported by four pillars; he is wearing an underrobe of violet and a mantle of red, both adorned with gold ornament and border. On his head is a golden crown; in one hand he is holding a sceptre, in the other the orb of the world, marked by the cross. His title is given: *Otto Imperator Augustus,* and close to him are standing four female figures, two on either side. These represent the four parts of his empire: Germania and Francia on the left, Italia and Alemannia (Swabia) on the right. They all wear long flowing gowns of blue color, covered as far as the knee by upper cloaks of green, violet, or light brown. Each, upright in dignity but with full assent, offers to the emperor a symbol of homage, the rounded orb of their individual rule. Here we may perhaps see the artist's remembrance of the *Notitia Dignitatum.*

Other manuscripts still surviving are also attributed to the Master's skill. Among them are five or six leaves of the *Codex Egberti;* one is that which describes the Massacre of the Holy Innocents. Another shows the Angel of the Annunciation. With wings widely spread, eyes alert and arm outstretched, he is eagerly declaring his message to the Virgin Mary, while she holds out her hands in surprise and wonder, trying to understand. Behind them rise the towers of Nazareth, medieval in their shaping.

At least three other works, critics believe, came from the same hand. Two of them are illuminated texts of the Gospels. One, formerly in the Sainte-Chapelle, but now in the Bibliothèque Nationale, Paris, was made either at Trier or at Echternach, near Trier. Coins on the page which introduces St. Matthew's Gospel point to a date about 985. On them appear Henry the Fowler, Otto I, Otto II, and a Henry whose naming is uncertain. Suggestion has seen in him Henry the Fowler, once more portrayed, or Henry the Quarreler, restored to his duchy of Bavaria. The latter theory seems more attractive. On another page Christ again appears in majesty, surrounded by a mandorla of gold; an inscription written in Greek proclaims: "Thy kingdom, O Lord, lasteth throughout all ages, and Thy dominion is from generation to generation." Around the Lord the Four Evangelists, each with his symbol, sit writing their books; Latin hexameter verses explain the meaning of the symbols. All reflect the life of Christ: the man by his birth into this world, the ox by its sacrifice in death; the lion which springs toward Heaven, and the eagle which rises Heavenward on its wings.

The second Gospel Book is in the John Rylands Library, Manchester. It holds pictures of all three Ottos, and since each one is entitled *Imperator,* the date must be placed after the coronation as emperor of Otto III in 996. Initial letters are elaborately adorned; purple, gold, red, blue, green, white, glow in splendid harmony.

The third work is a sacramentary, also from the ending of the tenth century and at Chantilly. It shows the same skill and inventive power in the painting of initials, in the intricate blending of color, in line unspoiled by confusion.

Lastly, we come to those paintings which more clearly reveal the vision of this century's latter years. All students of these years know the Book of the Gospels, once at Bamberg, but now in the

292 DEATH AND LIFE IN THE TENTH CENTURY

Bayerische Staatsbibliothek of Munich; it was made about 1000, probably at Reichenau, and it is called by the name of Otto the Third.

It is filled with scenes from the life of Christ. The Three Kings, one old, two much younger, with lively excitement offer their gifts; the Child holds out His little hand in blessing while the Mother gives hers in welcome. The background here is pure gold, marked by an enormous star, radiating color. Then come miracles in picture: the healing of the man possessed by evil, from whose mouth devils are flying in terror, only to fall into the water surging below; the calming of the storm, a portrayal of three scenes on a page, one of the Christ, weary to death and sunk in peaceful sleep, while a disciple is trying to arouse Him; another of two more, struggling with a billowing sail; and, finally, a fourth, watching with great awe the Master, now wide awake, as He hurls rebuke at two horned spirits of the winds, blowing their hardest.

The Transfiguration shows the Lord in glory, standing on a mountain bright with foliage and flowers. Above Him flash rays of golden light, coming from the hand of God the Father, held in blessing. On either side Moses and Elias look up in marvel, while the disciples John and James, bowed to the ground, hide their eyes in fear. Not so St. Peter; he is watching with all excitement and energy. The Entry into Jerusalem is matter of surprise and wonder to passersby, as they see Christ, calm and determined, ride forward on a donkey gazing earthward with melancholy eyes. The Washing of the Feet finds Peter with one foot in the basin, penitently begging the Lord to wash his hands and his head, if He will; the rest of the disciples, much younger than Peter, are evidently horrified by his bold words of refusal and the Master's stern rebuke. For the Garden of Gethsemane there is again a threefold picture on one page: Christ reproaches His slumbering followers; he lies prostrate on the ground in prayer; He receives the kiss of Judas. His devoted and overzealous disciple is clutching the servant of the high priest, about to cut off his ear; at the side men with swords and staves are drawing near.

From the Christ in this book of Munich we come to Otto the Third, who is given two pages lying open, right and left. On the one the emperor sits enthroned; on the other, four female figures, as at Chantilly, are approaching to render homage with their gifts. Once again they represent the four parts of empire. But here they come, not upright, but with bowed heads, and their names are different; they represent now Sclavinia, Germania, Gallia, Roma. Rome had gained a name for herself; and in 997 victory over the Slavic people had at last been won. Moreover, on the emperor's left side stand two bishops of the Church; on his right two warriors with sword and shield. The hand that holds the orb of the earth is now lifted in imperial dignity of Church and state.

The Four Evangelists are here again. But no longer are they bowed over their writing; their heads and their hands are raised in ecstasy. St. Luke, his eyes blazing with fire, his whole body alive with energy, is proclaiming to all the world the truth it must hear and must receive. Above him plunges and rears the winged ox, and all around the ox, in circles, of which the two lowest are supported by Luke's own upstretched hands, prophets and kings of the Old Testament cry aloud, and from their cry bursts flaming radiance.

Kings and prophets of the Old Testament and Evangelists of the New are here giving forth truth foretold under the Old Dispensation, confirmed by the New. Had not the Christ Himself declared: "Think not that I am come to destroy the law or the prophets; I am not come to destroy but to fulfill?" An inscription at the bottom of St. Luke's page runs:

Fonte patrum ductas bos agnis elicit undas:

From the wellspring of the patriarchs the ox draws
and brings forth waters for the lambs.

The ox is symbol of the Gospel; the faith of both Jew and Christian is symbolized here by streams of living water which flow from beneath the Evangelist's feet; from them beasts of the field, designed as lambs, bend to drink, symbolizing the people who are and shall be nurtured by a faith ever old and ever new.

Another Gospel Book of Otto III, now one of the treasures of Aachen cathedral, was made about the same time as that of Munich and in all probability at the same place. It was given to the emperor by Liuthar, a leader in the art of Reichenau. Here Otto once more sits in majesty, and the hand of God, clasping the cross, lays the crown of empire upon his head. The Earth, represented by a female figure, bowed at his feet, supports him and his throne. On each side stands a man with coronet and pennon denoting his rank; these represent the dukes of Otto's empire and they are yielding him their vow of service. Below are once more two warriors and two archbishops of his land. The page next to this one gives the name of the donor:

Hoc, Auguste, libro tibi cor Deus induat, Otto,
quem de Liuthario te suscepisse memento:

May God, O Emperor, clothe thy heart, Otto, with this book; forget not that from Liuthar thou didst receive it.

Otto, then, is here *rex et sacerdos,* appointed by authority of God Himself. So did painting of the eleventh century show his successor, Henry II, crowned by Christ.

5

Reliefs, sculptured for the adorning of covers of books, of reliquaries and of crosses, also survive from this time. At Paris, in the Musée Cluny, there is an ivory relief showing the Lord Christ between Otto II and the Empress Theophano, His hands laid in blessing on their crowned heads. It once decorated the cover of a book, and it shows Byzantine influence. Its date is about 982-83, and Otto is described as "Imperator Romanorum," a title assumed by him in 982. At his feet is kneeling, half-hidden by a footstool, a bearded man who in Greek words is praying the emperor: "Lord, help thy servant John." Was this, as has been suggested, that John Philagathos so deeply favored by Theophano and through her power in 982 given rule of Nonatula's abbey in Italy?

About the same time, between 980 and 983, was made the ivory panel of Christ in majesty, now in the Castello Sforzesco, Milan. On either side an angel is rapt in devotion; lower down are standing the Virgin Mary and St. Maurice, patron of Magdeburg; at the feet of the Lord kneel the Emperor Otto II and Theophano, who holds in her arms their little son.

The church of St. Gereon, Cologne, includes among its treasures another ivory which shows the Christ in majesty. He is giving His blessing to Saints Victor and Gereon, who bear the palm of martyrs in their hands. Below are standing the companions of St. Maurice, famous in story as the "Theban Legion," a band of Christian soldiers mustered in Egypt and put to death for refusing to disobey their creed.

From the Christ we come to His Mother, and find her in sculpture at Mainz and at Essen. The Altertumsmuseum of Mainz possesses a Madonna carved from ivory in the late tenth century, perhaps in Mainz, more probably in Trier. Did the hand of the Master of the *Registrum Gregorii*, as has been thought, picture the Virgin Mother's face here, with its serious, intent devotion? She sits upon a throne which encircles her head in high arching, and she holds her Child upon her lap; one hand is raised upright against her breast, the other rests upon the Christ. Her robe reaches to her feet; its sleeve hangs wide and loose.

The Golden Madonna of Essen was made at Cologne about 1000 and placed in Essen's convent of the Holy Trinity while Matilda, granddaughter of Otto the Great and his first wife, Edith, by their son Liudolf and his duchess, Ida of Swabia, was abbess there, from 973 until 1011. Albert Boeckler has some interesting words concerning this work. He compares the flickering light which plays about the golden sheen of its figures to that from clear water rippling over stones. "The human relationship between mother and child is not stressed here: the Mother is staring with unnaturally opened eyes, not at the Child upon her knee, but straight before her. She is deep in thought, meditating on that Mystery of Redemption of which she is the instrument." In her hand she is carrying the apple, and is therefore known by painters as the "new Eve."

This same Abbess Matilda of Essen gave to her church a processional cross. It is covered with gold from which sparkle precious stones and pearls; it bears the Christ Crucified. At His feet the serpent of Eden lies coiled and conquered. Further below are two little figures, portrayed in enamel, man and woman, each grasping a tall cross set between them. They are the Abbess Matilda and her brother Otto, duke of Swabia from 973 and of Bavaria from 976, until his death in 982. On the back of the cross, at its center, the Lamb of God stands with halo of victory. This Matilda-Cross was also made at Cologne, between 973 and 982.

The cathedral treasury of Aachen holds another cross, made at Cologne at the end of the tenth century; this is the Cross of Lothar II, king of Lotharingia from 855 to 869. Jewels shine out, red, green, and blue, small and great, over all its surface. At its center is a splendid cameo, cut on sardonyx, of the Emperor Augustus, his head wreathed in laurel, his hand bearing the standard of the eagle. Far below is the seal which gave the cross its name: the seal of that young King Lothar who aroused so great turmoil in Europe through his efforts to divorce his queen, Theutberga. On the other side again is seen Christ Crucified; above His head the hand of God the Father is reaching down to place upon it the laurel of victory. Within the circle of its wreath is the dove of the Holy Spirit; at the sides are figures of the Sun and the Moon, weeping bitterly, their light darkened by grief.

Two reliquaries—caskets for the guarding in due honor of sacred relics—lie among the treasures of Trier. It may be of interest here to note the respect shown by the great Gerbert for Egbert, archbishop of Trier, as a connoisseur of art; in Egbert's atelier while he was at Trier these reliquaries were created. In 987 Gerbert, then head of the school of Reims and secretary to its Archbishop Adalbero, wrote to Egbert in Adalbero's name concerning a cross ordered from Trier for the cathedral of Reims: "Your great and famed genius will enoble our scanty material"; and: "Please send that cross, worked upon, we hope, by your skill, to Verdun, where I shall then be staying, and, if possible, by November the first. As often as I look at it, my love for you will increase, day by day." The words are given to Adalbero, but the thought comes from Gerbert.

One of these reliquaries is in the form of a portable altar, dedicated to St. Andrew and made between 977 and 993; its inscription states that a sandal of the saint lies within its hollow interior. Gold, set with costly jewels, covers it; its four short supports rest on the backs of golden lions, holding rings in their mouths. Inlaid work of ivory and enamel add to its beauty; on its sides, alternating with symbols of the Evangelists, lions again appear. Upon the altar stands a model of the foot of St. Andrew, sheathed in gold; around and along it are strings of precious stones.

The other casket is that of the holy nail, said to have been taken from the cross of Christ; the shrine is itself shaped in the form of a nail. It, too, is radiant with enamel and gems. A third reliquary, made about 988 and now at Limburg on the river Lahn, enclosed, so tradition told, part of a staff of St. Peter; it bears the words: *Baculum beati Petri*. Its ornament of small jewels is arranged in triangular form; between these triangles lie gems of larger size, with portraits of popes of Rome and archbishops of Trier.

It hardly seems possible to omit all mention of the manifold work in art done for his see by Bernward, bishop of Hildesheim from 993 to 1022, although the best of it dates from the eleventh century. Illuminated texts, handicraft in gold, silver, and bronze, marked his episcopate. Under the guidance of the Late Antique and the Carolingian models he supervised the making of the famous bronze doors for his cathedral early in these ten hundreds. The wing on the left tells of the fall of man, in scenes from Genesis; that on the right, of his redemption, in scenes from the life of Christ. To the early eleventh century also belongs, we may think, the column of Hildesheim placed in St. Michael's church; around it in spiral curve were engraved miracles wrought by the Lord on earth. Probably it held the Paschal candle at Eastertide. In Hildesheim's Church of the Magdalen, at the end of the tenth or in the first decade of the eleventh century, Bernward placed two candlesticks of gilded silver; upon them naked men rode winged dragons, beasts were climbing through foliage intricately entwined. Critics have seen here an allegory, picturing man's effort to rise from the depths, the darkness of evil, to the clear light of Christian life.

Four works in ivory, created in this century, are of unusual interest. One is a vessel for holy water in the Domschatz, Aachen, of about the year 1000. An inscription, engraved at that time, gives the name of Otto, and the manner of the vessel's making points to Otto III. Around it run two bands, one higher, one lower, each holding eight figures of men. Percy Ernst Schramm (*Die deutschen Kaiser und Könige*, pp. 98 ff.) has interpreted their meaning in this way. Figures in the lower band are those of warriors, symbol of the emperor's secular power. Seven of those in the upper band are priests and monks, representing the Church. In this upper line Otto III sits enthroned, holding high the orb of the earth and the sceptre of majesty. Under the figure sitting on the emperor's right hand the word *Sanctus* appears in abbreviated form. This man represented in particular mention as "holy" is not Christ, for he wears the tonsure; he is St. Peter, prince of the apostles. Next to St. Peter, on his right, sits another priest, wearing both tonsure and pallium. These are the only three of the eight in the upper band who are sitting; the other five stand upright. Two of these five who stand are also wearing the pallium and are therefore archbishops; the two next have no pallium and no doubt are bishops; the one at the end seems to hold an abbot's crozier.

Who, then, is the priest, wearing tonsure and pallium, who not only is sitting, but is sitting on the right hand of St. Peter? He can only be the pope, perhaps Sylvester II. Therefore, in this representation St. Peter is sitting between the pope and the emperor, the pope on his right hand, the emperor, Otto III, on his left. The prince of the apostles thus binds together the powers of Church and state, while he gives the greater honor to the Church. But since the emperor finds his place among the priests of the Church, the only layman included in this upper band, once again we see him *rex et sacer-*

dos. As John Beckwith has remarked, the warriors in the lower band are guardians of the holy city of God.

The next three, panels in relief, are linked together as possibly created by one and the same artist, one of extremely individual and original genius. He has no name; Wilhelm Vöge, who has described his work, calls him simply "Ein deutscher Schnitzer des 10 Jahrhunderts."

Here we see, not the refinement, the beauty delicate and austere, the aristocratic courtliness of Byzantine and of Carolingian portraits and pictures; we see, recreated with all power, with all determination, the face, the feelings, the hopes and the fears, the sturdy strength and the weakness of humanity, definitely real, definitely German, as it could be seen by a Saxon worker.

In the Staatliches Museum, Berlin, there is an ivory relief of Christ in majesty, with the Four Evangelists. The face of the Christ is framed by thick hair, parted in the middle and falling flat on either side, with beard and moustache. It is alive with awareness and energy, the face of one simply rather than proudly born, wonderfully natural. So are the figures of the Evangelists, and here let us follow Vöge's leadership. Saint Matthew in perplexity is trying with all his might to understand the counsel or correction which an angel is administering as he points over the Evangelist's shoulder at the writing tablet on his knee. Saint Mark has entirely given up for a while; he is sitting as one lost, at the feet of his lion, while the lion is pondering how best to help him out. Saint John is doing what he can, with his head twisted round in desperation, to hear and comprehend the promptings whispered diligently by his eagle in his ear.

At Nürnberg, in its Germanisches Museum, another relief in ivory adorns the cover enclosing the *Codex Aureus Epternacensis,* the "Golden Manuscript of Echternach." This ivory shows Christ Crucified. Agony of suffering marks the face, but the hair and features are remarkably like those of the Berlin "Christ in Majesty." On one side of the cross stands Longinus with the spear, and, on the other, Stephaton with the sponge dipped in vinegar. Terra, the Earth, is crouching at the feet of Christ. Saints also are there: the Virgin Mary; Willibrord, patron of Echternach; Benedict; Boniface; Liudger; and, too, the king of Germany, Otto III, with his mother, Theophano.

Even more humanly real is the picturing on a diptych, a double panel of ivory, in the Staatsliches Museum, Berlin. It shows on one side the giving of the Tables of the Law to Moses by God, and on the other the Doubting Thomas. Moses is looking up in rapture of devotion, raising both his arms to receive this sacred burden of ministry for his people. The once unbelieving Thomas is reaching with all the effort he can make, his head thrown back, his foot lifted to support him, to clutch the robe which Christ with His left hand is drawing away to show His wounded side. Thomas is torn by penitence, by hope; Christ is looking down into his eyes with reproach, with question, with love. One can almost hear him saying, "Why, Thomas, why?"

We do not know that these three ivory panels were the work of one man. But they are full of a spirit entirely their own, and it is easy to believe that they came from one source.

CHAPTER ELEVEN

The Harvest in Learning

1

"It often happens that when the horror of tragedy piled upon tragedy wearies the mind, through this very horror the spirit in distraction does not utter the words it would naturally say; caught elsewhere by the image of its thought, it keeps silence where silence must be. He who would unravel the mystery of truth always craves quiet in perfect tranquility. So with me. As the hart desireth the water-brooks, so has my soul, trained in the elements of classic disciplines, longed for the work-filled leisure of philosophic meditation: leisure which I would use for the good of many."

With these words Abbo, abbot of Fleury in the last years of the tenth century, began the argument of his *Apologeticus*. They are bitter words. In a brief tracing of his life we may see the struggle of a man of this time: a monk vowed to tranquil round of prayer; an abbot called to direct and to reform monastic communities; a scholar devoted to learning; a politician fighting for his fellows; a citizen in a world of strife.

To Fleury's cloister of Saint-Benoît-sur-Loire, that monastery of ancient foundation reformed by Odo of Cluny in 930, Abbo had been brought as a child by his parents; there under Abbots Wulfad and Richard he had eagerly followed the threefold and fourfold paths of the liberal arts: grammar, rhetoric, and dialectic in the *trivium,* as a beginning, arithmetic, geometry, astronomy, and music in the *quadrivium,* the later course. The tenth century still followed this training in its schools. But the schools were attached to cathedrals, monasteries, and convents; their teachers were busy with those destined to become monks, priests, or nuns. There were exceptions; but these were few.

So keen was Abbo that Aimoin, monk of Fleury, who afterward

wrote his *Life,* declared: "As a boy he needed only one telling from his teachers; he caught, understood, and hid deep in his mind all that he heard."

When he was ready his abbot gave him boys of Fleury's cloister to instruct. Then he sent him to ripen his knowledge under the leading masters in France, to study philosophy at Paris, and under Gerbert at Reims. For a while he was also at Orléans, where he took private lessons in musical theory from some cleric, "at no little price."

Now he had a firm grasp of five of the liberal arts; rhetoric and geometry, of which he knew less, he did all he could to cultivate after his return home to Fleury. Time was scant; he was appointed *scholasticus,* director of its school.

His reputation was growing; Fleury's monks began to think of him as successor to their present abbot, Amalbert. Not all, however, were anxious to receive as their leader this learned brother, at the time some forty years old. They need not have worried; when in 985 upon Amalbert's death Brother Oylbold was elected to follow him, it was Lothair, king of France, we are told, who really decided the matter.

From without, indignation rose at the news. Gerbert wrote from Reims to Majolus, abbot of Cluny: "An intruder, they say, has laid hold upon Fleury, that abbey so revered for its holy Father Benedict! If you keep silence about this, Majolus, who will speak? And if this error is not corrected, what knave will not hope for the like?" Majolus wrote back that of course Oylbold was an intruder; he had been of bad repute before he was made abbot, and his supporters were certainly impious. But his character would get even worse if he were driven away from wholesome and holy influence at Fleury. "Besides," Majolus pointed out, "abbot of Cluny though I am, it is not for me to interfere in Fleury's affairs." Very courteous and prudent words, observed Gerbert. "But let us have nothing to do with Oylbold; and, if possible, let us get malediction cast upon his head by the pope at Rome."

Abbo himself was more charitable. Years afterward Abbot Oylbold wrote to him: "Through your letter my heart received joy; it banished from my mind and memory what I so greatly feared concerning you."

Just at this time a deputation arrived at Fleury from the abbey of Ramsey in Huntingdonshire, England, to ask if Abbo might come there to direct education in its school. Ramsey had been dedicated in 974 by its founder Oswald, bishop of Worcester and archbishop of

York. Now he was eager to gain this skilled and energetic scholar for its progress in learning. Oswald knew Fleury well. He had not only lived there in his student days, but there also he had received in religion the habit of Saint Benedict.

For nearly two years, in 986 and 987, Abbo taught Ramsey's monks, and in his leisure hours he wrote for them his *Quaestiones Grammaticae,* "Points of Grammar." Absence from Fleury healed his recent disappointment. He loved community life in East Anglia: the work, the house itself and its surroundings, its setting in solitude on the lonely marsh stretching far and wide; the wooded islands among its pools; the sunlight now and then breaking through the shadows.

His visit also gave him lasting friendship with Oswald and with Dunstan, archbishop of Canterbury. In days to come he was to write for the brethren of St. Edmunds Bury in Suffolk a *Life* of their patron, Edmund, king and martyr. He had heard the story from Dunstan himself, and to him he sent its finished script, praying for criticism and correction. For Dunstan he also made three poems, two of them in that triple acrostic form so dear to medieval versifiers. But it was Oswald who in England ordained him priest.

In 987 he was recalled to Fleury; shortly after his return Oylbold died, and the year 988 saw Abbo its abbot, struggling between busy action and his love for leisure and learning. Whenever prayer and the ordering of his community did not call him, he was reading, writing, or dictating. The work of his pen still remains to us, in print or in manuscript, carried out before or after his election as abbot: work on dialectic and grammar, on patristic literature, on Papal history, on canon law, on mathematics, chronology, and computus.

Much of his learning he used as a weapon in his battle for what he held the rights of his fellow man, whether lay citizen, monk, archbishop or king. Between him and his diocesan, Arnulf, bishop of Orléans (who must not be confused with the archbishop of Reims, another Arnulf who comes into the history of Abbo), there raged for years battle concerning disposal of the offerings and the tithes due to the Church. The conflict was not confined to Fleury; it was widely spread. To a friend, known to us only as G., Abbo wrote: "Those who seize dishonestly monies due to servants of God are not private individuals but learned teachers of Christian men, leaders of the people. By will of the bishops offerings made by folk of the Church, intended for the Church, go to support the horses and dogs of laymen, rather than pilgrims or widows and orphans, or churches in need of repair. Canon law concedes to the bishop one third or one quarter of the tithes; it seems strange to find him too greedy to be content with that."

So bitter grew the quarrel that, according to Aimoin, men in the service of Arnulf of Orléans attacked Abbo on his way to keep the Feast of Saint Martin at Tours and seriously wounded one of his escort.

About 992-93 a council was held at the abbey of Saint-Denis near Paris; its monks, like those of Fleury and many other monasteries, were angry for the same reason: the receiving of too large a share of offerings of the faithful and of tithes by the bishops of France for disposal at their own will, of too small a share by monastic communities. Bishops, monks, and laymen came from all directions and the debate was fierce. Vote was given in favor of the bishops. At once the monks, and laymen who were on their side, rose in rebellion and riot. The bishops fled for their lives; leaders of the tumult were excommunicated, and Abbo, once again home at Fleury, sat down to defend monastic privilege in an appeal to the kings of France, Hugh Capet and his son, Robert II. He had already prepared for this same defense a book of extracts from the decrees of popes, of synods and of councils of the Church; he had called it a *Collectio canonum*. It is interesting to note that Abbo mentions, amid his accusations against Arnulf of Orléans in his *Apologeticus*, his appeal to Hugh and Robert, Arnulf's harsh treatment of that Letald of Micy whom we have found writing verse; he declares, rightly or wrongly, that the bishop of Orléans treated Letald of Saint-Mesmin "in unjust and illegal manner, without thought of the reverence due to a priest."

In 991, as we have also seen, Arnulf, archbishop of Reims, had been condemned and deposed by the bishops of France gathered at the Council of Saint-Basle, and Gerbert had been consecrated in his place. At that council Arnulf, bishop of Orléans, had been chairman, directing its proceedings against the accused archbishop and against the Holy See itself. Abbo of Fleury, on the other side, had zealously defended both the archbishop and the pope, John XV, who had refused to condemn him.

Some years later, early in 996, Abbo crossed the Alps, bound for Rome and for audience with that same Pope John. Two reasons were urging him on. He wanted to gain confirmation of monastic privilege for Fleury in its dispute with its diocesan bishop; he also wanted to plead with the pope for the restoration of Arnulf to his metropolitan see of Reims, now held by Gerbert.

Gerbert noted this move with deep misgiving. "I am greatly surprised at the mission of the venerable A.," he wrote to Constantine, monk of Fleury (we may safely follow Harriet Lattin in reading "Abbo" here). "If Arnulf should be restored to Reims without any counsel from the bishops, then the power, the authority, the dignity of the bishops will be brought to nothing. . . . Those who consecrated" (a reference to Gerbert's own consecration as archbishop of Reims), "he who was consecrated, and those to whom he has himself given Holy Orders, all will be victims of slander; the very kings of France will appear guilty of each and every sin alleged."

Abbo gained nothing from John XV. In 997 he was once more in Italy, delighting in talk with John's successor, Pope Gregory V. Now he won for Fleury privilege and right, also Gregory's word that he was indeed restoring Arnulf as archbishop of Reims. A third request he did not gain, nor did he resent the pope's refusal. As we already have marked, he calmly carried back to France and to its king, Robert II, Gregory's message of complete opposition to his marriage with his kinswoman, Bertha.

Abbo died as he had lived, in the midst of monastic working, of study, of vigorous action and struggle. The year 1004 called him to the abbey of La Réole in Gascony for restoration of discipline among monks unruly and rebellious. The Basques were no friends of men of France and during his stay a fierce quarrel broke out. Its noise reached Abbo as he sat in his guest chamber enjoying an hour of leisure and deep in problems of mathematics. He went out with all speed to rebuke his own followers; amid the confusion of riot a Basque drove a sword into his side. One of his monks held him up as he dragged himself into the cloister; "with a face alert and almost smiling" he said to Aimoin, who was with him: "What would you do, if you were wounded like this? But don't be afraid; go out to our men and make them come in here to me; then this disturbance will quiet down." They came, and in a moment, as they stood silently around him, he passed from quarrel to the peace beyond. It was the thirteenth of November; in many places he is revered on that day as saint and martyr.

2

Filled as Abbo was with the spirit of learning, he must yet yield to Gerbert, who never for a moment forgot the joy stored for himself and others in the words of Cicero and Boethius, in the secrets of the liberal arts. Richer, his pupil at Reims, has described for us—in the third book of his *History of France*—Gerbert's devoted working as teacher in its Cathedral School during the eight years from 972 to 980. He not only discussed matter, and theory underlying it; he carried out and explained experiment, step by step. To reveal in greater force the fascination of astronomy, he made spheres for his students—"a very difficult business"; that they might observe the positions, the movements of stars and planets, he took them out at night to watch Nature at work in the heavens. For their study of mathematics he returned to the abacus, that board furnished with signs and figures which made calculation an easier and more exciting experience. *Fervebat studiis,* Richer wrote; "Passion for learning boiled within him." Thietmar of Merseburg wrote that he surpassed men of his time in knowledge of varied kind; a later age declared his dealings with magic and with Satan, so learned he was, so successful. William of Malmesbury told the tales.

Let us pass from fable to fact, and look at Gerbert in his letters. Here we find his requests for books, his gratitude for books sent him, his anxiety to get copies of manuscripts, his care for their safekeeping. Willingly he lent his own books and eagerly he demanded their return. He was continually giving instruction in the liberal arts by correspondence, including matters of medicine. To Constantine, monk of Fleury and, later on, abbot of Saint-Mesmin, Micy, he wrote letter after letter on mathematics. He bade Romulf, abbot of Sens: "Continue, then, as you have begun, and send me the waters of Cicero for my thirst; let Cicero come to our aid in our troubles." He reminded one Thietmar of Mainz: "Amid the grievous surging of cares, philosophy alone can give us some relief." He rebuked a man, unknown to him, who had inquired about medicine: "Do not expect me to treat of things which belong to doctors. I have indeed tried hard to gain knowledge of medicine; I have always declined to practice it."

Above all, one thinks of this greatest scholar of his age as counselor and teacher of young Otto the Third. To him the emperor, sixteen years old, wrote in the autumn of 997:

"To Gerbert, most skilled of masters and honored in the three divisions of philosophy" (physics, mathematics, and theology):

"We desire to attach to ourselves the excellence, revered by all, of your most kind love; and we call to us the abiding presence of so great a guardian, because your experience, the depth and the authority of your learning, have never despised our simplicity. Putting aside all misunderstanding, we would gladly give you the naked truth. We have finally decided of our own free will to tell you in this letter of our own choice and our special petition: that henceforth, as in the past, you give to us, untaught and ill-disciplined, your constant care both in writing and conversation; that you apply to us your zealous correction and in matters of the state your most trustworthy counsel. So, in this declaration of our will, which please do not reject, while we do indeed desire you to shudder at Saxon boorishness, we want you to incite our Greek subtlety to the study of Greek; since, if only encouragement be given, some spark of the keenness of the Greeks will be discovered in us. With humble prayer we beg that, bringing the flame of your knowledge in all its power to awaken our little spark, you will with God's help kindle within us the lively spirit of the Greeks."

"Please, will you explain that book" (of Boethius) "on arithmetic? And, Father, do write soon!"

It was a boyish, immature letter, but the emperor knew what he wanted. Already he had talked long with Gerbert: in Italy, while the summer of 996 still lasted; in Germany, where on some spring day of 997 Otto had welcomed him, a fugitive from Reims; where, during its hot summer and amid the crisis of battle against the Slavs, they had fallen again and again into discussion, question, answer and argument, on problems of their world and of the past. Now Gerbert did not hesitate; as Percy Ernst Schramm puts it, he became for the rest of Otto's short life an Aristotle for his Alexander.

Nevertheless, as contrast to this due praise, one has to admit that Gerbert, the devoted student who had dwelt among Arab men of genius, gave his world and the world of the future but scant knowledge gained from this association, no light won from Arab research in astronomy.

We have marked the school established by Abbot William for his monastery of Saint-Bénigne, Dijon; his work in education merits further notice. Here again we are indebted to the *Life* written by Rodulf Glaber. In 1001 Richard, duke of Normandy, asked the abbot to take charge of the monastery of Fécamp in his duchy; it was in dire need of reform. William consented, and the *Life* by Glaber describes his planning and its result:

"The father, seeing with a keen eye that not only in Fécamp but throughout Normandy, indeed throughout the whole of France, knowledge of song and chant, as well as of letters, was wholly wanting among peasants and of no account to clerics, set up at Fécamp schools for their aid. Here brethren of the abbey, well educated themselves and eager to labor for love of God were to give their service. This teaching was to be open free of charge to all who came to the monastery, to free men and to slaves, to the rich and the poor. Many of those who came were very poor, and they were fed as well as taught."

Until his death in 1031 William ruled both Saint-Bénigne and Fécamp, together with other abbeys. We may feel sure that in all of them the same custom was observed as a sacred duty. No persuading to enter religious life was allowed; but we are told that of the many who came to Fécamp "some became monks." The movement here begun was to reach countless abbeys of France.

4

From France it is natural to cross into Lotharingia and to look at two of its centers of learning in the tenth century; the diocese of Liège and, in particular, the monastery of Lobbes. Liège had suffered cruelly in the ninth century and in the earlier years of the tenth. During the winter of 881 it had been plundered by the Danes; its land of Lotharingia had been from 895 to 900 under Zwentibold a kingdom racked by rebellion; in 900 it passed to a German king of the Carolingian House, Louis the Child; in 911 it declared its allegiance to the Carolingian king of France, Charles the Simple; in 920 it was under the power of Gilbert as duke, even as "king"; in 925 it was a German duchy, governed by Gilbert under Henry the Fowler.

No wonder that schools in the diocese of Liège had fallen low through neglect. To make their situation even worse, in 920, upon the death of Stephen, bishop of Liège, a bitter struggle had broken out between two men ambitious to succeed him. Gilbert had supported one Hilduin as candidate; since at this time the duke was all-powerful, Lotharingia's clergy and people had followed his lead. Hermann, archbishop of Cologne, had consecrated Hilduin bishop. But Charles the Simple, who held Lotharingia as his by right of supreme rule, would have none of this; Hilduin had been a rebel against his sovereignty in the land. Charles as king had decided that

Richar, abbot of Prüm, should be bishop in Liège, and he had won his will; Richar had been consecrated for the see and there he remained. The victory was due to intervention by Pope John X, who in 921 had sternly rebuked Archbishop Hermann for his presumption in consecrating Hilduin: "We were not slow in our astonishment that you dared to act against reason, without the authority of King Charles. Surely you know that it is absolutely wrong to consecrate a bishop without royal mandate!" Richar in 922 had received from this pope the pallium as sign of lawful standing; Hilduin, sentence of excommunication.

Richar ruled until 945. Although individual scholars were at work in his diocese, he himself did little for its schools. These were revived under two later bishops, encouraged by the enthusiasm of Bruno, duke and archbishop in Lotharingia from 953 until 965. One of these was Éveracle, who held the see of Liège from 959 until 971. We hear of him from Anselm, who as canon of Liège cathedral wrote during the earlier half of the eleventh century a *History* of its bishops: "When for a long time among us the study of the liberal arts had faded from memory, Éveracle founded schools for the cloisters of his diocese. Yes, and he thought it proper to visit them frequently, to read passages from books to the older students, to press home with kindly heart the meaning of what he read, to promise to explain a hundred times to them whatever they had not understood. When he went to the royal Court, or traveled on some errand far from Liège, he would write letters to encourage the schoolmasters, and sometimes he would send merry lines of song in verse. To the younger ones, his children in the schools, whose lessons he loved to share, he would send word from abroad, often from Italy, even Calabria."

Éveracle was followed in 972 by Notker, that builder in Liège. But he, too, as bishop, cared for the schoolboys in his diocese: "When he went on journeys, short or long," Anselm tells, "he would take some of them with him, and all the books and other things which they needed for their lessons."

They grew up to do him honor. Anselm continues: "Many churches rejoiced to have as pastors men trained by him in their early years; among them were Gunther, Archbishop of Salzburg, Rothard and Erluin, who succeeded one another in the see of Cambrai, Haimo, bishop of Verdun, and Adalbold, bishop of Utrecht."

5

The close connection between the see of Liège and the abbey of Lobbes is nowhere more marked than in the story of Rather, one of the distinguished writers of this time. He is not of interest as a leader in education, but as a man of culture who used his wide learning in counsel and in rebuke to a multitude of people, including himself.

He was born near Liège in the later years of the ninth century; as child, youth and man he was in turn oblate, novice, and monk in Lobbes. Folcuin in his history of the abbey describes him in the year 920, when he was a little over thirty, as "its most quick-witted scholar." When, six years later, in 926 Hilduin, defeated in the struggle for the see of Liège, at last set out for Italy to ask aid from his kinsman Hugh, now king in that land, Rather gave up life as a monk in Lobbes to go with him. It was the beginning of a restless life of struggle, disappointment, and bitterness. In Italy he remained for years; finally in 931, through the pope himself, John XI, who interceded for him with King Hugh, he was consecrated bishop of Verona. His tenure was brief; his miseries were immense; so immense that when in 934 Arnulf the Bad, duke of Bavaria, invaded Italy, hoping to seize its crown, Rather was full of joy. Hugh, though he had allowed the election to Verona's see, had always been his enemy. It was Rather himself, then, who as Verona's bishop invited Arnulf to enter its gates. Once within, Arnulf's Bavarians fought for its possession against the troops of King Hugh; they were utterly defeated, and with their duke fled back to Germany; its bishop, Rather, was arrested and sent to live at Pavia, a lonely captive in its "Walbert's Tower."

There he remained two years and a half, full of wrath and writing a vivid tale of his sufferings; in 937 his imprisonment was exchanged for exile in Como. Two years passed; in 939 he was free once more, on his way toward his own Lotharingia. But he did not hurry. Some time he spent in Provence, desolate and humiliated; his only comfort, it would seem, came from a boy named Rocstagnus, whose father, struck by his learning, begged him to give his son lessons in grammar and classic works of literature. Rather did, and even wrote for his pupil a text-book; in wry humor he described it by a German-Latin title: *Sparadorsum*, "Spare the back." It might save Rocstagnus from a flogging in the future!

In 944, at the monastery of Saint-Amand, Laon, he was offered the office of abbot; he refused. At last he was in the abbey of Lobbes, allowed a stay there by Richar, bishop of Liège.

His stay was brief. Soon he was traveling back to Italy, called there by, of all people, his former enemy, King Hugh. A rival for the throne had risen in Berengar II, count of Ivrea, and Hugh's position had quickly become desperate. Two men of note had deserted him for Berengar: Manasses, bishop of Verona and other sees in northern Italy, appointed by Berengar as archbishop of Milan; and Milo, count of Verona. Perhaps, thought the king, Rather might aid him? Undoubtedly he was a man of courage and energy.

The call was welcome. Rather was weary of monastic round, longing for action; moreover, Italy, however deeply it had troubled him, was at least a more cultured land to live in than Lotharingia.

Promptly upon his arrival he was captured and held prisoner by Berengar. Relief came from Count Milo, relief not indeed hoped for by Rather, but born of stratagem. The count of Verona was beset by fear that Manasses would change his mind and turn again to support Hugh. This was the last thing which Milo wanted; it would do him much harm. In his anxiety he had decided that he would be safer with Rather as bishop in Verona than Manasses. Craftily he went to work, step by step, and at each step he won his will: the release of Rather, the removal of Manasses from Verona's see, and the appointing of Rather in his place.

For a second time, then, from 946 to 948 Rather was bishop of Verona; once again his experience of Italy was dismal. Clergy, peasants, slaves, so he told, by continual rebellion brought to nothing every effort he made to assert his authority. Count Milo, his fear of Manasses now quenched, was always stirring up revolt against his bishop, delighting in Rather's angry temper. "Day and night," Rather wrote later to Pope Agapetus II: "I was so wretched, so nervous, exhausted, weary of my life, that I would more gladly have been in that tower of Walbert at Pavia than in the cathedral of Verona, more gladly have been fasting under Hugh than feasting with Milo."

In 948 Hugh was no longer in Italy, and his son, King Lothar, sent peremptory order to Rather that he return immediately the see of Verona to Manasses. There was nothing to do but obey. A period of wandering, endless and aimless, now followed, year after year, from land to land. Again in 951 Rather entered Italy, as friend of Liudolf, duke of Swabia and eldest son of King Otto I, hoping that Liudolf would succeed in gaining support from Italian nobles and that perhaps he himself might return to Verona as bishop. Even that would be better than wandering.

But Liudolf gave him no aid. The same year Milo, count of Verona, by heavy pressure persuaded Manasses to yield his see in that city to another Milo, the count's nephew. Milo senior, according to Rather, had received support in this move from the pope himself. "I thought it better," wrote Rather in his letter to Agapetus, "to yield to your apostolic authority instead of to the count's majesty, and not to find fault with what you yourself had decreed. And so, released by the mercy of God from prison and exile, allowed my own free will, I am resolved to seek the solitude of a monastery, and there to hope that God may save me from cowardly spirit within myself and from the stormy tempest of my enemies; to search into the causes of my expulsion, alone and in penitence; to judge myself that I be not judged; to believe that what has been decreed by you has been decreed by God."

The monastery he sought was again Lobbes and he was there from December 951 until the summer of 952. Then King Otto I, eager that his younger brother Bruno, now nearing the end of his study at court, should receive some last preparation for his future work, called upon Rather. His name was already well known to Bruno, from Provence or from Lobbes Rather had written to him, asking to be allowed to enter his service. He had also sent with his letter the writing he had done at Pavia, his *Praeloquia,* as he had named it.

Soon, so Folcuin tells, Rather was "foremost among philosophers at the palace." The two royal brothers gave him good reward; on September 25, 953, when Bruno was consecrated archbishop of Cologne, at Aachen Rather received the vacant see of Liège.

Again he destroyed his chance. Again the clergy and people rose in anger; on Christmas Day 954 their rebellion reached its height. Reginar III, count of Hainaut, was working with all his strength to get his nephew, Balderic, elected bishop of Liège. Rather found resistance hopeless; "captain of its church though he was, he yielded before the storm," and in 955 Balderic was installed.

The exiled bishop now found refuge with another whom he had taught: William, son of Otto I, now archbishop of Mainz. At Mainz he spent his days again in writing. Next we find him head of some small abbey, probably that of Aulne near Lobbes. In 961 King Otto arrived in Italy on his way to imperial crowning; through pressure from Rome he used his influence to establish Rather in the following year as bishop of Verona for the third time. Seven years of renewed resentment, hatred, and disobedience on the part of his subjects followed; at length, defeated in synod, condemned in trial through the enmity of Nanno, another count of Verona, he could no longer remain. In his despair he wrote to Folcuin, then abbot of Lobbes, and asked if he might once more make the abbey his home. Would Folcuin send him horses and an escort for the journey? In 968 he arrived; Folcuin not only welcomed him but, with the consent of his community, he gave him tenancy of two minor abbeys and two little farms, dependencies of Lobbes.

It availed nothing. Rather heartily detested this patronage; "instigated by others" he did all he could to harm the abbot. Finally Folcuin decided to resign; the situation was unbearable and he knew well that Éveracle, bishop of Liège, would raise no objection. At once Rather took possession of the monastery; to keep it safe from attack by Folcuin's relations, men of high standing in the land, he raised around it bulwarks so strong that it looked like a fortress.

Happily in 972 Notker succeeded Éveracle and as bishop at once made inquiry into the doings at Lobbes. Folcuin was restored to office; Rather, found guilty of having usurped his abbacy, made peace with him and retired to live in Aulne. In 974 he died, while on a visit to Namur.

His life was filled by pen and paper; wherever he was, bishop in Italy or in Lotharingia, in prison, in exile, in monastery, words poured from his mind in a rushing stream, turbid and complex, carrying a freight of learned references gathered from works of the past, pagan and Christian, sometimes quoted at secondhand, more often taken from their original Latin text.

Men of all classes and callings were his passionate concern, kings, nobles, simple folk, bishops, priests, deacons, monks and their abbots. He did not write his words to them in love and sympathy; to all he sternly pointed out their duties, their proper relationship one with another, their sins and their vices. In his prison at Pavia he sat drawing in words a hideous picture of the clergy of Italy: neglectful of their flocks, given to worldly and seductive sport with horse, dog, and falcon, dressed like layfolk, adorned like women in ornament foreign and barbaric, stripped of God and clothed with the world; gambling with dice, players in place of priests, stage musicians in place of clerics, mimic actors in place of monks. What to them was holy office, saintly life, canon law or papal decrees? They lived for wealth.

Nor did he spare himself. He dissected his own conscience in an agony of self-accusation. While he reviled his enemies and wrote in misery his long lament on the injuries done to him, he knew that these were largely due to his own ambition, to his own arrogant, impatient temper. It is also true to say that he had warm praise for his friends, but especially for those from whom he received or hoped for help.

Albert Hauck has written of him: "Er war eine Genie der Reflexion. Er reflektierte über alles." Augustin Fliche and Émile Amann have pointed out his longing for reform in relations between the crown and the papacy, a longing which heralded the future. To the *Praeloquia* Amann finds no parallel in all medieval literature. Another comment upon this work from Pavia, given by one of Rather's own century, Liutprand of Cremona, tells us: "There with wit and polished humor he wrote a book on the unhappiness of his exile. Whoever reads it will find in it reflections very neatly suited for his own situation, reflections no less pleasing than profitable."

6

A few words may find place here concerning the tenth century's work in music and in languages, ancient and contemporary. Gerbert was an authority on music; Rather taught it. To Hucbald (c.840-930), monk of Saint-Amand in Flanders, Martin Gerbert in his *Scriptores ecclesiastici de Musica,* published in 1784, assigned the renowned work, *Musica Enchiriadis;* in the second volume of the *New Oxford History of Music* Dom Anselm Hughes places it in the same period but observes that it is now held anonymous. Hucbald was, indeed, highly praised for his skill in music by Sigebert of Gembloux, writing early in the eleventh century; he did compose a little work entitled *De Harmonica Institutione.*

More important is the question debated concerning the place in music's tradition of Odo, second abbot of Cluny. Recently Dom Pierre Thomas, in a learned lecture given at the Congress of Cluny in 1949 and published in the following year, with firm voice denied to this Saint Odo any of the treatises on music attributed to him, with the possible but doubtful exception of the *Tonale* (MS. 318, Monte Cassino). That, however, was his verdict only so far as the treatises were concerned. He declared with equal firmness that this Odo's rendering of song, his knowledge of the theory of music and his writing of hymns and antiphons, his encouraging of music in France, brought him renown which lasted the length of medieval days.

We turn to look at knowledge and use of language in this time. Montagu Rhodes James summed up the situation thus in regard to classical Greek: little knowledge remained to scholars; manuscripts were lacking; teaching by the Irish had almost ceased; the Greek East stood aloof from what they held the ignorant West; the Greek monks of southern Italy did not spread teaching of the ancient language of Greece.

Very possibly some Greek was picked up from men who had fled from their native lands to Otto's royal court; perhaps his brother, Bruno, learned a little from the Irish bishop Israel who taught him there. Others, like Liutprand of Cremona, learned Greek, we may think, from travel in the empire of the East.

From the thought of Greek we come to Notker Labeo, "the German," a nephew of Ekkehard I of Saint-Gall. This Notker, who lived from about 950 to 1022, taught at Saint-Gall and was an excellent Latin scholar. His pupils, unhappily, found this ancient language difficult enough. But, if they could not read Latin with some ease, how were they to study the pages of writers on the liberal arts? Notker found a solution of this problem and described it in a letter written during his later days to Hugh, bishop from 998 to 1017 of Sitten (Sion) in Jurane Burgundy. The letter was, of course, in Latin:

"I was so glad to hear by messenger of your good health. But, reminded that your request calls for answer, what can I say but that words from me must make up for action? I still want to please you; but we are held in the hands of the Lord, both ourselves and our work. Necessity, not our own will, carries us along. So I cannot do as you wish. I have given up all thought of that work of my own on the liberal arts which you wanted me to do; I can only enjoy them as means of learning for my pupils. . . .

"For their sake, then, I have dared to do a thing almost unheard of; I have tried to turn Latin writings on the liberal arts into our own language!"

We still have translations by Notker from Latin into Old High German: translations of Boethius, *De Consolatione Philosophiae;* of the Latin renderings by Boethius of Aristotle's *Categoriae* and *De Interpretatione;* of work influenced by Boethius, on logic and on rhetoric; of part of the *De Nuptiis Philologiae et Mercurii* by Martianus Capella; of the Latin Psalter. Comment, drawn by Notker from Latin sources, in German translation or in his own German words, flavors the whole; his lively thought and style gave doubtless delight to those who read him. The translation itself is not literal but rendered in free version, and the Latin does not run in the exact order of its original text.

7

There were, then, winds of learning to enliven and to fortify men of the tenth century. But they could not drive away mists of superstition which still lay dense on its lands. As the years went by and battle followed battle, against Hungarians, Saracens, and Slavs; as invasion, fire, and famine fell upon the empire of the West; as portents of evil yet to come appeared, in volcanic eruption, in the burning of St. Peter's itself in Rome; as the dreaded comet, always herald of tragedy, shone month after month bright in the darkness, men began to fear that surely the end of the world must be approaching; Antichrist, minion of Satan, would soon descend upon the earth; the trumpet of the Seventh Angel would sound and time would be no more.

Already in 954 Gerberga, wife of King Louis d'Outremer of France, was sending a petition to Adso (then scholar and teacher at Saint-Èvre, Toul, from 967 to be abbot of Montiér-en-Der in Champagne), praying him to explain what this rumor of Antichrist meant? In reply Adso wrote for her his *Libellus de Antichristo*.

It was based upon words of the Book of Daniel, of the Apocalypse, of the Second Epistle to the Thessalonians, of Biblical commentaries. The Antichrist, it told, will appear after the fall of the Roman Empire, which will endure as long as the line of Frankish kings holds rule. The last of these rulers will be the greatest of all, zealous in his governing. He will destroy the shrines of false gods; he will gather in the heathen for Christian baptism; under him the cross of Christ will reign in all temples of worship. In the end he will journey to Jerusalem; he will lay down his sceptre and his crown upon the Mount of Olives, and glorious will be his sepulchre. After his departing two great prophets, Elias and Enoch, will arise on this earth to prepare the faithful for war. Then will come the Antichrist, bringing tribulation such as never has been known. Every Christian soul will either deny God in this time of terror or will die by torture: torture of the sword, of fire, of serpents, of wild beasts. Three years and a half Antichrist will hold this power; then the Christ will come to cast him down to perdition, to raise to eternal joy those who have died for the faith, and in His mercy to give to the faithless a little time for repentance. Finally He will judge all men, in the hour appointed before time and worlds were born.

Years later, shortly after 960, Abbo of Fleury, then a young student, heard a preacher announce in Paris that Antichrist would come upon the earth in the year 1000, and that the Last Judgment of all souls would follow shortly afterward. Abbo, young though he was, sternly rebuked the preacher. Again, so the same Abbo tells, in the time of Richard, abbot of Fleury from 962 to 975, a letter arrived at the monastery from Lotharingia. It bore dreadful news: "A rumor is spreading through nearly the whole earth, warning all mankind that when in the future the Feast of the Annunciation shall fall on the same date as Good Friday, without any doubt this world will come to an end." His abbot instructed Abbo once again to make sharp denial.

Raoul Glaber, however, who has left us his record of the fears and forebodings of men between the years 900 and 1044, described portent after portent which gave rise to a belief that the end of this world of time would come in 1033: a thousand years, in contemporary dating, after the Passion of the Lord Christ. As that year drew near, death followed upon death in grim succession; the pope of Rome (Benedict VIII), the king of France (Robert II), the bishop of Chartres (Fulbert), the abbot of Saint-Bénigne (William), all departed this life. Then, too, "in all the world famine waxed strong and threatened nearly the whole human race, in the East, in Greece, in Italy, in France, in England." Raoul goes on to record a ghastly tale of men driven to kill one another, to prey upon human flesh, to devour anything and any creature weaker than themselves.

Such fears of world's ending, however, have beset all centuries and all generations of men. Superstition is hydraheaded; and it never dies. The years 1000 to 1033 came and went, and the world continued its course. Thietmar of Merseburg wrote in his *Chronicle* that in the thousandth year after Mary Immaculate bore her Child for our salvation, "a morning dawned radiant on the world." Glaber himself admitted that in the year 1030 "it seemed as if the world, shaking itself and casting off its old age, was putting on, here, there, and everywhere, the pure white robe of churches."

But perhaps the best, because the most natural, story of this fear is given us by Anselm in his *History of the bishops of Liège*. In 968 the German king, Otto I, was on campaign against Byzantine power in southern Italy, and Éveracle, bishop of Liège, was in the field for his support, with a regiment of Lotharingian soldiers. Suddenly at high noon the daylight began to fail and darkness to cover the earth. "It is the end of the world!" cried the terrified men, as cattle and birds sought shelter, and the horror of black shadow crept steadily around; "the Last Judgment is upon us!" Those who dauntlessly had stormed towns and crushed rebellion now ran through this unknown night to hide wherever they could, in barrels, in wooden chests, under wagons. The bishop stood alone, unafraid. Out of the night his voice called to them: "Warriors! you who have braved a thousand perils, courage! No danger faces you, no enemy! This is but harmless dark; in a little while it will be light and you will see the sun. All's well; come forth!"

They did, and found his words were true. The bishop had read his astronomy.

Perhaps those who have seen the sun shining on the snow gradually fade into the blackness of total eclipse, or have watched in past days the night of London fog slowly but surely blot out all streets and buildings at eleven in the morning, may sympathize with Otto's soldiers. Nevertheless, here in the tenth century good learning conquered ignorance.

So, in the year 1002, the sun of the third Otto's vision set and night fell on the Western empire; to disappear, as ever, in the rising of a new day.

TABLES

EMPERORS OF THE WEST

Charles III, the Fat:	881-87
Guy of Spoleto:	891-94
Lambert of Spoleto:	892-96
Arnulf of Germany:	896
Lambert of Spoleto:	897-98
Louis "the Blind," king of Provence:	901-2
Berengar of Friuli:	915-24
Otto I:	962-73
Otto II:	967-83
Otto III:	996-1002

EMPERORS OF THE EAST

Leo VI:	886-912
Constantine VII, Porphyrogenitus:	913-59
Romanus II:	959-63
Nicephorus II:	963-69
John I, Tzimisces:	969-76
Basil II:	976-1025

POPES OF ROME

John VIII:	872-82	John XI:	931-36
Marinus I:	882-84	Leo VII:	936-39
Hadrian III:	884-85	Stephen VIII:	939-42
Stephen V:	885-91	Marinus II:	942-46
Formosus:	891-96	Agapetus II:	946-55
Boniface VI:	896	John XII:	955-64
Stephen VI:	896-97	Leo VIII:	963-65
Romanus:	897	Benedict V:	964
Theodore II:	897	John XIII:	965-72
John IX:	898-900	Benedict VI:	972-74
Benedict IV:	900-903	Boniface VII:	974
Leo V:	903	Benedict VII:	974-83
Christopher:	903-4	John XIV:	983-84
Sergius III:	904-11	Boniface VII:	984-85
Anastasius III:	911-13	John XV:	985-96
Lando:	913-14	Gregory V:	996-99
John X:	914-28	John XVI, Antipope:	997-98
Leo VI:	928-29	Sylvester II:	999-1003
Stephen VII:	929-31		

KINGS OF GERMANY

Charles III, the Fat:	882-87	Henry I, the Fowler:	919-36
Arnulf of Carinthia:	887-99	Otto I, the Great:	936-73
Louis the Child:	900-11	Otto II:	961-83
Conrad of Franconia:	911-18	Otto III:	983-1002

KINGS OF FRANCE

Carloman:	879-84	Raoul of	
Charles III,		Burgundy:	923-36
the Fat:	885-87	Louis IV,	
Odo of		d'Outremer:	936-54
Neustria:	888-98	Lothair:	954-86
Charles the		Louis V:	(979)986-87
Simple:	(893)898-922(923)	Hugh Capet:	987-96
Robert I:	922-23	Robert II, the	
		Pious:	(987)996-1031

KINGS OF ITALY

Charles III, the Fat:	879-87	Rudolf of Burgundy:	922-26
Berengar of Friuli:	888-89	Hugh of Arles:	926-47
Guy of Spoleto:	889-94	Lothar, son of	
Lambert of Spoleto:	892-96	Hugh of Arles:	931-50
Arnulf of		Berengar of Ivrea:	950-61
Germany:	894(rival king);	Adalbert, son of	
	896	Berengar of Ivrea:	950-61
Lambert of Spoleto:	897-98	Otto I:	961-73
Berengar of Friuli:	898-900	Otto II:	961-83
Louis of Provence:	900-902	Otto III:	983-1002
Berengar of Friuli:	902-22		

KINGS OF BURGUNDY

Rudolf I:	888-c.912	Conrad	
Rudolf II:	c.912-37	the Peaceful:	937-93
		Rudolf III:	993-1032

KINGS OF PROVENCE

Boso:	879-87	United with	
Louis "the Blind":	890-928	Burgundy:	933-34 . . .

DUKES OF GERMANY

Saxony

Liudolf: died 866
Bruno (the elder son): 866-80
Otto (his younger brother):
  880-912
Henry: 912-19:
  king of Germany: 919-36

Under the crown of Germany:
  919-36
Under the crown of Germany
  (with Hermann Billung from
  c.960 acting as duke): 936-73
Bernard I: 973-1011

Bavaria

Liutpold: died 907
Arnulf "the Bad": 907-37
Eberhard, son of
  Arnulf "the Bad": 937-38
Berchtold: 938-47
Henry, brother of Otto I: 947-55
Henry the Quarreler:
  955-76; 985-95

Otto, grandson of Otto I:
  976-82 (also duke of Swabia)
Henry the Younger: 983-85
  (also duke of Carinthia)
Henry, son of Henry the
  Quarreler: 995-1004;
  king of Germany 1002-24

Franconia

Conrad: 906-11
Under the crown of
  Germany: 911-18
Eberhard, brother of Henry
  the Fowler: 919-39

Under the crown of
  Germany: 939 . . .

Swabia

[Burchard I: died 911]
Erchanger: 915-17
Burchard II: 917-26
Hermann I: 926-49
Liudolf, son of Otto I: 949-54

Burchard III: 954-73
Otto, grandson of Otto I:
  973-82 (also duke of Bavaria)
Conrad of Franconia: 983-97
Hermann II: 997-1003

Lotharingia

Gebhard: died 910
Reginar I: 910-15
Gilbert: 915-39
  (elected king in 920)

Henry, brother of Otto I:
  939-40
Otto of Verdun: 940-44
Conrad the Red: 944-53
Bruno: 953-65

Upper Lotharingia

Friedrich I:
c.959-78

Dietrich, son of Friedrich I:
978-1026

Lower Lotharingia

Godfrey of Lotharingia:
c.959-64

Charles: 977-91
Otto, son of Charles: 992-1005

Carinthia

Henry the Younger:
976-78; 983-89

Otto, son of Conrad the Red:
978-83; 995-1004

DUKES OF BOHEMIA

Wenzel: c.925-29 (935)
Boleslav I: 929 (935)-967

Boleslav II: 967-99

DUKES OF POLAND

Miesko I: died 992

Boleslav, Chrobry: 992-1025

ARCHBISHOPS OF GERMANY

Cologne

Hermann I: 890-925
Wikfried: 925-53
Bruno: 953-65
Folcmar: 965-69

Gero: 969-76
Warin: 976-85
Everger: 985-99
Heribert: 999-1021

Magdeburg

Adalbert: 968-81

Gisler: 981-1004

Mainz

Hatto I: 891-913
Heriger: 913-27
Hildebert: 927-37
Frederick: 937-54

William: 954-68
Hatto II: 968-70
Rothbert: 970-75
Willigis: 975-1011

ARCHBISHOPS OF REIMS, FRANCE

Fulk: 883-900
Hervé: 900-922
Séulf: 922-25
Rivals for archsee of Reims:
   Hugh of Vermandois: nominated and represented by deputy: 925-41; archbishop: 941-48

Artaud: archbishop: 931-61

Odalrich: 962-69
Adalbero: 969-89
Arnulf: 989-91 (expelled)
Gerbert: 991-98
Arnulf (restored): 998-1021

BISHOPS OF LIÈGE, BELGIUM

Stephen: c.903-20
Richar: 920-45
Hugh I: 945-47
Farabert: 947-53

Rather: 953-55
Balderic: 955-59
Éveracle: 959-71
Notker: 972-1008

TH

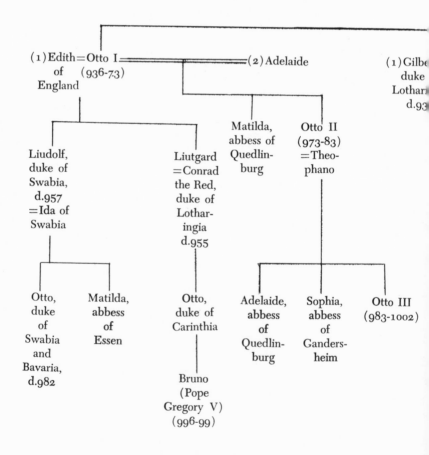

TTONIAN HOUSE

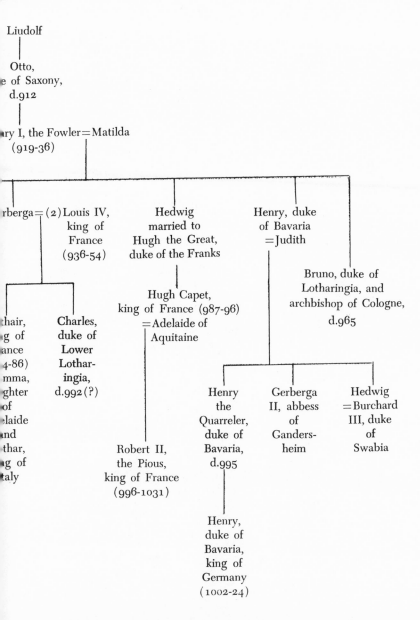

Liudolf

Otto,
e of Saxony,
d.912

ry I, the Fowler = Matilda
(919-36)

rberga = (2) Louis IV,   Hedwig   Henry, duke
king of   married to   of Bavaria
France   Hugh the Great,   = Judith
(936-54)   duke of the Franks
                                                        Bruno, duke of
                                                        Lotharingia, and
                         Hugh Capet,   archbishop of Cologne,
                     king of France (987-96)   d.965
                       = Adelaide of
thair,   Charles,   Aquitaine
g of   duke of
ance   Lower
4-86)   Lothar-
mma,   ingia,
ghter   d.992(?)   Henry   Gerberga   Hedwig
of   the   II, abbess   = Burchard
laide   Quarreler,   of   III, duke
nd   duke of   Ganders-   of
thar,   Robert II,   Bavaria,   heim   Swabia
g of   the Pious,   d.995
taly   king of France
                      (996-1031)
                                    Henry,
                                    duke of
                                    Bavaria,
                                    king of
                                    Germany
                                    (1002-24)

TABLE 1

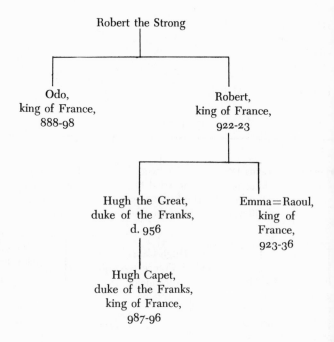

TABLE 2

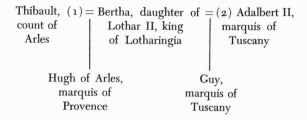

TABLE 3

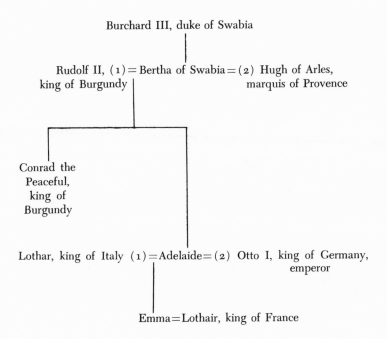

Burchard III, duke of Swabia

Rudolf II, (1) = Bertha of Swabia = (2) Hugh of Arles,
king of Burgundy   marquis of Provence

Conrad the
Peaceful,
king of
Burgundy

Lothar, king of Italy (1) = Adelaide = (2) Otto I, king of Germany,
emperor

Emma = Lothair, king of France

TABLE 4

Marozia, widow (2) = Hugh of Arles = (3) Bertha of Swabia,
of Alberic I   marquis of   widow of Rudolf II,
of Spoleto, and   Provence,   king of Burgundy
of Guy, marquis   king of Italy
of Tuscany

SOURCES
Selected, Primary and Secondary

AA.SS: Acta Sanctorum Bollandiana

AA.SS.OSB.:   Acta Sanctorum Ordinis S. Benedicti, ed. Mabillon

AHR: American Historical Review

BEC: Bibliothèque de l'École des Chartes

BEHE: Bibliothèque de l'École des Hautes Etudes

DA: Deutsches Archiv für Geschichte des Mittelalters

DHGE: Dictionnaire d'Histoire et de Géographie ecclésiastique

DVLG: Deutsche Vierteljahresschrift für Literaturwissenschaft und Geistesgeschichte

EHR: English Historical Review

Fonti: Fonti per la Storia d'Italia

HZ: Historische Zeitschrift

MGH: Monumenta Germaniae Historica

MIÖG: Mitteilungen des Instituts für Österreichische Geschichtsforschung

NA: Neues Archiv der Gesellschaft für ältere deutsche Geschichtskunde

PG: Patrologia Graeca

PL: Patrologia Latina

PLAC: Poetae Latini Aevi Carolini, M G H

PLMA: Poetae Latini Medii Aevi, M G H

RB: Revue bénédictine

SRG: Scriptores rerum Germanarum, M G H

SS: Scriptores, ed. Pertz, M G H

ZK: Zeitschrift für Kunstgeschichte

Chapters One to Five

Abbonis Bella Parisiacae Urbis: ed. with French tr. H. Waquet (1942).

————. ed P. de Winterfeld, PLAC, IV, i, 72 ff.

Acta Concilii Mosomensis (Mouzon) 995: Mansi XIX, 193 ff.; SS III, 654, 690 f.

Acta Concilii Remensis ad Sanctum—Basolum, auctore Gerberto archiepiscopo, 991: Mansi XIX, 107 ff.; SS III, 658 ff.

Adalbero, Remensis archiepiscopus: Epistulae: PL CXXXVII, 503 ff.

Adam of Bremen: History of the Archbishops of Hamburg-Bremen, tr. Francis J. Tschan (1959).

Amann, Émile: L'Époque Carolingienne (1947).

————, et Dumas, Auguste: L'Église au pouvoir des laïques (888-1057) (1948).

Annales Augienses: SS I, 67 ff.

Annales/de Saint-Bertin: ed. Félix Grat, Jeanne Vielliard et Suzanne Clémencet; intro. et notes par Léon Levillain (1964).

Annales Colonienses: SS I, 98f.

Annales Corbeienses: SS III, 1 ff.

Annales Einsidlenses: SS III, 137 ff.

Annales Fuldenses III (Mainz) auctore Meginhardo, cum Continuationibus Ratisbonensi et Altahensibus, ed. Fr. Kurze, 1891 (S R G).

Annales Hildesheimenses: SS III, 18 ff.

Annales Juvavensium Majores: SS XXX, 2, 742.

Annales Lobienses: SS XIII, 224 ff.

Annales Quedlinburgenses: SS III, 18 ff.; Continuatio (994-1025), ibid., 72 ff.

Annales S. Maximi Trevirensis: SS IV, 5 ff.

Annales Sangallenses Majores: SS I, 72 ff.

Annales Vedastini, ed. B. de Simson, 1909 (S R G).

Annales Weissemburgenses: SS III, 18 ff.

Annalium Alamannicorum Continuatio Sangallensis tertia: SS I, 52 ff.

Annals of Lambert of Hersfeld, ed. O. Holder-Egger, 1894 (S R G).

Arnulfi Remensis archiepiscopi Acta: PL CXXXIX, 1543 ff.

Barraclough, Geoffrey: tr. Mediaeval Germany (911-1250): Essays by German historians, I-II (1938).

————, ed.: The Origins of Modern Germany (1946).

————: History in a Changing World (1955).

————:The Mediaeval Empire: Idea and Reality (1959).

Baynes, N. H. and H. St. L. B. Moss: ed. Byzantium (1948).

Benedicti, monachi S Andreae in Monte Soracte: Chronicon, ed. G. Zucchetti: Fonti LV, 1920, 1 ff.; SS III, 695 ff.; PL CXXXIX, 9 ff.

Brooke, Christopher: Europe in the Central Middle Ages (1964).

Böhmer, Heinrich: Willigis von Mainz (1895).

Böhmer, J.F.: Regesta imperii II, ed. Ottenthal (1893).

Browning, Robert: The Ring and the Book, X, The Pope.

Calmette, Joseph: Le Reich allemand au Moyen Age (1951).

Cam, Helen M.: "The Adolescent Nations": Symposium, 7 ff.

Cambridge History of Poland, I (1950).

Cambridge Medieval History, III (1922), with maps; IV, i (1966).

Cambridge Medieval History, Shorter, by C. W. Previté-Orton, ed. Philip Grierson, I (1952).

Capitularia Regum Francorum II, ed. A. Boretius and V. Krause (1897).

Chronicon Farfense, Gregorio Catinensi auctore, ed. U. Balzani: Fonti XXXIII, 107 ff.; XXXIV, 1 ff. (1903).

Chronicon Salernitanum: SS III, 467 ff.

Constantine VII Porphyrogenitus: De Cerimoniis Aulae Byzantinae I (Bonn, 1829), 594.

Cross, S.H.: Slavic Civilization Through the Ages (1948).

Dahmus, Joseph: A History of Medieval Civilization (1964).

David P.: "Bohême": DHGE IX, 426 ff.

Dawson, Christopher: The Making of Europe (1932).

Deanesly, Margaret: A History of Early Medieval Europe, 476 to 911 (1956).

Destructio Monasterii Farfensis, ed. a Domino Hugone abbate: Fonti XXXIII, 1903, 25 ff.

Diehl, Charles, et Marçais, Georges: Le Monde Oriental de 395 à 1081 (1936).

Diplomata regum et imperatorum Germaniae, ed. Th. Sickel: MGH I (Conrad I, Henry I, Otto I); II, i (Otto II); II, ii(Otto III) (1879-93).

Diplomata Regum Germaniae ex stirpe Karolinorum IV (Louis the Child), ed. Theodor Schieffer (1960), 75 ff.

Duchesne, Louis: The Beginnings of the Temporal Sovereignty of the Popes (754-1073), tr. A. H. Mathew (1908).

Duckett, Eleanor S.: Saint Dunstan of Canterbury (1955).

Dümmler, Ernst: Auxilius und Vulgarius (1866).

Duprè-Theseider, E.: "Otto I und Italien": MIOG, Ergänzungsband XX, i (1962), 53 ff.

Dvornik, F.: The Making of Central and Eastern Europe (1949).

———: The Slavs: Their Early History and Civilization (1956).

———: The Slavs in European History and Civilization (1962).

Ebert, Adolf: Allgemeine Geschichte der Literatur des Mittelalters im Abendlande, III (1887).

Eckel, Auguste: Charles le Simple (1899), B E H E 124.

Falco, Giorgio: The Holy Roman Republic, tr. K. V. Kent (1964).

Favre, Édouard: Eudes, Comte de Paris et roi de France (882-898) (1893), B E H E 99.

Fawtier, Robert: Les Capétiens et la France (1942).

Fliche, Augustin: L'Europe occidentale de 888 à 1125 (1930).

Folz, R.: L'Idée d'empire en occident du Vᵉ au XIVᵉ siècle (1953).

Fonti per la Storia d'Italia (Fonti).

Ganshof, F.-L.: Feudalism, tr. Philip Grierson (1952).

———: Le Moyen Âge (1953).

Gay, Jules: L' Italie meridionale et l'Empire Byzantin (867-1071) (1904).

Gebhardt, Bruno: Handbuch der deutschen Geschichte, I: Frühzeit und Mittelalter, ed.[8] H. Grundmann (1962).

Gesta Pontificum Cameracensium, ed. L. C. Bethmann: SS VII 393 ff.; PL CXLIX, 9 ff.

Gesta Archiepiscoporum Magdeburgensium: SS XIV, 361 ff.

Ghellinck, J. de: Littérature latine au Moyen Âge, I - II (1939).

Giesebrecht, Wilhelm von: Geschichte der deutschen Kaiserzeit, I[5] (1881).

Gregorii V Papae Litterae de Synodo Papiensi (997): SS III, 694.

Grundmann, Herbert: Betrachtungen zur Kaiserkrönung Ottos I: Bayerische Akademie der Wissenschaften, phil. hist. Klasse (1962).

Haller, J.: Das Papsttum: Idee und Wirklichkeit, II (1951).

Halphen, Louis: Charlemagne et l'Empire Carolingien (1947).

———— "La Cour d'Otton III à Rome (998-1001)": À travers d'histoire du Moyen Âge (1950), 105 ff.

———— et Lot, Ferdinand: Recueil des Actes de Lothaire II et de Louis V, rois de France (954-987) (1908).

Hampe, K.: "Kaiser Otto III und Rom": HZ CXL, 1929, 513 ff.

————. Das Hochmittelalter: Geschichte des Abendlandes von 900 bis 1250[4] (1953).

————. Herrschergestalten des deutschen Mittelalters[6] (1955).

Hartmann, Ludwig M.: Geschichte Italiens im Mittelalter, III, ii (1911); IV, i (1915).

Hauck, Albert: Kirchengeschichte Deutschlands, III, 1958 (neunte, unveränderte Auflage)

Heer, Friederich: "Die 'Renaissance' Ideologie im frühen Mittelalter": MIOG LVII, 1949, 63 ff.

Hefele, J.-Leclercq, H. Dom: Histoire des Conciles, IV, ii, (1911).

Hélin, Maurice: Histoire des lettres latines du moyen âge, 1943; revised and tr. Jean C. Snow (1949).

Holtzmann, Robert: Geschichte der sächsischen Kaiserzeit (900-1024), ed. 4 (1961).

Holtzmann, Walther: König Heinrich I und die heilige Lanze (1947).

Jaffé, Ph.-Wattenbach, W.-Löwenfeld, S.: Regesta Pontificum Romanorum, I (1885).

Jahrbücher des deutschen Reiches: Uhlirz, Karl: I (Otto II), 1902;
Uhlirz, Mathilde: II (Otto III) (1954).

John the Deacon: Chronicon Venetum: Fonti IX (1890), 57 ff.; SS VII,
1 ff.; PL CXXXIX, 875 ff.

Johnson, Edgar J.: The Secular Activities of the German Episcopate
(919-1024): Univ. of Nebraska Studies, XXX-XXXI (1930-31).

Kleinclausz, Arthur: L'Empire Carolingien (1902).

Koebner, Richard: Empire (1961).

Labande, E.-R.: "Mirabilia mundi": Essai sur la personalité d'Otton III:
Cahiers de civilisation médiévale, VI, 1963, 297 ff., 455 ff.

Läwen, G.: Stammesherzog und Stammesherzogtum (1935).

Lauer, Ph.: Le Règne de Louis IV d'Outremer (936-54) (1900), BEHE
127.

————: Robert I et Raoul de Bourgogne, rois de France (1910), BEHE
188.

————: Recueil des actes de Louis IV, roi de France (1914).

Leflon, Jean: Gerbert: Humanisme et Chrétienté au Xᵉ siècle (1946).

Leo Diaconus: Historiae, ed. C. B. Hase, Corpus Scriptorum historiae
Byzantinae (1928), 87 ff.

Leyser, Karl: "The Battle at the Lech, 955: A Study in Tenth-Century
Warfare": History L, No. 168 (Feb. 1965), 1 ff.

Libellus de Imperatoria Potestate in Urbe Roma: ed. G. Zucchetti, Fonti
LV (1920), 189 ff.; SS III, 719 ff.

Liber Pontificalis: ed. L. Duchesne, II, 1892: III, revised C. Vogel, 1957.

Lintzel, Martin: "Zur Erwerbung der heiligen Lanze durch Heinrich I":
HZ CLXXI, 1951, 303 ff.

Lopez, Robert S.: "Still Another Renaissance?" AHR LVII, 1951, 1 ff.

————: "Some Tenth-Century Towns," Symposium, 4 ff.

————: The Tenth Century (1959).

————: Naissance de l'Europe (1962).

Lot, Ferdinand: Les derniers Carolingiens: Lothaire, Louis V, Charles de
Lorraine (954-91) (1891), BEHE 87.

————: Études sur le règne de Hugues Capet et la fin du Xᵉ siècle (1904), BEHE 147.

————: Naissance de la France (1948).

———— et Ganshof, Francois-L.: Les Destinées de l'Empire en Occident ii (768-888) (1941).

Lüttich, Rudolf: "Ungarnzüge in Europa im 10 Jahrhundert": Historische Studien LXXXIV (1910).

Mâle, Émile: Rome et ses vieilles Églises (1942).

Manitius, Max: Geschichte der lateinischen Literatur des Mittelalters I-II-III (1911-31).

Mann, Horace K.: The Lives of the Popes in the Early Middle Ages²: III-V (858-1048) (1925).

Mansi, J.D.: Sacrorum Conciliorum nova et amplissima Collectio, XVIII-XIX (885-1070).

Manteuffel, Tadeusz: "L'État de Mesco Iᵉʳ et les relations internationales au Xᵉ siècle": Revue Historique, CCXXVIII (1962), 1 ff.

Monumenta Novaliciensia Vetustiora: II, ed. Carlo Cipolla (1901), 197 f. (Fonti XXXII).

Morghen, Raffaello: "L'Età di Ottone III": Problemi, 13 ff.

Ohnsorge, Werner: "Otto I und Byzanz": MIÖG Ergänzungsband XX, i (1962), 107 ff.

Omont, H.: "Quatre bulles inédites des papes Silvestre II et Pascal II": No. I, 999-1003: BEC 50 (1889), 567 f.

Ostrogorsky, G.: History of the Byzantine State, tr. Joan Hussey (1956).

Parisot, R.: Histoire de Lorraine, I (1919).

Paulhart, Herbert: Odilonis Cluniacensis abbatis Epitaphium domine Adelheide auguste: MIÖG Ergänzungsband XX, ii (1962).

Peter, Damian, St.: De Principis Officio: PL CXLV, 830.

Pfister, Chr.: Études sur le règne de Robert le Pieux (1885), BEHE 64.

Poole, Reginald L.: "Henry I and the Holy Lance": EHR XXX (1915), 51 f.

Poupardin, René: Le royaume de Bourgogne (888-1038) (1907), BEHE 163.

Privilegium Ottonis Imperatoris, Feb. 13, 962: see Walter Ullmann: "The Origins of the Ottonianum," Cambridge Historical Journal, XI (1953), 114 ff.

Problemi comuni, I, dell'Europa post-Carolingia (1955).

Regino, abbas Prumiensis: Chronicon, cum Continuatione: ed. F. Kurze (1890) (SRG); SS I, 537 ff.

Rice, David Talbot: ed. The Dark Ages (1965).

Russian Primary Chronicle, tr. S. H. Cross: Harvard Studies in Philology and Literature XII (1930).

Sakellion, A.J.: ΕΠΙΣΤΟΛΑΙ BYZANTINAI: ΣΩΤΗΡ XV (1892) 117 ff. See Schramm, Percy Ernst: Byzantinische Zeitschrift XXV (1925), 89 ff.; HZ 129, 1924, 453 ff.

Schlumberger, G.: L'Epopée byzantine à la fin du dixième siècle, I-II (1896-1900).

Schmid, Heinrich F.: "Otto I und der Osten": MIOG.: Ergänzungsband XX, i (1962), 70 ff.

Schneider, F.: Rom und Romgedanke im Mittelalter (1926).

Schramm, Percy Ernst: Kaiser, Rom und Renovatio, I-II (1929), (Schramm, KRR): vol. I revised, with index and notes (1962).

—————— "Die Kaiser aus dem sächsischen Hause im Lichte der Staatssymbolik": MIÖG XX, i (1962), 31 ff.

Southern, R.W.: The Making of the Middle Ages (1953).

Symposium on the Tenth Century: Medievalia et Humanistica, Fasc. IX (1955) (Symposium).

Tellenbach, Gerd: Die Entstehung des deutschen Reiches (1943).

Ter Braak, Menno: Kaiser Otto III, Ideal und Praxis (1928).

Turville-Petre, G.: The Heroic Age of Scandinavia (1951).

Ullmann, Walter: The Growth of Papal Government in the Middle Ages (1955).

Uhlirz, Mathilde: "Die italienische Kirchenpolitik der Ottonen": MIÖG XLVIII (1934).

—————— "Das Werden des Gedankens der 'Renovatio Imperii Romanorum' bei Kaiser Otto III": Problemi, 201 ff.

——————: See Jahrbücher.

Wallace-Hadrill, J.M.: The Barbarian West, 400-1000 (1952).

Wattenbach, Wilhelm: Deutschlands Geschichtsquellen im Mittelalter: Deutsche Kaiserzeit, ed. R. Holtzmann, I, i-ii (1948).

White, Lynn, Jr.: "The Vitality of the Tenth Century": Symposium, 26 ff.

Chapter Six

Adalbert of Prague, St.:
    Passio: SS XV, ii, 705 ff.;
    Vita, auctore Johanne Canapario: SS IV, 581 ff.;
    Vita auctore Bruno Querfurtensi: SS IV, 596 ff.

Bernward of Hildesheim, St.:
    Vita, auctore Thangmaro: SS IV, 754 ff.

Brundage, J.A.: Widukind of Corvey and the 'Non-Roman' Imperial Idea: Mediaeval Studies XXII (1960), 15 ff.

Bruno of Querfurt: Vita Quinque Fratrum: SS XV, ii, 709 ff.

————: Epistola ad Heinricum II: ed. A. Bielowski, Monumenta Poloniae Historica I, 224 ff. Also printed in von Giesebrecht, Geschichte II, 702 ff.

Concilium Romanum pro Canonizatione S. Udalrici Augustani Episcopi: PL CXXXVII, 845 ff.

David, J.: Les cinq frères, martyres en Pologne, 1003; DHGE VIII (1935), 3 ff.

Flodoard: Les Annales, ed. Ph. Lauer (1906); SS III, 363 ff.; PL CXXXV, 417 ff.

————: Historia Remensis Ecclesiae: SS XIII, 405 ff.; PL CXXXV, 23 ff.

————: De Christi triumphis apud Italiam: PL CXXXV, 832.

Franke, W.: "Romuald von Camaldoli": Historische Studien CVII (1913).

Gerhard: Vita S. Oudalrici Augustani Episcopi: SS IV, 377 ff.; PL CXXXV, 1009 ff.

Kemp, Eric W.: Canonization and Authority in the Western Church (1948).

Liutprand of Cremona: Opera, ed.[3] J. Becker, 1915 (SRG); PL CXXXVI, 787 ff; SS III, 264 ff.; tr. F. A. Wright (1930).

MacKinney, Loren C.: "Tenth-Century Medicine as Seen in the Historia of Richer of Reims": Bull. of the Institute of History of Medicine (Johns Hopkins University) II (1934), 347 ff.

Nilus, St.:
Vita: AA.SS.Boll. Sept. VII, 279 ff.

Richer: Historiarum Libri IV (884-995), ed. et tr. R. Latouche (1930-37); SS III, 561 ff.; PL CXXXVIII, 17 ff.

Romuald, St.: Vita auctore Petro Damiano sancto, ed. G. Tabacco, Fonti XCIV (1957); SS IV, 846 ff.; PL CXLIV, 953 ff.

Ruotger: Vita Brunonis Archiepiscopi Coloniensis: ed. Irene Otto (1951), SRG: New Series X; SS IV, 252 ff.

Thietmar of Merseburg: Chronicon, ed.[2] R. Holtzmann (1955), SRG: New Series IX; SS III, 723 ff.; PL CXXXIX, 1183 ff.

Tschan, Francis J.: Saint Bernward of Hildesheim, I-III (1942-52).

Voigt, H. G.: Adalbert von Prag (1898).

Widukind, monachus Corbeiensis: Res gestae Saxonicae, ed. P. Hirsch (1935), SRG; SS III, 408 ff.; PL CXXXVII, 115 ff.

Chapter Seven

Abbots of Cluny: Documents and Lives:
Berno: Testament: AA.SS.OSB. V, 86 f.; PL CXXXIII, 857.
Odo: by John of Salerno: AA.SS.OSB. V, 150 ff.;
            PL CXXXIII, 43 ff.; Anonymous (11th century),
            ed. E. Sackur, NA XV (1890), 113 ff.
———— Occupatio, ed. A. Swoboda (Teubner) (1900).

Aymard: Testimonia: PL CXXXVII, 699 ff.

Majolus: by Syrus: AA.SS.Boll. Maii II, 668 ff.;
            PL CXXXVII, 745 ff.;
        by Odilo: AA.SS.Boll. Maii II, 684 ff.;
            PL CXLII, 943 ff.;
        by Nalgod: AA.SS.Boll. Maii II, 658 ff.

Odilo: by Jotsald AA.SS.OSB VI, i, 679 ff.; PL CXLII, 897 ff.

————: Epitaphium Adelheide auguste, ed. H. Paulhart: MIÖG Ergänzungsband XX, ii (1962).

À Cluny: Travaux du congrès scientifique (9-11 juillet, 1949) (1950).

Acta Sanctorum Belgii Selecta: ed. J. Ghesquière and C. Smet, IV, (1787).

Albers, Dom Bruno: ed. Consuetudines Monasticae Antiquiores, I-V (1890-1912).

——— "Le plus ancien coutumier de Cluny: RB XX (1903), 174 ff.

Balzani, Ugo: ed. Il Chronicon Farfense di Gregorio di Catino: La Constructio Farfensis e gli Scritti di Ugo di Farfa: Fonti XXXIII-XXXIV (1903).

Bavonis S. Vita: M.G.H. Script. rer. Merov. IV, 527 ff.

Benedict of Aniane, St.: Vita (by Ardo): SS XV, i, 198 ff.

Berlière, Dom Ursmer: L'Étude des reformes monastiques des Xe et XIe siècles: Bull. de l'Acad. royale de Belgique, Lettres XVIII (1932), 137 ff.

——— Monasticon belge I-II (1890-1928).

Bernard, Auguste, et Bruel, Alexandre: Recueil des Chartes de l'Abbaye de Cluny I (1876).

Chaume, M.: "En Marge de l'histoire de Cluny": Revue Mabillon, XXX (1940), 33 ff.

Chaussier, F.: L'Abbaye de Gorze (1894).

Conant, Kenneth J.: "Cluny in the Tenth Century": Symposium, 23 ff.

Dauphin, Dom Hubert: "Monastic Reforms from the Tenth Century to the Twelfth": Downside Review LXX (1952), 62 ff.

Evans, Joan: Monastic Life at Cluny, 910-1157 (1931).

Fayen, Arnold: ed. Liber Traditionum S.-Petri Blandiniensis, (1906).

Fliche, Augustin: La Reforme grégorienne I (1924).

Folcuin: Gesta abbatum Laubiensium: SS IV, 52 ff.; PL CXXXVII, 541 ff.

———: Gesta abbatum S. Bertini Sithiensium: SS XIII, 607 ff.

Ganshof, F.-L.: La Flandre sous les premiers Comtes (1949).

Glaber, Rodulfus: Vita S. Guillelmi abbatis S. Benigni Divionensis: PL CXLII, 697 ff.

Graham, Rose: "The Relation of Cluny to some other Movements of Monastic Reform": English Ecclesiastical Studies (1929), 1 ff.

———— and A. W. Clapham: The Monastery of Cluny, 910-1155: Archaeologia LXXX (1930), 143 ff.

Grierson, Philip: ed. Annales de Saint-Pierre de Gand et de Saint-Amand (1937).

———— "The Early Abbots of St. Bavo's of Ghent": RB XLIX (1937), 29 ff.

Hallinger, Dom Kassius: Gorze-Kluny I-II, Studia Anselmiana XXII-XXV (1950-51).

————: "Zur geistigen Welt der Anfänge Klunys": DA X (1953-54), 417 ff.

Hückel, G.A.: Les poèmes satiriques d'Adalberon (1901).
John of Gorze:
   Vita, auctore Johanne abbate S. Arnulfi Mettensis: AA.SS.OSB. V, 363 ff.; AA.SS.Boll. Feb. III, 690 ff.; SS IV, 335 ff.; PL CXXXVII, 239 ff.

Knowles, Dom David: "The Monastic Horarium, 970-1120": Downside Review, LI, 1933, 706 ff.

————: The Monastic Order in England, 943-1216 (1949).

Letonnelier, Gaston: L'Abbaye exempte de Cluny et le Saint-Siège (1923).

Mansi: Concilia, XVIII, 263 ff. (Council of Trosly, 909).

Marrier, M, and Quercetanus (Duchesne) A.: Bibliotheca Cluniacensis (1614).

Monumenta Broniensia: SS XV, ii, 646 ff.

Moreau, É. de, S. J.: Histoire de l'Église en Belgique II² (1945).

————: Les Abbayes de Belgique (VII-XII siècles) (1952).

Narberhaus, Josef: Beiträge zur Geschichte des alten Mönchtums und des Benediktinerordens, XVI (1930).

Sackur, Ernst: Die Cluniacenser, I-II (1892-94).

Schmitt, C.: Oddone di Cluny: Enciclopedia cattolica IX (1952), 65 ff.

Schmitz, Dom Philibert: Histoire de l'Ordre de Saint Benoît I (1942).

———— DHGE s. v. Bénédictin (Ordre).

Schultze, W.: "Gerhard von Brogne": Forschungen zur deutschen Geschichte, XXV (1885), 221 ff.

Sigebert, monk of Gembloux: Gesta abbatum Gemblacensium: SS VIII, 523 ff.; PL CLX, 591 ff.

———— Vita Wicberti: SS IV, 504 ff.

Smith, Lucy M.: The Early History of the Monastery of Cluny (1920).

Tellenbach, Gerd: "Zum Wesen der Cluniacenser": Saeculum, IX (1958), 370 ff.

————: ed. Neue Forschungen über Cluny und die Cluniacenser, von J. Wollasch, H.-E. Mager und H. Diener (1959).

Valous, Guy de: Le Monachisme Clunisien des Origines au XVe siècle, I (1935).

————: DHGE s. v. Cluny.

Williams, Watkin: Monastic Studies (1938).

Chapter Eight

Abbo of Fleury: Otto valens Caesar: PLMA V, ii, 469 ff.

Alleluia, dulce carmen: AH II, 41.

Alleluia (Easter) Sequence: Raby, Oxford Book, 135 f.; AH LIII, 69.

Alleluiatic Sequence: Brittain, Penguin, 162 ff.; Raby, Oxford Book, 148 ff.

"Anacreontic Song": Raby, Oxford Book, 137 ff.; PLAC IV, i, 430 f.

Analecta Hymnica Medii Aevi, ed. G. M. Dreves and Clemens Blume, II, XLVII-LI, LIII (1888-1911) (AH).

Berengarii Imperatoris Panegyricus: PLAC IV, i, 354 ff.; SS IV, 189 ff.

Bezzola, R. R.: Les Origines et la formation de la littérature courtoise en occident (500-1200), I, (1944).

Bloch, Hermann: "Beiträge zur Geschichte des Bischofs Leo von Vercelli und seiner Zeit": NA XXII (1897), 109 ff.; see also PLMA V, ii, 476 ff. and Schramm, KRR II, 62 ff.

Brittain, F.: The Medieval Latin and Romance Lyric to A.D. 1300[2] (1951).

————: ed. The Penguin Book of Latin Verse (1962).

Carmen in Assumptione Sanctae Mariae in nocte quando tabula portatur; Invitatio ad Orationem: PLMA V, ii, 465 ff.; von Giesebrecht, I, 897 ff.

Chailley, Jacques: L'École Musicale de Saint-Martial de Limoges (1960).

Clark, J.M.: The Abbey of St. Gall (1926).

Deus amet puellam: PLMA V, ii, 553 f.; Dronke, RELL I, 264 ff.

Dronke, Peter: Medieval Latin and the Rise of European Love-Lyric, I-II (1965-66) (Dronke, RELL).

Ecbasis cujusdam captivi per tropologiam: ed. Karl Strecker, 1935 (SRG); tr. with introduction: Edwin H. Zeydel, North Carolina Studies in Germanic languages and literature, No. 46 (1964).

Eia recolamus laudibus: Brittain, Penguin, 158 ff.; Notker, von den Steinen, II, 94.

Ekkehard IV: Casus S. Galli: SS II, 75 ff.; tr. (German) H. Helbling (1958).

Epitaphs in verse, of Otto I, Otto III, Crescentius: PLMA V, ii, 281, 341 f.

Erdmann, Carl: "Konrad II und Heinrich III in der Ecbasis Captivi": DA IV (1940-41), 382 ff.

Eugenius Vulgarius: Sylloga: PLAC IV, i, 406 ff.

Fickermann, Norbert: "Zum Verfasserproblem des Waltharius": Beiträge zur Geschichte der deutschen Sprache und Literatur, LXXXI (1959), 267 ff.

Franceschini, Ezio: "L'Epopea post-Carolingia": Problemi, 313 ff.

Gerbert, Verse: PLMA V, ii, 472 ff.

Grimm, J. and Schmeller, A.: ed. Lateinische Gedichte des X und XI. Jh. (1838).

Hartman of Saint-Gall: Poems: PLAC IV, i, 317 ff.; IV, ii (1098).

Heriger: Raby, Oxford Book, 170 f.; Waddell, Penguin, 160 ff.

Hauck, Karl: "Das Walthariusepos des Bruders Gerald von Eichstätt": Germanische-romanische Monatsschrift, N.F. IV (1954), 1 ff.

Hucbald of Saint-Amand: De Calvis: PLMA IV, i, 261 ff.

"Jam, dulcis amica, venito": Dronke, RELL, I, 271 ff.; Brittain, Penguin, 171 ff.; Raby, Oxford Book 172 f.; Emilio P. Vuolo, Cultura Neo-latina X (1950), 5 ff.

Leo of Vercelli: see Bloch, Hermann.

Letald of Micy: ed. A. Wilmart, "Le poème héroïque de Letald sur Within le pêcheur": Studi Medievali IX (1938), 188 ff.

Mabillon: Vetera Analecta (1723).

Modus De Heinrico: Die Cambridger Lieder, ed. Strecker, 57 ff.; see Mathilde Uhlirz DVLG XXVI (1952), 153 ff.

Modus Liebinc: Brittain, Penguin, 167 ff.; Raby, Oxford Book, 167 ff. ("The Snow-Child").

Modus Ottinc: ed. Strecker, Die Camb. Lieder, 33 ff.; PLMA V, ii, 480.

Notker "the Stammerer" of Saint-Gall: Poems, ed. Wolfram von den Steinen: Notker der Dichter und seine geistige Welt, I-II (1948); and: Notkers des Dichters Hymnenbuch, Lateinisch und Deutsch (1960).

Oriole, The: Raby, Oxford Book, 147; N. Fickermann, NA, L, 1935, 582 f.

O Roma nobilis: Brittain, Penguin, 155; Bernard M. Peebles, American Benedictine Review, I (1950), 67 ff.; Raby, Oxford Book, 140.

Quis dabit aquam capiti?: PLMA V, ii, 480 f.

Raby, F.J.E.: Philomena praevia temporis amoeni: Mélanges Joseph de Ghellinck, S.J. (1951).

————: A History of Christian-Latin Poetry² (1953).

————: A History of Secular Latin Poetry in the Middle Ages,² I-II (1957).

————: The Oxford Book of Medieval Latin Verse, newly selected and edited (1959).

Radbod: The Swallow: PLAC IV, i, 172 f.; Raby, Sec. Lat. Poetry I, 250 f.

Ross, Werner: "Die Ecbasis Captivi und die Anfänge der mittelalterlichen Tierdichtung": Germanische-romanische Monatsschrift, N.F. IV (1954), 266 ff.

Salamo III: Poems: PLAC IV, i, 296 ff.; 343 f.; 345.

Salus aeterna: Brittain, Penguin, 160 ff.; Raby, Oxford Book, 133 f.

Sancta Dei Genetrix: see Carmen in Assumptione S. Mariae.

Schumann, Otto: "Über die Pariser Waltharius-Handschrift": Festgabe K. Strecker (1941).

————: "Waltharius-Probleme": Studi Mediaevali N.S. XVII (1951), 177 ff.

Spanke, H.: "Aus der Vorgeschichte und Frühgeschichte der Sequenz": Zeitschrift für deutsches Altertum und Literatur, LXXI (1934), 1 ff.

Stach, Walther: "Waltharius": HZ CLXVIII (1943), 57 ff.

Steinen, W. von den: "Die Anfänge der Sequenzdichtung": Zeitschrift für schweizerische Kirchengeschichte, XL, iii (1946), 190 ff.; XLI, ii (1947), 122 ff.; see also s. v. Notker.

Strecker, Karl: ed. Die Cambridger Lieder (1926).

———: "Ecbasisfragen": Historische Vierteljahrschrift, XXIX (1935), 491 ff.

———: "Der Walthariusdichter": DA IV (1941), 355 ff.

Szövérffy, Josef: Die Annalen der lateinischen Hymnendichtung I (1964).

Vestiunt silvae: Raby, Oxford Book, 174 f.: Waddell, Penguin, 154 f.

Vinay, Gustavo: "Contributo alla Interpretazione della 'Ecbasis Captivi' ": Convivium (1949), 234 ff.

Waddell, Helen: Mediaeval Latin Lyrics, Penguin Classics, (1962, reprint of 1933 ed.).

Waldram: Song for Conrad I: PLAC IV, i, 328 ff.; ed. Walter Bulst: "Susceptacula regum": Corona Quernea, Festgabe Karl Strecker (1941), 121 f.

Walter of Aquitaine: Materials for the Study of His Legend, tr. and discussion of Waltharius by F. P. Magoun, Jr., and H. M. Smyser (1950).

Waltharius, ed. Karl Strecker, Otto Schumann and Norbert Fickermann: PLMA VI, i (1951), 1 ff.; Prologue: PLMA V, ii (1939), 405 ff.; ed. Karl Strecker, tr. (German) Peter Vossen (1947).

Watch-Song of Modena: Brittain, Penguin, 156 f.; Raby, Oxford Book, 141.

Zeller, Ulrich: Bischof Salomo III von Konstanz, Abt von St. Gallen (1910).

Zeumer, Karl: ed. M.G.H. Leges V: Formulae Merowingici et Karolini Aevi (1886) (Collectio Sangallensis).

Chapter Nine

Cena Cypriani: PL IV, 925 ff.

Chambers, E. K.: The Mediaeval Stage, I-II (1903).

Coulter, Cornelia C.: "The 'Terentian' Comedies of a Tenth-Century Nun": Classical Journal, XXIV (1929), 515 ff.

Du Méril: Les Origines latines du Théatre moderne (1897).

Euringer S.: "Drei Beiträge zur Roswitha-Forschung": Historisches Jahrbuch, LIV (1934), 75 ff.

Franceschini, Ezio: "Il Teatro post-Carolingio": Problemi, 295 ff.

Hardison, O. B., Jr.: Christian Rite and Christian Drama in the Middle Ages (1965).

Hennecke, Edgar: New Testament Apocrypha, ed. W. Schneemelcher, tr. R. McL. Wilson, I (1963): Protevangelium of James, 370 ff.

Hodie cantandus est: AH XLIX, 7 f.; Notker, ed. von den Steinen, I, 46.

Hraban Maur: On the Cena Cypriani to King Lothar II: M.G.H. Epp. V, 506: No. 52.

Hrotsvitha: Opera, ed.[2] Karl Strecker, 1930; ed. Paul de Winterfeld, 1902; SS IV, 302 ff.; PL CXXXVII, 939 ff.; tr. (English) Christopher St. John (1923); H.J.W. Tillyard (1923); tr. (French) Coecilia Vellini (1907).

Hudson, W. H.: "Hrotsvitha of Gandersheim": EHR III (1888), 431 ff.

Jones, Charles W.: ed. Medieval Literature in Translation (1950).

Kuhn, Hugo: "Hrotsviths von Gandersheim dichterisches Programm": DVLG XXIV (1950), 181 ff.

Lapôtre, A.: "Le Souper de Jean Diacre": Mélanges d'Archéologie et d'Histoire XXI (1901), 305 ff.

Levison, Wilhelm: M.G.H. Scriptores Merovingici VII, 142 ff. (on Hrotsvitha: Gangulf).

"Quem quaeritis in sepulchro?": AH XLIX, 9; Raby, Oxford Book, 136 f.

Spitz, Lewis W.: Conrad Celtis, The German Arch-Humanist (1957).

Symons, Dom Thomas: ed. and tr. Regularis Concordia (1953).

Terentius et Delusor: Hrotsvithae Opera, ed. P. de Winterfeld (1902), XX ff.

Walther, H.: Das Streitgedicht in der lateinischen Literatur des Mittelalters (1920).

Wiegand, Sister M. Gonselva, O.S.F.: The Non-Dramatic Works of Hrotsvitha, text, tr. and commentary (1936).

Young, Karl: "The Origin of the Easter Play": Publications of the Mod. Lang. Assoc. of America, XXIX (1914), 1 ff.

————: The Drama of the Medieval Church I (1933).

Vita S. Abrahae Eremitae: PL LXXIII, 281 ff.; Vita S. Mariae Meretricis, neptis Abrahae: *ibid.*, 651 ff.

Wattenbach-Levison-Löwe: Deutschlands Geschichtsquellen im Mittelalter, IV (1963), 467 ff.

Zeydel, Edwin H.: "Knowledge of Hrotsvitha's Works Prior to 1500": Modern Lang. Notes, LIX (1944), 382 ff.

————: 'Ego clamor validus': *ibid.*, LXI (1946), 281 ff.

Chapter Ten

Anthony, Edgar W.: Romanesque Frescoes (1951).

Beckwith, John: Early Medieval Art (1964).

Boeckler, Albert: "Ottonische Kunst in Deutschland": Problemi, 329 ff.

———— "Bildvorlagen der Reichenau": ZK XII (1949), 1 ff.

Broadley, H. T.: "A Reconstruction of the Tenth-Century Church of St. Cyriacus in Gernrode": Marsyas (New York), VI, (1950), 25 f.

Clapham, A. W.: Romanesque Architecture in Western Europe (1936).

Conant, Kenneth J.: "Excavations at Cluny": Speculum, IV (1929), 443 ff.; VI (1931), 3 ff.; XXIX (1954), 1 ff.

————: Carolingian and Romanesque Architecture (1959).

Evans, Joan: The Romanesque Architecture of the Order of Cluny (1938).

————: Cluniac Art of the Romanesque Period (1950).

Focillon, Henri: The Art of the West in the Middle Ages, ed. Jean Bony, I: Romanesque Art (1963).

Frankl, Paul: Die frühmittelalterliche und romanische Baukunst (1918).

Gall, Ernst: Cathedrals and Abbey Churches of the Rhine, tr. and adapted by Olive Cook (1963).

Goldschmidt, Adolph: Die Elfenbeinskulpturen aus der Zeit des karolingischen und sächsischen Kaiser, I (1914).

————: German Illumination, II (1928).

Grabar, André and Nordenfalk, Carl: Early Medieval Painting (1957).

Grodecki, Louis: Au Seuil de l'Art Roman: L'Architecture Ottonienne (1958).

Köhler, W.: "Die Tradition der Adagruppe und die Anfänge des Ottonischen Stiles in der Buchmalerei": Festschrift Paul Clemen (1926), 255 ff.

Mültherich, Florentine: "Ottonian Art: Changing Aspects": Acts, 20th Congress of the History of Art, I (1963).

Nordenfalk, Carl: "Der Meister des Registrum Gregorii": Münchner Jahrbuch der bildenden Kunst, III, i (1950), 61 ff.

Otto, Walter: "Reichenauer Goldtreibarbeiten": ZK XIII (1950), 39 ff.

Paulus Diaconus: S. Gregorii Magni Vita: PL LXXV, 57 f.

Purchardi Carmen De Gestis Witigowonis Abbatis: SS IV, 621 ff.; PLMA V, i, 260 ff.

Saalman, Howard: European Architecture, 600-1200 (1962).

Schnitzler, Hermann: Rheinische Schatzkammer (1957).

Schramm, Percy Ernst: "Zur Geschichte der Buchmalerei in der Zeit der sächsischen Kaiser": Jahrbuch für Kunstwissenschaft, I (1923), 54 ff.

————: Die deutschen Kaiser und Könige in Bildern ihrer Zeit, 751-1152, I (1928).

———— und Mültherich, Florentine: Denkmäler der deutschen Könige und Kaiser, 768-1250 (1962).

Swarzenski, H.: Early Medieval Illumination (1951).

————: Monuments of Romanesque Art (1954).

Vöge, Wilhelm: "Ein deutscher Schnitzer des 10. Jahrhunderts": Gesammelte Studien (1958), 1 ff.

Weisbach, Werner: "Les images des evangelistes dans l'evangelaire d'Otton III et leur rapport avec l'antiquité": Gazette des Beaux-Arts (1939), 131 ff.

Chapter Eleven

Abbo of Fleury: Opera: AA.SS.OSB. VI, i, 30 ff.; PL CXXXIX, 417 ff.

———— "Les Oeuvres inédites d'Abbon de Fleury": A. Van de Vyver: RB XLVII (1935), 125 ff.; Life of Abbo by Aimoin: PL CXXXIX, 387 ff.

Adso, Dervensis abbas: De Antichristo: PL CI, 1289 ff.

Allen, Roland: "Gerbert, Pope Sylvester II": EHR VII (1892), 625 ff.

Anselm: Gesta episcoporum Leodiensium: SS VII, 189 ff.

Constable, Giles: Monastic Tithes from Their Origins to the Twelfth Century (1964).

Cousin, Dom Patrice: Abbon de Fleury-sur-Loire (1954).

Dolch, Alfred K.: Notker-Studien I-II (1951-52). (Notker Labeo)

Dresdner, A.: Kultur- und Sittengeschichte der italienischen Geistlichkeit im X und XI Jahrhundert (1890).

Focillon, Henry: L'An Mil (1952).

Gerbert, Pope Sylvester II: Opera, ed. A. Olleris (1867); PL CXXXIX, 85 ff.; Epistolae, ed. Julien Havet, 1899; tr. (with his papal privileges as Sylvester II) Harriet P. Lattin (1961); see also Richer, Historiae III, cc. 46-55.

Glaber, Rodulfus: Historiarum Libri quinque (900-1044), ed. Maurice Prou (1886).

Hoffmann, Paul: Die Mischprosa Notkers des Deutschen: Palaestra. LVIII (1910).

Kurth, Godefroid: Notger de Liège et la civilisation au Xe siècle, I-II (1905).

La Salle de Rochemaure, Duc de: Gerbert, Silvestre II (1914).

Lattin, Harriet: The Peasant Boy Who Became Pope: The Story of Gerbert (1958).

———— "Astronomy: Our Views and Theirs": Symposium, 13 ff.; see also Gerbert.

Liudprandi Opera: ed.[3] J. Becker (1915).

MacCulloch, J. A.: Medieval Faith and Fable (1932).

MacKinney, Loren C.: "Tenth Century Medicine: Classicism and Pragmatism," Symposium, 10 ff., see also under c. 6.

Maître, L.: Les Écoles épiscopales et monastiques en Occident avant les Universités (768-1180)[2] (1924).

New Oxford History of Music II: Early Medieval Music, ed. Dom Anselm Hughes (1954).

Notker Labeo, "the German": Opera, ed. Paul Piper, I-III (1882-83); ed. E. H. Sehrt and Taylor Starck (1933-35).

Picavet, F.: Gerbert: Un pape philosophe (1897): BEHE (sciences religieuses IX).

Plaine, Dom François: "Les prétendues Terreurs de l'An Mille": Revue des Questions Historiques (1873), 145 ff.

Rather of Verona: Opera: PL CXXXVI, 9 ff.; Letters, ed. F. Weigle: M.G.H. Die Briefe der deutschen Kaiserzeit I (1949).

Stubbs, William: ed. Memorials of St. Dunstan: Rolls Series, No. 63 (1874).

Vogel, Albrecht: Ratherius von Verona und das zehnte Jahrhundert, I-II (1854).

Wallach, Luitpold: "Education and Culture in the Tenth Century": Symposium, 18 ff.

William of Malmesbury: De Gestis Regum Anglorum, ed. William Stubbs, I (1887), 193 ff., 203 f.

INDEX

Selected Ann Arbor Paperbacks
Works of enduring merit

For a complete list of Ann Arbor Paperback titles write:
THE UNIVERSITY OF MICHIGAN PRESS ANN ARBOR